HANS URS VON BALTHASAR:
HIS LIFE AND WORK

Hans Urs von Balthasar: His Life And Work

Edited by
David L. Schindler

COMMUNIO BOOKS
IGNATIUS PRESS   SAN FRANCISCO

Cover photo by © André Muelhaupt

© 1991 Ignatius Press, San Francisco
All rights reserved
ISBN 0–89870–378–6
Library of Congress catalogue number 91–73330
Printed in the United States of America

The Spirit meets the burning questions of the age with an utterance that is the keyword, the answer to the riddle. Never in the form of an abstract statement (that being something that it is man's business to draw up); almost always in the form of a new, concrete supernatural mission: the creation of a new saint whose life is a presentation to his own age of the message that heaven is sending to it, a man who is, here and now, the right and relevant interpretation of the Gospel, who is given to this particular age as its way of approach to the perennial truth of Christ. How else can life be expounded except by living? The saints are Tradition at its most living, Tradition as the word is meant whenever Scripture speaks of the unfolding of the riches of Christ, and the application to history of the norm which is Christ. Their missions are so exactly the answer from above to the questions from below that their immediate effect is often one of unintelligibility; they are signs to be contradicted in the name of every kind of right-thinking—until the proof of their power is brought forth. St. Bernard and St. Francis, St. Ignatius and St. Theresa were all of them proofs of that order: they were like volcanoes pouring forth molten fire from the inmost depths of revelation; they were irrefutable proof, all horizontal tradition notwithstanding, of the vertical presence of the living Kyrios here, now, and today.

Hans Urs von Balthasar, *A Theology of History* (New York: Sheed and Ward, 1963), 105.

Contents

Contributors

ELLERO BABINI teaches theological anthropology at the Studio Teologico Accademico of Bologna and is a member of the editorial board of the Italian edition of *Communio.*

GEORGES CHANTRAINE, S.J. is a professor at the Jesuit Faculty of Theology in Brussels and a member of the editorial board of the French edition of *Communio.*

HENRI CARDINAL DE LUBAC, S.J., one of the leading Catholic theologians of the twentieth century, now lives in retirement in Paris.

LOUIS DUPRÉ holds the T. Lawrason Riggs Chair in the philosophy of religion at Yale University.

MAXIMILIAN GREINER is Managing Editor of the German edition of *Communio.*

ALOIS M. HAAS is Professor of Early German Literature at the University of Zurich.

PETER HENRICI, S.J. is Professor of Modern Philosophy at the Pontifical Gregorian University, Rome and Director of the German edition of *Communio.*

POPE JOHN PAUL II.

CHARLES KANNENGIESSER holds the Katherine Huisking Chair in theology at the University of Notre Dame.

WALTER KASPER is Bishop of Rottenburg-Stuttgart, Germany and a member of the editorial board of the German *Communio.*

KARL LEHMANN is Bishop of Mainz, Germany, President of the German Bishops' Conference, and a member of the editorial board of the German *Communio.*

WERNER LÖSER, S.J. is Director of the Philosophisch-Theologischen Hochschule St. Georgen in Frankfurt, where he is Professor of Dogmatic Theology.

JOHN O'DONNELL, S.J. is Professor of Dogmatic Theology at the Pontifical Gregorian University, Rome.

MARC OUELLET, S.S. is Rector of the Grand Séminaire of Montréal and a member of the editorial board of the North American edition of *Communio.*

JOSEPH CARDINAL RATZINGER, a co-founder of the German edition of *Communio,* is Prefect of the Sacred Congregation for the Doctrine of the Faith.

JOHANN ROTEN, S.M. is Director of the International Marian Research Institute at the University of Dayton, Ohio.

DAVID L. SCHINDLER teaches metaphysics and fundamental theology in the Program of Liberal Studies at the University of Notre Dame, and is the Editor-in-Chief of the North American edition of *Communio.*

CHRISTOPH SCHÖNBORN, O.P. is Professor of Dogmatic Theology at the University of Fribourg, Switzerland, a member of the International Theological Commission, and a member of the editorial board of the German edition of *Communio.*

ANTONIO SICARI, O.C.D. teaches dogmatic theology at the Studio Teologico Carmelitano in Brescia, Italy and is a member of the editorial board of the Italian edition of *Communio.*

WOLFGANG TREITLER is Research Assistant at the Institute for Fundamental Theology and Apologetics at the University of Vienna.

Preface

The Christian, says von Balthasar, remains the guardian of the metaphysical wonder which is the point of origin for philosophy and indeed for authentic human existence. This wonder lies unacknowledged but alive in the child's first opening of its eyes to its mother's smile. Through that smile the child learns that "it is contained, affirmed and loved in a relationship which is incomprehensively encompassing, already actual, sheltering and nourishing".[1] The relationship, in other words, is *a priori* (616), and it calls forth a wonder at being permitted to be. Thus we come to the heart of von Balthasar: "This condition of being permitted cannot be surpassed by any additional insight into the laws and necessities of the world" (633).

"Being permitted": here is indicated the disposition that provides the unifying center of the great themes of von Balthasar's life and work: obedience, love, beauty, glory—and indeed suffering and passion and selflessness unto death. All of these are aspects of and responses to gift. Not gift in any vague or generic sense, but gift first as spoken by the trinitarian God in Jesus Christ and *received* into creation through Mary and the Church by means of the Holy Spirit.

Von Balthasar's theology, then, as a theology of wonder and gift, finds its form in the Christic-Marian-ecclesial *fiat.* The phrase he coined for the basic way or "method" of theology—namely, *"kniende theologie"*: praying or kneeling theology—applies to his own work. A theology whose first "method" is prayer does not exclude other (e.g., historical-critical) methods; but it nonetheless includes these only as it transforms them. It is the saints, says von Balthasar—those who have received the word of God into every fiber of their being—who alone, finally, have "warrant" to speak about God.

Von Balthasar's profound sense of gift, taking its beginnings from the divine *communio* revealed in Jesus Christ, inspires his reading of Western culture. The West, more ambiguously in the pre-Christian ancient world, more unequivocally in the modern period, has drifted from wonder (*Verwunderung*) in the presence of the mystery of being, to mere admiration (*Be-wunderung*). Human consciousness has shifted from Being to things, with a consequent loss of the gratuitousness which disposes one to approach the

---

[1] *The Glory of the Lord: A Theological Aesthetics,* V: *The Realm of Metaphysics in the Modern Age* (San Francisco: Ignatius Press, 1991), 616. All citations are from this volume.

The translation of *Herrlichkeit* (*The Glory of the Lord*), the first part of von Balthasar's great trilogy, is now complete in seven volumes (San Francisco: Ignatius Press, 1982–1991).

unseizable mystery of God, and indeed to perceive God's glory through all the fragmentary manifestations of beauty in the world. The instrumentalist-positivist cast of mind characteristic of so much of modernity represents merely an extreme form of this shift in consciousness.

But let von Balthasar speak for himself regarding the task which faces Christians:

> The Christians of today, living in a night which is deeper than that of the later Middle Ages, are given the task of performing the act of affirming Being, unperturbed by the darkness and the distortion, in a way that is vicarious and representative for all humanity: an act which is at first theological, but which contains within itself the whole dimension of the metaphysical act of the affirmation of Being. Those who are directed in this way to pray continually, to find God in all things and to glorify him are able to do so on particular grounds (that is particular graces) which allow them to perform their "creaturely duty" (as *Ruysbroeck, Bérulle* and *Condren* understood it). But in so far as they are to shine "like the stars in the sky", they are also entrusted with the task of bringing light to those areas of Being which are in darkness so that its primal light may shine anew not only upon them but also upon the whole world; for it is only in this light that man can walk in accordance with what he is truly called to be (648–49).

It is clear that this bringing of light is not merely a speculative task:

> All this will, of course, prove a hard test for Christians; if they want to be the teachers of our times, then they must learn to read the signs of the times. This age cannot be purified by fire if Christians are not ready to allow themselves to be tested in the same fire to see whether they are made of gold or of potash, whether their hearts and their work are of "gold, silver and precious stones" or of "wood, hay and straw" (1 Cor 3: 13). This is the ultimate truth: that Christians, as guardians of a metaphysics of the whole person in an age which has forgotten both Being and God, are entrusted with the weighty responsibility of leading this metaphysics of wholeness through that same fire. . . . They can only adequately answer God's universal engagement with the world in the love of Jesus Christ for them by lending their own love, in the *concretissimum* of the encounter with their brother, that universal breadth of Being which—consciously or not, explicitly or not—the metaphysical act possesses and is (654–55).

The mission of Christians today, then, is to give witness, in all aspects of their existence, to the metaphysical act: that is, to the act of love whose form is given in the suffering *fiat* of Jesus Christ. Any charge against von Balthasar of "nostalgia" or "restorationism" is simply impertinent. Christians are to read the signs of the times in the light of the Gospel. The inculturation of the Gospel which results will be a new inculturation, not the mechanical imposition of some earlier one. The inculturation will be creative, formed in the freedom of the Spirit. All of this will happen so long as the Christian does not cease to wonder, and to love.

Von Balthasar died suddenly on June 26, 1988, just a few days before he was to have been officially made a cardinal by Pope John Paul II. Like so much else in his life, it was an honor von Balthasar had accepted only in obedience. One is at a loss to try to summarize adequately all the achievements of this great theologian, surely one of the giants of our time. The purpose of the present volume is merely to help display his vision and the character and range of his service to the Church and to culture—so that he might more effectively become the only thing he ever wished to be: a John the Baptist refracting the light of him who is greater than we are and of whom we are unworthy, but who has loved us all unto death.

The papers in the present volume were for the most part prepared especially for *Communio,* and some have appeared in various *Communio* publications in North America and elsewhere. Regarding the pieces which appear in the appendix: that by Bishops Walter Kasper and Karl Lehmann is taken from their preface to a collection of studies on von Balthasar (many of them included in the present volume) published by the German *Communio;* the article by Henri de Lubac was written some twenty years ago in tribute to von Balthasar; and the telegram from Pope John Paul II and the homily by Cardinal Joseph Ratzinger were composed in connection with von Balthasar's funeral Mass in Lucerne.

Von Balthasar's "A Résumé of My Thought" was presented at a conference in Madrid prior to the annual *Communio* reunion in May 1988, just before his death. It is fitting that this was the last paper he himself had sent to the North American *Communio* for publication.

David L. Schindler
Notre Dame, Indiana
May 1, 1991

HANS URS VON BALTHASAR

A Résumé of My Thought

When a man has published many large books, people will ask themselves: What, fundamentally, did he want to say? If he is a prolific novelist—for example Dickens or Dostoevsky—one would choose one or another of his works without worrying oneself too much about all of them as a whole. But for a philosopher or theologian it is totally different. One wishes to touch the heart of his thought, because one presupposes that such a heart must exist.

The question has often been asked of me by those disconcerted by the large number of my books: Where must one start in order to understand you? I am going to attempt to condense my many fragments "in a nutshell", as the English say, as far as that can be done without too many betrayals. The danger of such a compression consists in being too abstract. It is necessary to amplify what follows with my biographical works on the one hand (on the Fathers of the Church, on Karl Barth, Buber, Bernanos, Guardini, Reinhold Schneider, and all the authors treated in the trilogy), with the works on spirituality on the other hand (such as those on contemplative prayer, on Christ, Mary and the Church), and finally, with the numerous translations of the Fathers of the Church, of the theologians of the Middle Ages, and of modern times. But here it is necessary to limit ourselves to presenting a schema of the trilogy: Aesthetic, Dramatic, and Logic.[1]

We start with a reflection on the situation of man. He exists as a limited being in a limited world, but his reason is open to the unlimited, to all of being. The proof consists in the recognition of his finitude, of his contingence: I am, but I could not-be. Many things which do not exist could exist. Essences are limited, but being (*l'être*) is not. That division, the "real distinction" of St. Thomas, is the source of all the religious and philosophical thought of humanity. It is not necessary to recall that all human philosophy (if we abstract the biblical domain and its influence) is essentially religious and theological at once, because it poses the problem of the Absolute Being, whether one attributes to it a personal character or not.

Translated by Kelly Hamilton.
Communio 15 (Winter 1988). © 1988 by *Communio: International Catholic Review.*

[1] In the trilogy, Hans Urs von Balthasar approaches Christian revelation under the aspect of its beauty (*Herrlichkeit*), goodness (*Theodramatik*), and truth (*Theologik*). See "English Translations of German Titles" in Appendix below for full titles.

What are the major solutions to this enigma attempted by humanity? One can try to leave behind the division between being (*Être*) and essence, between the infinite and the finite; one will then say that all being is infinite and immutable (Parmenides) or that all is movement, rhythm between contraries, becoming (Heraclitus).

In the first case, the finite and limited will be non-being as such, thus an illusion that one must detect: this is the solution of Buddhist mysticism with its thousand nuances in the Far East. It is also the Plotinian solution: the truth is only attained in ecstasy where one touches the One, which is at the same time All and Nothing (relative to all the rest which only seems to exist). The second case contradicts itself: pure becoming in pure finitude can only conceive of itself in identifying the contraries: life and death, good fortune and adversity, wisdom and folly (Heraclitus did this).

Thus it is necessary to commence from an inescapable duality: the finite is not the infinite. In Plato the sensible, terrestrial world is not the ideal, divine world. The question is then inevitable: Whence comes the division? Why are we not God?

The first attempt at a response: there must have been a fall, a decline, and the road to salvation can only be the return of the sensible finite into the intelligible infinite. That is the way of all non-biblical mystics. The second attempt at a response: the infinite God had need of a finite world. Why? To perfect himself, to actualize all of his possibilities? Or even to have an object to love? The two solutions lead to pantheism. In both cases, the Absolute, God in himself, has again become indigent, thus finite. But if God has no need of the world—yet again: Why does the world exist?

No philosophy could give a satisfactory response to that question. St. Paul would say to the philosophers that God created man so that he would *seek* the Divine, try to attain the Divine. That is why all pre-Christian philosophy is theological at its summit. But, in fact, the true response to philosophy could only be given by Being himself, revealing himself from himself. Will man be capable of understanding this revelation? The affirmative response will be given only by the God of the Bible. On the one hand, this God, Creator of the world and of man, knows his creature. "I who have created the eye, do I not see? I who have created the ear, do I not hear?" And we add "I who have created language, could I not speak and make myself heard?" And this posits a counterpart: to be able to hear and understand the auto-revelation of God man must in himself be a search for God, a question posed to him. Thus there is no biblical theology without a religious philosophy. Human reason must be open to the infinite.

It is here that the substance of my thought inserts itself. Let us say above all that the traditional term "metaphysical" signified the act of transcending physics, which for the Greeks signified the totality of the cosmos, of which man was a part. For us physics is something else: the science of the material world. For us the cosmos perfects itself in man, who at the same time sums up the world and surpasses it. Thus our philosophy will be essentially a meta-anthropology, presupposing not only the cosmological sciences, but also the anthropological sciences, and surpassing them towards the question of the being and essence of man.

Now man exists only in dialogue with his neighbor. The infant is brought to consciousness of himself only by love, by the smile of his mother. In that encounter the horizon of all unlimited being opens itself for him, revealing four things to him: (1) that he is one in love with the mother, even in being other than his mother, therefore all being is one; (2) that that love is good, therefore all being is good; (3) that that love is true, therefore all being is true; and (4) that that love evokes joy, therefore all being is beautiful.

We add here that the epiphany of being has sense only if in the appearance (*Erscheinung*) we grasp the essence which manifests itself (*Ding an sich*). The infant comes to the knowledge not of a pure appearance, but of his mother in herself. That does not exclude our grasping the essence only through the manifestation and not in itself (St. Thomas).

The One, the Good, the True, and the Beautiful, these are what we call the transcendental attributes of Being, because they surpass all the limits of essences and are coextensive with Being. If there is an insurmountable distance between God and his creature, but if there is also an analogy between them which cannot be resolved in any form of identity, there must also exist an analogy between the transcendentals—between those of the creature and those in God.

There are two conclusions to draw from this: one positive, the other negative. The positive: man exists only by interpersonal dialogue: therefore by language, speech (in gestures, in mimic, or in words). Why then deny speech to Being himself? "In the beginning was the Word, and the Word was with God, and the Word was God" (Jn 1:1).

The negative: supposing that God is truly God (that is to say that he is the totality of Being who has need of no creature), then God will be the plenitude of the One, the Good, the True, and the Beautiful, and by consequence the limited creature participates in the transcendentals only in a partial, fragmentary fashion. Let us take an example: What is unity in a finite world? Is it the species (each man is totally man, *that* is his unity), or is it the individual (each man is indivisibly himself)? Unity is thus polarized in the domain of finitude. One can demonstrate the same polarity for the Good, the True, and the Beautiful.

I have thus tried to construct a philosophy and a theology starting from an analogy not of an abstract Being, but of Being as it is encountered concretely in its attributes (not categorical, but transcendental). And as the transcendentals run through all Being, they must be interior to each other: that which is truly true is also truly good and beautiful and one. A being *appears,* it has an epiphany: in that it is beautiful and makes us marvel. In appearing it *gives* itself, it delivers itself to us: it is good. And in giving itself up, it *speaks* itself, it unveils itself: it is true (in itself, but in the other to which it reveals itself).

Thus one can construct above all a theological *aesthetique* ("*Gloria*"): God appears. He appeared to Abraham, to Moses, to Isaiah, finally in Jesus Christ. A theological question: How do we distinguish his appearance, his epiphany among the thousand other phenomena in the world? How do we distinguish the true and only living God of Israel from all the idols which surround him and from all the philosophical and theological attempts to attain God? How do we perceive the incomparable glory of God in the life, the Cross, the Resurrection of Christ, a glory different from all other glory in this world?

One can then continue with a *dramatique* since this God enters into an alliance with us: How does the absolute liberty of God in Jesus Christ confront the relative, but true, liberty of man? Will there perhaps be a mortal struggle between the two in which each one will defend against the other what it conceives and chooses as the good? What will be the unfolding of the battle, the final victory?

One can terminate with a *logique* (a *theo-logique*). How can God come to make himself understood to man, how can an infinite Word express itself in a finite word without losing its sense? That will be the problem of the two natures of Jesus Christ. And how can the limited spirit of man come to grasp the unlimited sense of the Word of God? That will be the problem of the Holy Spirit.

This, then, is the articulation of my trilogy. I have meant only to mention the questions posed by the method, without coming to the responses, because that would go well beyond the limits of an introductory summary such as this.

In conclusion, it is nonetheless necessary to touch briefly on the Christian response to the question posed in the beginning relative to the religious philosophies of humanity. I say the Christian response, because the responses of the Old Testament and *a fortiori* of Islam (which remains essentially in the enclosure of the religion of Israel) are incapable of giving a satisfactory answer to the question of why Yahweh, why Allah, created a world of which he did not have need in order to be God. Only the fact is affirmed in the two religions, not the why.

The Christian response is contained in these two fundamental dogmas: that of the Trinity and that of the Incarnation. In the trinitarian dogma God is one, good, true, and beautiful because he is essentially Love, and Love supposes the one, the other, and their unity. And if it is necessary to suppose the Other, the Word, the Son, in God, then the otherness of the creation is not a fall, a disgrace, but an image of God, even as it is not God.

And as the Son in God is the eternal icon of the Father, he can without contradiction assume in himself the image that is the creation, purify it, and make it enter into the communion of the divine life without dissolving it (in a false mysticism). It is here that one must distinguish nature and grace.

All true solutions offered by the Christian Faith hold, therefore, to these two mysteries, categorically refused by a human reason which makes itself absolute. It is because of this that the true battle between religions begins only after the coming of Christ. Humanity will prefer to renounce all philosophical questions—in Marxism, or positivism of all stripes, rather than accept a philosophy which finds its final response only in the revelation of Christ.

Forseeing that, Christ sent his believers into the whole world as sheep among wolves.

Before making a pact with the world it is necessary to meditate on that comparison.

PETER HENRICI, S.J.

Hans Urs von Balthasar: A Sketch of His Life

According to Pascal, "it is a bad sign when you see a man and immediately think of his books." The danger of focusing on the writer and forgetting the human being is almost unavoidable in the case of someone like Hans Urs von Balthasar, who wrote more books than a normal person can be expected to read in his lifetime. He more than once found it necessary to provide a survey or "statement of account" of his literary work, and constantly emphasized that he regarded his writing as a "sideline". After the death of Adrienne von Speyr, he was increasingly ready to make autobiographical statements, and yet these are too scattered and fragmentary to give a proper picture of Hans Urs von Balthasar the man. What follows, therefore, is a preliminary and inadequate attempt to draw a picture of this person as we knew, admired, and loved him.

Gifts

For all of us, he was a little too great. In conversation with a group of friends, whether standing up or, as he preferred, walking up and down, he was literally head and shoulders above everyone else. In his knowledge and judgment, too, he towered over those with whom he spoke. You had to look up to him. Without putting himself on a pedestal, he could see far and wide. And yet he never let you feel his superiority. He never spoke condescendingly, never looked down on anyone. Only occasionally did he seem to forget that others were not endowed with his own gifts and incredible capacity for work. His judgments of ideas and books could sometimes sound rash, harsh, even disparaging, yet, when this happened, he was simply expressing the high standards he demanded of himself, of his milieu, above all, of everything connected with the Church. "Only the best is good enough for you," he once told a young confrère, "in people, in ideas, in demands on yourself."[1] He

Translated by John Saward.
Communio 16 (Fall 1989). © 1989 by *Communio: International Catholic Review.*

[1] Citations without footnotes come from private communications. All works cited without author are by Hans Urs von Balthasar.

measured everything by his own great standards, and by those standards much fell short.

For all his greatness and towering knowledge, he was able to remain "uncomplicated", humble, indeed, childlike. (I shall come back to this later.) But he did realize and acknowledge his gifts. He saw them as just that—pure gift, something bestowed on him, for which he had to be thankful, which he had simply to put into service. (He himself, though, did not fully appreciate the sheer magnitude of the gift.)

Looking back at his youth, we can single out three great gifts which he received, so to speak, in the cradle.

Origins

The first is his family. He came from an old patrician family in Lucerne which had given his hometown army officers, statesmen, scholars, and churchmen— abbots and abbesses, canons, and a Jesuit provincial in Mexico. The foundation of the city and canton library of Lucerne went back to his forefathers. His father, Oscar Ludwig Carl von Balthasar (1872–1946), was the canton builder, responsible, among other things, for the St. Karli-Kirche, one of Switzerland's pioneering modern church buildings. Through his mother, Gabrielle Pietzcker (d. 1929), co-foundress and first general secretary of the Swiss League of Catholic Women, he was related to the Hungarian martyr-bishop, Apor von Györ, who was shot by Russian soldiers in 1944 for harboring some women refugees in his house. His younger brother Dieter served as an officer in the Swiss Guard. His sister Renée (1908–1986) was Superior-General, from 1971 to 1983, of the Franciscan Sisters of Sainte-Marie des Anges. At the Pension Felsberg, run by his grandmother, he spent a large part of his childhood in the company of an aunt who was only a few years his senior. Here cosmopolitan attitudes and trilingualism (German, French, and English) were taken for granted. Here, too, he became familiar with the witty conversation and sophisticated lifestyle of the English visitors; later on, during the First World War, with wounded French soldiers; and finally, in 1918, with the Habsburg imperial family as they passed through. Von Balthasar had connections with Protestantism through his grandfather, the cavalry colonel Hermann Pietzcker— "We used occasionally to pay a shy visit to his smoky, weapon-filled room."[2] In fact, three of his great-grandparents, on his mother's side, were Protestant.

As von Balthasar himself testified, his childhood and youth were pervaded by music, for which he had a quite extraordinary talent. He had perfect pitch, so that, after the death of Adrienne von Speyr, he was able to give away his stereo system on the grounds that he did not need it anymore: he knew all the

---

[2] *Unser Auftrag. Bericht und Entwurf* (Einsiedeln: Johannes Verlag, 1984), 30.

works of Mozart by heart; he could picture the score and hear the music in his mind. But let us hear his own words:

> From those first tremendous impressions of music, Schubert's Mass in E-flat (when I was about five) and Tchaikovsky's *Pathétique* (when I was about eight), I spent endless hours on the piano. At Engelberg College there was also the opportunity to take part in orchestral Masses and operas. However, when my friends and I transferred to Feldkirch for the last two and a half years of high school, we found the "music department" there to be so noisy that we lost our enjoyment in playing. My university semesters in poor, almost starving, post-war Vienna were compensated for by a superabundance of concerts, operas, orchestral Masses. I had the privilege of lodging with Rudolf Allers—medical doctor, philosopher, theologian, translator of St. Anselm and St. Thomas. In the evenings, more often than not, we would play an entire Mahler symphony in piano transcription. . . . When I entered the Jesuits, music was automatically over and done with.[3]

Studies

Just a few things need to be added to this story of a musical youth. In point of fact, for a long time, von Balthasar wavered between musical and literary studies. He once reminded the pugnacious editor of the *Schweizer Kirchenzeitung*, Alois Schenker, of their time together in high school at Engelberg. "At that time you were frightfully industrious, while I was spending all my time on music and Dante and standing on my bed in the dormitory at night trying to get enough light to read *Faust*."[4] It is unclear why he prematurely left the Benedictine high school to go to the much less musical Jesuits in a neighboring but war-torn foreign country. He was probably looking for a more demanding curriculum. The transfer may also have contributed to the final decision to take literature (and philosophy) at the university rather than music. But in Feldkirch, too, von Balthasar did not stay to the end. A year before graduating from high school, he and two fellow students from Switzerland decided that they had had enough of the classroom and secretly matriculated in Zurich. The course in German studies, leading to his doctorate in the fall of 1928, consisted of "nine university semesters, alternating between Vienna, Berlin, and Zurich".[5] His stay in Vienna was especially long. What fascinated him there was Plotinus, whom he encountered in the lectures of Hans Eibl, and who gave him his first access to theology. Later on, Plotinus was to be the

---

[3] Ibid., 31.

[4] "Über Amt und Liebe in der Kirche. Ein offener Brief an Alois Schenker", *Neue Zürcher Nachrichten*, supplement on "Christian Culture", no. 29 (July 17, 1953).

[5] *Geschichte des eschatologischen Problems in der modernen deutschen Literatur* (Dissertation, Zurich, 1930), 221.

object of his polemic, as was Indian thought, which he came across in the
Sanskrit and Indo-European courses which he was taking at the same time
(among others, with Helmut von Glasenapp in Berlin). In Berlin he also heard
Eduard Spranger and a course on Kierkegaard given by Romano Guardini,
which profoundly impressed him. But the most lasting impression from his
student days came from his Viennese friend, the convert and dissident disciple
of Freud, Rudolf Allers, who had found his way from psychoanalysis to
medieval philosophy and theology. "Opponent of Freud and free disciple of
Alfred Adler, he possessed and imparted the feeling for interhuman love as the
objective medium of human existence; in this turn from the 'ego' to the reality
of the full 'Thou' lay for him philosophical truth and psychotherapeutic
method."[6]

Faith

One final yet primary gift must be mentioned, a gift bestowed on him, so to
speak, in the cradle: a simple and straightforward faith, unassailed by any
doubts, a faith which, to the very end, remained childlike in the best sense. He
owed this to his family, especially his mother, who "day by day went to Mass
down the steep path from our house". He remembered "quiet, deeply moving
early Masses on my own in the choir of the Franciscan church in Lucerne
(where he was baptized and received his first Holy Communion) or ten
o'clock Masses in the Jesuit church, a church for me of overwhelming
splendor".[7] This piety remained unbroken through his days at high school
(just think what boarding-school piety, always rather rigid, must have meant
for someone with a feel for the real thing!). Even more amazingly, it survived
all the anti-Christian currents of his time at the university. "In Vienna, I was
fascinated by Plotinus, but then, in another direction, there were inevitable
contacts with psychological circles (including Freudians). Mahler's tortured
pantheism moved me deeply. Nietzsche, Hofmannsthal, George came into
view. Then there was the *fin de siècle* mood of Karl Kraus, the manifest
corruption of a culture in decline."[8]

It was his undoubting faith which led the student von Balthasar, in his
doctoral dissertation, to examine modern German literature theologically,
from the point of view of its attitude to the Last Things, to the soul's "final or
eternal destiny"—a bold undertaking not only because of its wealth of material,
but even more because the dissertation was submitted to, of all places, the
Liberal Protestant University of Zurich. In the foreword to his *History of the*

[6] *Rechenschaft 1965* (Einsiedeln: Johannes Verlag, 1965), 34.
[7] *Unser Auftrag*, 30.
[8] *Prüfet alles—das Gute behaltet* (Ostfildern: Schwabenverlag, 1986), 8.

Eschatological Problem in Modern German Literature (1929) (he says it is really just "an extract from a larger treatise"), the author includes an apology:

> The novelty, or perhaps one should say the rashness, of what I am attempting in this study perhaps explains the kind of trepidation I feel about submitting it for publication. It may seem strange, in an historical investigation, to use philosophy and theology to explain works of art, and *vice versa,* works of art, without much reference to their aesthetic qualities. The results of this method will be its only justification.[9]

These two hundred and nineteen dense pages were passed *summa cum laude.* It is hard to decide whether this proves the results of the method or the immensely wide reading of the author.

Sometime before the completion of his dissertation, von Balthasar's faith led him to the thirty-day retreat given by Fr. Friedrich Kronseder, S.J. in the summer of 1927 to a group of lay students at Whylen near Basel. This was to be the decisive turning point of his life.

The Jesuit

Before this retreat von Balthasar had not had the slightest thought of becoming a priest or entering a religious order. In the student circles he frequented — this is not long after the *Literaturstreit* — "it was seen as a real misfortune if someone changed courses and took up the study of theology". That is why the call of God struck him like lightning from a cloudless sky.

> Even now, thirty years later, I could still go to that remote path in the Black Forest, not far from Basel, and find again the tree beneath which I was struck as by lightning. . . . And yet it was neither theology nor the priesthood which then came into my mind in a flash. It was simply this: you have nothing to choose, you have been called. You will not serve, you will be taken into service. You have no plans to make, you are just a little stone in a mosaic which has long been ready. All I needed to do was "leave everything and follow", without making plans, without wishes or insights. All I needed to do was to stand there and wait and see what I would be needed for.[10]

Like St. Ignatius when he is discussing "the first occasion of election" (*Spiritual Exercises,* no. 175), von Balthasar compared this calling to that of Levi the tax collector and Saul the persecutor of Christians, to whom Christ's call went out in a totally unmistakable way, not because of their merits but because of their ignorance. "At that stage it was just a matter of surrendering myself. If I

---

[9] *Geschichte des eschatologischen Problems,* foreword.
[10] *Pourquoi je me suis fait prêtre.* Témoignages recueillis par Jorge et Ramón Sans Vila, ed. Centre Diocésain de Documentation (Tournai, 1961), 21.

had known then about the Secular Institutes' way of life, I might well have found the solution to my problem even in a secular profession, the problem, I mean, of how to put myself entirely at the disposal of God."[11] However, it was the path into the Society of Jesus which lay closest at hand. And so, after the completion of his doctorate, after his mother's premature and painful death, which she offered up for her son, after his younger sister's entry into a religious order, on November 18, 1929 von Balthasar entered the novitiate of the south German province of the Jesuits.

There then followed the regular formation of a religious: two years of novitiate under the direction of Fr. Otto Danneffel (his fellow novices included Alois Grillmeier and Franz von Tattenbach); two (instead of three) years of philosophy at Pullach near Munich and four years of theology at Fourvière near Lyons. These studies concluded with the double license in philosophy and theology. Von Balthasar never acquired a doctorate in these subjects.

Entry to a religious order meant, first of all, renunciation—the abandonment not only of music but also of literary and cultural life. Von Balthasar's account of Hopkins' loss of his poetic power on becoming a Jesuit is undoubtedly colored by autobiographical reminiscences. As Hopkins saw it, the Society of Jesus did not lay stress on the aesthetic, and brilliance did not suit Jesuits.[12] The normal studies of a religious were bound to seem dry and pretty dull to a young man like von Balthasar, accustomed to a very different world. He saw his philosophical studies as a "languishing in the desert of neo-scholasticism".[13] His teachers were the authors of the old Pullach *Institutiones Philosophiae Scholasticae* —Frank, Rast, Schuster, Wilwoll, solid neo-scholastics with a degree of openness to modern problems. Later he was to remember with particular gratitude the moralist, Johann Baptist Schuster, and proposed Maximilian Rast, by then spiritual director of the seminary at Sion, as the first investigator of the mission of Adrienne von Speyr.

Fourvière was not much more stimulating than Pullach. "Really nothing was heard of a *nouvelle théologie* in the lectures. (I am surprised by this myth dreamt up nowadays for poor old Fourvière!)"[14] And yet he found valued teachers like Henri Vignon and Henri Rondet (who was to carry out the second examination of Adrienne's mission) and fellow students and friends like Henri Bouillard and Donatien Mollat and younger men like Pierre Lyonnet, François Varillon, and Jean Daniélou. But the real problem was neither the teachers nor the students, but the theology itself. Looking back in 1946, still a Jesuit, he wrote:

---

[11] Ibid., 22.
[12] *Herrlichkeit. Eine theologische Ästhetik.* Bd. II: *Fächer der Stile* (Einsiedeln: Johannes Verlag, 1962), 736–41.
[13] *Rechenschaft 1965*, 34.
[14] *Prüfet alles*, 9.

My entire period of study in the Society was a grim struggle with the dreariness of theology, with what men had made out of the glory of revelation. I could not endure this presentation of the Word of God. I could have lashed out with the fury of a Samson. I felt like tearing down, with Samson's strength, the whole temple and burying myself beneath the rubble. But it was like this because, despite my sense of vocation, I wanted to carry out my own plans, and was living in a state of unbounded indignation. I told almost no one about this. Przywara understood everything; I did not have to say anything. Otherwise there was no one who could have understood me. I wrote the "Apocalypse" with a dogged determination, resolved, whatever the cost, to rebuild the world from its foundations. It really took Basel, especially the all-soothing goodness of the commentary on St. John, to lead my aggressive will into true indifference.[15]

Von Balthasar mentions there one of the great inspirers of his student days and indeed his entire work: Erich Przywara. He was never von Balthasar's teacher (he lived in Munich, not Pullach), but he proved to be "an excellent if exacting mentor. He made you learn the scholastic philosophy with an attitude of serene detachment and then go on (as he did) and deal with all the modern philosophy, confronting Augustine and Thomas with Hegel, Scheler, and Heidegger."[16] Von Balthasar was to meet Przywara again each year in the summer vacation, when he returned from Fourvière to Munich to finish a chapter of his *Apokalypse.* He then lived for two years with him when he was working on the *Stimmen der Zeit.* Out of gratitude he later published Przywara's early writings in three volumes—even though he had, in the meantime, expressed certain reservations about them.

With an even more undivided heart he paid the same debt of gratitude to his other great friend and inspirer (who likewise was never his teacher), Henri de Lubac. It was from him that he learned what theology really was and could be.

Luckily and consolingly, Henri de Lubac lived in the house. He showed us the way beyond the scholastic stuff to the Fathers of the Church and generously lent us all his own notes and extracts. And so, while all the others went off to play football, Daniélou, Bouillard, and I and a few others (Fessard was no longer there) got down to Origen, Gregory of Nyssa, and Maximus. I wrote a book on each of these.[17]

In addition to these, still under the influence of Przywara, came a translation of part of Augustine's *Enarrationes in Psalmos* and the preparation of a more

---

[15] Adrienne von Speyr, *Erde und Himmel. Ein Tagebuch. Zweiter Teil II: Die Zeit der grossen Diktate,* ed. and with an introduction by Hans Urs von Balthasar (Einsiedeln: Johannes Verlag, 1975), 195ff.

[16] *Prüfet alles,* 9.

[17] Ibid.

comprehensive Augustine anthology, for which von Balthasar read through Augustine's complete works while sitting through lectures with plugged ears.[18]

France introduced him not only to theology but to the great men of her literature—Péguy, Bernanos, and above all Claudel, with whom he had an unforgettable personal encounter. Von Balthasar would translate Claudel's *Satin Slipper* "at least five times". He worked on the translation of Claudel's lyric poetry for twenty-five years before it could appear in 1963 in its definitive version.

His Lyons student days also left him with a susceptibility to bowel and throat infections which would accompany him throughout his life and constantly give him trouble. Nevertheless, the most important aspect of those years was his preparation for the priesthood, which he saw as total availability. On July 26, 1936 he was ordained to the priesthood, with twenty-one of his confrères, by Cardinal Faulhaber. At his first Mass, celebrated for a small family group in a private chapel in Lucerne, he himself preached the sermon ("after all, you don't want to know how Fr. Gutzwiller preaches, but how I preach"). His text came from the words of consecration, which were also printed on his ordination card: "*Benedixit, fregit, deditque.* [Because he blessed, he broke, and because he broke you, he could give you.]"[19] He emphasized the breaking so forcefully that it remained in one's memory for life.

At the conclusion of his studies in 1937 he was sent first for two years to work on the *Stimmen der Zeit,* but above all to complete his own books. In 1939 he returned for a few months to Pullach for his tertianship under the direction of Fr. Albert Steger and again to make a thirty-day retreat. Fr. Steger was one of the first people in the German-speaking world to interpret Ignatian spirituality mystically rather than just ascetically. At the beginning of the war his superiors gave von Balthasar the choice of going either to Rome as a professor at the Gregorian University or to Basel as a student chaplain. In Rome he and three other fathers were to have established an institute for ecumenical theology—a plan which up to now has not materialized. Von Balthasar chose Basel—certainly not out of patriotism, but because pastoral work was closer to his heart than lecturing.

The Student Chaplain

To understand the next stage of von Balthasar's life properly, we must remember the situation at that time. In Switzerland the Jesuits were no more than tolerated, certainly not officially accepted. The constitutional prohibition of

---

[18] Ibid.

[19] *Das Weizenkorn. Aphorismen* (Einsiedeln: Johannes Verlag, 1953), 99.

any kind of work "in Church and school" and of the establishment of
residences was still in force. So it was through prominent individuals that the
Society of Jesus made its appearance in public. It would be rumored that these
men were Jesuits (basically everyone knew that anyway), and it was by them
that the Society as a whole was judged. There could be no institutional
presence; it was just not permitted, whether in educational institutions or in
Jesuit churches. The *Akademikerhäuser* of the student chaplains had the highest
profile. The magazine founded in these years by the Swiss Jesuits, the
Apologetischen Blätter (later called *Orientierung*), came out first of all as a kind
of underground newspaper. Juridicially, the Swiss Jesuits belonged to the
south German province of the Society, though, because of wartime circumstances, they were largely independent. In 1947 a Swiss vice-province was set
up. From the beginning of the war there was also a Swiss novitiate, first of all,
modestly beyond the Swiss frontier at Balzers in Liechtenstein, and then, just
as coyly, in the canton of Fribourg. Among the Swiss in this situation there
were no professors, hardly any "intellectuals", but mostly competent pastors.
A young confrère, who, at the commencement of his work, had already
written more books than all the others put together must have seemed like a
misfit or oddity.

Not that the Swiss Jesuits at this time lacked the intellectual and cultural
dimension. Swiss Catholicism was undergoing a cultural awakening, and
Jesuits like Richard Gutzwiller and Paul de Chastonay (to name just the two
best known) were well to the fore. In the early '40s student chaplaincy work
meant, above all, cultural work. This new development was given further
impetus by the war and the resulting cultural isolation, especially of German-
speaking Switzerland. Publishing flourished—it was a case of having to resort
to literary self-sufficiency. In reaction against Hitler's Germany, Catholics
turned more and more to French Catholicism.

This is the context in which von Balthasar's activities in Basel began. First
and foremost was his activity as an editor and translator. He took over the
editing of the "European Series" of the Klosterberg collection, a wartime
attempt to save Europe's cultural heritage. The series was to be comprised of
altogether fifty short anthologies. Von Balthasar himself was responsible for
ten of them: Goethe, Novalis, Nietzsche (three volumes!), Brentano, and
Borchardt. He translated Claudel, Péguy, the poetry of the French Resistance,
later also Bernanos and Mauriac. In 1943 the Zurich Playhouse—at the time,
with the exiled Horwitz, Ginsberg, Langhoff, Paryla, Becker, and Giehse,
probably the best German-speaking theatre in the world—staged the premiere
of his translation of *The Satin Slipper*. Von Balthasar himself collaborated in
the production in an advisory capacity. Other plays by Claudel followed.
Finally, in 1951, there was the first performance of Bernanos' *Carmelites,* also in
his version. Von Balthasar maintained friendly contacts with artists like Richard

Seewald, Hans Stocker, Albert Schilling, and Hermann Baur, who pioneered
the renewal of ecclesiastical art, undoubtedly the ripest fruit of the cultural
renaissance in Swiss Catholicism.

His work with students was also largely cultural. The student chaplain gave
lecture after lecture[20]—the distraction of television was still in the distant
future. In addition to an annual series of public lectures, he spent numerous
evenings debating in the various student societies, in particular, the culturally
orientated Akademische Gesellschaft Renaissance, of which he himself was a
senior member. In Zurich, Bern, and Freiburg, too, he was a frequent and
welcome guest at its meetings. The Studentische Schulungsgemeinschaft (SG),
which he founded in 1941, was also, as the name suggests, primarily aimed at
giving students a training in the philosophy of life. The list of those who
conducted courses and conferences included some distinguished names: Hugo
Rahner, Max Müller, Otto Karrer, Alois Dempf, Gustav Siewerth, Alfons
Deissler, Gottlieb Söhngen, Oskar Bauhofer, Josef Bernhart, Martin Buber,
Karl Rahner, Adolf Portmann, Yves Congar, Walter Dirks, Eugen Biser,
Henri de Lubac—the names, more or less, of von Balthasar's friends and
acquaintances.

But the Schulungsgemeinschaft was also an expression of von Balthasar's
pastoral activity, which was not confined to student liturgies (which, for the
time, took quite a modern form), regular sermons in the *Marienkirche,* and
countless conversations with individuals. The chaplain each year conducted
several retreats for male students and eventually—an innovation—for female
students as well. What is more, the retreats took the full Ignatian form of
exercises aimed at helping people make a decision about their state of life.
With many of these students and retreatants he established genuine, lifelong
friendships. Their conversations with him, detailed and often decisive for their
lives, were unforgettable. He liked to begin by inviting them to go for a walk.
Unforgettable, too, were the nightlong discussions among small groups of
friends. Unforgettable were the evenings on the training courses when he
would sit down at the piano and play, from memory, Mozart's *Don Giovanni.*

One at least of the students of this period must be mentioned by name:
Robert Rast (1920–1946), the person perhaps closest to von Balthasar. Like
von Balthasar, Rast was from an ancient Lucerne family, and also like him an
old pupil of the Benedictine high school at Engelberg. Having been awarded
top marks in his school-leaving examination, he went on to Basel and Freiburg
to study cultural philosophy—because it was the only way he could think of
bringing together his diverse cultural, musical, literary, and theological interests,
and because he felt called to be a Christian cultural politician, involved in the
"intellectual clash of contemporary Swiss Christian culture (the culture of the

---

[20] A list of these series of lectures can be found in *Unser Auftrag,* 62.

West) and National Socialism".[21] It was from Robert Rast that the idea came of establishing a Schulungsgemeinschaft. Rast took the initiative in setting it up and became its first leader. In addition to study, he devoted himself to literature. He wrote several articles, published a book, *On the Meaning of Culture,* and (in the Klosterberg collection) a selection of texts from Herder. Having taken his doctorate, after only eight university semesters (his course was shortened because of military service), he decided to join the Society of Jesus, but then, after only a few weeks in the novitiate, he succumbed to a serious lung disease. He spent a year at the sanitorium in Leysin, where he completed another and newly arranged translation of Lallemant's *Spiritual Doctrine.* On May 16, 1946, having taken his religious vows, he died. His grave in the cloister of the Hofkirche in Lucerne is only a step away from von Balthasar's.

Robert Rast was not the only one of von Balthasar's Basel students to find his way into the novitiate of the Society of Jesus. Two of his friends had preceded him, others followed. The students in Basel talked of "Jesuititis". Not all who entered the novitiate—some of them against von Balthasar's advice—stayed the course. This led to personal tragedies, bitterness, and much gossip. Von Balthasar's style was not everyone's cup of tea. For many it seemed too aesthetic, too demanding. He was successful with students of literature and history, with architects, a few lawyers, and some medical students. With scientists and science he never found the right approach. So it was inevitable that the dedication of his 1945 book, *Das Herz der Welt—Electis dilectis,* was seen as utterly elitist, and that von Balthasar himself should be regarded by many people as inaccessible and arrogant. He saw things differently. What he wrote at this time about Mozart in the Renaissance yearbook without doubt represents his own feelings: "So exclusive is the nobility of this genius that it excludes the common and includes in itself everything in the world.... Like everything really great, it is unenvious of anything or anybody, because it knows that greatness is esoteric of its very nature and has no need of the false and artificial charm of a 'circle'."[22]

The student chaplain's third sphere of activity was the encounter with Protestantism. Basel, the ancient city of the humanists, was a stronghold of the Reformation. Karl Barth taught at its theological faculty. Von Balthasar had already discussed Barth in the *Apokalypse.* Now he tried to take up again the failed dialogue about the *analogia entis* between Barth and Przywara. The idea was to take de Lubac's theology of creation as its starting point. It was the common love of Mozart which made their meetings easier and lay at the heart

---

[21] Hans Urs von Balthasar (ed.), *Der Ruf des Herrn. Aus Briefen von Robert Rast* (Lucerne: Räber, 1947), 21.
[22] *Spiritus Creator (Skizzen zur Theologie III)* (Einsiedeln: Johannes Verlag, 1967), 470.

of their abiding friendship. In addition to numerous private conversations,
Barth invited von Balthasar to take part in his seminar, and in 1949–1950 von
Balthasar gave a series of lectures on Barth in Barth's presence. The book on
Barth of 1951, "joyfully welcomed and approved"[23] by Barth, shows how
there could be a healthy rapprochement of the two points of view. Barth
became the third great inspirer of von Balthasar's theology. "Barth's doctrine
of election, that brilliant overcoming of Calvin, powerfully and permanently
attracted me."[24] But it was Barth's radical Christocentrism which exercised
the most lasting influence. By von Balthasar's own admission, the essays in
Verbum Caro, Theologie der Geschichte, and *Glaubhaft ist nur Liebe* are the fruit
and continuation of this ecumenical discussion.[25]

What von Balthasar was aiming at in these discussions, albeit in vain, was
nothing less than Barth's conversion. At that time in Switzerland contact with
Protestants almost invariably meant conversion. A quite exceptional wave of
conversions was attracting notice, and in Basel von Balthasar was notorious as
a "convert-maker". In fact, he played only a small part in the two most
sensational of his conversions, which took place at the very beginning of his
time in Basel. He had been introduced by a mutual friend to Professor Albert
Béguin and to a lady who wanted to be received into the Church—Adrienne
Kaegi-von Speyr. A close friend of Georges Bernanos, Béguin, from western
Switzerland, was a professor of French literature, and an authority on German
romanticism. He had been driven out of Nazi Germany and was teaching at
the University of Basel. Toward the end of the war, he returned to France to
take up the direction of the journal *Esprit.* He was baptized by von Balthasar
on November 15, 1940. The friend of his youth, Adrienne von Speyr, whom
von Balthasar had received into the Catholic Church two weeks previously,
was his godmother.

With Adrienne

The encounter with Adrienne von Speyr had a determining influence on the
rest of von Balthasar's life and work. This medical doctor, from an old Basel
family, had been born at La Chaux-de-Fonds in 1902. In 1927 she had married
a widower, the Basel historian Emil Dürr. After his accidental death, following seven happy years of marriage, she fell out with God and for years could
no longer say the Our Father. In 1936 she married again, this time to Dürr's
successor, Professor Werner Kaegi, with whom she lived until her death in the

[23] *Rechenschaft 1965,* 38.
[24] *Unser Auftrag,* 85.
[25] *Kleiner Lageplan zu meinen Büchern* (Einsiedeln: Johannes Verlag, 1955), 7; *Rechenschaft 1965,* 16, 35.

lovely house *Auf Burg* on the Münsterplatz in Basel. Later von Balthasar would be welcomed there as a guest. She was a woman with a good sense of humor, a lively mind, and a sharp tongue, socially popular, and devoted to her patients, especially the poor ones and those with psychological problems. Her conversion (in the offing since her childhood) caused a considerable stir in Basel, especially among her family and Protestant friends. Soon there was gossip about miracles, which apparently took place in her surgery. There were rumors about the visions she was supposed to have had. The regular and lengthy meetings with her spiritual director aroused the mistrust of his confrères and gave rise, understandably, to more gossip.

Soon the first fruits of this collaboration between the student chaplain and Frau Professor Kaegi came to light. On October 15, 1945, after a retreat in Estavayer (August 5–12), in a house in Wettsteinallee, the women's branch of the Community of St. John was founded with three postulants. At first, only a few people knew about the foundation. On its publication three years later, von Balthasar's much discussed book *Der Laie und der Ordensstand* made the new foundation more widely known. In 1947, with the help of an Einsiedeln friend, Dr. Josef Fraefel, Johannes Verlag was set up for the publication of Adrienne's works, which were having difficulties over the imprimatur. In the same year, Johannes Verlag published Adrienne's translation of *The Autobiography of a Soul* (*Theresia vom Kinde Jesu, Geschichte einer Seele*), with a preface by von Balthasar. A year later the much discussed and appreciated book on Our Lady, *Magd des Herrn,* was published, as well as the third volume of the commentary on St. John's Gospel, *Die Abschiedsreden,* again with a preface by von Balthasar. The remaining three volumes, which had to be revised at the insistence of the censor, could not be published until 1949. The last of these "early works", which made Adrienne von Speyr well-known, was the two-volume commentary on the Apocalypse of St. John, published in 1950.

Leaving the Jesuits

Meanwhile, the problems of Adrienne's confessor were multiplying. In 1945 his already advertised Christmas sermon on German Swiss Radio was cancelled at short notice because of the law about the Jesuits. Public astonishment at the decision led to the first discussion of this article of the constitution. Odermatt, editor of the *Neue Zürcher Nachrichten,* asked: Is Swiss Radio "school" or "church"? For the Swiss Jesuits, who in any case were having problems in Zurich, the incident was, to say the least, unpleasant. The years that then followed were to be a time of real crisis for von Balthasar. All his human ties were placed in question. To begin with, there were family troubles. His father had been gravely ill for quite some time and eventually died in June

1946. His godmother, the person to whom he most easily related in the family, who had always understood him, suffered her first stroke, was left paralyzed, and was given the last rites by him. On May 16, 1946 Robert Rast died in Leysin. Shortly before, von Balthasar had received news that his friend and mentor Przywara was suffering from a serious nervous disorder, so he set about trying to obtain for him the entry permit into Switzerland. In August von Balthasar was due in the normal way to make his solemn religious profession. However, at the same time, he was informed that the Society of Jesus could not take responsibility for Frau Professor Kaegi and the Community of St. John. Von Balthasar asked for the genuineness of her visions to be investigated, and for the postponement until then of his vows. On April 22, 1947 (the Feast of the Mother of God and the foundation feast of the Society of Jesus), he spoke in Rome for the first time and unsuccessfully with Father General Johann Baptist Janssens.

Meanwhile, von Balthasar's Lyons friends, and he himself with them, were coming under fire theologically. In the August issue of the *Revue Thomiste,* Michel Labourdette, O.P. had published a critical review of the two Lyons series *Théologie* and *Sources Chrétiennes.*[26] Critical remarks were made about de Lubac, Bouillard, Fessard, and Daniélou. The reviewer at first made a favorable mention of von Balthasar's study of Gregory of Nyssa, *Présence et pensée* (which had not appeared in the two series referred to above). But then, in his conclusion, he returned to it with a long quotation from von Balthasar's foreword, introduced as follows: "Theology, no more than metaphysics, does not lend itself to be judged according to the categories of aesthetics. I do not mean in its expressions, but in the universal value and permanence of the truths it defines. That is what is wrong, to give an example, with a brilliant and superficial page written by a very distinguished author."[27] Then follows the quotation from von Balthasar—from a text which, in later years, he would probably no longer have written in that form. In retrospect, it is noticeable how clearly Labourdette already recognized the aesthetic character of von Balthasar's theology (with reference to Daniélou, again for the first time, he spoke of a "dramatic theology"). Admittedly, what he meant by this, not entirely incorrectly, was an aestheticizing theology. Von Balthasar himself had not yet found his way to the true "seeing of the form" of God's glory.

By contrast to the elegant and delicate piece by Labourdette, the article by his Dominican confrère Garrigou-Lagrange, in the December issue of the *Angelicum,* seemed like a bombardment. "Where is the new theology going?" he thundered in his title. He concluded with this succinct answer: "It is going

---

[26] M. Michel Labourdette, "La théologie et ses sources", *Revue Thomiste* 46 (1946): 353–71.

[27] Ibid., 370.

back to Modernism."[28] Von Balthasar is not expressly mentioned in this second article, and so he did not take part in the controversy which eventually led to the suspension from teaching of de Lubac and Bouillard and to the encyclical *Humani generis*. And yet the suspicion surrounding his friend de Lubac had a most profound effect on him and his theological work. In theology, too, he could no longer move about freely. The book on Barth (and the ensuing controversy with E. Gutwenger about the theological concept of nature) can only be understood in the context of this consternation.

In mid-September 1947 von Balthasar was able to travel to Germany to accompany Erich Przywara back to Basel, where his friend slowly recuperated. On November 26, he spoke for a second time with the Father General, who sent him to Lyons for a discussion with Fr. Rondet. Rondet was unable to recognize the genuineness of Adrienne von Speyr's visions and the divine mission entrusted to von Balthasar. The Bishop of Basel, Franziskus von Streng, also had reservations about the Community of St. John, and even later would not withdraw them. In this hopeless situation, Father General told von Balthasar to go on retreat under the direction of Fr. Donatien Mollat, the Johannine specialist, and during that retreat to make his final decision. The retreat took place at the end of June 1948 at Barollières near Lyons. The decision, made with the agreement of the retreat father, was to leave the Society, if it was not otherwise seriously willing to test von Balthasar's mission. Then followed a painful eighteen months of waiting, during which von Balthasar tried in vain to find a bishop who would accept him, and his confrères tried in vain to make him change his mind. After a further exchange of letters with Father General, he left the Society on February 11, 1950.

How von Balthasar himself saw this departure and how hard it was for him comes out in the short printed statement sent to his friends and acquaintances and the long farewell letter written to his confrères.

> I took this step, for both sides a very grave one, after a long testing of the certainty I had reached through prayer that I was being called by God to certain definite tasks in the Church. The Society felt it could not release me to give these tasks my undivided commitment. . . . So, for me, the step taken means an application of Christian obedience to God, who at any time has the right to call a man not only out of his physical home or his marriage, but also from his chosen spiritual home in a religious order, so that he can use him for his purposes within the Church. Any resulting advantages or disadvantages in the secular sphere were not under discussion and not taken into account.

For his confrères he goes into more detail. It was a question, he says, of the conflict between his "interior certainty, reached in prayer" and his obedience

---

[28] Reginald Garrigou-Lagrange, "La nouvelle théologie où va-t-elle?" *Angelicum* 23 (1946): 143.

to the Society, in other words, the conflict between obedience to the Society and direct obedience to God. With references to St. Thomas and Cardinal de Lugo, Balthasar explains theologically that the resolution of this conflict is not to be found "absolutely and in every case in obedience to the order", and he concludes confidently:

> Whether it be hard or easy, whether or not it be understood, whether the prospects be fair or gloomy, whichever be the darker night — the obedience of staying or the obedience of going: What is that to the person who seeks the will of the Lord? And if *Spiritual Exercises,* no. 167 almost inevitably comes true, he will accept it with a grateful heart. And yet what does it matter to him? God ensures that such obedience, if practiced in a childlike way without "heroism" or arrogance, ends up, not at the edge, but at the very foundations of the Catholic Church.[29]

This astonishing certainty contrasts greatly with what he constantly impressed upon his students with regard to Ignatian obedience, especially when he was directing the Spiritual Exercises. Only now, as a result of the documents published since the death of Adrienne von Speyr, can we understand it properly. From these it becomes clear that for years and years von Balthasar had been confronted with a superabundance of charismatic attestation — multiple stigmatization, healings and other miracles, vision upon vision. The behavior of the seer herself never gave rise to any doubt about the authenticity of her experiences; on the contrary, it seemed to confirm them. But, above all, one realizes how much Adrienne, with her gift of knowing people's hearts, helped her confessor with his spiritual and pastoral work. One also sees how not only the common mission but also, even in the early days, the necessity of leaving the Jesuits emerged with such imperative clarity. Adrienne suffered the latter even more deeply, so it would seem, than von Balthasar himself. Looking back at his decision, he wrote: "For me the Society was of course a beloved homeland; the thought that one might have to 'leave all' more than once in a lifetime in order to follow the Lord, even an order, had never occurred to me, and struck me like a blow."[30] Toward the end of his life he asked for readmission to the Society of Jesus. It could not be granted him, however, because he attached to it the condition that future responsibility for the Community of St. John should also be taken over. On the occasion of his appointment as a cardinal, Father General wanted to offer him Sant'Ignazio as a titular church, but this too fell through because of canonical problems.

This is neither the time nor the place to subject Adrienne's charisms to a critical theological examination or to distinguish within them between divine

---

[29] Published in Italian translation in *Il Sabato* (July 23–29, 1988): 28.
[30] *Erster Blick auf Adrienne von Speyr* (Einsiedeln: Johannes Verlag, 1968), 38.

gift and what was possibly natural endowment—if such a separation is ever really possible. Two things, though, can be said in retrospect. If Adrienne von Speyr had a mission in the Church (and ecclesiastical statements of recent years seem to point in that direction), then, to carry it out, she needed the mediation of a priest like von Balthasar who could accept her visions with theological knowledge and a childlike simplicity of faith. Any encouragement of self-reflection (which he constantly avoided), any rash critical judgment, would have restricted the free flow of inspiration. On the other hand, the founding of the Community of St. John might possibly have worked out better if von Balthasar had not left the Jesuits. (During the retreat leading to his decision, he saw the mass of difficulties awaiting him as the only argument against the divine source of his mission.) And yet, in the Society, von Balthasar's theological work would scarcely have taken this form. In line with the "Gamaliel principle" (cf. Acts 5:34–39), the final judgment of von Balthasar's decision must be left to the future and thus to God.

The Final Years with Adrienne

After leaving the Society, von Balthasar was literally on the street. He had, first of all, to look for somewhere to live, and that meant, since his presence there was not welcome to the bishop, outside of Basel. Through the good offices of his friends, he was offered a vacant apartment on the Zürichberg, Im Schilf 11, from which he moved later to Titlistrasse 51. On the ecclesiastical side, the Bishop of Chur, Christianus Caminada, gave him permission to say Mass and, somewhat later, to hear confessions, so that he was able once more to give retreats. Yet it was only on February 2, 1956 that, at the urging of some of his lay friends in Zurich on the occasion of his fiftieth birthday, he was incardinated in the diocese of Chur. With this ecclesiastical home, he was at last able to move back to Basel and accept the hospitality of Professor Kaegi at Münsterplatz 4, where he had had a room since 1952.

A second, no less burdensome concern was his financial upkeep. To earn his living and to finance the publishing firm, which devoured rather than made money, he repeatedly undertook lecture tours of Germany. In February 1950 he went to Tübingen, Bonn, Bad Honnef, Maria Laach (where he renewed his religious vows in the hands of the abbot, for from this commitment he did not want in any way to be released), Andernach, Koblenz, Neuwied, Cologne, Essen, Münster, Paderborn, Stuttgart.[31] The following winter there were lectures in Freiburg, Bonn, Walberberg, Cologne, Düsseldorf, Hannover, Hamburg, Kiel, Göttingen, Marburg, Heidelberg, Baden-Baden, and in the

---

[31] Adrienne von Speyr, *Erde und Himmel. Ein Tagebuch. Dritter Teil: Die späten Jahre* (Einsiedeln: Johannes Verlag, 1976), 55.

early summer of 1952, "in sweltering heat", at various German universities. "It is no fun, but it is attracting a considerable number of people. In Freiburg there must have been about a thousand. There is a real vacuum, and anyone who finds the right words has hearers who are thirsting for Christ." The book *Die Gottesfrage des heutigen Menschen* gives an impression of the content of these lectures. Meanwhile, retreats were constantly being given; in 1950 four courses in Dussnang, Kerns, Colmar, and Mainz. Later the emphasis would be on retreats for theologians, and from 1958 onwards there were retreats for the *Cusanus-Werk,* each time with between forty and eighty retreatants.

Several university chairs were offered him: just before he left the Society, he was invited to succeed Guardini in Munich. When an offer came from Tübingen, the Congregation for Seminaries and Universities imposed a teaching ban on him because he had left a religious order. In any case, he turned down all offers. He had not been freed of one commitment in order to take on another which would remove him still further from his mission. The only chair which he might have accepted, at the philosophy faculty in Basel, was never offered him, though Karl Barth did invite him to come to the (Protestant) theology faculty. An entry in his diary, from the spring of 1954, conveys the atmosphere of the period.

> Many visitors. From time to time Reinhold Schneider, C. J. Burckhardt, Guardini, Heuss. I still have my room in Zurich. I am incardinated nowhere. Many courses—retreats or continuing education weeks—after Easter, at the Ascension, in June, end of July, beginning of August, in Spain, then in Louvain. I don't meet Adrienne until August 17 in Paris. From there we go to St. Quay. After the vacation more courses and conferences. So Adrienne is on her own a lot. This year she performed her last surgery in the Eisengasse. She was too ill to take it up again at home.[32]

This sounds like a terribly fragmented existence. And yet, in these years of his middle age, von Balthasar had found his own real center. It started with two little books, which on their publication caused quite a stir, and which even today are rightly regarded as milestones in the development of his thought: the already mentioned *Der Laie und der Ordensstand* of 1948 and *Die Schleifung der Bastionen* of 1952. In his fiftieth year, he focused his *Kleiner Lageplan zu meinen Büchern* on this central point, and then years later, *Rechenschaft 1965,* more aggressive and concerned with himself, starts off from it. The issue is the Church in the world, not a radiating of the Church's holiness into the profane world, but the leavening of the world from within in order to make visible God's glory which still shines in this world. The center of the Church, says von Balthasar, is where people usually see the periphery: her secular mission. That is why the defensive bulwarks must be razed to the ground and

[32] Ibid., 165.

spacious boulevards built from the rubble. This mission of the Church in the world must be carried out by the laity, who live completely in the world. But, to be able to fulfill that mission, they really must be "salt" and "leaven". They must live at the very heart of Christianity, in the shame of the Cross, in prayer, and renunciation. Here von Balthasar sees the role of the secular institutes, as proposed in 1947 by *Provida Mater,* and as the Community of St. John tries to put into practice.

All of von Balthasar's polemics revolve round this central point. They begin with the still quite peaceful exchanges of this period about the theological concept of nature and, with Karl Rahner, about the definition of the laity. Then, in a harsher tone, there is *Friedliche Fragen an das Opus Dei.*[33] (In *Schleifung der Bastionen* he had cited Opus Dei as an example of what he meant. He later heard, with relief, that it no longer regarded itself as a secular institute). Finally, there were the furious attacks of the post-conciliar period, of which *Cordula* became the best known. This *zelos* of the controversialist is not only the reverse side of his theological *eros* (think how sarcastic Karl Barth could be!). He was also concerned that there should be no abandoning or obscuring of the indissoluble bond between the Christian's mission in the world and his imitation of Christ Crucified—the "decisive test", witnessing to Christ in one's life and suffering.

By leaving his religious order, von Balthasar himself was again "in the world". His life was more the secular one of the ordinary Christian than that of a diocesan priest. Here, in retrospect, may lie the deeper significance, for his mission, of the decision to leave the Jesuits: lifestyle and mission came to coincide more closely. The center of his mission now also shed light for him on his earlier career, including his literary work. "It all may as well be literary gossip if it does not serve an ecclesial activity which is not self-chosen or self-appointed. That is the center: everything else—even if it came earlier—is arranged around it."[34] In the years of which we are speaking, being in the world meant above all concern for the return of men to God, as is shown by *Die Gottesfrage des heutigen Menschen.* But abiding at the Christian center meant above all prayer and contemplation. "The deeper that action is meant to penetrate, the deeper must be the contemplation that precedes and follows it."[35] That is why the chief obligation of the members of the Schulungsgemeinschaft was "a short time each day of recollection before God, of contemplative prayer". To help with this, in 1955 von Balthasar started a series at Johannes Verlag called *Adoratio.* He himself wrote the first volume in it, *Das betrachtende Gebet.* Significantly, the series languished after four volumes:

[33] "Friedliche Fragen an das Opus Dei", *Der christliche Sonntag* 16, no. 15 (1964): 117f.
[34] *Kleiner Lageplan,* 19. .
[35] Ibid., 20.

no collaborators could be found for it. And so von Balthasar constantly tried new series: *Lectio Spiritualis* (from 1958), *Beten Heute* (from 1972), *Christliche Meister* (from 1979). As early as 1948, at the same time as the book on lay communities, an essay appeared which was to fix von Balthasar's image for years to come: *"Theologie und Heiligkeit"*. The contrast drawn there between "sitting" and "kneeling" theology has become proverbial.

In his personal life, too, von Balthasar at this time was taken deeper and deeper into the center of Christianity, into the Cross. First of all, there was the collaboration with Adrienne, which demanded more of him as the years went by. After the great dictated biblical commentaries, there was much selfless secretarial work to be done. At the beginning of April 1956 he reports:

> Since January I have already copied one thousand manuscript pages: 1 Corinthians, Colossians, and a book about the states of Christian life. All seem excellent to me in their own way. I suppose this year I shall have to concentrate on this work if I am ever to see light at the end of the tunnel. There is also much I have to ponder before I can give my own opinion and get it ready for publication.

However quickly he thought he could do it at the time, the work never came to an end for him. Right up to the last years of his life, he had to sacrifice his vacations in order to complete more manuscripts. Being with Adrienne increasingly meant looking after a seriously ill woman. Again and again in his letters he says: "Frau Kaegi is very seriously ill." Since 1940 she had been suffering from heart trouble, to which, as time went on, more and more sufferings were added. Several times she had to (or was allowed to) experience dying, and from 1954 she could no longer leave her house in the Münsterplatz.

But von Balthasar's own health was also affected. Already in his early fifties he was constantly falling ill between the various journeys to give lectures or retreats. In the fall of 1957—Albert Béguin had died in May—a state of exhaustion laid him low for six months. "I really thought I was cracking up, but it now looks as if I am getting back to normal again. It is good to get *avertissements* of this kind." In the early summer of 1958 he had phlebitis for several weeks, and six months later illness overtook him completely and brought him to death's door. Paralysis of the limbs was correctly diagnosed as a symptom of a form of leukemia. Months of convalescence in Montana-Vermala restored him to health, but for years after he would be dogged by the after-effects of that illness. His hands functioned very poorly, he had difficulty standing and walking.

And yet he never stopped working. In the years of illness he completed the translation of Claudel's lyric poetry, translated Calderón's *Great Theatre of the World* for performance in Einsiedeln (though in the end another text would be used), and above all he began to plan his trilogy, the first volume of which appeared in 1961. At the end of 1958 he wrote for the first time: "I am trying to bring aesthetics and theology face to face. This is my first attempt at the high peaks. A tremendous theme, but who would be up to it these days? Where has *eros* got to in theology, and the commentary on the Song of Songs, which belongs to the very *center* of theology?" And yet, hardly recovered from his illness, he was inundated with secondary work. We have reached the end of 1960, the period of feverish preparation for the Council. "So many small things on every side mean fragmented commitment. Radio, television. Much haste, so much churning out, and the one thing covering up the other. One would rather be in a Charterhouse."

He could not now withdraw to a Charterhouse. However, he was not invited to the Council, and so, next door to Adrienne's sickroom, he was able to continue work undisturbed on his Aesthetic. The second volume in particular, with its twelve individual studies, gave him a great deal of joy, but also much work. Each had to be carefully worked on, though he was able to incorporate some which had been planned originally as separate pieces—the chapters on Denys, Dante, and Péguy. The first volumes of this theological *summa* (and also, I suppose, bad conscience about his absence from the Council) brought him many kinds of honors on his sixtieth birthday: the Golden Cross of Mount Athos, and honorary doctorates in theology from the universities of Edinburgh, Münster, and, after a suitable delay, Fribourg.

Before he could bring his Aesthetic to a conclusion, the year 1967, with the mortal illness of Adrienne, placed a second deep caesura in his life. For three years she had already been almost completely blind. Now, with cancer of the bowel, an infinitely slow, infinitely burdensome agony began—"dying with the drop counter, in slow motion",[36] from June to September. She died in the night of September 17, 1967—on her own, like her heavenly mentor, Ignatius.

For von Balthasar, a new phase of life began. He moved from the Münsterplatz to Arnold Böcklinstrasse 42, and from now on was able to move more freely. For the moment, he had his hands full with bringing out *Erster Blick auf Adrienne von Speyr* and preparing the first of the unpublished works for printing. The members of the Community of St. John were amazed, one might say stunned, by the superabundance of their foundress' charismatic gifts, of which, in her lifetime, they had had hardly an inkling. For the last twenty years of his life, von Balthasar was to devote himself to getting Adrienne's mission recognized by the Church. The private printing of the unpublished works cost him a fortune; at a first estimate he reckoned on at least 300,000 DM/Fr.[37] As for theological honors and the growing trust of the Pope, these he diverted, time after time, to Adrienne. This was how he

---

[36] *Erde und Himmel* III, 349.
[37] *Erster Blick*, 227.

understood the cardinalate and the reason why, albeit reluctantly, he accepted it. Back in 1965 he wrote: "Her work and mine cannot be separated from one another either psychologically or theologically. They are two halves of one whole, with a single foundation at the center."[38] So, before turning to the last years of his life, we must have at least a short look at this common work.

The Work

The Foundations

From what has been said, at least one thing is clear. Von Balthasar's most important works, at least in his own eyes, are not his writings but his foundations. Even less than the books, these were not planned in advance, nor were they his own initiative, and so he never undertook them on his own. For the most part, he just gave support to a foundation which did not begin with him.

The first foundation, the Studentische Schulungsgemeinschaft (SG for short), sprang from an idea of Robert Rast. Von Balthasar helped to put it into effect, and for more than twenty-five years carried on the work almost alone. He gave the annual introductory exercises, organized an annual conference and training course, alternating between philosophy and theology. Sometimes he himself led these, but he was in any case always there as a stimulating contributor to the discussion and a discreet focal point. When in 1947 the first members had passed through the scheduled four training courses and reached the end of their studies, they joined together in the Akademische Arbeitsgemeinschaft (AAG). Until 1979 von Balthasar was involved in this as spiritual advisor, and each year, to the end of his life, he gave its Advent day of recollection in Einsiedeln.

Like all of von Balthasar's foundations, these two fellowships are characterized by an absence of organization. They depend on friendship and the good will of their members. That is why, at the end of the '60s, with the interests of the generation of '68 lying elsewhere, the SG died out only to rise again to new life a short time later. The AAG was also affected, many of the "sixty-eighters" being friends of von Balthasar. In 1970 he decided to write a Christmas letter of energetic admonition. I shall quote just the central passage:

> In Christianity it is senseless to play off past, present, and future against each other, because the Christ event is eschatological and so transcends the boundaries of time. Early Christianity was in its own way extremely future-oriented precisely because of its constant pondering of the "past perfect" of the Cross and Resurrection, from which came the "indicative" and "imperative"

---

[38] *Rechenschaft* 1965, 35.

of the present. All the great renewals in the history of the Church have had this "temporal form". Only a Christian who ponders the sources (contemplation) stands a chance of attaining a genuine forward-looking attitude and the right kind of commitment (action). As we all know, the whole plan and purpose of the Spiritual Exercises is to provide preparation and training for apostolic, world-transforming action.

Of the next foundation, the Community of St. John, less needs to be said. We have already seen that von Balthasar regarded it as the center of his work. Its foundress and first superior was, nevertheless, Adrienne von Speyr, whereas von Balthasar was responsible for spiritual direction and formation. What can be said of the Community has been already explained elsewhere by von Balthasar himself and by one of the Community.[39]

It was disappointing for von Balthasar—perhaps the greatest disappointment of his life—that, like the branch of Tantalus, the foundation of the men's community, whenever it seemed to be in his grasp, time after time eluded him. The foundation of the priests' branch has its own history. No theology students were accepted into the SG, and yet, as early as 1944, von Balthasar was explaining to his future successor as spiritual advisor of the AAG the idea of "getting together a group of interested theology students and younger priests in parallel to the existing Schulungsgemeinschaft".[40] This eventually happened the year after. Von Balthasar's spiritual and pastoral care also extended to priests and theology students. Indeed, this was his predilection. This can be seen above all in the countless retreats, but also in the tireless, friendly patience with which he constantly made himself available to doctoral students and other inquirers. Letters were answered by return, and invitations to come and talk with him in Basel were warmly extended. In 1968, with the help of friends (and apparently through Adrienne's heavenly mediation—she had given him advance notice of this in 1952), he was able to acquire a holiday home for the community at Rigi-Kaltbad. As a result of this, his contacts with a group of younger confrères were to a certain extent institutionalized. Each year the "Rigianer" spent a few days of vacation with him. Yet it was only in 1983 that the priests' branch of the Community of St. John could be established. In the final years of his life von Balthasar was much concerned to build it up.

Johannes Verlag ought to be mentioned as a third foundation. Again this came about with the help of friends who formed the body of legal trustees. At first, it was intended for the publication of Adrienne's writings, but soon it was used to publish von Balthasar's own works as well. It also stood for a

[39] "Kurze Darstellung der Johannesgemeinschaft" (by a member of the Community) in *Adrienne von Speyr und ihre kirchliche Sendung.* Proceedings of the Roman Symposium, September 27–29, 1985 (Einsiedeln: Johannes Verlag, 1986), 49–57.

[40] Anton Cadotsch, "Dank an den Seelsorger", in *Hans Urs von Balthasar 1905–1988* (Basel, 1989), 25.

far-sighted publishing policy with regard to Church and culture that was independent of market forces and, in the best sense, had an alternative emphasis: *opportune, importune.* The publications of the company gradually developed in ten series or collections, which went from spiritual reading and the rediscovery of forgotten masters, via scholarly contributions to theology, to books of a topical kind, indeed real pamphlets. The history of this publishing venture, in which von Balthasar invested a good part of his working energy, still waits to be written. What can at least be said, without exaggeration, is that, without this publishing firm at his disposal, von Balthasar's own work would have been neither written nor published. Once again von Balthasar applied his working principle of a minimum of organization. He was often translator, editor, and publisher in one person, and the authors came mainly from his circle of friends.

The same is true of von Balthasar's last joint foundation, *Communio: International Catholic Review.* Let us hear what he himself has to say on the subject:

> In 1945 a request was made several times [through Adrienne] that "I should start a review." How I was to do this as a student chaplain was completely baffling to me. I saw no possibility of it at all. Then the answer came: "Not now. But still make plans and keep people in mind with whom it will be written." A year later again: "Don't forget the review!" I did not think of it seriously again. Then, one evening in a restaurant in the Via Aurelia in Rome, a few of us from the International Theological Commission decided to start the international review *Communio.* It was supposed to be launched first of all in Paris, but that fell through, and so it made its first appearance in Germany in 1973. It would never have occurred to me to link this journal, which today comes out in eleven languages, with what had been asked of me almost forty years earlier. When the founding group began to break up, I was left on my own, having been pushed, against my will, into a kind of coordinating role. Only then did it dawn on me that there might be a connection with that request in the past from heaven. The blessing that rests on this fragile network linking different countries and continents confirms me in this supposition, which slowly but surely became a sure conviction.[41]

Something else needs to be said here. Von Balthasar inconspicuously put a tremendous amount of work into this journal—correspondence, translation, revision. His friend, Franz Greiner, the executive editor of the German edition, knew this better than anyone. He died one year before von Balthasar.

---

[41] *Unser Auftrag,* 68f.

The Writings

Von Balthasar is without doubt one of the most prolific writers of our times. His bibliography includes eighty-five separate volumes, over five hundred articles and contributions to collected works, and nearly a hundred translations, not to mention numerous smaller pieces and the sixty volumes of the works of Adrienne von Speyr. This is not the place to draw even a general outline of this immense achievement. But a few biographical pointers may help the reader to order its individual parts more clearly.

Von Balthasar insisted time after time that his work was absolutely inseparable from Adrienne von Speyr's. Nevertheless, the earliest works came into being independently. To some extent one can see in them how much von Balthasar put of what was truly his own into his later work, and how much that work remains truly his very own, even if much is deepened or has a different emphasis. It never occurred to anyone to speak of von Balthasar I and II, though he himself once said that he "once thought, when approaching the end of the first stage, that a change of direction would be necessary".[42]

In addition to his dissertation and the *Apokalypse der deutschen Seele,* the monographs on Origen, Gregory of Nyssa, and Maximus belong to this early work, not to mention the even more specialized Patristic studies. Then there are the two books which come closest to university philosophy and theology. *Wahrheit* (1947) and *Karl Barth* still predominantly bear the mark of his studies and of the man himself, although Adrienne's influence is beginning to shine through in the idea of truth as revelation and in the doctrine of universal election. The same is more or less true of the collection of aphorisms *Das Weizenkorn* (1944), which in large part probably goes back to his student days.

This inconspicuous little book, together with the first thing to be written entirely under the influence of Adrienne's visions (*Das Herz der Welt,* 1945), was von Balthasar's real breakthrough work. Both books—initially, only in Switzerland—addressed a wide readership and were several times reprinted, while the *Apokalypse* was regarded from the outset as unreadable. *Das Herz der Welt,* his book about Christ, was written by von Balthasar in a very short time during the summer vacation of 1943 "on a rock in Lake Lucerne". The fact that sometimes the linguistic form is there for form's sake is a pointer to its origins. Adrienne was suitably critical: "You know, there are certain passages at the beginning that I find a little tepid. In other words, your enjoyment of word play, the sound of words, their analysis, their 'cognates', seems here and

---

[42] Address in Innsbruck, May 22, 1987, on the occasion of the award of the Mozart Prize by the Goethe Foundation (MS, 1).

there to leave the spiritual aspect in the shade. I'll ... gladly show you the passages if it will help."[43]

Then followed the writings revolving around Adrienne's mission: the already mentioned *Der Laie und der Ordensstand* and *Theologie und Heiligkeit* (both of 1948) and *Die Schleifung der Bastionen* (1952). Then there were the two monographs, *Therese von Lisieux: Geschichte einer Sendung* (1950) and *Elisabeth von Dijon und ihre geistliche Sendung* (1952), which explore a kind of *a posteriori* theology of mission. The two were later combined as *Schwestern im Geist* (1970). *Der Christ und die Angst* (1951) and the commentary on the questions on charisms in the *Summa Theologiae* (*Thomas von Aquin: Besondere Gnadengaben und die zwei Wege menschlichen Lebens,* 1954) provide a theological grounding for Adrienne's special graces. Finally, von Balthasar ventures to the heart of mission with the already mentioned *Das betrachtende Gebet* (1955) and the *Adoratio* series to which it belonged. Two monographs dating from this period helped to give Adrienne's mission an orchestration in the Church and the world. The first was about Reinhold Schneider (1953), "a dear friend, the only man in Germany (apart from a few Jesuits) who knows who Ignatius is, what his fundamental presuppositions were. Through him I made a bridge between my *Apokalypse* and *Der Laie und der Ordensstand.*" The second was a study of Bernanos, who utterly fascinated von Balthasar because "his focal point was not the intuition of God but the knowledge of hearts: the gaze of God on sinful man, who can and should be brought to fulfillment by the ministerial and mystical (confession and judgment). Bernanos here seriously presents descent as a way to God in imitation of the God who came down to us." The *Theologie der drei Tage* can be considered as the late-born child of this group of writings. Although it was written for a specific occasion (von Balthasar took the place of a contributor who had dropped out of the *Mysterium Salutis* handbook), it offers a theological exposition of Adrienne's Good Friday and Holy Saturday experiences.

Theologie der Geschichte (1950), several times reprinted and revised and finally taken up into *Das Ganze im Fragment* (1963) and *Theodramatik,* is an early expression of the very heart of von Balthasar's theology. Here the streams flowing from his own studies merge with the waters of inspiration received from Adrienne. The collected "Sketches in Theology" of 1960, *Verbum Caro* and *Sponsa Verbi,* revolve around this same central point. A first creative period comes to a close with these collections. It must be said, though, that they by no means give a very detailed or sharply focused picture of von Balthasar's main preoccupations as a theologian and pastor during the first years. Had one asked his Basel students for a description of his thought, they would undoubtedly have cited the key words "mission", "obedience", "contemplation", and

---

[43] *Unser Auftrag,* 80.

the themes of marriage in paradise and the empty hell, which were previously regarded as theological oddities. *Christlicher Stand,* though planned in about 1945, appeared only in 1977. Until then he had not published very much about obedience and marriage in paradise. The controversy about hell was left entirely to the final years of von Balthasar's life. At the time no one could have known how much these themes owed to the inspiration of Adrienne von Speyr.

Von Balthasar's second creative period, following his major illness, though considerably richer, is more easily surveyed. Its backbone is the great trilogy with its fifteen volumes (1961–1987). Then there is the multitude of occasional pieces, written as demanded by the current state of the Church. We have already seen how the Aesthetic (*Herrlichkeit*) began to take shape for the first time in 1958; here it should be added that in its origins it goes back much further. It can be found already *in nuce* in an essay of 1943 on the farewell trio in Mozart's *Magic Flute,* then, more explicitly, in *Wahrheit,* where the beautiful comes before the true. It would not be wrong to look for its first glimmerings in his disagreement with the ideas of Kierkegaard, whom he discovered through Guardini in Berlin. Von Balthasar could never forgive Kierkegaard for condemning *Don Giovanni,* and with it everything aesthetic, as unethical and anti-religious. Nevertheless, an aesthetic of God's glory blazing forth in the world became really possible only when von Balthasar came to see the descent of Christ, "the economic *id quo majus cogitari nequit*", as the form in which God reveals himself in the world. All the volumes of *Herrlichkeit* circle round this central point, perhaps most beautifully in the chapters on the holy fools and the steps of prophetic obedience.[44]

Theodramatik was conceived before the Aesthetic, and, in its origins, it perhaps goes back still further; it was certainly even closer to von Balthasar's heart. Leaving on one side his doctoral research and the *Apokalypse* (where there is at least a preliminary outline of the *Prolegomena* and *Das Endspiel*), the first approaches to the subject are to be found in lectures on the drama of Christianity which von Balthasar gave repeatedly from 1946–1947 onwards.[45] Then in 1950 he spoke of "his long envisaged philosophy and theology of the dramatic (of *actio,* of event—this ultimately comes down again to the old problem of action and contemplation)". Two years later he was able to report: "After that [the commentary on St. Thomas] comes, at long last, the subject I have been longing to write about for years: *Theatrum Dei* (the theology of the theatre)." As with the Aesthetic, the beginning of his work on this second part of the trilogy was marked by illness. From January to March 1973 he was "more or less completely ill, with high fevers, which leave one completely exhausted.

---

[44] *Herrlichkeit. Eine theologische Ästhetik.* Bd. III/I: *Im Raum der Metaphysik* (Einsiedeln: Johannes Verlag, 1965), 492–551; Bd. III/2, 1. Teil: *Alter Bund* (Einsiedeln: Johannes Verlag, 1966), 199–282.

[45] *Unser Auftrag,* 62, n. 3.

All I could do was read a pile of plays in bed for the *Prolegomena* to the Dramatic. If possible, I would like to have finished with the *Prolegomena* by the autumn, because I ought to be getting back to the theology." In volume II/2, he was able to bring in his theology of mission, and in volume III, another favorite theme, which accompanied him throughout his life: eschatology. He was supposed at one stage to take over the eschatology volume in the Herder *Handbuch der Dogmengeschichte.* As it turned out, however, he was only able to publish short essays on this fascinating subject.[46] In 1954 he wrote: "Everything here is tied together as in a knot, but the knot is so tight that it is hard to disentangle."

Theologik mattered to him less; indeed, he originally thought of not writing it at all. For the first volume, he fell back on a book which he had already produced in 1946: *Wahrheit.* That "First Book: Truth of the World", as it was subtitled, was supposed at that time to have been followed by a second, "The Truth of God". In *Theologik,* this followed, in two volumes, the reprint of the 1946 book. What, at the beginning of his labors, von Balthasar had not dared to hope for had become a reality: the trilogy was complete, with substantially more volumes than originally envisaged. The only volume which he had to abandon was the advertised concluding volume of the Aesthetic, *Ökumene.* This was so he could push ahead with *Theodramatik.* At the urging of friends, he agreed to follow the trilogy with a summarizing *Epilog* (1987). In his will he laid down that manuscripts left unpublished at his death should be destroyed: he had published everything that was to be published (a sensible instruction, when one thinks of how posthumous works are treated!).

Although he published everything that was to be published, a few works that had been planned for years remained unwritten. "The book on obedience", which he had constantly talked about since the '40s, was never written in that form. Its parts can be assembled from *Theologie der Geschichte* (the obedience of the Son), the Old Testament volume of the Aesthetic (the steps of prophetic obedience), and *Christlicher Stand* (the obedience of the Christian), with orchestration coming from the numerous passages about obedience in other writings. It is less easy to form an idea of "Encounter with Asia". From 1957 onwards the plan for this book, foreshadowed by the translation of Jacques Cuttat's *Begegnung der Religionen,* kept coming up. Von Balthasar, who in the past had studied Indo-European philology and Sanskrit, knew more about Indian thought than was imagined by those struck by his criticism of Eastern meditation techniques. The last issue of *Communio* which he planned and saw through to printing turned out to be on the subject of "Buddhism and Christianity". That was more than chance. In his final years, he had constantly pressed for work to be done on precisely this theme.

---

[46] Ibid., 81f.

Many things were left undone, probably most of his publishing plans. The *Lectio Spiritualis* and *Christliche Meister* were closest to his heart. Two things in particular concerned him here: once again, the spiritual tradition of the Fathers of the Church, and then the idea of "a continuous *German* spirituality".

> This was what preoccupied Goerres and Schlegel and the Romantics, but they knew too little. The role of the Jesuits from 1570 to 1770 is chiefly that of a foreign supremacy and a break in tradition. They have left almost *nothing,* in contrast to Luther, who was moved to the center, while Rhineland mysticism appears devalued and debilitated. What a scene of devastation! What an insoluble task! If only Wagner had been a Christian!

Expansion and Simplification

Honors

In the last two decades of his life von Balthasar became what he was already publicly regarded to be. After Adrienne's death, already close to retirement age, he did not for a moment entertain the thought of an *otium cum dignitate.* The publishing business was making more and more demands of him, and the last volume of *Herrlichkeit* was lying on his desk, unfinished. Translated into French, Italian, English, and Spanish, this work has determined the theological image which people have of von Balthasar. But it has another feature too. Since its establishment in 1969 to the end of his life, von Balthasar was a member of the Pope's International Theological Commission—although he asked to be discharged from it. At the second Synod of Bishops in 1971, on the ministerial priesthood, he worked as one of the theological secretaries and drafted the document on priestly spirituality.

Now he began to accumulate honor after honor. Also in 1971 he received the Romano Guardini Prize of the Catholic Academy of Bavaria. Two years later he was made a Corresponding Fellow of the British Academy, and on his seventieth birthday the French Academy made him an *associé étranger.* He received the translation prize of the Foundation Hautviller in Paris and the Gottfried Keller Prize of the Martin Bodmer Foundation in Zurich. In the fall of 1977, the first von Balthasar symposium took place at the Catholic University of America in Washington, and from then on he was constantly being invited to the U.S.A. (in 1980 to receive an honorary doctorate from the same university). In 1984 he was allowed to receive his highest honor, the International Paul VI Prize, from the hands of the Pope, and a year later, in honor of his eightieth birthday, a symposium was organized in Rome on "Adrienne von Speyr and her Ecclesial Mission". The nighttime celebration of his birthday at the Castel Sant'Angelo was overshadowed by the tragic death of his youngest nephew.

In 1987, in Innsbruck, he received his final honor: the Wolfgang Amadeus Mozart Prize, the rounding off of a life whose secret passion had been music. In his speech of thanks he reminisced:

> My youth was defined by music. My piano teacher was an old lady who had been a pupil of Clara Schumann. She introduced me to Romanticism. As a student in Vienna I delighted in the last of the Romantics — Wagner, Strauss, and especially Mahler. That all came to an end once I had Mozart in my ears. To this day he has never left those ears. In later life Bach and Schubert remained precious to me, but it was Mozart who was the immovable Pole Star, round which the other two circled (the Great and Little Bears).[47]

The Shorter Works

But his public passion was something quite different. It shines through the dignified and measured progress of the trilogy — there cannot and must not be an unpassionate theology. And it breaks through, unrestrained, in the smaller works of von Balthasar's final years. Constantly reprinted and translated into seven languages, these little books have carried von Balthasar's theology out into the world — even more than the trilogy, before which many people stand back in reverence and amazement. The first of the little books came out when Adrienne was still alive. It began in 1963 with *Glaubhaft ist nur Liebe,* a short flaring up of the fundamental idea of the trilogy, the positive counterpart to *Schleifung der Bastionen.* After the Council, the same passion breaks through in a less serene way. For twenty years von Balthasar had committed himself to the idea that the center of the Church was to be found where most see her periphery: in her committed action on behalf of the world. Now von Balthasar was to see openness to the world being misunderstood to mean adaptation to the world, catching up with the times. The center, the real heart of Christianity, was being forgotten, being lost altogether.

> The Church, they say, to appear credible, must be in tune with the times. If taken seriously, that would mean that Christ was in tune with the times when he carried out his mission and died on the Cross, a scandal to the Jews and folly to the Gentiles. Of course, the scandal took place in tune with the times — at the favorable time of the Father, in the fullness of time, just when Israel was ripe, like fruit ready to burst, and the Gentiles were ready to receive it on their open soil. Modern is something Christ never was, and, God willing, never will be.[48]

The former student chaplain dedicated the little book *Wer ist ein Christ?,* from which this passage is taken, to his friends from the Akademische

---

[47] Innsbruck Address, 1.
[48] *Wer ist ein Christ?* (Einsiedeln: Benziger, 1965), 30f.

Verbindung Renaissance. The tone is still sympathetic and conciliatory: "Thorough spring cleaning rarely succeeds unless the janitor or housewife takes a certain hectic pleasure in it. So we can make allowances for the emotional uplift affecting Christians today."[49] But the demands are uncompromising: "Failures, disappointments, setbacks, calumnies, contempt, and finally, as life's quintessence, major bankruptcy. This was Christ's daily bread and will always be the Church's fate in this world. Any man who wants to be a member of the Church must be prepared for such things, for no process of evolution will ever remove them." So all Christian engagement in the world leads to prayer. This is true for the laity as well as for secular institutes.

> [The Church's] most essential forces — prayer, suffering, faithful obedience, readiness (perhaps unexploited), humility — elude all statistical analysis. So the correct approach is that of those secular communities (*instituta saecularia*) which reject a direct (statistically measurable) apostolate in favor of a simple presence in the dechristianized world (*présence au monde*). Other communities which use all available means to attain positions of secular and cultural power in order (so they claim) to help the Church merely injure it; they make themselves and the Church, not unjustifiably, odious in the eyes of others.[50]

These last few sentences capture von Balthasar's basic tone in his polemical writings. They were little understood. Those who thought superficially in the categories of right and left, conservative and progressive, saw in them an about-turn, a judgment which he, according to taste, either rejected or warmly accepted. Those who were in his line of fire put it down to the bitterness and insufficient information of a lonely and outdated man. But bitterness is never apparent in the texts, just sometimes a grim humor that comes close to sarcasm. The fact that these controversial books were put down on paper with such a sharp pen and with such visible delight in writing perhaps made them more hurtful than was necessary. Von Balthasar confined his most pointed polemic, though, to articles and book reviews, which he never allowed to be reprinted: "Polemics ought not to be made eternal". Behind it all is background knowledge of every kind, as well as perhaps a too negative, injured view of the Church's situation, like that of his friend de Lubac, in addition to insufficient information about positive developments. Nevertheless, the unprejudiced reader of the polemical writings will find more balance in them than was visible to those who looked through the sieve of the media.

The "horn blast" of the *Bastionen* was followed by the "drumbeat" of *Cordula*. To all intellectual experiments in theology it opposes the "decisive

---

[49] Ibid., 29.
[50] Ibid., 105f.

test" of the love which goes as far as martyrdom. Just as Kierkegaard's
Either-Or became well-known through its "Diary of a Seducer", so *Cordula*
became famous because of the dialogue between a Christian and a well-
intentioned commissar—a biting, post-conciliar satire. The whole thing was
seen as polemic directed against Karl Rahner. In fact, it can be argued that
Rahner's "anonymous Christians" (not invented by him) are merely a peg on
which von Balthasar hangs a more general critique of what, at least at the
time, was a widespread attitude. Here we should say something about von
Balthasar's relations with Karl Rahner. They were never students together,
though in the summer of 1939 they did collaborate on the outline of a
dogmatics, which Rahner published in the first volume of his *Theological
Investigations.* Then they had various kinds of literary quarrels. Each reproached
the other for being humorless, and yet the mutual esteem was just as great. At
the time of their sixtieth birthdays, which fell quite close, they expressed their
mutual admiration and respect in a way that went far beyond mere politeness.
Years before, when the first volume of the *Investigations* came out, von
Balthasar expressed this opinion:

> This is surely the only book to justify today any kind of hope in this field.
> Seldom has the flame of theological *eros* climbed so high or so steeply. The
> closer he comes to finding himself, the more necessary it is for us to take him
> seriously and listen reverently to what he is saying. I am already looking
> forward to the volumes to come. I just hope that the Roman scalp-hunters
> don't finish him off first.

In 1969, three years after *Cordula,* he said again: "Rouquette's death has upset
me. I hope Rahner lasts out. What would be next?" A few months later they
began their occasionally controversial collaboration on the International Theological Commission. For all their mutual esteem, they never understood each
other at a really deep level. Rahner's starting point was Kant and scholasticism,
while von Balthasar's was Goethe and the Fathers. They remain a contemporary monument to the diversity of theology.

Cordula was followed five years later by *Klarstellungen* (1971), with its
eloquent subtitle, "On the Discernment of Spirits". It was published in paperback by Herder in order to reach a larger readership. *Der antirömische Affekt*
was published in 1974, again as a Herder paperback. This was a "two months
child": "Including reading, it was written between October 15 and December
25. You can tell that." And yet this book contains von Balthasar's ecclesiology
in nuce. As is clear from its ironic subtitle ("How can the Papacy be integrated
in the Church as a whole?"), this must not be read in a simplistic way. In *Neue
Klarstellungen* (1979) and *Kleine Fibel für verunsicherte Laien* (1980), von Balthasar
adopts a gentler tone. These are books of help and encouragement rather than
polemics.

Parallel to these books of controversial theology, von Balthasar published another series intended to lead the reader to the heart of Christianity. In the controversial books, he thundered against the *terribles simplificateurs*. In this other series he wanted to guide people to simplicity of faith—in and despite all the inevitable complexity of theology. Here too the starting point was a controversy, and again predominantly with Rahner. It surfaced first of all, in a peaceful way, at the meetings of the International Theological Commission. The issue was pluralism. Does one have to find some kind of consensus from the diversity of theologies, a diversity already evident in the New Testament? Or has the unity already been given, from the beginning, in Christ, a unity which can be unfolded into diversity? *Einfaltungen: Auf Wegen christlicher Einigung* (1969) and *Die Wahrheit ist symphonisch: Aspekte des christlichen Pluralismus* (1972) give examples of how from the Christian center "a tremendous panorama of freedom opens up! 'All things are yours'... the plurality of all the forms in the world and in history, including death and the future, is accessible to the Christian's thinking and acting, if indeed he surrenders himself with Christ to God."[51] The next book, *Katholisch: Aspekte des Mysteriums* (1975), in a way takes the place of the missing ecumenism volume of the Aesthetic in the sense that it shows how the distinctively Catholic doctrines belong to the heart of Christianity. Finally, with *Christen sind einfältig* (1983), everything leads to a simplicity of faith which does not exclude the fullness.

At the end, there was one last controversy, with the left, but mainly with the right. It was a last controversy about the things which are truly last: hope beyond judgment and possible damnation. Here von Balthasar's thought comes full circle. *Was dürfen wir hoffen?* (1986) and *Kleiner Diskurs über die Hölle* (1987) not only go back to Origen's *apocatastasis* and Barth's doctrine of universal election and give them an interpretation which is defensible from a Catholic point of view, but they also take up again the concern of the *Apokalypse* to incorporate everything possible in redemption in Christ. Looking back in middle age at this early book of his, von Balthasar wrote: "What a tricky job the angels will have on the last day! They will have to pick up God's truth in farflung places and surgically remove it from hearts where previously it had lived alongside darkness!"[52]

So now everything was rounded off. His life's work was finished. Everything, or almost everything, he had wanted to write and publish had been published. He was able to look towards death with confidence: in fact, after his sister's death, he was happy that he too would "soon be allowed to go home".

---

[51] *Die Wahrheit ist symphonisch. Aspekte des christlichen Pluralismus* (Einsiedeln: Johannes Verlag, 1972), 75.
[52] *Kleiner Lageplan,* 18.

The Final Years

Despite his apparently undiminished creative energy, von Balthasar's final years were more and more difficult. Back in 1962 he wrote on one occasion: "I am often tempted to weariness, because the goal is so far off, but then I pull myself together and get going again." In the '70s the complaints become more specific:

> Some help with the publishing would make everything easier. Without such help, the most basic things, time after time, just do not get done. But this is now the form of my life. How can I change it? (1971). With all the secondary chores (radio, lectures, endless mail), I scarcely get to read and work. And yet I would like to make progress with this "necessary Dramatic" (1974). I am not making much progress with my work. Too many odd jobs on all sides. The review on top of the publishing work is the last straw (1976). I'm free in principle, yet in practice less and less free for myself, because I am at everyone's beck and call—and you can't say No to everything (1976).

Then, in 1977, came a longer illness, and in 1978 he says again: "Work here is becoming increasingly difficult. Mail is growing immeasurably, visitors and so on too. And there is no point in getting away if you don't have any books. So I crawl along very slowly with the Dramatic." And again in 1979: "Nothing new here. I am almost completely tied up with lectures and articles of every kind. This prevents me from steering a straight course and getting on with my Dramatic. *Tant pis et tant mieux* —it probably won't be much good."

In 1980–81 came an operation for cataracts on both eyes, after which he had to learn "new sight". In 1983 he says again: "The number of what, for an old man like me, are very taxing retreats and other courses is increasing, and the mountains of mail have hardly subsided."

The size of his mail and the number of his visitors are an indication of how, in these final years, von Balthasar's sphere of life had widened. Three new circles of friends were being built up. First, there was his friendship with Don Luigi Giussani and his *Communione e Liberazione* movement, in which von Balthasar saw something similar to what he had been striving for with his own communities. He dedicated his 1971 book *In Gottes Einsatz leben* to them. It was also meant to be a word of warning, along the lines of what he had already set out in *Wer ist ein Christ?*

> After the humbling of hierarchical triumphalism, there still remains a more subtle, spiritual triumphalism, the triumphalism found in the ideology of communities or groups.... The humility of small groups is the Church's greatest need today, but it is also a great danger. On the one hand, there is

the temptation to be too involved in the world; on the other hand, there is the temptation of an enclosed autonomy. The only solution is openness to God's revelation in its unabbreviated Catholicity.[53]

The second circle of friends consisted of the doctoral students and young priests who from the '60s onwards had been working on von Balthasar's theology. Now more than forty dissertations have been written. The first two were submitted in 1970 in Rome and Milan. Gladly and tirelessly, von Balthasar always gave them every conceivable kind of information. He was somewhat surprised that so much academic research could be extracted from his totally unacademic work (and somewhat saddened that no one dared to give his ideas further development). He praised the finished work with perhaps excessive selflessness and did all he could to help them into print. Many of these doctoral students remained his lasting friends.

The third circle of friends, the widest in scope, came to him through the journal *Communio*. Year after year he organized the small meeting of the various editions in Basel. Year after year it was he who was the undisputed central reference point of the larger international meeting. He made stimulating suggestions about each of the themes proposed, pointed out difficulties, and was able to name suitable authors—whether living or from the past. Only the friends themselves know of the trouble he took to build up and hold together this "fellowship" (*communio*!) of the twelve editorial teams from very different cultural backgrounds. Only they too can tell of the countless conversations on the fringe of the meetings.

It was after his return from the 1988 international editorial meeting in Madrid, which was preceded by a symposium on his theology, that news reached von Balthasar of his appointment as a cardinal. Though tired and ill again, he this time accepted, out of obedience to the Pope, what to him was an embarrassing honor. He also undertook the journey to Rome to be measured for his cardinal's robes (which, as previously with his theologian's soutane, he would have left in Rome). But he knew in his heart that heaven had other plans. "Those above", he wrote to a friend, "seem to have a different plan." Death came gently upon him. He more than once had to see those closest to him suffer an agony lasting months—"a death with the drop counter". But he himself was allowed to pass away in a moment and while he was still fully active. It happened as he was preparing to celebrate morning Mass. Like his father St. Ignatius, he was alone and unnoticed. The date was June 26, 1988, just two days before his elevation as a cardinal. In his study of St. Thérèse of Lisieux, he had once remarked: "Who *can* die? The person who finds it hardest is perhaps the one whose consciousness is alert, whose self-control has

---

[53] *In Gottes Einsatz leben* (Einsiedeln: Johannes Verlag, 1971), 104.

penetrated the deepest fibers of his soul...."[54] Death came gently to him. On his desk lay, completed, the manuscript of the book he had chosen as that year's annual Christmas gift to his friends: *Wenn ihr nicht werdet wie dieses Kind* (*Unless You Become Like This Child*). That is his true legacy.

John

How can one sum up in a few words a life so rich, work so abundant? Von Balthasar gave the name "John" to his most important foundations, to the "center of his work": the Community of St. John and the Johannes Verlag. It was not the name of his patron saint. That was St. John the Baptist, "the friend of the Bridegroom" (Jn 3:29), together with the valiant martyr-soldier Ursus (the bear!). No, by "John" he meant the beloved disciple. At the end of the retreats he gave to students in the '40s, he would also give an exposition of the last chapter of St. John's Gospel—with such an expressive tone of voice that it still rings in one's ears today: "If it is my will that he remain until I come, what is that to you?" Twenty years later he put it down on paper:

> The two of them run "together". That is the first thing to say. It is an indispensable truth which is not invalidated by the second point, namely, that love, in its more unrestrained way, "runs ahead", while office, which has many things to consider, reaches its destination later. Love sees what can be seen (from outside), but lets office go in first. Office looks closely at everything (including what is not visible from outside) and, from the position of the napkin which had been on his head, reaches a kind of *nihil obstat*. Office lets love go in, so that love (by seeing the signs, by seeing what Peter has discovered?) may reach faith.... Peter has his task as servant, the rest is not his affair. It is not his business to know exactly where the boundaries between the official Church and the Church of love are to be found. The Church of love will "remain" until the Lord comes again, but how and where, only the Lord knows.... The last thing said to the servant Peter, the last word of the Lord in the Gospel, is the watchword for the Church and theology in every age: "What is that to you?"[55]

Von Balthasar saw his mission to be the Johannine Church, which both runs ahead of the Petrine and gives it precedence. The fact that running ahead and giving precedence may each be prominent at different times just shows the unity of the mission. Both are only possible with the attitude of the beloved disciple. Of love not much can be said, though von Balthasar included it in the title of his best known book. In human terms, love showed itself in the

---

[54] *Schwestern im Geist. Therese von Lisieux und Elisabeth von Dijon* (Einsiedeln: Johannes Verlag, 1970), 105.

[55] *Theologie der drei Tage* (Einsiedeln: Benziger, 1969), 190–92.

way he preferred "fellowship" (*communio*), indeed friendship, to structures and organization. It shone through his theological *eros,* in his wonder at *id quo majus cogitari nequit,* but also in his jealous protection of the prerogatives of God. And it constantly fed itself, unnoticed by the world and even by friends, on the "silence of the Word".[56]

---

[56] *Die Stille des Wortes. Dürers Weg mit Hieronymus* (Einsiedeln: Johannes Verlag, 1979).

ALOIS M. HAAS

Hans Urs von Balthasar's "Apocalypse of the German Soul"

AT THE INTERSECTION OF GERMAN LITERATURE, PHILOSOPHY, AND THEOLOGY

> "Everything which is good and beautiful belongs to us."
> —Justin (*Apol.* II, 13)

> "Our thought and love should penetrate the flesh of things like X-rays and bring to light the divine bones in them. This is why every thinker must be religious."
> —Hans Urs von Balthasar (*Das Weizenkorn*)

Hans Urs von Balthasar was by no means well-known for divulging autobiographical details. He was sparing in the use of such information. In fact, he relativized it as far as possible in favor of the mission given to the Christian, a mission which in every case claims permanent "predominance" over all psychology.[1] Nevertheless, in private conversation, he occasionally liked to point out with some irony that he was really a professional scholar of German literature and not a theologian. The point of this self-definition was that theology was later to determine his scholarly and cultural writings both from within and from without. As a professional scholar of literature he was called and sent to become a theologian. A tension is thereby expressed which was to shape not only von Balthasar's theological work, but especially his work in German literature.[2] The "predominance of mission" of which von Balthasar

---

Translated by Michael Waldstein.

[1] Cf. *Kleiner Lageplan zu meinen Büchern* (Einsiedeln: Johannes Verlag, 1955), 12. Many who had personal contacts with von Balthasar may have been irritated by his uncompromising orientation toward what he called mission and by his consequent disinterest in the psychological in the widest sense. I have always felt his attitude is in the highest degree refreshing and purifying.

[2] One can speak of this work in literature only in inclusive terms. Nevertheless, the

speaks in his *Kleiner Lageplan zu meinen Büchern*[3] can be felt quite early and clearly in his work in literary criticism. One can speak of a true theological *a priori* that impregnates all of von Balthasar's literary-philological works, including those in German literature.[4]

Far from skewing von Balthasar's orientation as a literary critic, this theological *a priori* attests that he is a theologian with an interdisciplinary orientation, a theologian to whom nothing in art, philosophy, or theology is foreign and who, with his eyes on the *renouveau catholique* in France,[5] calls out to the German and Protestant Kierkegaardians who "tragically" sever the aesthetic from the moral-religious: "Is the *fact* that great art is Christian a problem?"[6] This question optimistically expresses the assumption that even, and precisely, great poetry is fundamentally Christian. Such an assumption is not likely to be accepted today,[7] for example by the theory of realization proposed by Dorothee Sölle that "what unconditionally concerns us" realizes and "hides" itself "in the profaneness of artistic form" and that it is the task of theology "to uncover this hidden reality".[8] The conditions under which a relation

---

literary interest can always be felt in von Balthasar in two ways: as an interest in issues and objects normally studied by literary scholars (literature) and as an accompanying methodological interest in literary scholarship (which von Balthasar always drew upon when the occasion permitted).

[3] *Kleiner Lageplan,* 12.

[4] This fact needs to be interpreted. The theological *a priori* does not, at root, violate literature: in this perspective, the form that represents its content can simultaneously be viewed and interpreted as provisional (which is the case with all historical reality) and as irreducibly definitive—in short, in its unquestionable finitude. This is precisely the cinematographic character of all "myths" as images.

[5] In this context one should mention von Balthasar's works on French literature, especially his monograph on Bernanos and the translations of Bernanos, Péguy, etc.; cf. *Rechenschaft* 1965 and the bibliography of von Balthasar's publications compiled by B. Widmer (Einsiedeln, 1965) and C. Capol, ed., *Hans Urs von Balthasar: Eine Bibliographie 1925–1980* (Einsiedeln: Johannes Verlag, 1981). This mediation of French literature to the German-speaking world has not been sufficiently recognized.

[6] *Kleiner Lageplan,* 16.

[7] The reason is simply that von Balthasar lets the whole fulless of literary, philosophical, and theological mythical formations converge toward an explicitly Christian mythic, while contemporary literary theology clearly tends toward a philosophical mediation between religion and literature. Even among literary scholars, von Balthasar is not likely to be accepted. K. A. Horst (*Kritischer Führer durch die deutsche Literatur der Gegenwart. Roman-Lyrik-Essay* [Munich, 1962], 456) diagnoses "an intelligent and sensitive intolerance in the essays of Hans Urs von Balthasar. True integration cannot be achieved in this way, because the phenomena are circled, but not truly assimilated." Horst probably gained this impression from von Balthasar's essay, *Die Gottesfrage des heutigen Menschen* (Vienna: Herold, 1956) which he reviewed quite unfavorably in *Neue Zürcher Zeitung.*

[8] Dorothee Sölle, *Realisation. Studien zum Verhältnis von Theologie und Dichtung nach der Aufklärung* (Darmstadt-Neuwied, 1973), 20. (It is typical of the dilletantism of contemporary

between ("autonomous")[9] literature and religion (Christianity) is conceded are dogmatically formulated as follows by Walter Jens, who continues and develops Sölle's theses in explicit opposition to Karl Barth's alleged rejection of art:

> We cannot, it seems, do completely without it [art], and in fact, we *really* cannot do without it, if theology is to experience how not only the Christian, but in the wider sense *homo religiosus,* man with his relation to the eternal, fares in the secular, emancipated, and godless world which is nevertheless in need of the hidden God: in his fear and finitude, his guilt and tragedy, his sin and scepticism. Only in art, especially in literature, do we see the "other" in the midst of the secular, in non-religious speech, with the help of a *theologia concretissima;* what becomes visible is the most hidden thing, that which gives authenticity to man; the totality of human existence suggests itself, however enigmatically; in the moment of success something "unconditional" appears behind the conditioned, a "final ground", a metaphysical factor which gives meaning and which gives to the described facts their value, their significance in the plan of a whole which is evoked after the manner of a sign.[10]

Von Balthasar would certainly have opposed such a secularized, dissolved, conceptually and theologically vague definition of the meaning of the relation between theology and literature, which in the end makes literature the *ancilla* of theology. For von Balthasar, theology was in a completely different sense *concretissima.* For him Christianity was never a matter of an "autonomous", "emancipated", or otherwise secularized anonymity, qualified by much fine print and hidden in the world of facts and life. It was always concretely a matter of opening oneself to faith or refusing this faith. This thematically articulated Christianity would never rest content with an arcane "absolute" that "unconditionally" concerns us,[11] rather, it bases itself without any compromise on the revelation which occurred in Jesus Christ and which is ines-

---

literary theology that a work whose purpose is so fundamental is not even familiar with von Balthasar's *Apokalypse. See* Dorothee Sölle, "Thesen über die Kriterien des theologischen Interesses an Literatur", in *Almanach für Literaturwissenschaft und Theologie* 4 [Wuppertal-Barmen, 1970], 206.) Sölle's theses are guided by a largely secularized concept of "theology" ("Theological concepts are those that speak of the human person in his or her totality and relate human existence to eternal, i.e., authentic, life") coupled with an absurd "discovery of non-religious interpretation which must be achieved by theology".

[9] What is meant by "autonomous" is the aesthetic identity of literature which is basic for contemporary literary products. Cf. D. Mieth, "Braucht die Literatur(wissenschaft) das theologische Gespräch? Thesen zur Relevanz 'literaturtheologischer' Methoden", in W. Jens, H. Küng and K. J. Kuschel, eds., *Theologie und Literatur. Zum Stand des Dialogs* (Munich, 1986), 164–77.

[10] W. Jens, "Theologie und Literatur. Möglichkeiten und Grenzen eines Dialogs im 20. Jahrhundert", in *Theologie und Literatur,* 52.

[11] Cf. thesis 6 by D. Sölle, *Realisation,* 207.

capably thematic, redeeming us from sin and guilt. Such a Christianity is, in the end, the decisive shibboleth of any Christian literature and "theology of literature"[12] deserving this name—regardless of the problems that arise in the fundamental question of whether Christian aspects of literature can be documented only in explicit references to the salvific event, Jesus of Nazareth, or also implicitly and in a hidden way. Nothing is thereby said against a form of "theology of literature" that attempts to bring to light the hidden Christian nature of literature. On the contrary, such a theology is made possible only through explicit Christianity which knows about its own character, and which is able to articulate the fundamental options and aims of this character and to perceive these even beyond the historical phenomenon of thematically "Christian" literature.

I

In his theological work, Hans Urs von Balthasar again and again engaged implicitly or explicitly in a "theology of literature"—often from new perspectives. His extensive interest encompassed the French (and English) literature of modernity and was never limited to German literature. For this reason one must see his interest in German literature as integrated into his fundamental intention of regarding literature as such as theologically relevant. In the context of the current discussion about a theology of literature, it must be pointed out that this attempt is not a usurpation or an expression of inappropriate missionary zeal,[13] but simply a necessary widening of the breadth of perception proper to theological research. The fact that literature can become a *locus theologicus* is, in Christian terms, not a phenomenon of "bringing home" or "baptizing" in the sense of co-opting literature, but simply a (frequently forgotten) fact within the Christian duty to perceive things. Christians must examine everything they meet in culture, without undue regard to their own sensibility or that of others: "Test everything, keep what is good" (1 Th 5:21).

In the case of von Balthasar, however, the concern with literature cannot be seen exclusively under the aspect of Christian duty. Intense musical sensitivity

[12] In the careful form in which D. Mieth, "Braucht die Literatur(wissenschaft)", uses this concept, it need not arouse suspicion. I would go further than Mieth to accept a position of theology in which it confronts literature with an "evaluation"—provided it does so in full literary competence and in uncompromising recognition of the artistic quality of the literary work. "Evaluation" is, after all, not identical with a procedure that violates "religious freedom". Quite to the contrary, a theological evaluation of a literary myth must clarify its origin in the subjective freedom of its creator in order to understand this product and thus to "evaluate" it.

[13] Contrary to the concerns and fears expressed in the discussion of D. Mieth's theses.

and artistic talent predestined him for an objective and congenial concern with the arts (music and fine arts). If one may so speak, his aesthetic sensibility was part of his mission—a combination which, one can anticipate, would make him suspect both to theologians and to literary scholars and philologists (to the extent that they took notice of his contributions at all). In fact, the anticipation that von Balthasar's studies on literature would not be recognized by philologists is quite correct. In the discussions about method that began in the '60s and '70s his name was never mentioned. A few scholars of old German literature—Fr. Ohly and his school: M. Wehrli, K. Ruh, W. Haug—appealed at some points to *The Glory of the Lord*. However, the full theology of literature contained in this work, accompanied by all the methodological tools and corresponding case studies, still needs to be made the subject of an intensive study. At this point what we can give is only a few (quite provisional) indications about von Balthasar's work as a scholar of German literature who had theological objectives.

If I see things correctly, there are, roughly speaking, three perspectives in which von Balthasar concerned himself with literature. The first perspective is eschatological,[14] the second transcendental-aesthetic[15] and the third theo-dramatic.[16] In what follows we will pursue the first of these in a cursory and admittedly eclectic fashion without due regard for the complexity of problems of method and content.

II

Quite impressive, from the point of view of both method and content, is von Balthasar's three-volume *Die Apokalypse der deutschen Seele,* which grew out of his Zurich dissertation[17] written under the direction of Robert Faesi.[18] The

[14] This perspective will be discussed below. On this subject, see now H. Vondung, *Die Apokalypse in Deutschland* (Munich, 1988), 14, n. 17, who accuses von Balthasar of "not making use" of the opportunity to write a truly thematically oriented analysis of "The German Apocalypse", "even though he integrated much material and mediates many important insights". We shall be concerned with these "important insights".

[15] In this context one would have to analyze von Balthasar's *The Glory of the Lord: A Theological Aesthetics,* which focuses less on the flow of literary mythical formations than on their "form" (*Gestalt*).

[16] This investigation would have to focus especially on *Theo-Drama: Theological Dramatic Theory,* I: *Prolegomena* (San Francisco: Ignatius Press, 1988) which unfolds the allegory with which *Apokalypse* closes, namely, the allegory of the world as a play.

[17] *Geschichte des eschatologischen Problems in der modernen deutschen Literatur* (Zurich, 1930); *Die Apokalypse der deutschen Seele,* 3 vols. (Salzburg, 1937–1939); the first volume was republished under the title, *Prometheus. Studien zur Geschichte des deutschen Idealismus* (Heidelberg: F. H. Kerle, 1947).

[18] Cf. M. Brauneck, ed., *Autorenlexikon* (Reinbek, 1984), 158. "Robert Faesi, born April

few who have read this work—most quit after the first volume—attest to von Balthasar's great skill in interpreting difficult literary-philosophical problems (especially those of German idealism, the modern immanentist thought in literature and philosophy), and note (in a positive sense) the difficulty of the text.[19] His teacher Faesi noted in a review (1937) that "von Balthasar's work makes high demands, but it also satisfies high demands."[20] In scholarship on German literature the work had hardly any echo at all—apart from Faesi's review and the careful review of Werner Milch, who criticizes von Balthasar's method and his interpretation of Goethe. Theodor Haecker's unjust outcry is well-known:

> *Die Apokalypse der deutschen Seele* is even more embarrassing than Söhle's manure pit, because it has completely different pretensions. The comparison between Stefan George and Isaiah—yes, Isaiah—is a horrible blasphemy; no, it would be a blasphemy, if George reached that level, but he doesn't. It is simply trash. It is not even "literature", which presupposes a sense of quality. This is what he lacks. He can't write a "sentence".[21]

Otto Friedrich Bollnow, who wrote two very positive reviews of the whole work, characterizes its contents as follows: "It is an analysis, on a grand and

---

10, 1883 in Zurich, died September 18, 1972, in Zollikon near Zurich, studied German literature, became *Privatdozent* at the University of Zurich in 1911, professor from 1922 to 1953. Faesi, whose work documents itself in scholarly analysis of literary forms and traditions, dedicated himself, above all, to Swiss tradition, fusing fiction and historical facts in graphic anecdotes." For this and other references I am indebted to Josiane Aepli. In comparison with Emil Ermatinger, Faesi was considered more liberal in spirit toward his students. He does not have a special interest in a theology of literature. See, however, his "Der Heilige in der modernen Dichtung", in *Zeitschrift für Deutschkunde* 40 (1926): 34–49, and his poem, critical of religion, "Logen, Gogen, zeitgemässe Theologen", in his *Ungereimte Welt gereimt* (Zurich, 1946): 57f.

[19] The following reviews of *Apokalypse der deutschen Seele* have come to my attention (I am indebted to Dr. Nikolaus Largier for research): M. Schmaus, in *Ärzteblatt für Süddeutschland* 5 (1938): 54; *Archives de Philosophie* 13 (1939–1940): Suppl. 54; H. Richtscheidt, in *Blätter für deutsche Philosophie* 13 (1939–1940): 336; W. Milch, in *Chronik des Wiener Goethevereins* 43 (1938): 48; O. F. Bollnow, in *Die Literatur* 40 (1937–1938): 183; idem, in *Die Literatur* 41 (1938–1939): 761–63; K. Thieme, in *Hochland* 36.2 (1939): 158–1962; *Kölnische Volkszeitung* (April 16, 1939); A. Delp, in *Scholastik* 16 (1941): 79–82; L. Gläser, in *Schönere Zukunft* 12 (1936–1937): 1173; *Seele* 19 (1937): 238; R. Jelke, in *Theologisches Literaturblatt* 60 (1939): 270; F. Knorr, in *Zeitschrift für deutsche Geisteswissenschaft* 1 (1938): 378. An announcement by von Balthasar himself appeared in *Schönere Zukunft* 14 (1938): 57–59. A sympathetic and positive review by J. Lesser appeared probably in the daily *Vaterland* in 1939 or 1940. The dissertation was at least acknowledged by T. Spoerri in his *Die Götter des Abendlandes. Eine Auseinandersetzung mit dem Heidentum in der Kultur unserer Zeit,* 4th ed. (Berlin, 1932), 130.

[20] R. Faesi, "Apokalypse der deutschen Seele", in *Neue Zürcher Zeitung* (August 1, 1937): 1382; on January 13, 1942, there is another review of *Apokalypse,* signed O. B. I am indebted to the archive of the *Neue Zürcher Zeitung* for these references.

[21] T. Haecker, *Tag- und Nachtbücher* (Frankfurt, 1975), 240; Haecker refers to a passage in *Apokalypse,* III, 47f.

ambitious scale and worked out to the smallest detail from a Catholic perspective, of the entire history of the idea of immanence, i.e., of the tendencies that understand the world and life purely out of themselves while avoiding the positing of anything transcendent."[22]

On the other hand Karl Thieme is irritated already by the title, by this ". . . iridescence of language which is hard to take if one is a friend of clean thinking. This iridescence continues throughout the sixteen hundred pages of the work; it results in a maze of equivocations and makes it exceedingly difficult throughout to determine what the author really wants to say."[23]

Despite these more or less aphoristic reviews, the harvest is rather meager. Von Balthasar's extensive first work did not get a reception that would have corresponded to the intention of the study on the same level, namely, the intention of "remaining within the condition of objective, almost uninvolved depiction, while aiming directly at challenge and unconditional decision".[24] In fact, this statement focuses on something decisive for method—which is what interests us here. The theological *a priori,* which reviewers called von Balthasar's "Catholic standpoint",[25] defines the pattern of questions, and is the light in which the work analyzes and interprets literary, philosophical, and religiously shaped texts. Even more, it is an insinuation addressed to readers to see themselves confronted with a question in the literary, philosophical, and theological positions on the "final attitude", a question that is not essentially different from the question von Balthasar addresses to the texts themselves. This question expresses a genuinely Jesuit motif of the Ignatian *Spiritual Exercises* that lets all reflection on the world and on humanity result in helping one to decide for God's ever-more—which must be given honor before all, precisely because of its transcendence over all.

The vehicle of this choice is decision, which penetrates through the wealth of the human world of images and thereby finds its way to a "final attitude". In reality, this final attitude only ratifies that for which creation and man, who is present in it, are "disposed"; ratifies it in such a way "that the only reason to desire or keep one thing or the other is the exclusive service, the honor, and glory of his divine majesty".[26] Thus an Ignatian aesthetics manifests itself already in the goal of *Apokalypse*—an attitude which, *mutatis mutandis,* was not foreign to the baroque Jesuits and their aesthetic-literary products. However, the time of publication—shortly before the outbreak of World War II—was not favorable to the *magnum opus* of the young Jesuit. Decisions had been

[22] O. F. Bollnow, *Literatur* (1938–1939), 761.

[23] K. Thieme, *Hochland,* 158.

[24] Preface to *Prometheus.*

[25] See note 22 above.

[26] Ignatius of Loyola, *Die Exerzitien,* trans. Hans Urs von Balthasar, 9th ed. (Einsiedeln: Johannes Verlag, 1986), 11, n. 16. Cf. *Kleiner Lageplan,* 5.

made in such a way that the Germans were no longer able to "save"[27] their
"souls".

III

If one had had the patience to read *Apokalypse der deutschen Seele* thoroughly,
then its critique of ideology in a Christian spirit would have come out more
clearly. There are, however, limits in the work itself that impede a reading
purely in terms of a critique of contemporary tendencies. When von Balthasar
appeals to the "mythical interpretation"[28] of George's school,[29] he follows a
mode of interpretation whose recourse to historical analysis in terms of
intellectual history is subject to the suspicion "that it considers the timeless humanity of fated limit-situations . . . [as] the exclusive content of literature", and that it detaches "great poetry as the timeless dialogue of the
leaders of humanity . . . from the historical tradition which remains without
significance."[30] On the other hand, one must take note of von Balthasar's
emphasis that what is called "spirit" by the school of intellectual history is to
be understood in the direction of a "*concrete* spirit". For von Balthasar,
eschatology is "knowledge about the standing of the concrete spirit before its
own . . . final reality".[31] For this reason—for the sake of this concreteness of
the person—he prefers the concept "soul" to that of "spirit"; "soul" refers to
"the most concrete personal reality", soul in the sense of "saving souls".[32]
Now, this most concrete reality of the core of the person is something hidden;
it is "veiled"[33] from the outside as something interior. The soul stands "before
itself even as before a closed door".[34] The term "apocalypse" serves in this
context as a concretely charged concept for eschatology and intends, in the
etymological sense, "revelation" "becoming manifest". Thus, *Apokalypse der
deutschen Seele* signifies the movement toward the final meaning, the flashing
up of the eternal destiny of the human person, revelation as the completion

[27] *Prometheus,* 4.

[28] Ibid., 15.

[29] Ibid., 16.

[30] P. G. Völker, "Die inhumane Praxis der bürgerlichen Wissenschaft", in *Methodenkritik
der Germanistik. Materialistische Literaturtheorie und bürgerliche Praxis* ed. M. G. Gansberg and
P. G. Völker, 2nd ed. (Stuttgart, 1971), 63. Völker's stereotype can hardly be applied in its
entirety to von Balthasar, if one remembers how von Balthasar treats war-poetry in detail
and how the critique of ideology is, after all, an orientation of his study.

[31] *Prometheus,* 11.

[32] Ibid., 4. On what follows, see the excellent dissertation by J. Gesthuisen, *Das Nietzsche-
Bild Hans Urs von Balthasars. Ein Zugang zur "Apokalypse der deutschen Seele"* (Rome, 1986),
47.

[33] *Prometheus,* 3.

[34] Ibid., 6.

and truth of the person.[35] In volume one, the gigantic work undertakes, in a more or less structured sequence of monographs and individual analyses, a review of the history of German idealism as a whole (Lessing, Herder, Kant, Fichte, Schelling, Novalis, Hölderlin, Schiller, Goethe, Jean Paul, Hegel). In volume two, it turns to the history of life-philosophy (*Lebensphilosophie*) in the second half of the nineteenth century (Bergson and Klages, Hoffmansthal, George, Spitteler, Rilke, and many others), culminating in a confrontation of Nietzsche and Dostoevsky. Finally, in volume three, the work turns to modern existentialist philosophy (many poets, Scheler, Husserl, Heidegger, Rilke, Karl Barth). It is a review, not as an indifferent portrayal, but in the sense of a judgment which intends the definitive refutation or cancellation of the idea of immanence by showing its failure even in its most extreme possibilities. The intention of the whole work is to examine how far modern philosophical and poetic creativity as a whole can grasp the movement of transcendence—which is rooted in human nature—as a movement in which that toward which the person transcends truly manifests itself. The fact that the result was largely negative did not throw the young Jesuit off-course. The demonstration of a fundamental contradiction in modernity's interpretation of meaning between "complete transfiguration of the world, the divinizing of the earth", on the one hand, and "pure falling, the path into nothingness and judgment", on the other, signals a fundamental contradictoriness of "dimensions of world history" whose "negativity" is "positivity".[36] An image for this contradictoriness is the Cross which encompasses and surpasses the entire dialectic between life and death. In this way all the myths of German intellectual history find themselves in a *reductio ad crucem*.

> The distention of existence between "life" and "spirit", between "Prometheus" and "the goddess soul", between existential and ideal truth, between earth and heaven, this distention of existence, which imparts to it its *final attitude* and its full truth, is a crucifixion. The "contradiction" of the entire dialectic of idealism (vol. one), like the "contradiction" between nature and spirit (vols. two and three) is *mythically* and concretely the crossing of the beams of the Cross. "For when the center has been lost in a circle", Bonaventure says, "it can only be found through two lines at right angles." And when the Letter to the Ephesians lays out the dimensions of the world, "that you may be enabled with all the saints to comprehend what is the breadth and length, the height and depth", Origen applies this dimension to the Cross. "The one who is crucified with Christ and extended with him is the one who comprehends the breadth and the length, the height and the depth with him." Augustine follows him. Christ gives to the world its form (*Gestalt*) and its law by *living* in the Cross that which the Cross expresses as an image.

[35] See *Prometheus*, 12.
[36] *Apokalypse*, III, 434.

This is why even "Prometheus bound" and "Dionysus crucified" find their
enlightenment in it.[37]

These statements clarify the methodological principle of "enlightenment"
in von Balthasar's interpretation of the philosophical and poetic myths of
idealism, life-philosophy, and existentialism. Completely removed from any
apologetic combative strategies, it is the self-unmasking of the myths in the
light of the myth of the Cross.

> After this reduction of the crucial myths of German intellectual history to
> the myth of the Cross, one must see the sense in which this myth is the final
> form (*Gestalt*) of the world and therein provides the parameters of the final
> human attitude. For it does not seem self-evident that an "accidental"
> historical event like the crucifixion of a "man" in a corner of the Roman
> Empire antecedently conditions and determines not only the entire course
> of world history, but, more profoundly, the inner reality of *every* human
> being, in fact, the entire ontological structure of every person. If that is
> correct, then all being and all possible thought proves to be Christian . . . [38]

The final mythical image which von Balthasar finds for this self-unmasking
dialectic of world events and interpretations is the category of play, as it is
presented in the allegory of the world play in the baroque, and especially in
Hoffmannsthal. "The word that expresses, at one and the same time, the
immense splendor of the rising surf of the world and the falling emptiness of
hollow foam is *play*. For 'play' means that the tragedy of the world, all the
way down to its hell, is embraced by a contemplative weighing vision, that it
is 'play *in front of* . . . ' and not something absolute."[39]

After this baroque relativizing of all worldly immanence, von Balthasar
picks up a mythical image of Hoffmannsthal's *Grosses Welttheater*: the great
redeeming gesture of the angel who points upward towards the world's judge:

> *Hinauf! Vor Meisters Angesicht!*
> *Bereitet euch auf ungeheures Licht.*
>
> Up! Before the master's face!
> Prepare yourselves for tremendous light.[40]

IV

If one is not aware of the labor involved in working out a comprehensive
portrayal of modern mythical proposals of meaning and their intended self-

[37] Ibid., 434–35.
[38] Ibid., 435.
[39] Ibid., 442.
[40] Ibid., 449.

unmasking, one cannot evaluate the literary, philosophical, and theological achievement of von Balthasar's first (three-volume) work. I am convinced that the hour has not yet come to assess its true importance in both method and content. A likely charge to be brought against it is that it is simply a final, albeit quite respectable, return to baroque principles of interpretation, deployed in an attempt to relativize and integrate modernity and its dynamism of emancipation, from a Christian perspective. Within the framework of secular structures of thought—to which Christians of all denominations are accommodating with increasing timidity—such a charge will be seen as correct. Yet in the context of a Christian faith that insists on the universal validity of its content, one is confronted with the inescapable duty of—congenially!—interpreting and examining philosophical, poetic, and theological interpretations of the world. No Christian can be dispensed from this duty if he wishes to bear that name rightly. From this perspective von Balthasar's first work presents itself in both its method and content as a successful attempt to review the eschatological myths of modern German intellectual history. The deepest intentions of that history receive from its own materials the formal meaning of a final option for or against the Christian God—on the presupposition that what is Christian is simply inescapable.

On this presupposition it is clear, of course, that the vehicle of portraying such an apocalypse (such a self-disclosure of the facts to be portrayed) cannot simply be the methods of literary criticism, philosophy, or theology. All insistence on a monism of method signifies a narrowing of perspective. Yet even a pluralism of method that proceeds by way of mere addition cannot reach the ambitious goal of interpreting the mythical self-disclosure of myths. The *sum* of philosophical, artistic, and theological points of departure cannot reach the "veiled inner space" of the "soul", because all these disciplines "do not speak a direct language in speaking of what is final; they only point and 'mean' ".[41] The method required for reaching the "apocalypse" of the "soul" is therefore "neither philosophical nor theological nor literary in the proper sense"[42] but mythical: its point of convergence is "historically concrete existence".[43] The contextual event in which the individual branches of science meet is a process in which they go beyond each other toward this point of convergence: "Just as literary theory in our opinion goes beyond philosophy, so philosophy goes beyond art; both of them (like theology) transcend toward historically concrete existence. Precisely this point toward which all three transcend shall be the geometric place of these studies."[44]

Von Balthasar's awareness of method, which is quite developed, relies on

[41] *Prometheus*, 7.
[42] Ibid.
[43] Ibid., 9.
[44] Ibid.

Ernst Bertram's *Versuch einer Mythologie,* a study of Nietzsche which he considers indispensable

> ... because myth, image, and mirror become the only thing "objective" that an existing subject holds before itself to understand itself, or that lies as a mediating "objective" medium between two subjects (in the end God and the soul) engaged in an existential and dialogical conversation.... Myth [which thus takes on great importance] remains *between* philosophy and art as truly objectively valid, though not to be clarified into concepts, as the monological or dialogical word of the soul's depth.[45]

Already in the preface to his dissertation von Balthasar acknowledges that he realizes the "novelty" and "daring" of the attempt to tell "the history of the eschatological problem as a history of myths".[46] "The manner in which philosophy and theology are here employed to elucidate works of art and in which these works are, conversely, used without consideration of their aesthetic qualities for investigating the history of the eschatological problem may appear strange. The success of this method will be its only justification."[47]

Von Balthasar even speaks of a "syncretism of method"[48]—which has become a postulate of philological research in the interdisciplinary search for an appropriate interpretation of texts. In a presentation of his work in 1945 he still had to admit that his studies in *Apokalypse der deutschen Seele* " ... attempted to combine poetry, philosophy, and theology from Lessing to today in a global Christian interpretation—to the insurmountable consternation of all orthodox scholars."[49] Today, he would be able to point out triumphantly—if the "specialists" who always speak of interdisciplinary work were serious about it—that his approach was interdisciplinary when such a thing was still a scholarly scandal. The triumph would be cheap if von Balthasar had not long since been proven correct. All those who insist today—with naïve immediacy —on the autonomy of literature and the power of mythic formation proper to it, should not do so without honestly coming to terms with von Balthasar's work, exemplary as it is both in its method and its content.

Although von Balthasar rightly distinguishes his work from philology and literary criticism, it must be emphasized that he would not have written this pioneering work if he had not been trained in literary criticism. The structure of his detailed analyses could demonstrate this point. When he portrays recent German intellectual history in terms of its myths, "in a picture book, as it

[45] Ibid., 16.
[46] *Geschichte des eschatologischen Problems,* 3.
[47] Ibid., preface.
[48] Ibid., 211, n. 1.
[49] "Es stellt sich vor: Hans Urs von Balthasar", in *Das neue Buch* 7, (1945): 44; quoted by Gesthuisen, *Das Nietzsche-Bild,* 98, n. 109.

were",[50] he looks at the "indivisible stream of images and formations"[51] and appeals to

> ... the living soul ... that is able to reimmerse the form that stands before itself into the creative process that gave rise to that form. It transforms the fixed pictures magically into a living succession; it can give the life that gave birth to them back to the mythical formations of its own apocalypse. This is no longer an aesthetic contemplation of constructs, but itself a renewed, repeated, and deepened apocalypse of the soul.
>
> ... As Bergson liked to show, the human spirit cannot sketch this wealth except by a cinematographic method. The individual pictures of the film represent the once-living movement.[52]

This method contains in embryonic fashion what the inimitable title of one of von Balthasar's books intends as an epitome of historical experience: *Das Ganze im Fragment* (The whole in the fragment).[53] It is now being understood clearly as a justified methodological principle that the entire ensemble of humanistic disciplines barely suffices for pursuing this objective.[54] The individual image—which must never be frozen into a fixed "form" (*Gestalt*) in this context—must provide the point of departure in which the efforts of all philologists, philosophers, and theologians begin concentrically, as it were. In this way the historical product is reimmersed into the origin that gave it birth in order to become truly visible—at least for a moment that fulfills what Nietzsche demands for historiography as a living connection of history and the present:[55] the historical figure in the mirror of its own apocalypse—toward the eschaton. Nietzsche's demand is thereby both fulfilled and rejected in Christian terms: in the rejection of all "return of the same" and in the mythical visibility of the "eschaton".

---

[50] *Prometheus*, 15.

[51] Ibid., 16.

[52] Ibid., 17, 16.

[53] *Das Ganze im Fragment. Aspekte der Geschichtstheologie* (Einsiedeln: Benziger, 1963).

[54] See V. Knapp, "Ästhetik und Dramatik. Zu den Prolegomena der *Theodramatik* von Hans Urs von Balthasar", in *Literaturwissenschaftliches Jahrbuch der Görresgesellschaft* (Neue Folge 15; Berlin, 1974), 261; quoted by Gesthuisen, *Das Nietzsche-Bild*, 98, n. 109.

[55] See K. Anglet, *Zur Phantasmagorie der Tradition. Nietzsches Philosophie zwischen Historismus und Beschwörung. Eine Studie auf der Grundlage der zweiten und dritten Unzeitgemässen Betrachtung* (Würzburg, 1989).

CHARLES KANNENGIESSER

Listening to the Fathers

The young Jesuit Hans Urs von Balthasar became acquainted with the Fathers of the Church through the mediation of Fr. Henri de Lubac. The encounter occurred at Fourvière between 1933 and 1937. A theology student at the time, von Balthasar had earlier distinguished himself by an astonishing creativity, precocious and concentrated, in the fields of musical aesthetics and German literature. He had taken a liking to spending time in the company of such men of genius as Johann Sebastian Bach and Friedrich Nietzsche. The great merit of Henri de Lubac was that he attracted his student's attention to the truly inspired dimension of the work of the Fathers. Von Balthasar showed all the signs of an exceptional openness to the most diverse cultural values; he was to recognize himself in these Fathers. These founders of the tradition of Christianity in the West had been capable of assuming the essential values of their culture and transforming them, putting them at the service of the Gospel that they preached. Von Balthasar had sufficiently surveyed the abyss into which the German soul tended to let itself be drawn by its apocalyptic inclinations and its metaphysical despair. He now found in the example of the Fathers a restorative synthesis, a constructive work which laid a mystical foundation that would endure for centuries.

Inflamed by this incandescent paradigm, he plunged into the diligent study of Origen and Gregory of Nyssa as into a crucible in which were fermenting the nascent energies of future Christian ages. Carrying with him his aspirations and his questions as a young intellectual of the twentieth century, he became a contemporary of the most eminent thinkers of the ancient Church.

Two facts strike one at the outset in considering this encounter between von Balthasar and the Fathers. On the one hand, von Balthasar finds it normal to interpret the Fathers in terms of their most daring initiatives. On the other hand, he develops his own theoretical synthesis in his contact with the Fathers. Thus the Swiss theologian's most original contribution to the study of the Church Fathers results precisely in releasing this study from its marginal status in the field of theological research. With this step he rejoins the fertile intuitions of Fr. de Lubac. Von Balthasar's work thus takes its place alongside

Translated by Esther Tillman.
Communio 16 (Fall 1989). © 1989 by *Communio: International Catholic Review.*

that of an Yves Congar, of the two brothers Hugo and Karl Rahner, and of Jean Daniélou, to name but the best known of his contemporaries in the field of theology. In a generation which survived the slaughter of World War I and grew to maturity amid the turmoil of ideas surging through Europe in the aftermath of this war, von Balthasar shared the lively sentiment of a possible Catholic and theological renaissance. It was a feeling common to the most open minds in the Church of the '30s. From the poetic invention of the convert Paul Claudel to the popular veneration of the "little" St. Thérèse, von Balthasar was continually observing new signs, precursors in his eyes of a fundamental restoration of Catholic thought that was fully modern. His personal project as theologian was to enter into the framework of such a hope. The Fathers of the Church were to become in some way his most authoritative spokesmen.

Through his more systematic organization and the more directly philosophical nature of the basic questions he brought to his reading of the Fathers, he distanced himself somewhat from his eminent teacher of Fourvière. He likewise stayed on the fringes of the more knotty documentary and pedagogical inquiries of a Congar or a Karl Rahner. These latter had at heart the demonstration of the theological theses, ecclesiastical or anthropological, which necessitated a substantial investment in the study of the Fathers. Thanks to such efforts, certain limits of neo-scholastic teaching would be successfully surpassed. But the spontaneous attitude of von Balthasar, appealing directly to the Fathers, was turned toward modernity in crisis in its essential principles, rather than toward competing pedagogical models in the narrow framework of clerical formation. In common with Jean Daniélou, he addressed himself to a cultured public that retained no ghetto mentality. If his work on the Fathers takes a very different direction from that of Daniélou, it is probably less because of his motivation than for the reason that these two authentic apologists of contemporary Christianity were of decidedly different temperaments. Fr. Daniélou spent the resources of his patristic knowledge in all directions, on all fronts of the war of ideas where an indefatigably lively faith would challenge the ideologies of the day. Von Balthasar focused his contemplative eye on trying to merge the demands of modernity, as he experienced it, with the spiritual and metaphysical treasures of the Fathers whose meaning he kept probing. To the "Pauline" virulence of the born polemicist Jean Daniélou, he somehow opposed the mystical rhythm and emphasis of a more "Johannine" discourse.

His main publications on the subject of patristics saw the light of day after von Balthasar had left the Jesuits, at the beginning of 1950. Believing himself obliged to make such a decision at the level of his institutional commitment, the Swiss theologian in no way modified his doctrinal commitment. On the contrary, free to organize at his convenience the mission that he assumed in the service of the Church, he reinforced his close ties with the Ignatian identity which had been built up in him since 1929 through the practice of the Spiritual Exercises. His principal work on Gregory of Nyssa, *Présence et pensée,* was essentially completed before 1939. It was published by Beauchesne in 1942, two years before Daniélou's *Platonisme et théologie mystique.* In an essay that did not appear until 1954, "La Source scellée" (title borrowed from the Song of Songs 4:12), he was to observe, "No Father of the Church is less platonist than Gregory of Nyssa."[1] But this remark, aside from any specialized scholarship or connotation, sprang from von Balthasar's metaphysical comprehension of Gregory's thought, the Ignatian background of which merits emphasis. If the immanent "presence" of God in this world reveals to us something of the divine "essence" itself and helps us comprehend why all creation aspires to rejoin its Creator, the "thought" of God, the saving Logos, reveals to us the divine *"ex-sistence"*, the pure Act of absolute love which draws God to the very heart of this world, on the Cross. In fact the world takes its real meaning only in a Christocentric perspective. It is true the author seems more inclined to invoke John Henry Newman or the Claudel of *Les Cinq grandes Odes* and *Le Soulier de Satin* to illustrate his vision of the divine reality as understood according to Gregory of Nyssa. However, the Ignatian meditation on the Two Standards and the contemplation on love that concludes the *Spiritual Exercises* outline the unvarying backdrop of his interpretation.

Likewise a work with the prophetic title *Schleifung der Bastionen,* published in 1952, remained wholly impregnated with the corporatist and social fervor of Henri de Lubac's *Catholicisme* which had appeared fifteen years earlier. With exemplary clarity von Balthasar demonstrated the absurdity of a "Bunker-Church" retreating within itself for fear of being besieged by a hostile world. In a human universe which the Fathers revealed to him as being Christocentric, such isolationism made no sense. The bastions therefore had to come down; the Church had to be opened to the world. Von Balthasar was literally ten years ahead of Vatican II.

A similar continuity could be observed between "Le Mysterion d'Origène" in the *Recherches de Science Religieuse* of 1936 and 1937 and its publication in the form of a work arranged by Fr. Duployé twenty years later in the Cerf editions. This volume, *Parole et mystère chez Origène,* reintroduces one of the most powerful essays ever conceived on the thought of Origen. But rather than evaluating this brilliant synthesis in relation to the happy years spent in the studious retreat of the scholasticate at Fourvière, one must perceive in it a sign of the full theological maturity of its author, toward the end of the '50s. "Origen is still for me the most inspired and open of all those who interpret and love the Word of God ... I never feel as much at ease as [I do] with

---

[1] "Der versiegelte Quell".

him."[2] This confidence which introduces the work precedes an original reconstruction of Origen's entire doctrine of the Logos. This doctrine is taken up again by von Balthasar across sacramental categories. The Word is at work making God intelligible. At the same time he enables us to know him as well as the knowledge itself. He is at once the revealer and the whole revelation of God, the divine sacrament of an ineffable God. In his Incarnation this Word also becomes the symbol of himself. "The Word made flesh will therefore be his own symbol. . . . "[3] Von Balthasar's conceptual lyricism, unfolding the lucidity and ubiquity of the mystery of Origen's Logos, recalls the passionate accents of the heroes of universal thought to which he refers: Heraclitus, Nietzsche, or even Hegel celebrating the final *"Aufhebung"* of the world in God. Just as he had subtitled the 1941 work *Kosmische Liturgie,* on Maximus the Confessor, *Höhe und Krise des griechischen Weltbilds bei Maximus Confessor,* so he prefigures with his essay on Origen what will become his own theological vision of the world in *Herrlichkeit,* published in 1961.

The study of the patristic structures therefore imbued von Balthasar with a style of thought and a loftiness of view which allowed him to take up the challenges of modernity without turning his back on it. This contemporary of Sartre and of Boris Vian celebrated the existentialism of Gregory of Nyssa on the threshold of the '50s. In 1939 when ideologies were about to plunge Europe and the world into the horrors of "total" war, he enunciated unequivocally in "Patristik, Scholastik, und wir" the thesis of an epochal rupture that would put an end to the classical tradition handed down from the Church Fathers. The day was to come, in 1947, when he would thoroughly examine the genesis and the faith motivation of the Rule of St. Basil, discerning in it the model of the "secular institutes" then in full gestation.

Thus von Balthasar has made a great contribution to the expansion of patristics integrated into the movement of contemporary theology. It would be quite as correct to observe that patristics, by way of return, contributed in a decisive fashion to the development of von Balthasar the theologian. Fascinated, as he had to be, by the *Confessions* of St. Augustine, the Swiss interpreter of the Fathers did not hesitate to change himself into an Augustine *redivivus,* composing a theological paraphrase of Books ten to thirteen of the *Confessions* in *Theologie der Geschichte,* published in 1959, or again in *Das Ganze im Fragment. Aspekte der Geschichtstheologie,* which appeared in Einsiedeln in 1963, and, in French, under the prophetic title *De l'Intégration.* The "decisive test"—a favorite expression of von Balthasar's—of the present time took form and meaning, in the eyes of this disciple of the Fathers, in the light of the founding struggle of the Fathers by which they surmounted the *aporia* of reason in

---

[2] *Parole et mystère chez Origène,* arr. P. Pie Duployé (Paris: Ed. du Cerf, 1957).
[3] Ibid., 46.

antiquity and set free the creative dynamism of the whole Christian tradition.

The one whom von Balthasar studied the most thoroughly, among several generations of these Fathers, was unquestionably Maximus the Confessor. As early as 1941, von Balthasar dedicated to him the work mentioned above as well as a study on *Die Gnostichen Centurien des Maximus Confessor*. Again and again he took up the study of Maximus until 1961, when he collected his works on this Father under the earlier title of 1941, *Kosmische Liturgie,* simplifying the subtitle: *Das Weltbild Maximus des Bekenners.* One would readily surmise a secret collaboration between his modern interpreter and the inspired Byzantine monk of the seventh century, who so perfectly combines "the glory and the Cross" in his tragic destiny and his spiritual achievement. Like Maximus, but under the cover of a theological neutrality fortified and guaranteed by the Fathers, von Balthasar was constantly on the lookout, denouncing without hesitation the doctrinal implications of the most diverse currents of thought running through his Church and his time. There would perhaps be good reason to attempt an interpretation of such an extraordinary theologian by comparing him to Augustine ready to die as he contemplated the verses of the Psalter on the walls of his death chamber in a city besieged by the Vandals, or to the septuagenarian Maximus allowing himself to be mutilated by his jailers rather than deny one iota of his doctrine on the incarnate Word. Each time, a form of Christianity, bearer of these men of genius, was doomed to disappear in short order. But these men were resplendent with the fire of their intellectual synthesis. The equal of the Fathers, von Balthasar has become from this day forward the shining symbol of a vanished Christian culture. His work remains no less significant for the humble laborers of the Church anxious to participate today in her intimate dynamism beyond the baroque or romantic periods of the Catholic restoration of yesteryear.[4]

---

[4] A solid and penetrating analysis of the relationship of von Balthasar to patristics is that of Werner Löser, *Im Geiste des Origines: Hans Urs von Balthasar als interpret der Theologie der Kirchenväter,* Frankfurter Theologische Studien, 23 (Frankfurt am Main, 1976). The author shows well how each of the initiatives of von Balthasar placed him in the movement or at the forefront of the study of the Fathers as it was developing in France.

JOHANN ROTEN, S.M.

The Two Halves of the Moon

MARIAN ANTHROPOLOGICAL DIMENSIONS
IN THE COMMON MISSION OF
ADRIENNE VON SPEYR AND HANS URS VON BALTHASAR

Introduction

In spite of an honorary degree from the Catholic University of America[1] (the only one) and an Anglo-Saxon Festschrift,[2] in spite of a very active publishing house busily occupied with making his many writings available[3], and in spite of *Communio*,[4] Hans Urs von Balthasar's thinking is far from having received an adequate reception in this country. Von Balthasar's fame in the United States is that of the theologian of beauty[5] and the "contemplative spirit"—author of a well-known and still up-to-date book on prayer;[6] his

Communio 16 (Fall 1989). © 1989 by *Communio: International Catholic Review*

[1] In early October 1977, Hans Urs von Balthasar made several presentations at the Catholic University of America ("Catholicism and the Religions"; "Christian Prayer"; "Current Trends in Catholic Theology and the Responsibility of the Christian"; and "Response to My Critics" published in *Communio: International Catholic Review*, 5 (Spring 1978): 6–14, 15–22, 69–76, 77–85). On that occasion, an honorary Doctorate of Humane Letters was conferred on him, for which he thanked CUA with the dedication of volume III of *Theo-Drama* (III: *Die Handlung* [1980]).

[2] J. Riches (ed.), *The Analogy of Beauty: The Theology of Hans Urs von Balthasar* (Edinburgh, 1980)—with interesting contributions on such topics as von Balthasar's "Analysis of Faith", Reflections on his Christology, the exegetical approach, the Mary-Peter relationship, his interpretation of Goethe, Hölderlin, and Hamann, and the sometimes combative opposition between von Balthasar and Rahner. (A festschrift is a volume of learned essays contributed by students, colleagues, and admirers to honor a scholar on a special anniversary.)

[3] Ignatius Press in San Francisco. The driving forces behind the translation of von Balthasar's works into English are Joseph Fessio, S.J., who wrote his doctoral dissertation on von Balthasar's ecclesiology (Regensburg, 1974), and John Riches.

[4] *Communio: International Catholic Review* — the English version — is in its sixteenth year (1989). It was launched by von Balthasar and a group of friends in 1972. See, for instance, "Communio: Ein Programm", in *Internationale Katholische Zeitscrift/Communio* 1 (1972): 4–17.

[5] Michael Waldstein, "An Introduction to von Balthasar's *The Glory of the Lord*", in *Communio* 14 (Spring 1987): 12–33. The German original, *Herrlichkeit. Eine theologische Ästhetik,* was published between 1961 and 1969.

[6] Hans Urs von Balthasar, *Prayer,* trans. Graham Harrison (San Francisco: Ignatius Press, 1986).

reputation is that of a combative opponent to Rahner[7] and a sometimes acid critic of the widespread anti-Roman complex.[8] Above all, von Balthasar is recognized as a *monumentum aere perennius,* towering with culture, erudition, and prolific writing, and chastised at the same time for his hermetic and convoluted style.[9]

All of this represents—*honi soit qui mal y pense*—but the tip of the iceberg! A second expedition into this truly theological continent is long overdue. Let us mention only a few of the many avenues still to be investigated: von Balthasar, the author of probably the greatest synthesis of Catholic theology[10] during this century; von Balthasar, the explorer of the highly dramatic relationship between human and divine freedom in salvation history,[11] the insightful portrayer of God's own hermeneutics[12] and loving kenosis,[13] but maybe, above all, the psychological and theological symbiosis with Adrienne von Speyr and his profoundly Marian mental structure.

In this paper I would like to address the last two mentioned aspects: the psychological and theological symbiosis with Adrienne von Speyr and—largely because of this symbiosis—Hans Urs von Balthasar's profoundly Marian mental structure. There is ample evidence that not only von Balthasar's Marian theology but—even more deeply—his personality structure, his habits of the heart, and his intellectual framework as well have been influenced and co-shaped by Adrienne von Speyr. Furthermore, it can be shown that Hans Urs von Balthasar's personality structure and his Mariology are intimately related and concurrent. Finally, since Hans Urs von Balthasar's thinking and writing correspond very definitely to what Metz calls a "theological biography",[14]

[7] See, for instance: L. Roberts, "The Collision of Rahner and Balthasar", in *Continuum* 5 (1968): 753–57; W. Rowan, "Balthasar and Rahner", in J. Riches (ed.), *The Analogy of Beauty,* 11–35, and James J. Bacik, "Hans Urs von Balthasar: A Contemplative Spirit", in *Contemporary Theologians* 16 (1988): 1–6.

[8] See: Hans Urs von Balthasar, *The Office of Peter and the Structure of the Church* (San Francisco: Ignatius Press, 1986).

[9] See, for instance, Charles Meyer, "Review of a Theological Anthropology", in *The Jurist* 28 (1968): 383.

[10] In the fall of 1987, von Balthasar published the sixteenth and last volume, *Epilog,* of his *"magnum opus"* begun in 1961, the trilogy, *Glory of the Lord* (7 volumes), *Theo-Drama* (5 volumes) and *Theo-Logic* (3 + 1 volumes).

[11] This is the main theme of *Theo-Drama,* the second part of von Balthasar's systematic theology. It is based on the phenomenology of the second transcendental (goodness) and uses as explanatory framework the categories of drama and dramaturgy.

[12] The basic assumption of part three of von Balthasar's theological synthesis, *Theo-Logic* (3 volumes: I: *Wahrheit der Welt* [1985]; II: *Wahrheit Gottes* [1985]; and III: *Der Geist der Wahrheit* [1987]) is that God has his own hermeneutics, his Spirit being *the* Truth.

[13] See: Hans Urs von Balthasar, "Theologie der drei Tage", in *Mysterium Salutis* III/2 (Einsiedeln: Benziger, 1970), 133–327.

[14] See: J. B. Metz, "Theologie als Biographie?" in *Concilium* (May 1976): 173.

there should not be any doubt about the inner cohesion and the corresponding *consecutio actuum* of spiritual experience, Marian "existential"[15] and Marian thinking.

Here is, therefore, one of the reasons why this paper fits the broader context of Marian anthropological dimensions: a rightly understood Mariology is no more and no less than the reflective contemplation of a theological anthropology *in actu*. A second anthropological dimension will be expounded at the end of this paper, as a result of the developments we will make.

A Common Spiritual Journey

When Hans Urs von Balthasar and Adrienne von Speyr first met in 1940, they were both in their thirties, and well established in their respective careers.[16] She was a Protestant, a practicing physician, and among the first women doctors in Switzerland, married for the second time to Werner Kaegi, and with charge of the two sons of her first husband. He, Hans Urs von Balthasar, was a Jesuit, brilliantly trained in literature, music, philosophy, and theology, coeditor for four years of the *Stimmen der Zeit* in Munich, having already widely published, and in the process of translating into German Claudel and Péguy, and now beginning to serve as a student chaplain at the University of Basel.

Their first encounter, which eventually led to Adrienne von Speyr's conversion and baptism on November 1, 1940, holds a key experience which will become the leading principle of all the twenty-six years of their common spiritual journey. Von Balthasar reports as follows:

> When I showed her that the expression *Thy will be done* does not mean we offer God what we are able to do ourselves, but rather that we offer him our willingness to let what he does take over our lives and move us anywhere at will, it was as though I had inadvertently touched a light switch that at one flick turned on all the lights in the hall. Adrienne seemed to be freed from the claims of restraint and was carried away on a flood of prayer as though a dam had burst.[17]

[15] Used here in a Heideggerian *"sensu lato"*, meaning ontological characteristics determined by existentiality (see: K. Rahner, "The Existential", in *Sacramentum Mundi* 2: 304–6).

[16] Adrienne von Speyr, born September 20, 1902, in La Chaux-de-Fonds, died on September 17, 1967, in Basel. Hans Urs von Balthasar, born August 12, 1905, in Lucerne, died on June 26, 1988, in Basel.

Adrienne's first husband was Emil Dürr, history professor at the University of Basel and widower. After his death in 1934, Adrienne married in 1936 his student Werner Kaegi, the biographer of the famous Jakob Burckhardt. He too was a professor of history at the University of Basel.

[17] *First Glance at Adrienne von Speyr* (San Francisco: Ignatius Press, 1981), 31.

The time of their common spiritual journey, from Adrienne's baptism in 1940 until her death in 1967, can be divided into three periods:[18]

1. The period between 1940 and 1944, which von Balthasar calls the training stage, was mainly devoted to Adrienne's initiation and rooting in the Christological mysteries. It was also a highly demanding school of "being used" (*EuH*, I, 8: *Gebrauchtwerden*) by God through countless visions, bilocations, emanations of light, ecstasies, and exterior stigmatizations. Finally, the feminine branch of the St. John's Community originated during this same period.

2. The second period (1944–1948) was marked by the so-called "great dictations", and represents a harvest of approximately thirty-five major writings dictated by Adrienne von Speyr. It was also a time of intensive work towards the establishment of their common secular institute, and, for Hans Urs von Balthasar, a growing awareness that he would eventually have to leave the Society of Jesus in order to more closely follow St. Ignatius.

3. During the later years, from 1949 until Adrienne's death, there are but few salient events to be mentioned. Adrienne's forces were rapidly declining; she became powerless (already in 1940 she had had a severe heart attack, and now developed a serious case of diabetes, had weight problems, suffered from growing numbness in her feet), and after 1964 gradually lost her eyesight. Besides that, Adrienne's theological mission after the years of the "great dictations" seemed to be largely accomplished. After his departure from the Jesuits, Hans Urs von Balthasar spent six years in Zurich until 1956. He then returned to Basel where he lived with the Kaegis until Adrienne's death.

These twenty-six years of a common spiritual journey did not pass without imposing definite priorities on von Balthasar's life and work. In all of his successive retrospectives[19] he will regularly acknowledge them and always mention the Community of St. John as his prime and foremost concern. As a second concern, he lists his publishing house (Johannes Verlag), thanks to which he will disseminate Adrienne von Speyr's literary bequest. Von Balthasar considers the publication of these works as probably the most important accomplishment of his life. He goes even so far as to maintain that people's

---

[18] The following subdivision reflects the biographical and autobiographical volumes of Adrienne von Speyr's posthumous works, published in 1985 with the explicit approbation of Pope John Paul II (see: Hans Urs von Balthasar, *Unser Auftrag: Bericht und Entwurf* [Einsiedeln: Johannes Verlag, 1984], 7). They are entitled *Erde und Himmel*. Teil I: *Einübungen* (1940–1944); Teil II: *Die Zeit der grossen Diktate* (1944–1949); Teil III: *Die späten Jahre* (1949–1967). In the following footnotes we will often refer to them and use the abbreviation *EuH* I/II/III. The number after that of the volume (I–III) refers to paragraphs and not to pages.

[19] The successive retrospectives give a helpful overview of the evolution of von Balthasar's thinking and work. 1955: *Kleiner Lageplan zu meinen Büchern* (Einsiedeln: Sonderdruck Johannes Verlag, 1955), 20p; 1965: *Rechenschaft 1965* (Einsiedeln: Johannes Verlag, 1965), 83p; 1975: *Ancora un decennio* (Milan: Jaca Book, 19), 47p; 1984: *Unser Auftrag*.

attention will be drawn to his own writings only after having given serious consideration to Adrienne von Speyr's work.[20] This intimate conviction is underscored in a practical way by the Annunciation angel who told Adrienne after her first Paschal experience in 1941: "In certain things Hans Urs' attention will also be fully claimed; both of you, at the given moment are to be ready to sacrifice the last of what you have and to do so smilingly and acquiescently, because you are not allowed to be cowards at any time, neither in small nor important matters" (*EuH*, I, 53). It may be surmised that everything in this common spiritual journey was nothing less than the intellectual and contemplative, the mystical and practical transposition of the above-mentioned key message into their very lives and works.

Objective Intimacy

To speak about von Balthasar's and von Speyr's mission means to point out first of all the deep human friendship that united both. It appears to be a special form of what von Balthasar calls *"Rühmung der Endlichkeit"*,[21] a sign that God glorifies those who are united for the exclusive joy of God himself. This friendship is an integral part of von Balthasar's and von Speyr's mission and message, yet without being self-centered; it constitutes an additional and generous proof of God's willingness to be present in this double figure of priest and mystic.

It may be said that this friendship stood entirely under the sign of gratitude: "Thanks for your benediction, thanks for your help, thanks for your friendship", says Adrienne von Speyr in early April of 1941, hardly five months after her baptism (*EuH*, I, 45). On September 13, 1967, four days before her death, Adrienne expresses these grateful feelings for both of them: "I wish you a bright and beautiful future . . . and hope that you will remember the many wonderful things we were able to accomplish together" (*EuH*, III, 2379).

Especially in the beginning, the nature of their close and mutual relationship is the object of a careful and open discernment to avoid all possible shortcomings. But no, there is nothing in their friendship that could have prevented them from being totally open and free for God, no "emprise" over von Balthasar on the part of Adrienne, much less any sensual dependence (*EuH*, I, 58).

[20] M. Albus, "Geist und Feuer: Ein Gespräch mit Hans Urs von Balthasar", in *Herder Korrespondenz* 30 (1976): 73.

[21] *"Rühmung der Endlichkeit"* stands for the observation that finite reality is not a negative concept but signifies a specific plenitude of being: *"Soyez béni, mon Dieu . . . qui avez fait de moi un être fini à l'image de votre perfection. . . . "* (Hans Urs von Balthasar, "Philosophie und Theologie des Lebens", in *Schriften der Schweizerischen Hochschulzeitung* [Zurich, 1938], 47). Von Balthasar cites Claudel, whose affirmation of the concrete he fully shares.

There is a certain need for support and clarification; Adrienne, especially in the beginning, hungers for theological information and welcomes von Balthasar's presence during her mystical experiences. She feels the urge to communicate and to share her experiences—"with the Bible in the hand, as she puts it, and shows most of the time great respect for her confessor's requests that she sleep in her bed and not on the floor" (*EuH*, I, 54). Conversely, Adrienne draws von Balthasar's attention to his own faults and weaknesses, for instance, his uneven, unbalanced approach to people and his lack of "winning sympathy or affection" (*EuH*, I, 962). She shows—at times—even more concern about the state of von Balthasar's spiritual health. She perceives that he is no longer living in the "total love" of God; she observes darkness setting in on his soul, and notes the "lack of prayer" (*EuH*, II, 1260). Once, as von Balthasar during one of their dictations showed signs of tiredness and distraction, Adrienne reminds him of his duties as her spiritual director: "I can do it only in an absolute openness towards you; I have to be able to make my soul transparent to the very core in front of you. You should not close your mind to what is happening, because I must pray and contemplate in front of you. This can happen only in perfect love" (*EuH*, II, 1595).

Even prayer reflects their psycho-spiritual symbiosis, so much so, that von Balthasar's prematurely interrupted *action de grâces* troubles Adrienne. "She noticed only then", remarks von Balthasar, "to what extent our prayer formed a unity, in an obvious way, without any of us being conscious of it" (*EuH*, II, 1634).

Obviously, there were tensions in this friendship as in any other human relationship: sometimes Adrienne would have the feeling of being abandoned by Hans Urs to carry the burden of their common work all by herself (*EuH*, I, 349). At one time Adrienne was afraid to confront Hans Urs—out of fear the confrontation could destroy their friendship (*EuH*, I, 121).

One of the most impressive episodes of this friendship goes back to the Lent of 1944 and is related by von Balthasar in these terms:

> She [Adrienne von Speyr] fell silent and remained so for a long time, then all at once she seized my hand again and put it in an invisible hand. She did it twice. Both times, she said afterwards, that it had been the Lord's hand. As soon as she had recovered a bit, she added: "You cannot imagine how beautiful it is, to be able to put somebody's hand in the hand of the Lord. I would like to do nothing else for all eternity" (*EuH*, I, 1034).

We mention the purely human aspects of this relationship only in order to better highlight what we would like to call the *objective intimacy* of Adrienne's and Hans Urs' friendship. It means that whatever they have in common transcends purely human mutuality and points beyond them towards their common mission. Take for instance this remark by Adrienne von Speyr:

"Sometimes I feel like a twin, who is waiting for her twin brother." What Adrienne von Speyr means is a person able to understand her and answer her questions with authority, able to guide and sustain her.[22] The key to the deeper understanding of this sentence is given by SPN[23] himself, whom Hans Urs von Balthasar had asked (through the mediation of Adrienne von Speyr, of course)[24] why Adrienne had to wait for so long until her conversion. Here is Ignatius' explanation: "Was Hans Urs von Balthasar's mission already laid down, was he ready for it? Adrienne had to wait because she was to receive her education as a Catholic from Hans Urs; only then could their missions be combined and united."[25]

The Right Combination

So, what really matters is the common work based on their common mission. This mission is essentially theological, in the comprehensive meaning of this word. It means to receive and to transmit, to ponder, "interpret", and to implant the word of God in human reality.

The common mission of Hans Urs von Balthasar and Adrienne von Speyr expresses itself in three types of activities.

The first, and theologically speaking the most original and fruitful, one was in Adrienne's dictations to Hans Urs von Balthasar, who left us with a description of this almost daily work between 1944 and 1960:

> Almost invariably she dictated for twenty minutes or half an hour each afternoon.... She would read the verse, close her eyes, reflect for a few seconds and then begin to dictate continuously, usually very quickly, so that being a poor stenographer, I followed only with difficulty and frequently had to ask her to pause for a moment.... Soon she was so accustomed to dictating that she spoke fluently, and in the last years what she dictated was often ready for direct publication. I later made a fair copy of all that had been dictated, making insignificant changes ... but nothing of her thought was ever changed.[26]

---

[22] Adrienne von Speyr, *Das Allerheiligenbuch:* Teil II (Einsiedeln: Johannes Verlag, 1977), 256.

[23] SPN = Sanctus Pater Noster; with this name Adrienne von Speyr and Hans Urs von Balthasar designate their common mentor, St. Ignatius of Loyola, who appeared frequently to Adrienne.

[24] Adrienne was gifted with the very special charism of "transposition", i.e., the ability for the forty-five-year-old woman to retrieve past states of consciousness, e.g., that of a fifteen-year-old teenager and to converse in this state with her spiritual director. See: Adrienne von Speyr, *Geheimnis der Jugend* (Einsiedeln: Johannes Verlag, 1966), 7.

[25] Adrienne von Speyr, *Geheimnis der Jugend,* 54.

[26] *First Glance,* 98–99.

In the dictations, highest priority was given to its pure transmission[27] of the word, which means its pure and unadulterated reception and objective transmission. Adrienne insisted on an ecclesially precise rendering, and von Balthasar's contribution and task was to protect and liberate her from any self-reflective tendency and to make sure that the whole process took place in the context of trustful obedience towards the Church, represented in the event by Adrienne's spiritual director.[28] The initiative is all Adrienne's where the contents and the formulation of her message are concerned. Von Balthasar was amazed by the originality and cohesion of her theology (*UA,* 52). Among the most important Scripture dictations, there is the Gospel of John (1944–45), Apocalypse (1946), Genesis (1946), the First Letter of John (1946), the First Letter of Peter (1946), the Letter to the Ephesians, and the Song of Songs (1947). Concerning the importance of Adrienne's written work—in 1985 there were sixty volumes—von Balthasar notes: "The prophetic charism of Adrienne von Speyr reveals its ecclesial fecundity mainly in those of her writings which explain the divine revelation. These works should be received first."[29]

Second, the pastoral "pendant" to the theological mission bears the name of *Gründung* (foundation). The foundation corresponds to the mission Adrienne received from Mary, a mission that took on its spiritual profile and form under the guidance of Ignatius and eventually became a tangible reality in the spirit of St. John. The principle initiative again originated with Adrienne von Speyr. Von Balthasar, evermore convinced of the divine origin of this mission, eventually consented to the most difficult of sacrifices and left the Society of Jesus (*UA,* 46).

It is not our purpose to enter into details about the foundation of the Community of St. John, its spirituality, rules, and different branches. It was to be composed of lay people, women and men, and priests, the best ones, able to occupy key positions in society, strong enough to be situated in the difficult position between world and monastery (*EuH,* I, 120): the whole was to be very demanding and entrusted to Mary (*EuH,* I, 107). The Spiritual Exercises held in the summer of 1945 (August 5) in Estavayer-le-Lac were to mark the official foundation of the Community.

In Adrienne's visions and imagery, the genesis of the Community was experienced and described as a time of pregnancy, where the foundation

[27] Von Balthasar distinguishes between objective and subjective mysticism. All mysticism has to be trinitarian, Christological, and ecclesiological: a special charism in the service of the *Word* (objective mysticism), experienced in a fashion proper to the mystic (subjective mysticism), as developed in Adrienne von Speyr's *Das Wort und die Mystik.* Teil I: *Subjektive Mystik* (Einsiedeln: Johannes Verlag, 1970); Teil II: *Objektive Mystik* (Einsiedeln: Johannes Verlag, 1970).

[28] *Unser Auftrag* (hereinafter referred to as *UA*), 50–51.

[29] "Adrienne von Speyr (1902–1967)", in *Geist und Leben* (1985): 66.

became the child, Adrienne its mother, and von Balthasar its father. She was encouraged by Ignatius and von Balthasar to talk about this pregnancy and to further explore the different facets of the relationship between man and woman united for a common mission (*EuH*, II, 1655). Very insistently, the common apostolic work was presented to both Hans Urs and Adrienne as a complementarity of man and woman. New insights, proposals, and initiatives were mostly Adrienne's forte, whereas von Balthasar acted as a theological filter, thanks to his knowledge, wisdom, and caution. Adrienne, the more practical and versed in the ways of the world, took care of the worldly needs and of the worldly character of their foundation, whereas von Balthasar subjected all this to the *scrutinium* of the Church's experience and norms. Ignatius, who insisted that he should be more communicative and give Adrienne more responsibility, didn't always appreciate von Balthasar's prudence and restraint: "Adrienne von Speyr needs trust and love, she hasn't received much during her life" (*EuH*, II, 1643). Also, the common work was the opportunity for Ignatius to confirm their double mission: "In any case Hans Urs could point out to Adrienne that their double mission has been officially confirmed. It is a new basis for fecundity into and within the Church" (*EuH*, II, 1645). Concerning the wound Adrienne received at the age of fifteen and which she vicariously bears for Hans Urs von Balthasar, Ignatius observed that this was appropriate in a double mission. Since both were virginal, this was the way for the woman to be marked by the sign of the man (ibid.). The very concrete symbolism of man and woman was retranslated into theological categories: to explain her mission with Hans Urs von Balthasar, Adrienne compared herself to the Church, which was given to Christ by God the Father (in the comparison, "Christ" means von Balthasar), to be his companion on earth in order that he may have on earth a sign of the presence of the Father (*EuH*, II, 1729). There is nothing presumptuous about these comparisons. They are sustained by an overwhelming sense of mission, an existence understood only within religious categories and constantly measured against and retranslated by them. Very revealing in this respect is von Balthasar's remark regarding their common mission: "Adrienne literally took refuge with me; in fact, she was looking for the *situs* of community and of common ground, where the will of God was to reveal itself" (*EuH*, II, 1319).

Third, the common mission was no obstacle to each one having his or her own mission: Adrienne's was that of passing on the Word of God into the world; von Balthasar's own personal mission was that of a theologian, speaker, writer, chaplain, and retreat master. Adrienne participated intensely in these activities through her prayer, her counsel, and especially her suffering. "Adrienne prays a lot for me and my apostolate", remarked von Balthasar. "Time and again she makes me the gift of an entire night (that is to say, of prayer). Evidently, these graces are immediately passed on to our common works" (*EuH*, II,

1307). But most of the time she wouldn't give her secret away, calling it *"les petites cachotteries de l'amour"* (*EuH*, II, 1360).

Although not always enthused about his writing—she once questioned whether von Balthasar did it for himself or for others (*UA*, 79–80)—she didn't refuse her spiritual support altogether (*EuH*, II, 1360). There are examples cited in Adrienne's diaries according to which she assumed personally von Balthasar's indispositions: "coughing, nausea, sore throat, and the like", to free her spiritual friend for his work (*EuH*, II, 1215, 1265, 1325). She also corrected the galley proofs of his books, gave her opinion on publications he asked her to read and made suggestions for his talks and homilies (*EuH*, III, 2052; *UA*, 62; *EuH*, I, 765). And when finally in 1972 von Balthasar succeeded in founding the now world-renowned review *Communio*, he was reminded of a request made by Adrienne as early as 1945 to launch a Catholic journal (*EuH*, II, 1439 and 1643).

Adrienne had a very special place in the retreats von Balthasar frequently gave. She helped him from a distance and communicated her observations through the telephone. Often without knowing the participants, she drew von Balthasar's attention to possible vocations and made suggestions about the manner in which to take care of certain personal problems or difficulties (*EuH*, II, 1573). "She was so intensely in Einsiedeln with us", says von Balthasar, "that she even knew whether the participants were sleeping or preoccupied and troubled" (*EuH*, II, 1284). This form of participation was often accompanied by intense suffering: "It was a continual pushing and pulling—a matter of life and death! She had the impression of experiencing for the first time in her life what spiritual exercises really meant" (*EuH*, I, 1077).

Sometimes Adrienne became the messenger and go-between. She communicated to Hans Urs what Ignatius had to say about his apostolic work and its fruition: "Hans Urs' seed will come up, beautifully and abundantly, yet he should not try to reckon with time, because the laws of growth are hidden in God" (*EuH*, III, 2161). The result of this mission, however, cannot be isolated from the double mission of Adrienne von Speyr and Hans Urs von Balthasar. "The spiritual fecundity of the man will be put into the flesh of the woman, in order that it may become fruitful. In this sense, Hans Urs von Balthasar's fecundity was laid into the wound which Adrienne von Speyr had received for him" (*EuH*, II, 1680).

In his book, *Unser Auftrag* (*Our Task*) (1984), von Balthasar thoroughly reports on the common mission and the different aspects of their spiritual legacy. One of its explicitly stated purposes is to prevent any separation whatsoever between his own work and that of Adrienne von Speyr. The book wants to furnish the proof "that this is in no way possible, neither in terms of our theology nor in so far as the institute is concerned" (*UA*, 11). Von Balthasar and von Speyr understand their common work as being complementary, just as the two halves of the moon complement each other. Each one had to grow in his (or her) own way first before the "right combination" (*EuH*, II, 1993) could finally be achieved. The archetype of this "right combination" is to be found in Mary and John, brought together by the crucified Lord himself to form the original virginal cell of the Church. Von Speyr and von Balthasar perceived their unity and complementarity in the same perspective of salvation history and therefore built the whole spirituality of St. John's Community around these two figures (*UA*, 101–97). Double missions draw their strength and character from completion based on difference, as Mary had once told Adrienne: *"C'est un autre chemin, mais c'est le même but"* (*EuH*, I, 325). And since Adrienne's mission was not primarily geared toward mystical experience as such, but had to be the interpretation of what she was allowed to experience, the double mission—involving the representative of the Church—became inevitable.

The double mission is complementary in terms of their respective gender roles, and there is ample evidence in von Speyr's posthumous works that this man-woman relationship was consciously reflected upon between the two. The role of the woman (Adrienne von Speyr) was perceived as radically solitary and exclusive: the woman alone bears the fruit and brings it forth, she even has to bear the man's impossibility to participate in these acts. On the other hand, the act of generation is not egotistical and inconsequential since all subsequent developments are already contained in it (*EuH*, I, 122). Furthermore, the respective roles of man and woman are directed towards the reaping of a common fruit. For Hans Urs von Balthasar and Adrienne von Speyr this common fruit was specifically the secular institute, christened the "child". Here is how Adrienne announces the "conception of the child": "And then we have also received a gift—because everything is in common, given to both of us—so great and overwhelming, that I do not know whether I will ever be able adequately to relate it, even though it is mine as much as it is thine" (*EuH*, I, 123). This is, therefore, how Adrienne von Speyr and Hans Urs von Balthasar conceived the roles of man and woman in and for the kingdom of God—like two halves of the same moon—different and somehow terribly estranged from each other—making the other suffer because of it—and yet fruitful only together.

Undivided Theology

It should be expected that at least where von Balthasar's theological thinking and writing is concerned, a clear and definite distinction could be made between his work and that of Adrienne. But such is not the case. According to von Balthasar himself, there are topics and thematics in his work after 1940 which, in spite of intense studies, did not play any major role before that time. Even more explicitly, he affirms that it would be a hopeless enterprise to cleanly separate Adrienne's part from his own part in the writings after 1940.

Among the common topics to which he makes reference there is the Johannine Christology, and at its center "the obedience of love" in its most mysterious and paradoxical consequence, which is Christ's descent to hell, the *locus* of sin itself (*UA,* 54–55). It is important to know that the bridge between this Christology and von Speyr's ecclesiology is founded in Mary and in Mariology.[30] Within the ecclesiological context we find such typical Speyrian themes as the theology of the sexes, the Christological fundamental notion of mission, holiness as related to the communion of saints and to prayer, and mysticism as a gift given for the benefit of the whole Church (*UA,* 53–61). All these topics and many others influenced the whole of von Balthasar's writings up to his own death.[31] More specifically, there are twelve themes (with the exclusion of the Marian themes) that reflect Adrienne von Speyr's direct influence on von Balthasar's opus. I would like to mention them briefly:

1. The first and most important is without a doubt Adrienne's Paschal experiences. These are reflected constantly in the publications between 1945 (*The Heart of the World*) and the fifth and last volume of *Theo-Drama* in 1983.[32] The booklet, *Der Christ und die Angst* (1951), for instance, goes back to Adrienne's supernatural states of anguish.

2. The theological notion of truth is based on a Johannine concept of truth as understood by Adrienne von Speyr (*UA,* 82), and is developed in most recent writings such as the first two volumes of *Theo-Logic* in 1985. Within the same context, there ought to be mentioned *Convergences* (1969); *Truth is Symphonic* (1972); and *Christen sind einfältig* (1983).

3. Von Balthasar's theology of the Christian states of life is largely a theologically articulated emanation of the common foundation and, among other aspects, of Adrienne's strongly defended position on the two states of life. The contemporary problematic of obedience to the Church and commitment to one's professional life is dealt with in the book on Reinhold Schneider, published in 1953.

4. In the context of mysticism, and especially that of the theology of

[30] See: Adrienne von Speyr, *Magd des Herrn,* written in 1946 (Einsiedeln: Johannes Verlag, 1948); translated into English as *The Handmaid of the Lord* (San Francisco: Ignatius Press, 1985).

[31] In his most recent works, von Balthasar almost exclusively refers to Scripture and Adrienne's writings.

[32] Note: the years given here and following refer to the original German publication, not the English translation.

mission, there are writings which would never have been produced, according to von Balthasar, without Adrienne von Speyr's theology of mission. This is true for *Schwestern im Geist* (1970). Von Balthasar's commentary on the *Summa Theologiae* II, qs. 171–82, published in 1954, was called forth by his confrontation with Adrienne's charismatic and mystical gifts.

5. The writings dealing with the theology of history (*A Theology of History*, 1959, and *Man in History*, 1963) are to be attributed in large part to Adrienne's "consequent Christological centering of history" and to the "universalization of the Christ event" through the Spirit and the doctrine of mission (*UA*, 84).

6. The publications on Catholic universalism reflect not only the intellectual kinship between Przywara, de Lubac, and von Balthasar, but also the spiritual congeniality with Adrienne von Speyr (see *Schleifung der Bastionen*, 1952, *Engagement with God*, 1971, and *In the Fullness of Faith*, 1975).

7. The often-treated topic, theology and holiness, receives its first impulse from the study of the Fathers, but even more so from the participation in the daily life of Adrienne von Speyr, who unites both, theology and holiness, in the admirable synthesis of her life as a physician and a mystic. It is from her that von Balthasar receives the idea to address the unity of both in a book on the French writer Bernanos in 1954.

8. The immediate reason for the elaboration of *Prayer* (1955) is to be found in Adrienne von Speyr's commentaries on Scripture. They are the expression of listening to the infused and autonomous action of God's word in the human person.

9. Von Balthasar considers the Johannine notion of glory (as presented in his work, *The Glory of the Lord*) which binds together the notions of Cross and Resurrection, as one of the most central themes expressing the common mission. He points out that the central Johannine vision of his whole work is in complete harmony with Adrienne's writings and her comments on the Gospel of John (*UA*, 91). Adrienne von Speyr's small booklet, *Das Licht und die Bilder* (The light and the images), is—according to von Balthasar— conceived according to the same basic outline and pattern as *The Glory of the Lord.*

10. There also exists a high degree of correspondence between Adrienne's overall Ignatian and Johannine theology and the central notions of mission and the ongoing confrontation between finite and infinite freedom, as expressed in *Theo-Drama*. Adrienne von Speyr's obedience to her mission (cf. *Sendungsgehorsam*) is in itself a living testimony of this tension between the two freedoms; it is a real confrontation of divine and non-divine freedom in man.

11. A further common topic deals with the ecclesial function, or office, and the priesthood. The conjunction made by Adrienne between Mary and John and her idea about the priesthood and the role of Peter, become the object of a

whole series of von Balthasar's articles[33] and are reflected especially in his *The Office of Peter and the Structure of the Church,* published in 1974.[34] It is within this broader context that the Marian thinking of both, Hans Urs von Balthasar and Adrienne von Speyr, is to be found.

12. Once more, explicit mention should be made of Christ's obedience in its Ignatian-Johannine form of existence. It was again Adrienne who laid down the Christological foundation of obedience according to John and who was called to reproduce it to its outer existential limits in her own life (*UA,* 95). Von Balthasar has written widely on obedience.[35] The core element of his theology on obedience is to be found in a section of his volume on the Old Testament called "The Stairway of Obedience".[36]

The convergences pointed out in these twelve aspects are but a few major examples of the symbiosis in work that existed between von Balthasar and Adrienne von Speyr. Their factual importance is all the more striking as it is witnessed by von Balthasar himself (*UA,* 81–96).

The Marian Personality Structure

The highly effective presence and influence of Adrienne von Speyr on von Balthasar's life and work is particularly striking where von Balthasar's Marian attitude and thought is concerned. It can easily be verified that important sources of his Mariology are the theology of the Fathers,[37] Scripture,[38] anthropology,[39] the Ignatian theology and spirituality,[40] as well as the thinking of theologians he met during his studies.[41] Yet the most decisive influences are due to Adrienne von Speyr and, as we shall see, not only because of her rich insights into the mystery of Mary, but primarily as a consequence of her

---

[33] See, for instance, B 187, 207, 210, 230, 232, 239, 246, 321, 331 in *Hans Urs von Balthasar; Bibliographie 1925–1980,* compiled by Cornelia Capol (Einsiedeln: Johannes Verlag, 1981), 32p.

[34] *The Office of Peter and the Structure of the Church* (San Francisco: Ignatius Press, 1974).

[35] See: A. Schilson and W. Kasper, *Christologie im Präsens: Kritische Sichtung neuer Entwürfe* (Freiburg, 1974) on von Balthasar's "Christology of Obedience", 63ff.

[36] *Herrlichkeit. Eine theologische Ästhetik.* Bd. III/2: *Theologie,* Teil 1: *Alter Bund* (Einsiedeln: Johannes Verlag, 1966), 199–283.

[37] See: *Theodramatik* II. *Die Personen des Spiels,* 2. Teil: *Die Personen Christus* (Einsiedeln: Johannes Verlag, 1978), 276–87.

[38] Ibid., 260–68.

[39] See: "Maria in der kirchlichen Lehre und Frömmigkeit", in *Kirche im Ursprung, zusammen mit Josef Kardinal Ratzinger* (Freiburg, 1980), 45–48.

[40] Von Balthasar underwent the whole *ratio studiorum* of the Jesuits, translated the *Spiritual Exercises,* and was himself a much sought after Ignatian retreat master.

[41] Foremost were E. Przywara and Henri Cardinal de Lubac, but also to some extent M. Scheeben.

existential bond with Mary, in which von Balthasar has an important and rewarding part.

Most of von Balthasar's specific and autonomous Marian writings[42] were published after the death of Adrienne von Speyr, although Mary's presence is discernible in almost all of von Balthasar's major publications before that time.[43] It is often overlooked that between 1944 and 1960, even though his own Marian production may be modest, von Balthasar participated in the dictation and editing of at least fifteen major titles of Adrienne's works, all of which contain major sections on Mary.[44] As coauthor and witness he was deeply marked by Adrienne's Marian theology. The notion of mission (synonymous with the theological concept of person) is typical of von Speyr's Ignatian-Johannine theology. And it is this notion of mission which is central in all of von Balthasar's articles and essays on the relationship between Mary and the Church, especially Mary's becoming the Church under the Cross. Here again we find pure von Speyr doctrine, as von Balthasar himself admits it (*UA*, 93).

But not only does the core of von Balthasar's Mariology have a strong Speyrian profile; in seemingly secondary points also we are able to detect interesting parallelisms, for instance, both use the symbol of the "three Marys" and that of "The Lady of the Mantle". In 1950 Adrienne wrote[45] *Drei Frauen und der Herr*[46] to symbolize the total act of faith in the totality of revelation: Incarnation, Passion, and Resurrection. Von Balthasar uses this image in a similar sense[47] as the perfect feminine attitude of the creature in front of its God, as the symbol of the lovingly believing Church. Our Lady of the Mantle, an old iconographical Marian motif,[48] is often present in Adrienne's

---

[42] Of a total of approximately thirty specific and autonomous Marian writings, only one was written in the '40s (1944), and three in the '60s (1960, 1961, 1963) before Adrienne's death.

[43] This is true for such major works as *Herz der Welt* (Zurich, 1945), translated into English as *The Heart of the World* (San Francisco: Ignatius Press, 1979); *Theologie der Geschichte* (Einsiedeln: Johannes Verlag, 1959), translated as *A Theology of History* (New York: Sheed & Ward, 1963); *Das betrachtende Gebet* (Einsiedeln: Johannes Verlag, 1955), translated as *Prayer* (San Francisco: Ignatius Press, 1983); and *Glaubhaft ist nur Liebe* (Einsiedeln: Johannes Verlag, 1963), translated as *Love Alone: The Way of Revelation* (London: Burn & Oates, 1968).

[44] They rank from the commentary on St. John (vol. 3, 1945) to the highly inventive monograph *Maria in der Erlösung* (1958).

[45] "Wrote" means dictated.

[46] Adrienne von Speyr, *Drei Frauen und der Herr* (Einsiedeln: Johannes Verlag, 1978), translated into English as *Three Women and the Lord* (San Francisco: Ignatius Press, 1986).

[47] See: *Theodramatik* II/2: 256; *Die Wahrheit ist symphonisch* (Einsiedeln: Johannes Verlag, 1972), 112–14; *Spiritus Creator* (*Skizzen zur Theologie III*) (Einsiedeln: Johannes Verlag, 1967), 201–4. For English titles, see list on pages 299–305 below.

[48] See, for instance, W. Beinert and H. Petri, *Handbuch der Marienkunde* (Regensburg, 1984), 187, 203, 786, 868, 941.

visions in different colors and forms, symbolizing the grace and light God has
bestowed upon Mary and the protection she gives to Adrienne von Speyr, to
Hans Urs von Balthasar, and their "child" (e.g., *EuH*, I, 3; *EuH*, III, 2122).
Von Balthasar uses this motif to symbolize Mary's ecclesial identity, especially
to signify Mary's Yes as the total Yes of "spouse-mother-Mary-Ecclesia".[49]
Thanks to Mary's mission, the Church is enabled to give light, warmth, and
security.[50]

Von Balthasar owes another very striking feature of his Mariology to
Adrienne von Speyr: the openness and obviousness with which he speaks
about Marian apparitions. In fact, his first Marian article in 1944, and one of
his more recent ones,[51] deal with the subject. There can be no doubt that this
is largely the result of Adrienne von Speyr's "wonderful intimacy with the
Mother of God". As von Balthasar recalls it: "Adrienne is not afraid of these
apparitions. Apparitions have, this is her explanation, always a strangely
natural way of fitting the patterns of everyday life, so much so, that they are
received—in spite of the awe and amazement they provoke—as something
obvious and matter of fact" (*EuH*, I, 3). The presence of the Mother becomes
for Adrienne a "wonderful habit" (*EuH*, I, 50); it is expressed in different
ways, oscillating between the "real presence of what is seen" and other forms
of presence where Adrienne perceives Mary as an "image", for instance, that
of a well known apparition, like Lourdes (e.g., *EuH*, I, 256; *EuH*, I, 508-9).

Von Balthasar's incarnational approach to revelation, his stress on the
factual, concrete, and personal dimensions of his Marian thinking, is echoed
by Adrienne's own and identical beliefs: "Where Mary is absent—says
Adrienne—Christ too becomes unreal and abstract. If you deprive him of his
love for his mother, it is as if you would deprive him of the terrestrial basis of
his love" (*EuH*, I, 519). Listening to these words, who is not reminded of von
Balthasar's own words about the motherless Church that becomes an inhuman
Church![52]

Our present concern, however, is not to compare Mariologies—it would
mean to force open doors!—but to make a step further into the wonderfully
amazing relationship between Hans Urs von Balthasar and Adrienne von
Speyr. Thanks to this relationship, it can be shown that von Balthasar's Marian
writing is but the outside view of a deep and lasting existential bond between
Mary and himself. Yet, the link between Mary and Hans Urs von Balthasar is

---

[49] *Love Alone,* 62–65.

[50] *Elucidations,* (London: Society for Promoting Christian Knowledge, 1975).

[51] "Die Erscheinung der Mutter", in *Schweizer Rundschau* 44 (1944): 73–82, and "Maria—
das Urbild der Kirche: Zu den Erscheinungen der Mutter des Herrn", in *KNA, Katholische
Korrespondenz* 15 (April 10, 1984): 2–3.

[52] The well-known sentence: "Without Mariology, Christianity threatens imperceptibly
to become inhuman", from "The Marian Principle", in *Elucidations,* 72.

Adrienne von Speyr. It is a highly rewarding experience to observe the extent to which Mary's presence in Hans Urs von Balthasar's life is altogether discreet and intense, encouraging and full of motherly attentions. And it is Adrienne who "channels" and mediates Mary's intentions and reactions for von Balthasar. Mary's role is that of a mother: "She possesses a kind of helping omnipresence" (*EuH,* I, 197). And her special attentions are usually directed more towards the common apostolate than towards the persons, but not exclusively so. In Adrienne's interpretation of her own destiny towards Catholicism and the double mission with Hans Urs von Balthasar, Mary and Hans Urs von Balthasar are closely related. She, Adrienne, puts it in these words: "Without Jean (meaning probably St. John), no Hans Urs; without Hans Urs, no Mother of God; without the Mother of God, no Christ . . . " (*EuH,* I, 220).

Among the truly touching attentions Mary has towards Hans Urs von Balthasar, there is the story about the roll of bandaging material. Adrienne is bandaging her bleeding hand while Mary holds the bandaging roll. At the completion of her work, Adrienne suddenly knows that she has to give Hans Urs von Balthasar the remaining bandaging material. She does so, telling him that Mary had it in her hand and that he should treat it respectfully and consider this gift as a pledge and obligation. And ever since, von Balthasar carries the bandaging roll in a small holder knit especially for him by Adrienne as a tangible sign of his commitment to the common mission (*EuH,* I, 422; *EuH,* I, 422, n. 16). In a different situation, Adrienne, whose confession von Balthasar is hearing at that moment, sees how Mary stands next to her confessor and puts her hand on his shoulder (*EuH,* I, 613). In still another example, Adrienne sees how Mary, standing next to Hans Urs von Balthasar— and somehow within him—receives Holy Communion. "This was absolutely new to her: that Mary receives the Lord fully in each one of those who take communion, whereas the person himself receives him only partially" (*EuH,* I, 608). On two occasions, Adrienne takes Hans Urs von Balthasar's hand and puts it in Mary's hand and tells him afterwards that Mary gave him her blessing (*EuH,* I, 720). There are other examples which show how much it is Mary who unites Adrienne and Hans Urs' mission. Von Balthasar narrates a common pilgrimage to Einsiedeln and adds: "I was kneeling at a certain distance from her (Adrienne). Afterwards she told me: 'Did you sense that Mary for a certain time had been kneeling between the two of us, praying with us? Our prayer was as if included in hers'" (*EuH,* I, 936). On another occasion, von Balthasar asks Adrienne how he could improve his spiritual life. She answers: "We cannot constantly think about ourselves and—at the same time—have the Lord as our center. We have to free the center of our being for him. And there is only one means to accomplish this: we must put our hand in the hand of Mary . . . " (*EuH,* II, 1400). Mary approves of their prayer and its Marian orientation by the wonderful gesture of taking their rosaries in her hands (*EuH*, II, 1214). She is also present in von Balthasar's process of discernment before leaving the Society of Jesus. During a retreat in Barollière in July, 1948, von Balthasar often kneels in front of the altar painting which represents Mary giving instructions to St. Ignatius. Von Balthasar comes to understand himself as integrated in this chain of command: that is, personally receiving orders from St. Ignatius, who passes on to him the Marian message of self-abandonment (*EuH*, II, 1998).

As mentioned earlier, Mary frequently shows herself to Adrienne as the patroness of their common apostolic work. During the inauguration ceremony of their first community residence (Wettsteinallee) in Basel, Mary is perceived by Adrienne standing behind von Balthasar and holding the child in her arms during his homily (*EuH*, II, 1368). Sometimes Mary holds big and small houses—other symbols for the St. John's Community—in her arms (*UA*, 40–41, especially n. 8). The group picture should be remembered: Adrienne and Hans Urs, the "child"—and behind them, the Mother of God. It is summarized in the following account of one of Adrienne's Marian visions: "We both want to love you [words addressed to God], to serve you, and thank you for the Church you have entrusted to us—these last words: for the Church you have entrusted to us . . . had suddenly been said by Mary, that is, we [Mary and Adrienne von Speyr] spoke them together, and for the fraction of a second she [Mary] placed the child [ours], you [Hans Urs von Balthasar] should know, on my arms, but it was not only the child, it was the *Una Sancta* 'en miniature' . . . " (*UA*, 78).

The Marian intimacy of their common mission, its Marian contents and structure is perhaps best expressed in an experience which took place during a visit to Notre Dame in Paris, where Adrienne was overwhelmed with the certitude of Mary's protection for their mission: " . . . Mary will mediate between us and the Catholic world in which we shall minister. She will be the contents which are to be mediated, even though the appropriate vessel for it is not yet ready. Mary sustains us and she will be sustained by us. She will show us how this has to happen. The attitude, the self-abandonment of the Mother is what we will have to mediate and to transmit" (*EuH*, III, 2046).

But we have not yet reached the bottom of what could be called the graced intimacy between Hans Urs and Mary, channelled and mediated always by Adrienne. Let us mention first that Adrienne's trust and confidence was based on von Balthasar's closeness to God and Mary: "If the Lord and his Mother didn't hold your hand forcefully—she says—it would be very dangerous for me, because in this moment I view God entirely through you. But it would be absurd to think that you could show me another but the true God" (*EuH*, II, 1750). Von Balthasar's intimacy with Mary—we have pondered the expression—takes on sometimes almost refreshingly childlike forms; as during a telephone call with Adrienne who is—at that moment—in the company of Mary. Von

Balthasar sends her greetings, and the Mother answers with an "incomparable gesture", so that Adrienne exclaims delightedly: *"O vous auriez dû voir ça!"* (*EuH*, II, 1723). After one of her raptures, Adrienne confides: "I saw Mary's Assumption . . . and I saw you—up there, kneeling very close to the Mother" (*EuH*, II, 1352).

Was von Balthasar's relationship with Mary even more intimate? St. Ignatius (SPN) remarks on January 15, 1947: "Hans Urs should remember during his whole life, that he has spoken with the Mother of God. This was a great, great grace" (*EuH*, II, 1717). Has Mary actually spoken to Hans Urs directly, in what we could term a Mariophany, or at least in a dialogue, in an actual exchange of words between the two of them? Our source on this point is not clear, not unequivocal: "SPN comes with the Mother, and the Mother wants to talk with Hans Urs. She gives him her blessing. The Mother loves Hans Urs. She says that she has received a lot from him. She says thanks to him for whatever he has daily given to her. For many years he hasn't forgotten her, not even for one day. Conversely, she had been with him every day. . . . She also would like us to return to her everything we received from her, not for her to keep it, but in order for her to distribute it all over the world" (*EuH*, II, 1717). Whatever the true nature of this event, it is and will remain a very explicit proof of Mary's affection for Hans Urs, and an encouraging confirmation of the common mission and the thoroughly Marian character of the common apostolate of Hans Urs von Balthasar and Adrienne von Speyr.

All the aforementioned facts and events tend to confirm that von Balthasar's thinking and writings are in fact a theological biography, where it would be impossible to separate the spiritual from the theological, the existential from the intellectual. And as we have been able to observe, this inner unity and cohesion has constantly been influenced and shaped by Adrienne's own mediation; more precisely, Adrienne's influence is not primarily her own, but that of Ignatius and that of Mary, thanks to Adrienne's "incredibly intimate relationship" with Mary (*UA*, 21). And when in 1940 she meets von Balthasar for the first time, she knows that it was because of him that during a Marian vision at the age of fifteen she had received the wound (*EuH*, II, 1637, 1645, 1680). This wound is the symbol of their common ecclesial fecundity, a fecundity rooted and conditioned in a thoroughly Marian personality structure.

It is this Marian personality structure that von Balthasar discovers during the retreat of 1929, which eventually led to his entry into Jesuit religious life. It is the discovery of the *fiat*: "All I had to do was to abandon everything and to wait to be used."[53] The ordination souvenir will go a step further and be even more explicit: *"Benedixit, fregit, deditque"* meaning that the destiny of the servant is intimately related to that of his master. A second conversion will

---

[53] *Pourquoi je me suis fait prêtre* (Tournai, 1961), 19–22.

occur after von Balthasar's encounter with Adrienne. God's own Prometheus—
the author of the monumental *Apokalypse der deutschen Seele,* 1937–1939,[54]
—will become the humble stenographer, taking down God's word transmitted
to him by Adrienne, and the proud and self-conscious aristocrat will eventually have to leave his spiritual homeland, the Society of Jesus, following
thereby the will and call of God, again expressed in the visions and words of
Adrienne. This is what we mean by Marian personality structure. The Marian
personality structure is not only the main thematic of von Balthasar's life; it
also has thoroughly shaped the epistemological framework of his philosophy
and theology. The key word in all of von Balthasar's thinking and writing is
Yes, the affirmative answer, the positive attitude, the acceptance, and the *fiat*
of obedience and love. Obedience and love are symbolized by Ignatius and
John, two principal figures in the Speyr-Balthasarian world of concepts and
images. Yet it is Mary who holds the position in the middle between Ignatius
and John, thus bringing obedience and love together into a living unity. Von
Balthasar's epistemological Yes is a deeply realistic one: it is a Yes to reality in
its concreteness and totality, the affirmative and joyous acceptance of God's
incarnational challenge to humanity, the creature's ready self-recognition as
creature, and the truly Catholic affirmation of all dimensions in the relationship between God and the human being. The three terms: affirmation (as *fiat*),
concreteness, and totality contain all of von Balthasar's major intellectual and
spiritual insights. Ultimately, *fiat* stands and falls with the never ending life
cycle of trinitarian love, the totality is grounded in the *"universale concretum"*
of the God-Man Jesus Christ, and concreteness is synonymous with *ecclesia,*
the historically concrete presence of Christ's Spirit among us. Von Balthasar's
thinking and writing have been labeled a "theological phenomenology". He
wants to show reality as the glass house, transparent and translucent to God's
grace. He sees himself like John the Baptist with the oversized forefinger on
Matthias Grünewald's "Crucifixion" in Colmar, Alsace. To point out and to
show, that is the theologian's main concern.

The Second Anthropological Dimension

There is, no doubt, a high degree of convergence between the significance of
this double mission and the main axis of von Balthasar's theological thinking.
Hans Urs von Balthasar and Adrienne von Speyr represent, in a multi-shaded
way, the incarnation and human concretization of the primacy of God's
descending love and the subjective-objective evidence of faith, of God's entry

---

[54] *Apokalypse der deutschen Seele. Studien zu einer Lehre von den letzten Haltungen.* Bd. I: *Der
deutsche Idealismus* (Salzburg: A. Pustet, 1937); Bd. II: *Im Zeichen Nietzsches* (1939); Bd. III:
Die Vergöttlichung des Todes (1939).

into human flesh and the unrestricted Yes of the purest of creatures. Their unity is the human symbol of Christ's descent into the hell of *kenosis* and man's self-divesting in the *Sequela Christi,* of God's masculine-generative redemption and man's feminine-receptive longing for redemption. They are kneeling and sitting theology united; the overflowing abundance of revelation carried in the womb of the woman and the representative function of the man, called upon to interpret and formulate — all these aspects of a complementary thematic can be found in the different facets of the double mission. One might ask what is first: the experience of the mystic Adrienne or the thinking of the theologian von Balthasar? We tend to say the first: Adrienne's objectively receptive action receives and passes on God's word, in tune, however, with the equally ecclesially objective theological action on behalf of this word by von Balthasar.

The central elements of the common theological anthropology are illustrated in the relationship between their respective personalities. There is first of all the unity of man and woman, expressed in their mutual interdependence. More important still is their common feminine-receptive dependence from and orientation towards the common origin and source of their double mission. And where their mission is objectified in the common foundation of the St. John's Community, the roles are again different, based on their being man and woman. Even the Church of Peter and the Church of Mary — office and institution and all-encompassing motherliness — are reflected in their providential relatedness, reproducing thus the one and only intention of the founder through the complementarity of their functions.

The bond between Adrienne von Speyr and Hans Urs von Balthasar is a specific expression of the living and unswerving bond between God and the human person. Yet, in this case, the *admirabile commercium* between heaven and earth is not realized on behalf of a single person, but of humanity in its full and complete expression, as embodied in man and woman, united in God's will for a common mission. And this mission, again, is nothing else — in its form, process, and realization — but the perfect embodiment of the patristic notion of *"anima ecclesiastica".* Because, if woman and man *together* represent the fullness of human being, then there is no doubt that the full expression of ecclesial attitude (*anima ecclesiastica*) is, according to the horizontal dimension, that of man and woman, and as such the full expression of creature in its vertical relationship with the Creator.

And this is, therefore, our second anthropological dimension, as announced at the outset of this presentation. It seems that the example of Adrienne von Speyr and Hans Urs von Balthasar could usefully address the present discussion in the Church about gender roles. Not that a case should be made of it and that it should be abused to prove hasty conclusions about the masculine and feminine psychology and nature. It could, however, suggest that the personal and interpersonal realities will find their proper place and appreciation only in the transpersonal. The relationship between Adrienne von Speyr and Hans Urs von Balthasar stands and falls with their common directedness towards the source of their common vocation, God, as he expresses himself through Ignatius and Mary, and towards the hopeful result of their double mission, the "child". It is in the name of and because of this transpersonal reality that difference in unity between man and woman may coexist and even become fruitful. "The greater the difference between man and woman", says von Balthasar, "the greater also the possibilities of love and fecundity."[55] Under one condition, however—that this complementary difference be grounded in the ever greater reality of trinitarian love and fecundity.

If feminist concerns are not merely a matter of hierarchic functional uniformity, then the example of Hans Urs von Balthasar and Adrienne von Speyr could be a challenging illustration—not necessarily to be copied as such!—of the best possibilities the Church has to offer to men and women, granted that both be shaped and permeated by the common fundamental Marian personality structure. Among the incarnational signs of God's presence in this world, the example of Hans Urs von Balthasar and Adrienne von Speyr should not be ignored, because: "Wherever in Christianity Mary appears" —says Adrienne von Speyr—"everything abstract and distant, all veils and obstacles disappear, and every soul is immediately touched by the heavenly world. Mary, the purest among all imaginable creatures, does not mediate anything whatsoever of the heavenly truth without the cooperation of the senses."[56]

---

[55] "...Je verschiedener die Ausprägungen von Mann und Frau in der identischen Menschennatur sind, umso vollkommener und fruchtbarer kann Einigung in der Liebe sein", in *Gedanken zum Frauenpriestertum,* Man. (Basel, 1987), 3.

[56] Adrienne von Speyr, *Magd des Herrn,* 2nd ed. (Einsiedeln: Johannes Verlag 1969), 182.

The Community of St. John

A Conversation with Cornelia Capol and Martha Gisi[1]

Nearly half a century has passed since you came to know Hans Urs von Balthasar. At that time, in the early '40s, he was working here in Basel as student pastor. This is also the period in which he began to work with Adrienne von Speyr and in which the plan for the foundation of a spiritual community began to take shape. How did you come to know Hans Urs von Balthasar?

M. Gisi: When I studied Romance languages I came across Claudel and Péguy, and, in connection with these two representatives of the *renouveau catholique* in France, certain questions about Catholicism posed themselves to me, a Protestant. So I looked up the local student pastor, Herr Doktor von Balthasar. He immediately realized that my concern was existential, and he mentioned books I should read, among them Erich Przywara, *Crucis Mysterium,* and especially Karl Adam, *Die Kirche Christi.* Claudel, he remarked, would be a good way to come to the Church; but at the same time he warned, "Yes, but with Claudel you must be careful. All of that is not so clear with him, for example, his understanding of love." At any rate, I left with an armful of books, and I returned with many questions, which he answered. And then he told me he knew a lady in Basel whom I should meet because she was forming something that could interest me. She was a doctor. Then he gave me her phone number, and so I met Adrienne.

C. Capol: At that time I was really far from Basel and already had a profession. A lengthy illness came upon me during that period, and I thought during its course: When I get through this I want to make the Spiritual Exercises. At that time—it was 1944—Fr. Richard Gutzwiller was active in Zurich, a famous preacher and master of the Spiritual Exercises. Everyone would have liked to have made the Spiritual Exercises with him. And so, when the occasion presented itself, I registered, but at the last moment I found out that the

---

Translated by Michael Waldstein.

[1] This conversation took place in February 1989 in Basel's Arnold Böcklinstrasse where Hans Urs von Balthasar lived and worked until his death. Cornelia Capol, who for many years assisted in his work for Johannes Verlag, and Martha Gisi are among the founding members of the Community of St. John.

exercises were not to be directed by Fr. Gutzwiller, but by a certain Herr
Doktor Hans Urs von Balthasar, whose name did not mean much to me. I had
read his translation of Claudel's *Way of the Cross,* but that was all I knew about
him. Nevertheless, I went there with many misgivings, and, as is customary
during a retreat, I asked to talk with him. He asked me what I wanted to do
with my life—I had already looked in the direction I eventually took—and he
said, yes, he knew something. And then in this first meeting he talked about
the planned community. The whole following year I did not get in touch
with him, contrary to what we had agreed. And when he once again conducted
Spiritual Exercises in the spring of 1945 I called him up and asked him for
permission to come once again. He was, I must say, rather ungracious and said,
"Spiritual Exercises are something one does only once." There were some
difficulties, I confessed. And he: "Well, then come!" The difficulties were the
following: at home I talked about the future community, which did not
exactly further a good atmosphere. My father thought, "Such a foundation is
a great risk, and you with your weak health—this is irresponsible." The final
argument almost convinced me. Well, at any rate, I went once more to the
retreat and presented my father's objections to "the Herr Doktor" as we called
him. He reflected a little, and then said, "If I were your father, I too would say
that it is a great risk." And then: "How often were you sick last year?"
     "I had the flu once."
     "Do you consider your illnesses tragedies?"
     That was a completely new question for me.
     "I don't think so", I answered.
     "Then I see no obstacle."
     This was the end of our conversation. We did not talk about it anymore. In
June 1945 I went to Basel for the first time for a meeting on the Münsterplatz.
We talked about obedience, and when we came together again in the evening,
we really already had the certainty that in August there would be the first
common Spiritual Exercises.

*If I understand rightly, these were the founding Exercises in August 1945, conducted for
the little community by Hans Urs von Balthasar in Estavayer. For the true foundation,
this is what* Unser Auftrag [2] *reports, took place already on December 8, 1944.*

M. Gisi: Yes, that is correct. We met in the chapel of the student house in
Herbergsgasse on December 8, 1944. The Herr Doktor was there and preached:

---

[2] In the little book *Unser Auftrag* (which was published in 1984 for the occasion of a
symposium about Adrienne von Speyr held the following year in Rome), Hans Urs von
Balthasar reports, "On December 8, four students and I met with Adrienne, who had a bad
cold, in the chapel of the student house on a Marian feast; 'afterwards we met at Adrienne's
and talked about the Community . . . '" (44f).

how in the Immaculate Conception of the Mother of God something absolutely essential took place without anybody knowing it, completely hidden, in secret; in the same way a seed was to be sown that day for something which would come into the open later and be of service to the Church. It was something invisible and not comprehensively knowable. We would not be able to know where it would take us; we only had to be ready. He then gave us the eucharistic blessing, after which we went up to the Münsterplatz, where Frau Professor Kaegi (as we used to call Adrienne) lived, in order to talk all together about what we should do practically. We decided—of course at the suggestion of the Herr Doktor and Adrienne—to meditate every day for a certain time, to begin in the morning and to conclude our day's work in this way. We wanted to attempt to live our whole lives in the light of this meditation. This was the very beginning.

Let us look at the time before this. Had the student pastor Hans Urs von Balthasar ever thought of founding a secular institute or did the initiative come from Adrienne von Speyr?

C. Capol: The Herr Doktor would definitely say that. I mean, that Adrienne had the idea. If one looks at her journals—of which we did not, of course, know anything at that time—she is the one who is commissioned for the foundation. Of course, it is to happen together with him, but really she was to lead him there. Of course, one could raise many questions here. On the one hand he already knew about the importance of such lay communities—at that time he already took care of the Schulungsgemeinschaft which he had founded together with Robert Rast at the beginning of the '40s,[3] and perhaps he had planned something similar for women. Still, the Community of St. John was somehow born from Adrienne.

M. Gisi: I still recall when I was with her for the first time—we were standing on the great terrace by the Rhine—she explained to me what she was really

[3] Already in 1941 von Balthasar, together with the later Jesuit Robert Rast, had founded the Schulungsgemeinschaft which later became the Akademische Arbeitsgemeinschaft. In a handwritten account Rast reports the founding idea, "At some point, I think it was in the fall of 1940, two people, the student pastor and a student in the first semester, were walking— *modo magistri discipulique,* in the manner of teacher and student, one would have said if one had seen them—from Basel into the surrounding hills and mountains. Both had the feeling that something uncommon must happen. . . . In the green of nature the little village Whylen came up opposite them. This produced a strong memory in the *magister,* for he had made a decisive retreat there in the Michaelsinstitut, an academic institute that dedicated itself to philosophical and religious education. With enthusiasm and a little sadness about the now defunct institute he told about the work accomplished there. The idea burst into flame in the *discipulus:* this must be realized now, among us! Despite some misgivings the plan was adopted mutually and without much discussion. . . . This was the birthday."

intending: to gather people who completely serve the Church, not as nuns, but as people who stand out there in life, who practice their professions, who are effective in their professions, and who in all this see their lives in the light of the daily meditation of the Gospel.

C. Capol: If one looks through the notes made in this period one always finds the instruction, "Go on with the child (that is, the Community) go on!" It finally went on when the Community was founded on December 8, 1944, and it has gone on since.

Yes, it has gone on to the present. But who could know this then? If one considers the little group: a student pastor, a doctor, and four young women who wanted to found a spiritual community, what personal expectations accompanied you at that time? Did you have solid trust in this plan, or were there already such things as doubts?

M. Gisi: I was completely decided. It all made sense to me from the beginning — the whole path somehow lay clear before my eyes. I was also certain that I wanted to participate. Right from the beginning I trusted the Herr Doktor and Adrienne. Perhaps I did not see it so much in practical terms, but I thought to myself: One can let oneself be led by these two, because I realized that everything was motivated by the will to commit oneself wholly and completely for the Gospel in the Church. The reality stood in the foreground, not the person; and I guess that this gave me my trust. Well, perhaps one asked oneself on occasion whether ambition did not play a certain role in oneself, I must confess that.

C. Capol: I too found here precisely what I had ultimately been looking for; I found it here much more fully formed than I could ever have imagined. That I knew practically nobody in Basel, neither the Herr Doktor nor Adrienne, nor my future sisters, this troubled me at times. But one thing was clear to me: If you don't take this step you can pack your bags with your whole religion. And then the first Spiritual Exercises with him were a great experience for me, because a man was speaking here who disappeared behind the Gospel. At first I thought: My God, one might as well set up a record player there, that's how much his personality stood in the background; so often I had experienced it differently in retreats.

So there were both things: I was certain in the matter . . . but there were also moments in which I asked myself: Do I belong here? I came from somewhere quite different and was not a student. Yes, at times I thought: Don't step beyond your limits! But then one thing led to another. Also, in the spring of 1945, I met Adrienne for the first time in Einsiedeln, on March twenty-first, the feast of Bruder Klaus. She asked me all kinds of questions, what I was reading and doing, and I answered her as well as I could, but I had the feeling that I had failed the exam. But then the Herr Doktor said good-bye with the words: We will meet at such and such a date. This came as a complete surprise to me, and it took some time for me to realize everything.

You just said, "Don't step beyond your limits!" In all the surprise about your own decision, what was the reaction of your family, of your parents and brothers and sisters?

C. Capol: With my brothers and sisters it varied much. My younger sister, who later unfortunately had a fatal accident, was completely understanding and helped me a lot. My younger brother was completely different: when he picked me up from the train station after the Spiritual Exercises I mentioned, he could not stop telling me the whole way back how stupid it was for women to enter a monastery or do similar things. In all that, he didn't know a thing. My father did not want to hear anything about it, and yet it was with him that I had the feeling: If I give in now, he will be the first to be disappointed. My mother, who was secretly hurt that I, the eldest, simply went away like that, told me shortly before her death: "If I know that any of my children are happy, you are the one." Later on my parents participated very much in our growth.

M. Gisi: In the beginning I did not say anything at home, because my parents would not have understood. For I came from a Protestant family and had converted shortly before. When the time arrived I really hesitated to take the final step; of course, I did not say anything about it. It was quite clear to me that I had to enter despite all misgivings. Then Adrienne arrived with her car and said, "So, pack your books here into the laundry basket; I'll take them along straight away. I am driving to the Wettsteinallee anyway." This is where she had rented the house. Well then, I packed my books, and she drove away with the basket. And from the moment that my books were over there I no longer feared the threshhold. I sort of followed after them.

C. Capol: Yes, her insight into people was extraordinary, she really had a good sense. At the end of August I still wrote to her about some difficulties. Then I got a postcard with the words, "The one who lays his hand to the plow and looks back is not worthy of me. Cordial Greetings, A. K." That was all.

They gave us some free time in the new house, about two weeks. After that the Herr Doktor blessed the house, and we were given a kind of rule of the house. Among other things, we were to call each other by our first names, but use the formal address, "Sie".[4] This custom is still observed and is almost an anachronism in similar communities. Adrienne explained the rule as follows: there must be a certain reverence for the person of the other, for her and for her path as someone consecrated to God. The immediate relationship with God should not be disturbed by other overly intimate human relationships. We have frequently talked about this in recent times with our younger members. They too want to keep the formal address.

We have come to a new aspect, the daily life of the young Community and its guidance by Adrienne von Speyr and Hans Urs von Balthasar. How close and direct was their guidance, since as a doctor and student pastor they had many duties?

M. Gisi: It was a very close cohesion, with personal consultations and conversations. At that time we received the so-called "points" from Adrienne.[5] She came to us almost every day in this first period and interpreted the Gospel of Mark—mostly after seeing her patients during the day, around three o'clock, before she made housecalls. Her interpretation of Scripture became very concrete at times. I can recall that she said—we had probably complained that we hardly had time for lunch and always had to rush back to the university or to work, "Yes, the disciples and the Lord also did not always have time to eat, because they had to preach, but they did not complain." In short, her interpretations always had a very concrete relation to our lives, our difficulties, and stupidities which we would perhaps never have realized otherwise. We have remembered these things; they got under our skin very much at the time.

Did you not experience this at times as a rather authoritarian correction?

C. Capol: Now and then perhaps. But you know, Adrienne was a woman whose authority one could bear, because she really had authority. She was a strong woman, but never authoritarian for her own sake, but it was always only in the service of the goal; one could sense this clearly. She was a woman who knew what she wanted—with us also.

And how was your relationship with Hans Urs von Balthasar in this time?

M. Gisi: At the beginning we saw him very little. We went to his morning Mass in the student house, and in addition he gave us the so-called seminars, at least at the beginning. The first book we read together was Scheeben, *Die*

---

[4] *Sie* is the formal address for "you" in German.
[5] In *Unser Auftrag*, von Balthasar tells about "points", mostly biblical pericopes which Adrienne gave to the members of the Community for meditation.

Herrlichkeiten der göttlichen Gnade (The glories of divine grace) and also the Letter to the Romans and other texts. We all took good notes, and of course we talked about the chapters that made a deep impression on us. All of that stopped abruptly when he was no longer student pastor, at least, daily Mass with its daily homily and also the regular seminars. Lectures on all kinds of topics were something we could, of course, always hear from him; and he often invited people: Romano Guardini visited us more than once, as well as Reinhold Schneider, Gertrud von Le Fort, Fr. de Lubac, and others. In addition we went to the theatre, to concerts, and to lectures by other people.

C. Capol: Adrienne also often sent us to other countries, to France or Italy—later to England—with a real program—not always described in full detail—of what we should see and assimilate. Her concern was not only the deepening of our religious life, but also the broadening of our cultural horizon: these were to go hand in hand, to enhance each other and to interpenetrate. At that time Basel was mostly Protestant; it was only in the middle of the last century that the first Catholic community since the Reformation came to be. Catholics here were simple people, domestic workers from Alsace, dayworkers and soldiers from central Switzerland who were stationed in Basel, in short, a rather random collection. On this basis one can understand Adrienne's ideas of a community of young, educated women.[6] The point was to grow into a diaspora in Basel and to show that Catholics need not be stupid. The issue (this is still true today) is not academic degrees but spiritual alertness.

We have reached a completely new set of questions that I would like to follow up on—even though they lead us away from the direction of our conversation—namely, the history of the Community of St. John. Nevertheless, it is perhaps the central fulcrum of our topic: I mean the spiritual orientation of the Community of St. John. One name has been mentioned, John; another should be added, Ignatius. Could one say that in Ignatius the influence of the Jesuit Hans Urs von Balthasar made itself felt?

C. Capol: No, I think this has a completely independent prior history in Adrienne. Many years before—in Leysin—when she was still a Protestant, she gathered a group of young people around herself and gave talks to them. One, among other themes, was the Jesuits. How she got the idea to talk in a circle of young Protestants about obedience, about *reservatio mentalis* and other matters, nobody really knows. Yet one can say with certainty that there was something Ignatian in her long before she met the Herr Doktor. Later she also dictated

---

[6] Von Balthasar notes Adrienne's founding ideas in *Unser Auftrag*: "... She especially sees different circles: a 'core group' of most educated, a 'second circle of less educated, of helpers, finally, a third circle that loosely belongs to the Community—the best persons able to undertake any important positions in public life' " (40).

the commentary on Ignatius' autobiography which was perhaps stimulated by him, but was her own work. One can certainly say that Ignatius was a point of contact for them in which they met.

M. Gisi: I believe what the Herr Doktor's and Adrienne's reflections had in common with the view of St. Ignatius lies in the idea of obedience as following the obedient Christ. This is really the central idea. And when one speaks in this context about our community one can understand obedience only in the light of this theology: obedience as following the crucified Lord. This is what was alive in him and in Adrienne as something coming from Ignatius, and it is here that one can see the true core of their Ignatian thinking and faith.

C. Capol: It is this Christological element that ties them so closely to Ignatius. One must not overlook that obedience serves in them also as the basis and orientation of the other counsels. If one were to reduce it somehow to the sociological dimension—obedience as an organizational aspect so that everything functions better—one would take away the ground beneath their work.

St. John gave his name to the Community. What is his significance?

M. Gisi: This leads us back again to the Cross. John stood under the Cross as the disciple who loved Jesus most and who probably understood him best. It is to him that Christ entrusted the Church on the Cross in the form of Mary, according to the famous text, "Behold, your mother." And this Marian and Johannine attitude under the Cross was what we too were to have before our eyes.

C. Capol: In our statutes John is spoken of as the disappearing center between the hierarchical Church and the Church of love, that is, between Peter and Mary. John is the one who brings both together and who disappears with his love into Peter.[7] This is an aspect which was again and again stressed by both: that, at all costs, the Community likewise should not present itself as a community or even as an ecclesiastical institution. You understand what I mean: John is there in the moment of the Cross—and nevertheless another occupies the highest place at a later time. This is what we desire as a characteristic of the Community of St. John: the ability to disappear into the Church. One can only let oneself be penetrated by such a thought; it can hardly be portrayed to the outside.

---

[7] These ideas are extensively presented in Adrienne von Speyr, *Johannes IV: Die Geburt der Kirche* (Einsiedeln: Johannes Verlag, 1949), chap. 21.

What does this spirituality mean in life? How does this disappearing take shape concretely?

M. Gisi: I don't want to speak grandly now, but according to our rule there should be more love in the world. For example, in the workplace we attempt to adopt a different attitude than people who live exclusively in the secular world, in that we help where we can, we radiate confidence, or we don't join in certain things—such as the hunt for good positions, which is customary today—or we take on work which nobody else wants to do. But really, still more important than all this is the idea that something of the grace given to us could be communicated to our environment through the presence of one of our members without anyone being conscious of it, not even the person concerned.

C. Capol: At this point people might ask themselves: Where does this confidence come from? Precisely in the contemporary situation, where everybody is talking about the end and destruction of the world, when only fears seem to exist in the world, we have the task of living a Christian trust in the innermost sense. Of course, one cannot aim at this, as if it were a virtue, but the strength is given when one is fed every day by the Church, when one lives out of her mysteries and her treasures. One need not, in the first place, point to the Community, but it should be possible to let those treasures of the Church flow that are offered to everyone. To clarify our manner of life, here is a more practical point: almost all of us are active in secular professions and have relatively good salaries. These salaries must not remain lying with us; all of that must go away again and again. In this context, Adrienne insisted very much on anonymity. As far as possible, the recipient should not know where the help comes from. This is perhaps a material aspect of "disappearing".

From here, from the point of view of the perspectives of a life lived in the world as you sketched it, let us attempt to go back to the point of our chronicle of the Community of St. John. As you said, the work of the Community of St. John took on concrete form already in 1945, two years, that is, before the ecclesiastical recognition of secular institutes by Pius XII.[8] *This means that at the time of its foundation the Community lacked all canonical recognition of such an enterprise. Didn't this cause a certain restlessness?*

C. Capol: I know that the Herr Doktor later mentioned on occasion that the appearance of the document and its novelty surprised him, although it lay in his line. No, I think he and Adrienne were simply of the conviction that they had to found such a community, the form of which would then manifest itself

---

[8] In the canonical statute *Provida Mater* which was followed by other documents in later years.

in the course of time. For the foundation was not their plan, but a commission which they did not know in advance. It had rather to be carried out step by step in obedience and in ever-renewed readiness. You, Martha, formulated this so beautifully during the symposium in Rome.

M. Gisi: Yes, negatively the point is this, in Adrienne's words, "If one wants to drive away the Spirit anywhere, then one should begin by creating rules."

But today there are rules of the Community of St. John. When were they composed?

C. Capol: They came very late. Early on there existed sketches for statutes—already in the '50s there was a first "outline" of the Community—but all of these were steps on our path. What we call our statutes today only came to be after Adrienne's death (1967). There is an extensive manuscript of her reflections and notes on this. Before her death, the Herr Doktor integrated much of that into the statutes that were completed before his own death. He did not want their theological foundation changed any more.[9] The more practical directives, however, can be adapted to the demands of the time.

That would mean that there is a certain free space for changes, of course. Is this the case and have there been such corrections?

C. Capol: I want to say that at root the same course has always been followed, but our founders also saw that many things perhaps had to be expressed differently to correspond to new circumstances and to avoid certain reactions. A little example: the Herr Doktor was quite surprised a little while ago that certain people were irritated by the word "academic". This thinking in terms of rank was somehow quite foreign to him. By "academic" he meant the thorough training in apostolically meaningful and effective professions, not social stratification. He finally left out the word. In this sense there really were corrections, but not corrections of the course.

M. Gisi: Practical things have changed, but the spiritual line has remained the same. For example, at the beginning we had to create an absolute separation from the family, a separation which really hurt. This is no longer the case today. All can visit their families and talk to them on the phone. Why things developed this way I don't know. Perhaps it was necessary at the beginning to give contours to the whole thing. Later, one could allow many things, because

---

[9] The second part of *Unser Auftrag* offers "A Sketch: The Community of St. John", in four chapters, the first of which contains "statutes for all"—this is what is meant by "theological foundation". It is followed by guidelines for the individual branches of the Community of St. John.

the foundation had now been laid. In addition, in all these years, primarily due to the influence of the Herr Doktor, the entire idea of secular institutes has changed and taken shape. Adrienne still stood—how should I say it—more strongly under the inspiration of the monastic life. She wanted—this is how she formulated it once—a cloister of the heart which must then be expressed in the practical sphere.

C. Capol: By no means must one think that the founders wanted to turn the members into radio-controlled persons. They were given responsibility; this responsibility made lived obedience possible, which is not a reduction of the person but the opposite: his liberation.

The rules of the Community of St. John mention not only general rules, but also a priestly and a male branch which was to come to be next to the female branch that was founded first.

C. Capol: On several occasions, when Adrienne was still alive, there were beginnings of a male branch, but it never came to be. A house was once intended for it in Zurich; evidently everything did not work out. We don't know exactly what happened. Only at the beginning of the '80s—especially in Germany—great interest grew among young priests who were dissatisfied with current theological studies and who made frequent use of the offer of the Herr Doktor's courses and lectures after retreats. This was the origin of the priestly branch which was officially founded in 1983.

M. Gisi: When the founding of a male branch was attempted, it became evident that there were great difficulties in its practical realization, at least in Switzerland. For a man who stands in life and has perhaps an exposed profession it seems hardly possible here to live in a full Christian commitment. The time was probably not yet ripe for it. In Latin countries there have been men for several decades who live a full professional lifestyle as celibates. What makes the matter even more difficult: in various countries there have always been people interested in the male branch, but if they are too dispersed they cannot form a community. "With one person alone I cannot form a community", the Herr Doktor used to say.

But the female branch has grown more or less steadily?

M. Gisi: Also with the women, things went very slowly, and both founders saw this as quite right. For the matter should not be pushed ahead, but should develop organically. The first new members came from the Spiritual Exercises which the Herr Doktor gave to students. Others came later because a priest had told them about the Community or because of the books of our founders. On the whole, it went very slowly, partly because one could not accept people who hoped that they could lead a quiet and retiring life. There have been such cases. But when those concerned realized that things were different, in fact, that they perhaps had to live alone and in a very exposed fashion, they left again.

C. Capol: This is also the reason why we have fixed an age limit of thirty for entry into the female branch. There are always older women who see a kind of refuge in such a community, which is not a sufficient basis for such a life. One also makes sure that the members have a certain psychological equilibrium. The statutes speak of the ability to live without unusual difficulty in a group one has not chosen. Why should such communities be spared tensions that must be borne, as everywhere, in patience and love?

How many members does the Community of St. John have today?

C. Capol: This is a question we do not like to answer. Not because we are ashamed of being few in number. But it belongs to the essence of a secular institute not to divulge the number and names of members and things of this sort. The Herr Doktor always insisted on this, even with regard to Roman statistics. According to him, it contradicts the nature of such institutes to turn them into institutions within the institution. They should live and work within the world, and so it is better if they don't appear in any lexicon.

Perhaps better known than the Community of St. John is Johannes Verlag. In a circle of friends Hans Urs von Balthasar once said of you, Frau Capol, that his work would not have been possible without you. I think he thereby wanted to thank you for your work in the publishing house. Let us speak briefly about this work. Where the name of the publishing house comes from is probably clear.

C. Capol: Of course, the name has the same background as the name of the Community. But I want to add that the practical occasion of the founding of the publishing house was Adrienne's commentary on John. The Herr Doktor wanted to publish this four-volume work, and no publishing house would take it at that time. So, together with a friend he founded Johannes Verlag. Still, I think he had been playing with the idea of founding a publishing house before that. *Kleiner Lageplan zu meinen Büchern* (A brief overview of my books), which he published on his fiftieth birthday, shows how the whole publishing venture unfolds around a central idea, even though there were unexpected and curious fruits, for example, art books and collections of poems, etc.

What is this central idea?

C. Capol: To let the treasures of Christian thought come to life—Christian thought not only of our own time, but of all centuries—to awaken joy in this treasury. The first collection, *Christ heute* (Christian today), attempted to do this for contemporary theology. Later there were the series *Sigillum, Lectio Spiritualis, Horizonte, Kriterien*. A final great series is *Christliche Meister* (Christian masters). In that series he attempted to bring old and new sources of Christian tradition closer to people today, from the Apostolic Fathers, to Irenaeus, Augustine, Pascal, and, finally, Paschasius Radbertus and Aelred of Rievaulx. He often translated and abridged the texts in order to make the message intelligible to people today. Among these witnesses are many women, the last one being Elizabeth of the Trinity, whose message about the general priesthood and ministerial priesthood he introduced to German readers (in the series *Theologia Romanica*).

It is an amazing idea that a theologian, almost alone, founds a publishing company that keeps going for over forty years and that can show an impressive list of titles. Where did he get all the technical and entrepreneurial skill?

C. Capol: This has always remained a question for us. Somehow something new was always there. Certainly he had an incredible nose for important texts. For example, when St. Thérèse of Lisieux' autobiographical writings came out in their original form in France he was able to get hold of the rights for a book which has practically remained our bestseller until today. Then he also knew how one makes books—Jakob Hegner's beautiful books certainly left their mark, and he had published his own works for a while with Hegner. How and where he acquired all his knowledge about graphic layout, types of paper, and typefaces I do not know—probably on the side, like many other things. I often heard about our next program only from the printers. Of course, I must add that in the Benziger Verlag in Einsiedeln, which at that time printed almost all our books, we had a very efficient and dedicated manager, Oswald Rohner, who achieved astonishing things for us. In addition, in that period the director of Benziger was a former member of the Studentische Schulungsgemeinschaft who was willing to put part of the technical and organizational strength of his company at the disposal of Johannes Verlag.

You mention a friend who accompanied the founding of the publishing house.

C. Capol: Dr. Josef Fraefel, he was one of his fellow students and lived in Einsiedeln. They knew each other from their student days in Vienna and had come close to each other through music. Dr. Fraefel, a lawyer, was also a glowing admirer of Mozart. The founding of the publishing house in Einsiedeln was also connected with the eventual incardination of the Herr Doktor in the diocese of Chur. All books with theological content were presented for ecclesiastical approval in Chur. He continued seeking this imprimatur to the very end.

I should think that the founding of such a publishing house—and certainly its continuation—would be an economic problem.

C. Capol: Somehow it has always worked out. Of course we have had helpful friends and sponsors, especially a lady who sponsored us for many years and who often had to dip her hand deeply into her purse. In addition, the Herr Doktor did not draw a salary from his work as an editor and his royalties flowed back immediately into the publishing house. Also the office was not a burden for the publishing house, the Community provided it, together with secretarial help. Still, it was not always easy to make ends meet. In this respect Johannes Verlag is not a model for future foundations, even though we always met our obligations.

An editor and a secretary—these are really the most primitive means. Was there not on occasion much confusion, full of hectic activity in the face of an unlimited sea of work?

C. Capol: Often there was a lot of work, but the Herr Doktor was an incredibly calm person who was never hectic. The whole thing was tight but calm. Of course I had difficulties at the beginning. I had not been in the Community for a year when I received his first shorthand manuscript to be typed, a long essay about the *studium generale.* He was evidently content with the typescript, the shorthand manuscripts multiplied, also the manuscripts of Adrienne's works (I owe much to her, by the way, about "how one works"!). Later there were translations to be looked through. The first was the autobiography of St. Thérèse of Lisieux which I mentioned above—which had to be practically retranslated like many other things. That often went so slowly that he had to help too. At the beginning I also had difficulties with his speed. At that time when I asked, when faced with two different tasks, which I should do first, he answered in a matter-of-fact manner, "Both." But the work was always thrilling and beautiful, and as time went on I slowly adapted to his tempo. On the whole it was an almost silent cooperation, we hardly talked about work. Yes, it was like that for more than forty years.

Yes, for more than forty years you have done this work, and now it is to continue, as the Community is to continue and to thrive. We have groped through the last five decades, and now we have reached the present again. I am tempted to throw a tentative glance into the future. What are the perspectives without Hans Urs von Balthasar and without Adrienne von Speyr?

C. Capol: We will attempt to continue in their spirit, and according to our founders this means in the ecclesial spirit. For they never wanted to claim a special spirituality for us. It has become very clear to us that it will not always be easy, but so many positive things are springing up that we must not fall into pessimism—not at all. Agreed?

M. Gisi: You know, what was valid at the Community's foundation is really still valid today. I can recall when Adrienne once said to the Herr Doktor, "I would like to see what the Community looks like in ten years." He answered her, "That is presumptuous."

WERNER LÖSER, S.J.

The Ignatian *Exercises* in the Work of Hans Urs von Balthasar

The *Spiritual Exercises* of St. Ignatius of Loyola is still considered among the most important works of spiritual literature. Even today, in fact ever more so, people who are striving for spiritual renewal rely on this book for help. It is, of course, not easy to deal with this book. It is no surprise that in the course of time many essays and books have been published on its interpretation and practical use. Such efforts are not lacking today. Dimensions of the Spiritual Exercises that had been overlooked or forgotten are made fruitful again. Historical investigations help us to understand certain sections of the text better. Theological interpretations bring out the overall meaning of the Exercises. Among the many voices that speak about the Ignatian Exercises one is little heard—that of the Swiss theologian Hans Urs von Balthasar. To point to this voice is the goal of the present essay. Section one of the essay throws some light on the biographical background. Section two, the central section, is concerned with the interpretation of the Exercises in von Balthasar's theology. Section three suggests, finally, in what sense von Balthasar's entire theological conception is shaped by options that stem from Ignatius' Exercises. In this way, the impression which this article intends to communicate will gain immediacy and life.

Biographical Aspects

Henri de Lubac once called Hans Urs von Balthasar "a fervent disciple" of St. Ignatius.[1] This statement is strongly confirmed by a look at von Balthasar's work and path; even more, it provides a key to understanding them.

In the summer of 1927 von Balthasar (at that time a student of German literature and philosophy) made a thirty-day Ignatian retreat in Whylen near Basel under the direction of Friedrich Kronseder, S.J. During this retreat he decided to enter the Society of Jesus after the conclusion of his studies. He did

Translated by Michael Waldstein.
[1] Henri de Lubac, "Un temoin du Christ dans l'Eglise: Hans Urs von Balthasar", in *Paradoxe et mystère de l'Eglise* (Paris, 1967), 185. (Reprinted below, 271–88.)

so in 1929. A few decades later he recounted that the retreat of 1927 was the crucial turning point of his life.[2] In order to suggest the dimensions of this event, he made use of the concepts of the Exercises: he came to know and to grasp God's will in the sense of "the first occasion of making a good choice".[3] It became clear to von Balthasar at that time that choice is the center of the *Exercises*. Von Balthasar's later studies confirmed this insight, and he stressed it again and again.

Von Balthasar lived in the Society of Jesus for over twenty years and thus came to know from within this order that lives out of the spirituality of the Exercises. When von Balthasar left the order in 1950, this was not a turning away from Ignatius; according to von Balthasar's conviction, it happened in obedience to a new mission, namely, the founding and leading (together with Adrienne von Speyr) of the Community of St. John. He later wrote, "What Ignatius wanted in his time clearly meant for me from then on, 'world-community' (secular institute); the difficult sacrifice demanded by the transition was accompanied by the certainty of serving the same idea with greater exactness."[4]

Even after leaving the Society of Jesus, von Balthasar remained in many ways tied to it; as he said in 1965, it was "his most dear and self-evident home".[5] At times this connectedness also expressed itself in concerned criticism.[6] To the end of his life, von Balthasar always worked both theoretically and practically with the Exercises. In 1955 he recounted, "I often gave talks at retreats and conferences about the idea of the Exercises, about their philosophical and dogmatic foundations, about the encounter between Ignatius' thought and modern thought in a theology of choice. The most important thing always happens, of course, during the Exercises themselves: one cannot 'lead' them without also receiving them anew from the origin."[7] Ten years later, in 1965, he wrote, "I translated the *Exercises*[8] and gave about one hundred retreats; if anywhere, this is where Christian joy lives. If anywhere, this is where it becomes clear what being a Christian means in its 'origin': listening to the word that calls, and becoming free for the expected answer."[9] Von Balthasar's personal journey and pastoral activity were thus shaped in a

---

[2] See *Por qué me hice Sacerdote,* ed. J. and R. M. Sans Vila (Salamanca, 1959), 29–32.

[3] See *Por que me hice Sacerdote,* 29; and *Spiritual Exercises,* no. 175.

[4] *Rechenschaft* 1965 (Einsiedeln: Johannes Verlag, 1965), 35.

[5] *Erster Blick auf Adrienne von Speyr,* 4th ed. (Einsiedeln-Trier: Johannes Verlag, 1989), 38.

[6] See, e.g., *Der antirömische Affekt: Wie lässt sich das Papsttum in der Gesamtkirche integrieren* (Freiburg: Herder, 1974), 296f.

[7] *Kleiner Lageplan zu meinen Büchern* (Einsiedeln: Johannes Verlag, 1955), 6, n. 1.

[8] Ignatius von Loyola, *Die Exerzitien. Aus dem Spanischen übertragen von Hans Urs von Balthasar,* 9th ed. (Einsiedeln: Johannes Verlag, 1986).

[9] *Rechenschaft* 1965, 8.

special way in Ignatian terms. This suggests the context within which his theological endeavors concerning the Exercises become intelligible.

The Exercises *in von Balthasar's Theology*

There are few, at least among the theologians of our century,[10] who as frequently offered incidental or thematic theological treatments of Ignatius' Exercises as von Balthasar. The number of studies expressly dedicated to themes of the Spiritual Exercises is considerable. The most important of these are presented below.

Works surrounding von Balthasar's Theological Studies

The Translation of the Spiritual Exercises

Von Balthasar's translation of the *Exercises* first came out in 1946 and has gone through many editions. In a postscript the translator gives an account of the manner of translating. It was his intention "to reproduce, whenever possible, the authentic tone of the original".[11] This tone is characterized by brevity and strictness as well as by the inner dynamism of "ever more" and "toward".

> The comparative (*más, mejor,* etc.), as the increase open toward what is above, is the true rhythm of life and thought of the founder of the Society of Jesus. Disinclined toward the static positive and superlative, he sees in the non-closure of "more" the distinctively divine (*deus semper maior*) but also the distinctively creaturely in the face of God (*ad maiorem Dei gloriam*).[12]

Von Balthasar calls the "open comparative" the "spiritual password of the *Exercises*".

The Exercises *and Theology*

In 1948, soon after translating the *Exercises*, von Balthasar published an article in the journal *Orientierung,*[13] in which he emphatically pointed to the theology of the Exercises as still not sufficiently noticed and containing permanently relevant accents. Ignatius, the article argues, though not a professional theologian, had a new access to the Gospel, moved by God's Spirit; this access is expressed

---

[10] See esp. E. Przywara, *Deus semper maior. Theologie der Exerzitien,* 2nd ed. (Vienna-Munich, 1964); G. Fessard, *La dialectique des Exercises Spirituels de Saint Ignace de Loyola,* 2nd ed. (Paris, 1966); K. Rahner, *Betrachtungen zum ignatianischen Exerzitienbuch* (Munich, 1965).

[11] Ignatius, *Exerzitien,* 95.

[12] Ibid.

[13] "Exerzitien und Theologie", *Orientierung,* 12 (1948): 229–32.

in the Spiritual Exercises. In a special way he could therefore enrich academic theology and make it fruitful. For this reason it would be well if theologians paid new attention to the Exercises to receive their theological contents. Ignatius had "an eminent 'mission of teaching' in the Church".[14] The profits of this mission have not been sufficiently gleaned either by the Church as a whole or by the Society of Jesus.

> One would be very much mistaken about their importance, if one simply limited it to the area of *praxis,* of *ascesis,* an area with which professional dogmatic theologians need not concern themselves. This has been done long enough, really for centuries, and so the Exercises have never been submitted to penetrating theological study. The flood of literature on the Exercises remains almost entirely stuck in pastoral and ascetical aspects; only few had the idea that the Exercises *must* contain decisive pointers and points of departure for theoretical theology as well. Suarez attempted in his time to construct a sort of theological spirituality of the Society; most recently Erich Przywara has undertaken the same synthesis in his monumental work, *Deus semper maior: Theologie der Exerzitien* (Herder, 1938–1940). In general, however, even within the Society of Jesus, there is a certain dualism between a theoretical philosophy and theology with a specifically pre-Ignatian form (not even Molina, Lessius, Lugo, Lallemant, and Rodríguez are exceptions) and an Ignatian pastoral method. A great number of Jesuits, by the way, are Thomists, either of the old or the newer form (Maréchal).[15]

In the remaining sections of the text von Balthasar unfolds three concepts around which the theology of the Exercises revolves: choice, indifference, and obedience. If one thinks them through in their content and connections, new and hitherto unnoticed accents in the understanding of God, humanity, and the Church emerge. To unfold and support these accents is the object of the studies presented below, in fact of the overall conception of theology developed by von Balthasar.

Interpretation of Motifs and Texts Taken from the Spiritual Exercises

The Christian State of Life

The most extensive and significant study written by von Balthasar on the theology of the Exercises is *The Christian State of Life.* A first version was completed around 1945, but the book was not published until 1977 and then only in a reworked form.[16] In its more than 400 pages it presents itself as

---

[14] Ibid., 230
[15] Ibid.
[16] *Christlicher Stand,* 2nd ed. (Einsiedeln: Johannes Verlag, 1981).

an extensive meditation on the foundations and background of the meditations of the *Exercises* on the "call of Christ" (*Exercises,* 91); about the
response that must be given to this call, if one "wants to let oneself be
grasped by it" (*Exercises,* 97); and the choice with which this call confronts
one: to follow Christ our Lord "into the first state which consists in
following the commandments" for which he gave us the example in his
obedience to his parents, or "into the second state, which consists in the
perfection of the Gospel" when he left his family "in order to be free in the
pure service of his eternal Father". All this "in order that in every state or life
which God our Lord gives us that we may choose it, we may be able to
arrive at perfection" (*Exercises,* 135), of Christian love, of course.[17]

Von Balthasar sees the core event of the Exercises in self-abandonment to
God's call, in choosing God's choice. Through all the texts he wrote on
Ignatius' Exercises this position runs like a red thread. The choice is made into
a "state" and thus has a concrete ecclesial dimension. In this context, "state"
refers to three things: (a) the general state of Christians, (b) the differentiated
state of life as a priest, a person with vows, or a married person, and (c) "the
concrete standing here and there within this state".

> This threefold gradation of the call—the call to the state of being in the
> Church, the call to a state within the Church, and finally the call to a
> concrete standing-place within this chosen state—manifests something like
> an analogy of the call that first of all makes a Christian a Christian by calling
> him out of the world, places him into a definite state by a new unique,
> second, and later call, in order to give him permanently a Christian life in
> this state through the concrete, ever-present quality of the call. The doctrine
> of the call thereby becomes the indispensable completion of a doctrine of
> the Christian states. It could seem at first that it faces the doctrine of states of
> life as the subjective side faces the objective side. But the above shows that
> this delimitation cannot be successfully carried out, because the call of God
> in the first place creates the standing of the Christian in each case and is the
> very substance of this standing.[18]

Ignatius surpassed the ancient and medieval doctrine of the spiritual life,
which circled around a schema of the ladder of perfection independent of the
concrete call of God, by understanding Christian perfection completely in
terms of obedient listening to God's call, completely in terms of choosing
God's choice. The encounter of the listening and choosing person with the
calling and disposing God is an ever-actual event of freedom and love.

In his work *The Christian State of Life,* von Balthasar made expressly clear
and unfolded systematically what is contained in the new spiritual teaching of

---

[17] Ibid., 7.
[18] Ibid , 318.

the Exercises: the God who chooses and calls out of love; Jesus Christ in his archetypal obedience to the Father; the Holy Spirit, who bears the Father's will
toward Christ; and thus: the triune God of love; further, the Church, which
unfolds from Christ in the midst of the concrete order of creation, sin, and grace
into a mutuality of states of life; finally, the human person who comes to God
and to himself by letting himself be sent into the state chosen for him by God.

The Christian State of Life is a large-scale systematic meditation and reflection on the motif of "choice", which is central in the Exercises. What Ignatius
offers with the utmost brevity is here placed into larger theological contexts
and clarified in its implicit contents. This procedure is characteristic of von
Balthasar's approach to Ignatius in general. One finds it also in shorter texts.[19]

"Three Forms of Abandonment"

The correct fundamental disposition of the creature in the face of the choosing
and calling God is abandonment (*Gelassenheit*) or—which is the same—
indiferencia or disposability. Von Balthasar often sketched it, most recently (a
few years ago) by explicitly going back to the Ignatian Exercises in the essay
"Drei Formen der Gelassenheit" (Three Forms of Abandonment).[20] The essay
speaks of "three forms" because it first deals with the abandonment of the
Christian who is making the Exercises, then with the abandonment (readiness)
of Mary, who is again and again called upon in the Exercises as the mediatrix
of prayers, and finally with the abandonment of Jesus Christ, the incarnate
Son of the Father. The three forms objectively belong together in their
distinction, and they point to each other.

Abandonment is the openness without which the one who is going through
Exercises cannot choose. In the "first week" as well as in the "second to fourth
week" of the Exercises what is at issue is *indiferencia:*

> ... the Exercises use the entire "first week" for cleaning out the sinful
> disorder; in the process, perhaps for the first time, a life is penetrated by the
> light of the divine judgment, by the full seriousness of the Cross. However,
> this first week of purification is not an end in itself, but preparation: removal
> of all illusions about things constructed and reached out of one's own
> power, humiliation to the point of insight into one's own perdition—if
> existence did not still hang on the unbreakable thread of God's grace (no.
> 71). The meditations on sin do not only create a great emptiness, they open a

---

[19] Cf. the discussion of the motif of choice in other texts, e.g., *Theodramatik* II. *Die
Personen des Spiels,* I. Teil: *Der Mensch in Gott* (Einsiedeln: Johannes Verlag, 1976), 278;
"Endliche Zeit innerhalb ewiger Zeit", in *Homo creatus est* (*Skizzen zur Theologie V*)
(Einsiedeln: Johannes Verlag, 1986), 38–51.

[20] "Drei Formen der Gelassenheit", in *Homo creatus est,* 31–37.

gaping abyss and, through deep fright at one's own disorder, they make yearning for a true order of life possible. In the double meaning of *disponer,* the first meaning is reached in the first phase of the rhythm of the exercises: to dispose oneself through (indifference) that the second meaning may prevail: that God dispose of me. The second to fourth week serve this second meaning: in the meditation on the life, Passion, and Resurrection of Jesus, in following from situation to situation, Christ's choice will happen and will be understood by me "if I am not deaf to his call" (no. 91). He chooses; we choose what he chooses for us. We know now "how we are to prepare (*disponer*) ourselves, so that in every state or life which God our Lord gives us to choose (*nos diere para eligir*) we may come to perfection" (no. 135). We have been created for this reality that has been chosen for us by God from eternity; by choosing God's choice we realize our own idea as it exists in God, and this is supreme freedom.[21]

While in medieval and late medieval piety "abandonment" had been understood as an attitude characterized largely by passivity, it transforms itself in Ignatius into an "active indifference" which remains in an actively open posture of listening and is, at the same time, ready to let itself be sent into action.[22]

Confronted with God's call, *indiferencia* transforms itself into obedience. The Exercises address the reality of obedience in the "Rules for Thinking with the Church";[23] in the constitutions written by Ignatius for the Society of Jesus and in his letters this obedience appears thematically.

In Ignatius the "theology of obedience" springs without a doubt from the Second Week of the exercises (which already makes itself felt in the meditations on the call and on the standards and in the "three modes of humility") as a noble passion to serve the crucified Lord precisely in his weakness and to allow the spirit of "the true bride of our Lord Christ, which is our holy mother, the hierarchical Church", to take shape in us as concretely as possible, by taking over her readiness and obedience (*Exercises,* no. 353).[24]

"To Love the Church?"

A famous chapter of the *Exercises* contains the "Rules for Thinking with the Church" (no. 352–70). In the great essay "To Love the Church?" von Balthasar explained the meaning and limits of the ecclesial sense and worked out the

[21] Ibid., 32–33.

[22] See *Exercises,* nos. 352–70.

[23] *Herrlichkeit.* Bd. III/1: *Im Raum der Metaphysik.* 2. Teil: *Neuzeit,* 2nd ed. (Einsiedeln: Johannes Verlag, 1975), 465.

[24] "Christologie und kirchlicher Gehorsam", in *Pneuma und Institution* (*Skizzen zur Theologie IV*) (Einsiedeln: Johannes Verlag, 1974), 160, n. 16.

essential theological contents of Ignatius' rules.[25] Above all, he made it clear that only the Marian character of the Church, which Ignatius points to in rules 1 and 13, can serve as a foundation for assent to the Church. In the "rules" Ignatius lists

> a whole list of Catholic objectivities that are to be "praised", all the things that had been thrown overboard by the Reformation: frequent reception of the sacraments, liturgical devotions, evangelical counsels and vows concerning them, "stations, pilgrimages, indulgences, jubilees, bulls concerning crusades and the lighting of candles in churches", fasting, external penance, decorations in the churches, veneration of images, etc. If one looks closely (and realizes the brilliant sense of humor in this list) one realizes that what is at issue is a fundamental attitude: obedient readiness before "the true bride of Christ" and her ordinances, "ever ready to find reasons in defense of her and in no way for resistance against her"—even in the face of abuses (362), for effective improvements can be found, not through public contestation, but only through prudent personal commitment. The elements of landscape and atmosphere are not defended in their crude materiality, but as a "living area" around the mother's house and in it; and it is characteristic that Ignatius does not speak of "love *for* the Church", but of readiness before her, evidently in order to be drawn into her love for Christ, and through Christ for all human beings.[26]

However, von Balthasar also reminds us of the Church's Petrine character when speaking of the meaning of the ecclesial sense. The Marian and Petrine elements together constitute the inner dimensions of the Church founded by Christ.

> It was only late that obedience emerged in the foreground for the founder and his first companions, namely, in the measure in which the new Christian all-readiness expressly offered itself to the visible hierarchical Church as an instrument at its disposition. The Pope thereby became the steward of this readiness, the true "father general" of the new Society, and the Society became the eminent instrument of the ecclesial Counter-Reformation. Without denying the universal principle, "finding God in all things", these "things" now became mainly the things of the Church Militant. If the first core of the *Exercises* is the "discernment of spirits" in view of the right choice of God's will for my life, its final word is *"alabar"*, the praise and fundamental assent and approval of ecclesial things: Ignatius praises them, just as Francis in his "Canticle" had praised the elements of nature as transparent for God. Ignatius praises them in all simplicity and in an act of a son's chivalrous faithfulness to "the true bride of Christ our Lord, which is our holy mother, the hierarchical

---

[25] "Die Kirche lieben?", *Pneuma und Institution,* 162–200.
[26] Ibid., 188–89.

Church". He loves her with a slight tinge of humor, at any rate with wise patience....[27]

The original relevance of the ecclesial sense in Ignatius manifests itself in the context of "choice". This sense must become effective especially in the moment when the "state" or "life" is chosen in which one is to serve God and human beings (no. 170). At the very beginning of *The Christian State of Life* von Balthasar points to this fact.[28] According to von Balthasar, the "ecclesial sense" does not exclude criticism of the Church. However, criticism does her justice and is helpful to her only if it stems from identification with the Church's true nature as posited by Christ.

"Two Modes of Faith"

In a study from the year 1967 von Balthasar compared two modes of faith, that of Martin Luther and that of Ignatius of Loyola.[29] Both sought, through all ecclesial tradition and institution, the immediate encounter with Jesus Christ, in order to shape their lives anew out of the experience of his saving work. Martin Luther derived Jesus Christ's salvific importance "for me" from the Pauline doctrine of justification, but adopted a more negative attitude toward meditations on the life of Jesus from which the concrete contents of obedient following are derived. Ignatius, on the other hand, has the person going through the Exercises abandon himself to God's call in the context of meditations on the life of Jesus. This approach shows itself most clearly in number 53 of the Exercises. Von Balthasar writes that the relation between the master who calls and the disciple who follows

> comes from the Pauline faith in the substitution of the sinner on the Cross (*"moriendum pro meis peccatis"*: *Exercises*, 53) and from the dialogue (*"colloquium"*: 53–54; 61; 63) between the Lord and friend crucified out of love and the person without love and faithfulness, which is myself. From this strongly emphasized *pro me* the question immediately emerges, *"quid ego... agere debeam pro Christo"* (53), ["what should I do for Christ?"]; however, this question can be answered only where, beyond comprehension, the call to follow makes itself heard (95f.) and where the unusable sinner, contrary to all expectations, becomes usable for his Lord on the basis of the pure grace of the Cross (and not of any synergism!).[30]

[27] *Herrlichkeit* III/1:2, 462.

[28] See *Christlicher Stand,* 7.

[29] "Zwei Glaubensweisen", in *Spiritus Creator* (*Skizzen zur Theologie III*) (Einsiedeln: Johannes Verlag, 1967), 76–91.

[30] Ibid., 86.

However, Ignatius has us meditate not only on Christ on the Cross, but on Christ as he meets us in the multitude of the mysteries of his life. Modern exegesis has shaken trust in the texts of the Gospels, but has also opened up possibilities of seeing the mysterious content of Jesus' earthly life in a retrospective vision from Easter, e.g., when it speaks of "implicit Christology" in the life of Jesus. Von Balthasar considers this contribution of modern exegesis sufficient for bringing to bear the concerns of Ignatius.

> In their life-of-Jesus meditations, the Spiritual Exercises emphasize in late medieval fashion a strongly pictorial illustration of scenes. However, they do so only in order to allow the person who prays to reach in each scene the full personal concreteness of the call to follow. This is also the goal of the entire practice of indifference as readiness. One can even say that nowhere in the Catholic sphere is there a stronger interior contact with the positive concern of contemporary theological exegesis than in the concern of Ignatius in the face of the call of Jesus' divine word to place the person into the eschatological decision of life, in order to move him to a corresponding form of selling everything (in order to find everything in following).[31]

According to Ignatius' instructions, the meditation of the *mysteria vitae Christi* must employ all senses and powers. At the end of the day—as he expressly recommends—there should be an *applicatio sensuum.*

> The "application of the five senses" that concludes every theme of meditation in the Ignatian Exercises does not rise above the concrete form (*Gestalt*) which is seen in the Gospels (nos. 121–25), for the text explicitly demands that we should "see the persons with the inner eyes in recollection and meditation"; "hear what they are saying"; with the sense of touch "embrace and kiss the places in which the persons enter and where they remain"; and through such sense-experience come to the smelling and tasting of the "infinite fragrance and sweetness of the Godhead". Ignatius does not speak, therefore, (like Origen and, after him, Bonaventure) of spiritual senses that grow in the soul when the bodily senses have been laid to rest. The human person is a unity of body and soul and all faculties of sense are borne, according to Thomas Aquinas, by the one and only spiritual soul; thus they have *within themselves* a spiritual dimension, even a graced dimension, if the person has been grasped by grace and the gifts of the Holy Spirit.[32]

An extensive account of the Ignatian doctrine of the *applicatio sensuum* (including its prehistory and its reception) is found in the first volume of *The Glory of the Lord,* which is concerned in general with the perception of the form (*Gestalt*) of revelation. The "application of the senses" in the Exercises intends to familiarize the person (who is going through the Exercises and

---

[31] Ibid., 90–91.
[32] "Das Schauvermögen der Christen", in *Homo creatus est,* 54–55.

choosing) in all the layers of his being with the character of Jesus Christ, so that the choice can concretely orient itself by Jesus Christ. In this context, poverty plays a great role. Von Balthasar points out that

> already in the first meditation on the life of Jesus, Ignatius lays his finger on following "in enduring all injustice, all shame, and all poverty"; at the highpoint of exercising a choice of life in abandonment, he demands "the most complete humiliation" which consists in this, that I "ever more wish for poverty with the poor Christ, ever more shame than honor with the Christ full of shame, and that I ever more desire to be considered an imbecile and a fool for Christ's sake, who was first considered such, more than to be considered wise and clever in this world".[33]

Discernment of Spirits

In the Exercises there are two series of "rules for the discernment of spirits" (nos. 313–27; 328–36). Von Balthasar dealt with these as well, especially in the third volume of *Theologik,* which came out in 1987 and which unfolds a theology of the Holy Spirit. In the chapter that discusses the working of the Holy Spirit in the Church there is a lengthy section on the discernment of spirits, in the course of which von Balthasar recalls Ignatius' rules.[34] Being moved by the spirits was for Ignatius himself the point of departure of his spiritual path. In order to choose God's will, the spirits had to be discerned. Ignatius was able to make use in this context of the experiences and texts of earlier masters of the spiritual life. What is characteristic of Ignatius' rules for the discernment of spirits, according to von Balthasar, is their orientation toward choice. Thus he writes, after recalling the content of the rules in summary fashion,

> All these rules are primarily directed toward the central process of the exercises, the choice of the way of life appointed by God for the individual person, in which choice the harmony between human and divine freedom must make itself present in its purity: for "in every life or state which God our Lord gives us for us to choose, we should be able to reach perfection" (*Exercises,* 135). For this fragile coordination which is endangered by human impurity, this pure and limpid (*pura y limpida*) coordination of most free divine offer and most free human consent—this is the main concern of the Exercises—must not be clouded by anything, if it is to succeed in all truth.[35]

---

[33] *Herrlichkeit* III/1:2, 495.

[34] *Theologik* III: *Der Geist der Wahrheit* (Einsiedeln: Johannes Verlag, 1987), 360–62.

[35] Ibid., 361. A fundamental work which also moves into currently urgent and concrete areas appeared under the title, "Vorerwägungen zur Unterscheidung der Geister" (Preliminary reflections on the discernment of spirits), in *Pneuma und Institution,* 325–39.

Ignatius provided for a person going through the Exercises to entrust himself
to the company and guidance of a retreat master. According to von Balthasar,
it is the task of this master in the process of the discernment of spirits to bring
to bear the Spirit of God inasmuch as that Spirit meets one in the givens of the
institutional Church.

> This discernment of spirits is apparently highly subjective, and the master is
> accordingly forbidden to mix his own opinions into the dialogue between
> God and the soul (no. 15). Nevertheless, since a life within "the sphere of the
> holy mother, the hierarchical Church" (nos. 170; 353) is to be chosen, it is
> indispensable that there be a control of this subjectivity through the objec-
> tivity of the official Church, embodied in the retreat master who must
> examine on his part a person's discernment of spirits in the light of ecclesial
> knowledge of the discernment of spirits (nos. 8–10; 14). It will not be
> enough to say that "human reason" is here simply "sufficient, supported, and
> illumined, however, by the light of faith, which on its part stems from God,
> and one cannot contradict the other, because truth necessarily agrees with
> truth" (*Directorium* of 1599, 28:5); one must call this "light of faith" more
> precisely as the grace of a discernment specifically bestowed on the retreat
> master by the Holy Spirit. This gift is connected with the objective spirit of
> ecclesial office so that, in fact, subjective and objective spirit cannot contra-
> dict each other here, if both together listen to the inspiration of God's
> Spirit.[36]

Locating the Exercises in the History of Theology

It is characteristic of all of von Balthasar's endeavors concerning the Exercises
that he situates them within the history of theology and spirituality. In some
cases the frame is large; in others it covers a short period of time.

"Homo creatus est"

The "Principle and Foundation" of the *Exercises* begins with the sentence,
"Man was created to praise, reverence, and serve God, our Lord, and so to save
his soul" (no. 23). In the essay, "Homo creatus est", von Balthasar interprets
this sentence by placing it in the widest context of the history of philosophy
and theology.[37] His concern is to show that in Ignatius' Exercises the Christian image of God and humanity is expressed with a new and unaccustomed
clarity. The Old Testament and New Testament contours of the understand-

---

[36] *Theologik* III, 361; cf. also "Autorität", in *Klarstellungen, Zur Prüfung der Geister* (Freiburg:
Herder, 1971), 85f.
[37] "Homo creatus est", in *Homo creatus est*, 11–25.

ing of God and humanity are brought to bear again without hindrance after being through centuries shaped by assimilation to more philosophically determined views. The opening sentence of the "foundation" expresses the meaning of being human in two ways: on the one hand, to praise, to reverence, and to serve God; on the other hand, to save one's soul. In the second purpose a motif makes itself heard that had a long pre-Christian as well as Christian history. According to this motif, the origin and destiny of the human person is disclosed in longing for happiness. This is the path chosen by the Platonism of Plato and Plotinus and by the idealist tradition of Western metaphysics. At all times Christian theologians oriented themselves by this model of thought and life that stresses the movement of eros and transcendence of the human spirit. Von Balthasar mentions especially Augustine, Gregory of Nyssa, then Thomas Aquinas; from our century, Joseph Maréchal and his disciples. Despite all the differences between their philosophies and theologies, they agree in positing the experience of God as the fulfillment of their longing for happiness. In extreme cases it is not excluded that means and end reverse themselves and that God becomes a means for reaching the longed-for bliss. When this happens, man becomes the measure of all things, theology becomes anthropology.

The "foundation" of the Exercises also mentions the striving for salvation and blessedness as a human destiny, but only in the second place. In the first place there is the praise and service of God. These attitudes and acts characterize the understanding of humanity in the Bible, first of all in the Old Testament—the Psalms document it with full clarity—then also in the New Testament, which speaks of Jesus Christ. Jesus' life and death is entirely praise, reverence, and service. In the situation of death on the Cross, these are completed. The line to the Cross is a descending line. The distance of the incarnate and finally crucified Jesus from the Father, which can only be thought in a trinitarian theology, is the final ground of the possibility of the God-given distance and self-standing of the created human person before God. The person rightly lives this situation of createdness if he lives in praise, reverence, and service and lets himself be sent, at the same time, with Jesus into serving others. Ignatius clearly gave first place to the theology and anthropology that think in terms of descending *agape,* and he gave the subordinate place to the theology and anthropology of ascending *eros.* While the medieval theologians were still struggling for a balance of these theologies and anthropologies, the emphasis has become clear in Ignatius. It is important, however, that the line of *eros* is not simply dropped, but integrated into the whole. The entire medieval world of thought remained within

the attempt to reach a balance between the biblical glorification of God and the blessedness of God in antiquity. Ignatius is distinct from this balance inasmuch as he pinpoints "praise, reverence, and service" as the goal of creation, even in the final sentence of the "foundation" according to which one must choose with indifference, *"lo que más nos conduce para el fin que somos criados"* (that which brings us most to the goal for which we were created). Only in a short final phrase and as if by the way does he mention that one thereby "saves one's soul" and reaches salvation. It must also be noted that Ignatius demands from the beginning the transcending of all selfish strivings for the sake of reaching that indifference which is the presupposition of pure praise and pure reverent service, and that this effort throughout the Exercises has as its aim that I make what God has chosen *for me* my own choice (no. 135), and thus that I choose "praise, reverence, and service" from "generous" love of God as the goal of my life. For this reason he can juxtapose and mention in one breath, almost by the way, *"amor y alabanza"* (no. 15), *"amar y servir"* (no. 233), *"en todo amar y servir"* (no. 363). Just as the Psalmist who praises and serves God has the Shema, the main commandment, in his ear, so in Ignatius, throughout the Exercises, the love of God is present in a hidden and nevertheless effective way, in such a way, however, that he thinks and especially acts always for God and his glory (for all forms of prayer and choice in the Exercises are in an eminent sense action, which becomes clear already from the comparison with bodily exercise in the first preliminary remark). Love finally emerges thematically in the "meditation for obtaining love" (nos. 230–37) while the concept of "blessedness" still remains unmentioned; this concept need not be mentioned, because the entire blessedness of the person clearly lies already in the *Suscipe* (no. 234) which answers God's abounding love. If one has given all one's own to God, because one returns what one has received, what more can one ask for? "Give me your grace and your love and that is enough for me." [38]

In this way Ignatius went beyond the theology of the ancient Church and the Middle Ages, and thereby brought biblical thought to bear in a new way. If one surveys the entire argument, one sees that, according to von Balthasar, Ignatius is decisively important in the attempt to find a correct mediation between Western metaphysics and Christian theology inasmuch as Ignatius freed theology and anthropology again from the embrace of philosophy, not by abandoning philosophy, but by inserting it into the primarily theological overall picture.[39]

Ignatius of Loyola and the Baroque Glory of Representation

According to von Balthasar, Ignatius is of towering importance in the history of spiritual theology.[40] He received strong stimuli from (late) medieval

[38] Ibid., 23–24.

[39] For an essay that moves in a similar direction, see "De arriba", in *Homo creatus est*, 26–30.

[40] See the chapter, "Ignatius von Loyola und die Barockherrlichkeit der Repräsentation", in *Herrlichkeit* III/1:2, 455–66.

tradition, but placed new emphases. These emphases concern especially the understanding of "indifference" (*indiferencia*). The great representatives of medieval piety, known to Ignatius from his reading of meditations on the life of Jesus (Ludolf of Saxony, the *Imitation of Christ,* the *Ejercitatoria de la vida espiritual* by Garcia de Cisneros, and other writings) understood this fundamental attitude as "becoming empty" and as readiness to "transcend beyond all other creatures into immediacy with God". Ignatius was the first to include an active cooperation of the person with the omnipotent and all-active God. Between God and man there is an *analogia entis* or rather an *analogia libertatis.* Von Balthasar described Ignatius' step beyond his predecessors as follows:

> It is absolutely decisive that Ignatius, when he followed out the idea of indifference in all its Christian radicality, did not take over its metaphysical formulation by the Germans, especially Eckhart. Even when it is thought and lived without any subtraction, Christian indifference does not imply the hylomorphic schema of antiquity: form (God) and matter (creature). In this way, indifference need not be practiced in the direction of the annihilation of the creature's own being and will, a direction that, with more or less strength, has given to spirituality from Eckhart to Fenelon hidden monothelite not to say oriental-pantheist parameters. By contrast, the true mystery of Christian revelation consists in this: that the completion of the kingdom of God, namely, "God all in all", "I live, yet not I, Christ lives in me", may be sought as God's universal causality in the creature's active cooperation — in indifference, abandonment, and service. This cooperation cannot remain in the condition of indifference as *mere* "letting it happen"; rather, God's particular will, which is actively to be grasped and realized, must also actively be sought. For this reason, indifference, which stands at the end of Rhineland mysticism, stands at the beginning in Ignatius and heightens itself in the Second Week of the Exercises through the central event of the "choice". In the analogy of freedom between God and the creature, man chooses "what God our Lord gives to us to choose; he freely and spontaneously consents to the particular choice that has been made for us in God's eternal freedom".[41]

Ignatius' thought and work had a far-reaching history of reception. Of course it was not possible to absorb his fundamental intuitions in all areas. The best situation in this regard was offered by the great culture of the baroque. However, one-sided tendencies made themselves felt when the Reformation had to be resisted. In theological terms (Bellarmine), and those of ecclesial politics, the concern of bringing to bear the Church's form of poverty was pushed too much into the background in the Counter-Reformation.[42] The

[41] Ibid., 457–58.
[42] See ibid., 463f.

principle of active indifference was usually received in one-sided fashion by the spiritual teachers and schools of the Society of Jesus. Some took up the element of "indifference" and interpreted it in the sense of the mystical tradition (L. Lallemant), others concentrated on the element of "activity", but understood it as achievement-oriented asceticism.

> The indifferent openness to the choosing God could easily be interpreted in earlier terms, e.g., in terms of the "mystical" tradition that was alive everywhere. Already during his own lifetime, Ignatius had to struggle hard against this tendency (Fr. Araoz and the Spanish contemplatives and quietists), while later it achieved a sublime and subtle height in the doctrine of *Fr. Baltazar Alvarez* (cf. the biography by Fr. De Ponte) and in the *Doctrine Spirituelle* of *Fr. Louis Lallemant* and his school. True listening to God's internally spoken word and to the movements and gifts of the Holy Spirit is rightly given a central place; however, the one-sidedness shows itself in a fearful concern with personal contemplation and a reduction of active apostolic commitment. Along the lines of ancient monasticism and German mysticism, action and contemplation are again dualistically split, and the superiority of [passive] contemplation is defended in a literal sense. When the leadership of the order began to suspect and condemn the mystical tendency, it gave an impetus to the opposite tendency that placed the emphasis, relatively correctly, on the spontaneity of human action in the analogy of freedom and choice and thus gave the word to active asceticism (represented by the "Guide to Perfection" of *Fr. Rodríquez*). As an unsuspected but necessary consequence, it misunderstood Ignatian indifference as an achievement, which is a Stoic and Buddhist misunderstanding. This deformation can be recognized in the practice of distance from the created world and in the resulting pseudo-ethical raising of the person over the world of fellow human beings which is judged to be merely apparent, insignificant, and perhaps even dangerous. This tendency endangers the true exposed Christian encounter between I and Thou. Both of these possible extremes are forms of escape from the narrow and steep charism that had been given to Ignatius.[43]

From this text it becomes clear that part of Ignatian spirituality is a closely intertwined unity of action and contemplation. The person who meditates and goes through the Exercises encounters a God who "works" arduously,[44] who chooses the person that turns to him and who sends the person into cooperation on behalf of other human beings and the world. In Ignatius the person is ordained toward this binitarian event of contemplation and action.[45]

[43] Ibid., 465–66.
[44] See the exercise, "Meditations to Attain Love", in *Exercises,* nos. 230–37, esp. 236.
[45] Von Balthasar repeatedly thought through and discussed this interpenetration of contemplation and action; see "Aktion und Kontemplation", in *Die katholische Schweizerin 29*

Theology out of the Spirit of the Exercises

Not only did von Balthasar frequently take up texts and motifs of the Ignatian Exercises to interpret them in terms of larger theological contexts; he shaped his own theological conception out of the spirit of the Exercises. He explicitly states on occasion that this is the case; as a rule it remains unspoken. Of course, the one who is familiar with Ignatius' Exercises finds their fundamental options at every step in von Balthasar's theological conception. The dimensions of von Balthasar's work are extraordinary. At the center one finds, apart from the five volumes of *Theologische Skizzen,*[46] the numerous volumes of the trilogy; more precisely, *The Glory of the Lord, Theo-Drama,* and *Theo-Logic.* It is not easy to give a brief sketch of the content of these many volumes. I will venture to pinpoint, more briefly still than von Balthasar himself did in the *Epilog* to the trilogy,[47] the central thought out of which the whole is formed and to relate it to the fundamental Ignatian intuition.

The decisive thing is what one can summarize in the words *analogia libertatis.* This phrase "analogy of freedom" is patterned after "analogy of being". In the traditional understanding, "analogy of being" refers to the specific relation between God and the world, Creator and creation, in the horizon of the question of how they are related to each other in their being. *Analogia libertatis* also refers to the relation between God and world, Creator and creation. However, being is now understood as freedom, so that the issue is now the togetherness of infinite divine freedom and finite human freedom. This shift of emphasis from the question of being to the question of freedom was probably brought about in von Balthasar through the encounter with Ignatius' thought; for Ignatius too is centrally concerned with the confrontation between the free human person and the free God—in the process of choice. Theology from the point of departure of *analogia libertatis* also means: emphasis on the action of the triune God on behalf of the world, an action that can in no way be deduced; and simultaneously, emphasis on the Marian, ecclesial, and personal presence with God in the sign of indifference or following. *Analogia libertatis* signals the program of a comprehensive new shaping of Christian theology as a whole, which is possible, of course, only in dialogue with the great tradition of Christian theology. The decisive question faced by such a theology is this: how is it possible that human freedom lives itself out to the point of closing itself against God, while God at the same time

---

(1942), 115–20; "Aktion und Kontemplation", in *Geist und Leben* 21 (1948), 361–70; repr. in *Verbum Caro* (*Skizzen zur Theologie I*), 2nd ed. (Einsiedeln: Johannes Verlag, 1965), 245–59; "Jenseits von Aktion und Kontemplation?" in *Pneuma und Institution,* 288–97; *In Gottes Einsatz leben,* 2nd ed. (Einsiedeln: Johannes Verlag, 1972), 53–56.

[46] *Verbum Caro, Sponsa Verbi, Spiritus Creator, Pneuma und Institution,* and *Homo creatus est.*

[47] *Epilog* (Einsiedeln-Trier: Johannes Verlag, 1987).

respects such human paths and integrates them in saving fashion into his own life? To answer this question, von Balthasar placed a trinitarian theology of the Cross at the center of his work. Through the Cross God remains, in the face of the drama of history, the God of merciful and glorious love.

This theology makes the claim of being an ontology made concretely possible only through the Gospel, which both surpasses and integrates the ontology developed by Western philosophy. The three parts of the trilogy show how the great themes of Western metaphysics are transformed in such an ontology. The first focuses thematically on beauty, the second on freedom, the third on truth.

The theology of the Ignatian *Exercises* is not the only impulse that gave its specific profile to von Balthasar's theology, but without a doubt it had special weight. Once again, in the twentieth century, Ignatian theology has thus been able to bring to bear its power of inspiration in a surprising way, now in the field of dogmatic theology.

ANTONIO SICARI, O.C.D.

Hans Urs von Balthasar:
Theology and Holiness

Hans Urs von Balthasar dealt with the topic *theology and holiness* for the first time exactly forty years ago in an essay published in *Wort und Wahrheit*.[1] In 1960 it was later amplified and transformed, and thus entered as a part of the first volume of *Skizzen zur Theologie: Verbum Caro*.[2]

Whoever is familiar with the further enormous output of this author knows how much the concerns expressed then have remained constant in his thought and how hard Fr. von Balthasar has tried to apply the solutions hinted at then, up to the last statement he dedicated to this topic in 1987 in the journal *Communio*.[3]

It is another matter to answer the question whether theology in general, and theologians in particular, have really taken note of those provocative suggestions or have at least grasped their weightiness. When dealing with "holiness", it will perhaps instinctively be said that it is not our place to judge. But since the holiness demanded by Fr. von Balthasar of theology and of theologians is an objective rather than a subjective matter, or even a "methodological" rather than an ascetical and moral one, it is not presumptuous or offensive to say that the work explicitly demanded then has still not been completed, if one excepts the experience of Fr. von Balthasar himself—an experience that in this regard is unique in its kind.

And nevertheless, we still have to confess that meanwhile the Second Vatican Council has been able to give a strong impetus to the renewal of theology.

It is thus first of all worthwhile to pose the terms of the "question" anew as they were presented in the first article to which we referred.

"Here", von Balthasar says, "we understand the title 'theologian' in the fullest sense as that of a doctor of the Church whose office and mission consist

Translated by Stephen Wentworth Arndt.

Communio 16 (Fall 1989). ©1989 by *Communio: International Catholic Review*.

[1] "Theologie und Heiligkeit", in *Wort und Wahrheit* 3 (1948): 881–96.

[2] *Verbum Caro* (*Skizzen zur Theologie I*) (Einsiedeln: Johannes Verlag, 1960). English edition: *Explorations in Theology*, vol. I, *The Word Made Flesh* (San Francisco: Ignatius Press, 1989).

[3] "Theology and Holiness", *Communio: International Catholic Review* 14 (Winter 1987): 341–50.

in explaining revelation in its fullness and completeness and thus in consider-ing dogmatics as the central point of his activity."[4]

Bearing this definition in mind (and in particular the fact that the theologi-cal activity is considered in its proper sense as an ecclesial "office and mission"), the author observed that in the first centuries of the Christian era it is not difficult to perceive a unity between knowledge and life such that the figures of the "doctor", the "pastor", and the "saint" are normally combined in the same person so that one witnesses the emergence of "total personalities".

It is evident that not all doctors were pastors and vice versa, and that not all doctors and pastors were saints and vice versa. Nevertheless, the most signifi-cant personalities almost naturally assume these offices and missions.

In particular, for the entire first millenium, the great dogmatic theologians are also some of the great saints: they are "total theologians". This fact exhibits several qualities essential to theological work: (1) The defense of a "full conception of truth" (or "canon of revealed truth") offered by the Gospel, according to which "the archetype of truth is the person of Christ himself who designates himself as the truth", so that "to walk in the truth" is "the modality in which believers are in the possession of the truth".[5] (2) The certainty of doctrine, in that the "theological totality" gave to the teaching of those great saints/dogmatic theologians "a profound tranquility and certainty" —today we say *ecclesial credibility.* (3) The unitary character of the disciplines, such that in their theological output it is almost impossible to find that dualism between dogmatics and spirituality which will later become characteris-tic of the entire following period of high scholasticism.

The problem begins when theology first finds itself with "an abundance of philosophical truth" and then with the development of the secular sciences of nature and of spirit.

In the first great theologians of mature scholasticism (Albert, Bonaventure, Thomas), the "concern for the whole" remains fundamental at least "as presup-position and atmosphere" (but also as a directive force in the progression of thought), and theology still succeeds in sacramentally transfiguring science, which is becoming autonomous, and in irradiating it from within. But then one witnesses the ever cleaner division between dogmatic theologians and spiritual theologians, between dogmatics and spirituality: (1) The overload of earthly philosophy is foreign to the spiritual theologians, for whom theologi-cal study will become more and more "a prolonged exercise of penance"; they then set out on the secondary road of the "science of the Christian life". (2) Dogmatic theologians, on the other hand, dedicate themselves more and more to describing and grounding theology as a rational science in the face of the

---

[4] *Verbum Caro,* Italian edition, 200.

[5] Ibid., 200–201.

other sciences that are in the process of development; they then develop an ever more subtle and satisfied ability in mastering the data of revelation and those of the human sciences together. "The divorce between dogmatic theology and spiritual theology thus threatens both the first and the second with sterility", especially in more recent centuries.[6]

With much bitterness von Balthasar observes: "That Bremond could simply set about writing an *Histoire littéraire du sentiment religieux* without even having to mention the contemporary situation of theology as a dogmatic science at all is a fact that of itself falls into line with the alarming problems of the history of the Church." The damage done is evident to all.[7]

Abandoned to themselves, spiritual theologians in some way feel constrained to describe their experience of God purely subjectively (although it was perhaps objective): "they no longer dared to be dogmatic theologians", and they feel spiritual precisely in the sense that they do not want to have any dogmatic pretenses or to make an attempt at dogmatic science (in the case of conflict they are humbly ready to submit their judgment and the data of their experience in the trusting expectation that God makes "the truth" and the orthodoxy of his devoted ones "triumph").

Their reflection on the objectivity of revelation is timid, and, even if they attain the dignity of "doctors of the Church", they are never such from a dogmatic point of view. In some cases, even the Bible frightened them.

Even more serious is the fact that the dogmatic theologians in turn render their task ever more objective and scientific, from which they too easily tend to exclude (or bracket): (1) the duty of giving an existential covering to their teaching (in this way the specific character of Christian truth and often the living organic character of all revelation are infected); (2) one's own organic insertion in the ecclesial body, with a growing difficulty in perceiving and conceiving the reciprocity of offices and charisms (cf., for example, the recent conflicts between theology and the Magisterium or, in general, the relation between theology and Church); (3) their "office" of dogmatically questioning the experience of the spiritual theologians, not only to integrate it, but also to allow it continually to fructify and renew the dogmatic process itself. In conclusion, if the spiritual theologians no longer dare to be dogmatic, the dogmatic theologians no longer dare to be spiritual.

The dogmatic theologians, however, have also cultivated, so to speak, a secret vice: not only do they no longer have pretensions of holiness but, in the course of the centuries, they have passed from a certain regret to an ever more dangerous pseudo-theological justification of not infecting the neutral purity of the science with too much devotion and subjectivization.

[6] Divo Barsotti in the preface to the Italian edition of *Verbum Caro*, 12.
[7] Ibid., 207.

In the essay to which we have been referring, Fr. von Balthasar offered an outline of how to move decisively towards a "new unity", first of all by describing
the existential placing of the saint from the point of view of those problems that
theology is continually called to confront theoretically, then showing how the
experiences of the saints should be accepted and utilized in a reconstruction of
fundamental theological treatises, and finally establishing the most comprehensive point of view: the question of the "doctrine of faith" understood as a
personal dialogue between bride and groom, between the Church and Christ.

But before taking up and systematizing or amplifying these indications
which seem to us prophetic and in need of repeating even today, forty years
after their formulation, it is perhaps necessary to mention a further question
and a further possibility.

Fr. von Balthasar would allow me to say that one perceives in his essay of
that time a sort of reserve that could be overcome only later, something that
needed to be said, but on which it was advisable not to insist yet, having
recourse rather to illustrations. I should like to be very frank in my formulation:
a theologian who demands a necessary bond between holiness and theology
(and this in the very person of the theologian himself) is placed in a strange
position—*he exposes himself.* And he, together with his own theology becomes,
so to speak, subject to judgment and even to blackmail: "Where then is your
holiness? What is your 'spirituality'?"

Besides being indiscreet, this simple question is, however, unjustified: what
a saint least knows how to do is to speak of his own holiness.

He should then have recourse to objective descriptions: to speaking of the
holiness of the Church, to demanding for this "ecclesial holiness" the right to
be a theological subject, to offering its already existent saint-theologians as
examples, and so forth.

But nevertheless, where theology is "theological activity" in the strict sense,
this objective "holiness" should show itself subjectively. And thus the problem
returns. In other words, in periods in which the bond between holiness and
theology is habitually broken, whoever wishes to speak of it should have
begun to experience it and—in order to speak of it—has to expose himself.

For this reason, he is tempted to renounce the entire project unless something happens to him to unify, so to speak, the subjective and the objective
aspects so as to permit him to speak freely of both the objective and subjective
holiness of the theologian with respect to himself.

This "something" is well known in the history of the Church and is an
event that can be described in this way: between the subjective holiness that
the theologian should have *in actu* and the objective holiness (of the Church of
which the theologian is a living member) there is inserted the contagion, both
objective and subjective at once, between different ecclesial subjects whose
experience and mission is unified by the Spirit.

When recently discussing the relations between "Theology and Church", Joseph Cardinal Ratzinger made this observation:

> Talk of the connection between theology and holiness is not sentimental or pietistic, but has its foundation in the logic of things and has on its side the testimony of all history. Athanasius is not thinkable without the new experience of Christ had by Abbot Anthony; nor Augustine without the passion of his road toward Christian radicality; nor Bonaventure and the Franciscan theology of the thirteenth century without the enormous new reactualization of Christ in the figure of Francis of Assisi; nor Thomas Aquinas without the passion of Dominic for the Gospel and evangelization; and one could continue thus throughout the whole history of theology.[8]

We can thus understand whence arises the new discussion of the relations between holiness and theology, dogmatics and spirituality, that Fr. von Balthsasar initiated in 1948. His encounter with Adrienne von Speyr dates from 1940, and even from that time his writings open up to the grace and mission arising from such an encounter.

In the preface to the volume *A First Glance at Adrienne von Speyr,* Fr. von Balthasar explicitly declares:

> I, . . . was without hesitation already making use of the insights she shared with me in the first books I wrote after her conversion. . . . On the whole I received far more from her, theologically, than she from me, though, of course, the exact proportion can never be calculated. . . . I also strove to bring my way of looking at Christian revelation into conformity with hers. If it had been otherwise, many an article in *Explorations in Theology* and, especially, the basic perspective of *Herrlichkeit* would never have existed. . . . Today, after her death, her work appears far more important to me than mine, and the publication of her still-unpublished writings takes precedence over all personal work of my own.[9]

In a report on his own theological output drafted in 1965, von Balthasar had already realized: "Adrienne von Speyr . . . laid the foundations for most of what I have published beginning from 1940. Her works and mine are not divisible psychologically or philologically. They are two halves of a whole that has a single foundation at its center."[10]

Ten years later he realized again that only with time would it be possible to verify "how strongly the intuition of this woman has influenced my books".[11]

---

[8] Joseph Cardinal Ratzinger, "Theology and Church", *Communio,* Italian edition, 87 (1986): 101.

[9] *A First Glance at Adrienne von Speyr* (San Francisco: Ignatius Press, 1981), p. 13.

[10] *Rechenschaft 1965* (Einsiedeln: Johannes Verlag, 1965), 35.

[11] *Noch ein Jahrzehnt* (Man.).

It would be an injustice to history as well as to the extraordinary intelligence of Fr. von Balthasar to think of this relation solely from the point of view of "spirituality" or to believe that "dogmatics" has issued from it in an impoverished state and become arbitrary.

The depths von Balthasar has received from the spiritual experience and the objectively mystical teachings of von Speyr have found a place and a rigorous systematization in his dogmatics. By way of example, it suffices to think of the celebrated *Mysterium Paschale* (of 1968): 250 pages inserted into the dogmatic course *Mysterium Salutis* (a text also published separately and known as *Theologie der drei Tage*). This so singular and unfathomable "communion of missions" has been all the more in his case the highest expression of a "theological style".

Thus, it is not only out of humility but from living theological conviction that Fr. von Balthasar wrote in his report of 1975:

> The works of von Speyr, almost all of them dictated, come to about a third of the books written in my own hand; a weaker third is constituted by books published in my name; a more voluminous third by books translated by me for my publishing house.
>
> If I now ask my heart, there are among these many latter some that are dearer and more important to me than my own books. They are works of my friends like Henri de Lubac and Louis Bouyer, of great poets like Claudel, Péguy, Bernanos, not to mention Maurice Blondel or Ignatius, Calderón and John of the Cross. . . . [12]

Von Balthasar thus confesses that he loves those books of his above all in which the *"communio sanctorum"* is most evident (the two volumes of "Styles"—of twelve great theologians—in *Herrlichkeit;* the volume on Origen; the translations of the poetry of Claudel).

We do not fear saying that von Balthasar is perhaps the only existing theologian who considers his "translations" (always "situated" and commented on by him) as an integral and not a secondary part of his own theological work. We can even say more: von Balthasar considers his whole enormous output secondary with respect to the living work of weaving ecclesial ties and forming people in holiness. He has written this confession:

> My activity as a writer remains and will always remain in the economy of my life a secondary product and *"faute de mieux".* At the center there is a completely different interest: the work for the renewal of the Church with the formation of new communities that unite radical Christian life according to the evangelical counsels of Jesus with existence in the midst of the world . . . in order to give new life to living communities.
>
> My entire activity as a writer is submitted to this work; if the writer

[12] Ibid.

should fail because of the urgency of the work of which I have spoken, to
me it would seem that I have lost nothing but gained much.

At bottom, this is self-evident for one who stands in the service of the
Cause of Jesus which, concretely, is the Church.[13]

"If the writer should fail because of the urgency of the work (of forming
new communities), to me it would seem that I have lost nothing"—this
expression, which merits emphasis because it is an uncensurable judgment
made by a man on himself and on his own task in the Church, is all the more
impressive if one reflects on several facts. Von Balthasar wrote it in 1975 (and
today we must still add the enormous output of these last thirteen years),
when it was a question of a theological output of which, already in 1975, de
Lubac wrote: "Here we are concerned with a work that has immense and
profound proportions such that the Church knows no other like it in our
times." And he added that even all the themes of Vatican II had been anticipated by him in the most precise way. He then concluded by comparing such
a work to "a vibration that proceeds from a single center and is diffused in all
directions of space".

"Von Balthasar", de Lubac said already twenty-three years ago, "calls all
writers and poets, philosophers and mystics, ancients and moderns, and Christians of all denominations to produce their notes since, for him, all voices are
necessary to compose the catholic symphony for the greater glory of God."[14]

It is in this very broad way, in this living and broad *communio sanctorum*,
that von Balthasar has been able to situate his work as a theological writer. We
mean all of this when we speak of the relations between "holiness and
theology". The examples given may suffice.

The problem of the relations between holiness and theology, between
dogmatics and "spirituality" (in the broadest sense of the word), cannot be
only a problem of the work and personal life of Fr. von Balthasar, even if it
cannot be forgotten to what extent he himself has lived it and shown how well
this road can be traveled.

We now arrive at the most difficult task: briefly systematizing the most
important data for a reconstruction of their unity.

First of all, however, it is perhaps necessary to render explicit a problem
that is only hinted at implicitly in the texts to which we have referred: on
closer inspection, the separation between dogmatics and spirituality has its
basis in a separation artificially induced by interpreters within revelation itself.

[13] Ibid. Published in Italian edition: *Il filo Arianna attraverso la mia opera* (Milan: Jaca
Book, 1980), in the chapter "Ancora un decennio", which dates from 1975, 47ff.
[14] Henri de Lubac, "Un témoin du Christ dans l'Église: Hans Urs von Balthasar", in
Paradoxe et mystère de L'Église (Paris, 1967). For an English translation, see below, Appendix,
271–88.

This is a question that permits noteworthy reflections. Here we shall strip it to the bones using a single issue as an example: think of ecclesiology, on the one hand, and of the Gospels, on the other (the extreme field limitation is deliberate here).

It escapes no one that in ecclesiology only certain general statements of principle are usually drawn from the Gospels: the preaching of the kingdom, the establishment of a New Covenant with a new people, the universality of the offer of salvation, the conditions of succession, the "gifts" deposited in the ecclesiastical institution, and little more.

The entire rest of the Gospel, in particular the encounters of Jesus with other men, *the whole "episodic mass", is in fact abandoned to "spirituality"* (although it is precisely an account and primary expression of *communio:* think of Mary, the different disciples, Nicodemus, the Magdalen, the Samaritan woman, Zacchaeus, the rich young man, and the like).

In fact, it is spirituality that reflects and writes constantly and abundantly on these "encounters" (and also, we may add, on the miracles, the parables, the events of the Passion, the Easter appearances, and so forth), whereas dogmatics does not know what to do with them or, if it confronts them, treats only their problematic aspects. Hardly anything is recovered in Christology in the attempt to extract from them a few indications of the identity and mission of Jesus.

How serious such a separation is, even in the way revelation is received and reflected on dogmatically, will stand out if a serious consequence is observed, one which we can only indicate here.

There is often in theology a question of a legitimate pluralism or of a plurality of theologies that are already present in Scripture. What is forgotten, however, is that this real plurality is not a plurality of theological theories but a plurality of "theological encounters" of which the texts (and the eventual theories) are a testimony.

> In every encounter and in every qualitatively distinct mission, Jesus crea-
> tively establishes a particular reality with unmistakable contours: Peter
> and John, Paul and James, Martha and Mary of Bethany, the Magdalen,
> Lazarus, the Samaritan woman. These constitute irrepeatable unities that are
> clearly impossible to add together, realities of singular encounters in
> which, nonetheless, the invisible Jesus is wholly manifested from time to
> time.[15]

But how does it stand with the alleged theological pluralism if the multi-plicity of encounters and approaches is exactly what is neglected, while there passes into the foreground a multiplicity of presentations abstracted from the

---

[15] "Spiritualità", in the Italian edition of *Verbum Caro,* 236.

one and only Christ, and thus a multiplicity of theories, and thus again a multiple possession of eventual theologies on the Christ-idea?

Let us now try to synthesize in a schematic way what the strong points are that derive from a rediscovered unity of theology and holiness, and thus between dogmatics and spirituality (whether in an objective or subjective sense).

1. First of all, the unity between theology and holiness is rediscovered at the source by recovering, so to speak, the identity of Jesus as the sole "theologian". He is the sole "interpreter" of the Father, and for him alone it has been possible "to express the original discourse of God about God (*theology*) in humanly comprehensible language. But the Son has been able to do this only by emptying himself in listening obedience to the Father, to the point of exhausting his own personal word in the silence of death. In order to be able to fulfill this task, he has been sanctified by the Spirit in the truth and has prayed for and obtained the prolongation of this "sanctification" in his disciples and witnesses.

There is an even deeper need never to forget that theology requires holiness because it "leads into" the intimate life of God where the true and original "theology" takes place of itself, consisting entirely of trinitarian relations.

Through Christ this original holy "theology" is opened to the world and pronounced in the world: whoever wishes to participate in it—beginning with the "man Jesus" himself—must let himself be attracted by and worthily involved in these holy trinitarian relations. This is all the more the case as one seeks to "specialize" (which is precisely the task of the theologian) in explaining these relations to the Church that is already living from them.

2. In the Church, therefore, the only witness that can be given is to the Sole Witness, letting oneself be "sanctified" adequately by his Spirit to the point of offering one's own life. Since it is a question of receiving the revelation that God is love, knowledge can only be loving knowledge, and loving knowledge can only be attained in practiced love which thus becomes an *instrument of knowledge.*

3. Even that particular witness which is expressed in virtue of a "charism of teaching" (and properly gives rise to "theological output") will be adequate only if the one who "speaks of God" assumes the interior form demanded by the word.

"There is no place in the face of revelation for any scientific 'objectivity' that is objective and thus uninvolved: there is a place only for the personal reciprocity of Word and faith, of Christ and the Church." Therefore if one truly "understands", one is holy, and—reciprocally—if one is holy, one "understands".

4. Prayer is thus "the only realistic attitude before the revealed mystery". "Even the attitude of knowledge can never transcend this attitude of prayer. Knowledge can never distance itself from the initial prayerful attitude in order then to apply itself to cognitive activity."

It should be noted well, however, that "prayed theology does not mean affective theology as opposed to a rigorously scientific one. One should think with accurate precision and correctness, i.e., in such a way as to render all that is due to that one, single reality, incomparable in content and method, which is the personal revelation of the Son of God."

5. In order to escape every dualism and not to confuse this "prayed theology" with external attitudes required of the theologian as an outer covering of his scientific activity (even if it is a necessary covering), one must grasp its urgency within the content of revelation itself. At its highest point revelation is the Word of God made man, but a perfect (free) response is necessary for this becoming man: "the faith of Israel reaches fulfillment (and is transcended) in Mary who in this way becomes the prototype of the believing Church and 'seat of wisdom'."

Von Balthasar maintains:

> This is the proper origin of the theology of the Church. This wisdom of the Marian Church consists in making place in oneself from the beginning for the word of God with the *fiat,* in meditating on it in the heart, in letting it grow, in bringing it to the world in the form of man, and in entrusting it to humanity. *In this, Mary is also the prototype of the whole theology of the Church, and for this she is honored by the Fathers with the title "Theologos".* From this is derived the primary connotation of every theology of the Church: it can move only in the circuit of word and responding wisdom, of revelation and ecclesial obedience, a wide circle given the fact that it embraces every truth, because in the Logos of God is founded the *logos* of every purely human knowledge, of every wordly science.... From this it follows further that every ecclesial theology as a response to the infinitely free and gratuitous Word of God must be adoration, thanksgiving, in brief, doxology. Given that it moves in the circuit of divine invitation and of human response, it cannot be separated even for a second from the character of the word as personal appeal; it cannot even for a second transform and reduce the infinite speaking subject to a neutral object, not even under the pretext of separating the content of everything said from him who speaks, who is God....
>
> *To cultivate this theology by following Mary* cannot be the privilege of the "saints" (whose theology is then rejected as a spirituality not to be taken seriously) but *must be the fundamental act of every theologian whether layman or "professional".* [16]

This "Marian prototype" will have to continue to subsist through the whole evolution of the theological work, which will maintain its unity in this way, whether at the level of meditative theology, at the level of didactic theology

---

[16] "Dalla teologia di Dio alla teologia della Chiesa", *Communio,* Italian edition, 58 (1981): 15–16.

(or catechetical theology, in which the meditative moment is united to the pedagogical), or at the level of "combative" theology (since the Word always provokes resistance).

6. Before sketching the methodological consequences of this approach in the successive points (7–10), it seems we must further radicalize the whole discussion by adding this final observation: *the essential element of the whole previous reflection is given, in our opinion, by the realization that the Christ-Mary relation (speaking-listening), and thus the Christ-disciple, Christ-community, and Christ-hagiographer relation, is not only the extrinsic condition of revelation but also the "content" of revelation, a content into which each one should enter who wishes to treat of revelation as such.* (To this effect, it will never be sufficiently emphasized that for the second Person of the Trinity—although incarnate—the "relation" is "constitutive" of the person. And that should be applied analogically even to the relations that he actualizes "in this world").

7. This "praying theology", which is founded on a total involvement in that which is revealed, has enormous *methodological* relevance: it in fact permits the dogmatic theologian to maintain a firm balance.

It permits him correctly to confront the most serious and fundamental theological question that determines numerous other questions. It is a question of understanding that:

> Dogmatics is not a "connecting link" between revelation and something else, e.g., human nature and reason or philosophy. . . . In order to investigate the nature-supernature relation man has no need to exit from the ambit of faith, to become a mediator between God and the world or revelation and reason, to set himself up as judge of the relation between world, nature, and the supernatural.
>
> It is enough for him to understand the "sole mediator between God and man: the man Jesus Christ" and to believe in him "in whom everything in heaven and on earth was created", "everything through him and for him". . . . The Christian does not need to exit from the center that is Christ in order to communicate him to the world, to understand his own relation with the world, or to construct bridges between revelation and nature, philosophy and theology. . . . That is what the saints know. They do not leave their center in Christ for an instant. . . . If they philosophize, they do so as Christians, i.e., as believers, as theologians.[17]

It is especially urgent that this conviction be rediscovered today by theologians.

8. Therefore, the theologian's proper placing with respect to "holiness" is what provides him existentially with a set of conceptual instruments. And he discovers, whether objectively or subjectively, that the category that pervades all revelation and thus all theology, as Scheeben has rightly seen, is that of the

[17] *Verbum Caro,* Italian edition, 215.

"indissoluble marriage", beginning with the foundational one between the
human and divine natures in Christ, as the revelation of the trinitarian love
that is poured out on the world.

9. In particular, theology is learning to depend on its center (a Christological and thus trinitarian center) in order to explain all existence and history. In
doing so, it understands that it must take up and make use of the experience of
the saints, as well as let itself be guided thereby, insofar as they appear *logically*
as the living and permanent interpretation of the Word made flesh.

10. In this way, the great tripartition of the Creed will be recovered in
order: (a) to explain the doctrine of creation in relation to the Father (beginning
thus from his relation to the Son made man), and then making use of the
saints' experience of God's paternity of the world in life, prayer, and message;
(b) to explain Christological doctrine, especially in its "passiological" core,
making use of the numerous ecclesial graces of believers' participation in the
Passion of Christ; and (c) to explain the pneumatological doctrine as a
"proclamation of Christ in the heart of the Church and of the believer" in
such a way as to take up in it the whole of ethics, ecclesial piety, liturgy,
sacramental theology, and even apologetics, taking care finally to introduce
into this doctrinal complex *the archetypical figure of the saint and not that of the
sinner* as often continues to be done.

In conclusion, then: theology takes place beginning with the living insertion of the theologian within the Church ("conversion", "new beginning of
thought"); and this living insertion is both an assumption of objective
("communal") holiness and a gift/task of subjective holiness. It is from this sole
point of view that theology can firmly maintain its identity and wholeness.

> If such a witness of Christ has received the charism of "teaching" . . . then his
> discourse about God (*theo-logia*) will necessarily and analytically be informed
> by a life dedicated to complete self-giving in order to stand credibly before
> the world. . . . And perhaps the degree to which he commits his life to
> bearing witness will be more fruitful than the limitations of his formulations
> and deficiencies which one is willing to forgive him because of the integrity
> of his bearing witness.
> . . . When a science calling itself theology ceases to stand in the following
> of the apostolic witness and, thereby, in the mission of Jesus and in the
> sanctity that supports it, then that science has ceased to be of importance for
> the believing Church.
> . . . Only "theology" as the unity of sanctity and witness born in the life
> of the Church earns its name.[18]

---

[18] "Theology and holiness", 346–47, 348.

GEORGES CHANTRAINE, S.J.

Exegesis and Contemplation in the Work of Hans Urs von Balthasar

Last year I asked a German priest of the Community of St. John, founded by Adrienne von Speyr with Fr. von Balthasar, what relevance his belonging to the Community had to his ministry. He replied to me: "Thanks to the works of Fr. von Balthasar and Adrienne we have learned how to contemplate God in the Scripture and consequently how to exercise our ministry in God." The simplicity and vigor of this response impressed me, and remained in my memory. I have subsequently been able to observe its accuracy with regard to other priests. Let us try to be as explicit as possible about it, knowing in advance that part of the essence of the thing will escape us, for here we touch on the very mystery of God's communicating himself to man. First we shall inquire why this priest had not learned to contemplate God in the Sacred Scriptures; next in what way the work of Fr. von Balthasar assisted him in this matter. We shall then examine what bond connects exegesis and contemplation in the theology of von Balthasar, and why exegesis and contemplation can be thus durably renewed after a crisis introduced in the sixteenth century.

Exegesis and Contemplation from the Sixteenth Century to our Day

Why, then, had this priest not learned contemplation during his years of formation? He provided me with the beginnings of an answer. "In school, we learned scientific exegesis. How is that to foster personal prayer and the life of our faithful?" This sort of experience is common in the Church. Most future priests receive, in seminaries and faculties of theology, a biblical instruction that no longer prepares them for preaching and gives them no help in prayer. The exegetical method is estranged from the spirit in which the Church reads and understands Sacred Scripture in her liturgy. At the time of the last Synod (1987), we were able to ascertain one result of such exegetical formation. A priest criticized the proposals to be submitted to the Pope because only two of them contained any scriptural citations. Someone else acknowledged the fact,

Translated by John Lyon.
Communio 16 (Fall 1989). ©1989 by *Communio: International Catholic Review.*

adding: "These proposals exactly reflect the work of the Synod. Scripture had no role therein." Such a deficiency is most serious. Surely the Fathers drew inspiration from Sacred Scripture more than once. Let us even assume that the literary style of the Synod does not facilitate citations from Scripture. But that Sacred Scripture should not be cited in the course of a month points out that it does not inspire the pastorate. Such indeed is the dichotomy to which the young priest of the Community of St. John drew my attention.

The causes of this dichotomy are known. They date at the latest from the sixteenth century. Although in practice exegesis and contemplation had not yet been separated for most people, still the division already prevailed in the conditions of work and in the methods used. This was so for intellectual reasons, but also because of a spiritual drift. We all know that the old exegesis tied together the story that is told and the spiritual reality that animates it, contains it, comes to light, and yields itself there. From another point of view, it tied together the literal and the spiritual senses. The spiritual reality presents itself under three aspects in the spiritual sense: the mystery of Christ and of the Church, its appropriation by the faithful, and its ultimate and heavenly manifestation in God. Within the spiritual sense then, there are three meanings: the allegorical, the tropological, and the anagogical. Now, with the development of theology since the thirteenth century, the allegorical sense had had a tendency to become autonomous, detaching itself from both the literal and the anagogical sense. For St. Thomas, however, theology was still called *sacra pagina.* But when, in the sixteenth century, the theological opponents of Erasmus wished to discredit him, they labelled him a *grammaticus,* or philologist. The "theologian" of that time found in Scripture certain timeless ideas which he developed systematically according to the teaching of the Church. The impetus of faith, which actuated his intelligence from within the search for God, tended from that time on to specialize in a mystical theology, or in a mysticism. Perhaps Meister Eckhart attempted to graft mysticism onto the intellectualism of St. Thomas. He did not, however, correct that intellectualism, but rather hastened the separation between theology and mysticism. By the sixteenth century, this separation had been accomplished. Keeping a close eye on the *Alumbrados,* the inquisitors of Salamanca would impose on Ignatius of Loyola, who appeared to them to be one of their own, the study of theology. Fifty years later, Teresa of Avila would be limited to commenting on the "Our Father", because a poor woman without a doctorate did not have access to the text of Scripture. Assuredly, religious persons of the epoch continued to draw from Scripture the substance of their prayer and their knowledge of God. Because of the conditions of their work and the spiritual drift of the times, however, they were put in the position of developing a subjective mysticism—a mysticism, one wants to say, in which the experiences and states of the subject were interpreted as graces from God, rather than as a lived exegesis of the mysteries of the Lord.

Luther perceived this spiritual situation. Though the task was virtually hopeless, he wanted to restore to theology its spiritual objectivity by rooting it in Scripture. He based it on the word of God perceived as objective spirit, but this amounted to tearing it out of the ecclesial subject considered as subjective spirit, and thus as necessarily sinful. For him, contemplation became purely dogmatic; mysticism was excluded as proceeding from the subjective spirit. By this same move, contemplation lost its Marian interiority and its internal mystical unfolding in allegory, tropology, and anagogy. Finally, who receives the word? The believer who by faith identifies himself with the objective spirit? But what, concretely, is that if it is not the Church? Kant and Hegel will propose two different answers. For Kant, it is the transcendental subject; for Hegel, Absolute Spirit. With the first, the transcendental subject determines the conditions for the possibility of both theoretical and practical knowledge in such a way that contemplation is impossible. The subject does not stop expressing itself and creating itself according to its conditions of possibility. The meaning it determines is its own. But is it the meaning of reality? According to Hegel, the Absolute Spirit expresses its own conclusion and knows itself in its movement, in its internal logic. Contemplation is restored, but it is not the contemplation of Scripture. Meaning is extracted from fact by reason; it is not the meaning of the fact itself. As with Luther before, dialectic brings about meaning. Its speculative Good Friday is the supreme moment.

In these different ways the idea is forged of an objectivity of the literal sense, which quite simply becomes the meaning of Scripture. That is objective which is not theological or spiritual. And what is objective is what is true; thus everyone thinks according to a common universal mentality. What is scientifically determined is objective; and that is scientific which explains phenomena without expressing an opinion about reality. This Kantian perspective does not impose itself in all cases; the universal mentality seems exempt. As a consequence, the theological and spiritual is a matter of choice, which no one can contest without shackling liberty. Here is the root of pluralism. In a word, that meaning is objective which is determined by faith purified from facticity. Thus to pull together the Lutheran inheritance, it was necessary that the meaning of the last things, the eschatological realities, should be conceived by the exegete as being imposed upon Jesus. Jesus, according to the eschatological school, thought of his life within the framework of contemporary Jewish eschatology. That which in the ancient exegesis was the object of anagogy is now thought of according to the standard of historical objectivity, that is, it is historically conditioned. It is neither a gift, nor the presence of the Father's will, nor the mission given through the Spirit. In Catholicism, at least in France, the meaning determined by faith (Bultmann) has been understood as subjective rather than objective. Pluralism found a theological foundation here. Consequently it has gathered strength, and the exegete is taken to be the theologian, if not the true theologian.

Such exegesis ignores contemplation. In none of its three meanings is its objectivity that of contemplation. It is, in various modalities, that of the subject, confronted with the biblical text without reference to the Catholic Church except as subjective, since methodologically the act of reading is done beyond the Church's purview. It is the objectivity of a subject who is able freely to determine who he is. He can even decide to be Catholic. But this decision does not originate in the act of reading; it is not determined by the history told by the Bible in such a way that the light thus received for the decision would also be that in which the biblical text should be interpreted. In such a spiritual context the progress of Heinrich Schlier, initially Bultmannian, is highly significant. Schlier allowed his mind to be made up by the meaning of the Faith to the point where he discovered in it the truth of the Catholic Church. It is this which gives his exegesis its contemplative tone. Exegesis and contemplation are no longer separate for Schlier. Without foregoing scientific precision, the exegete has, as it were, rediscovered traditional exegesis but at a new price. To such an exegesis the remark of the young priest which I cited at the beginning of my account does not apply.

The Ecclesiastical Milieu

This brief review of the connection between exegesis and contemplation has as its only purpose to remind us of some essential references, to heighten our awareness of rational and spiritual conditions which impinge on Catholic thought, and to introduce us to the work of von Balthasar.

Two remarks before proceeding, in order to avoid two misunderstandings—one concerning what has been said and the other about what will be said. First of all, I have had no intention of considering the evolution of theology since the sixteenth century as catastrophic. The specialization of the disciplines responds to a requirement of discursive reason. Each epoch creates its problems and tries to resolve them. The permanent task of the theologian is to maintain the presence of contemplation within discursive advances and changing problematics. This was assured by those theologians or philosophers who, since the sixteenth century, perceived the conditioning of thought and tried not to let themselves be determined by it. Near to our own time, we recall Johann Möhler, Scheeben, Newman, Blondel, and Bruaire, to speak only of those who are deceased.

Secondly, the work of von Balthasar does not present itself as the Blessed Isles which one comes upon abruptly in the middle of a stormy sea. It is positioned in the midst of an exceptional theological and spiritual flowering.

In order to refresh our memory, let us run through the list of contemporaries and near-contemporaries to whom von Balthasar dedicated his works: Karl Barth, Henri de Lubac, Reinhold Schneider, Martin Buber, Paul Claudel, Charles Péguy, Georges Bernanos, Thérèse of Lisieux, Elizabeth of the Trinity, Marie of the Trinity, Adrienne von Speyr, Romano Guardini. Yet, in the totality of his life's work, his books take third place, after the Community of St. John, founded by Adrienne von Speyr, and after the

> ... translation of what, in the great theological tradition, appeared to me important for contemporary Christians to know and assimilate. I began with the Apostolic Fathers, Ireneaus, Origen, Gregory of Nyssa, Maximus, Augustine; then, moving through the Middle Ages with Anselm, Bonaventure, St. Thomas, and the great English and Flemish mystics, came by way of Dante, Catherine of Siena, John of the Cross, Bérulle, Pascal, to our own time and Thérèse of Lisieux, Madeleine Delbrêl, Claudel, Péguy, Bernanos, Henri de Lubac (10 volumes), and Adrienne von Speyr (60 volumes).[1]

Twice we have mentioned Adrienne von Speyr. Her work is crucial for the contemplation of God in Sacred Scripture. This Basel physician, originally Protestant, became a Catholic under the tutelage of Fr. von Balthasar, whom she had as a confessor for the rest of her life. She dictated to him an immense quantity of work, particularly some important scriptural commentaries, of which the main ones are devoted to John: his Gospel (in four volumes), his epistles, and the Apocalypse. She enjoyed the gift of prophecy which, in Paul's meaning, is the gift of interpreting Scripture, seeing in it the mystery which it unfurls. As was the case with certain prophets of the Old Testament, this gift affected her whole being, body and soul. In this fashion she has understood the mysteries of the Lord, particularly the Paschal Mystery, and that of Mary. With her, the spiritual experience is not subjective, but objective, for she hands over in a symbolically incarnate fashion the mystery of the Lord in order to increase the believing understanding of mystery in the Church. This same gift, amplified by the knowledge of the heart, *cardiognosis,* allowed her to know the situation of men, living and dead, in God's eyes.

In what way do these exceptional gifts concern us and clarify our subject? In two ways, at least: first, with Adrienne, that which is extraordinary disappears in order to be put at the service of all. Thus, who could predict the experiences which inspire the servant of the Lord? Next, this gift of prophecy is given through Adrienne to the whole Church. It is, as it were, the divine response, prevenient and superabundant, to a deep need whose nature and historical fullness we have analyzed. With a bit of humor, one might even conclude (in seeing that God made his gift to the Church through her) that the spiritual and intellectual crisis is deeper than we thought.

[1] See *Hans Urs von Balthasar: Bibliographie, 1925–1990* (Einsiedeln: Johannes Verlag, 1990).

Adrienne von Speyr found in her confessor, Fr. von Balthasar, a theologian who was predisposed to contemplate the mystery of God in Scripture. Ignatius of Loyola had formed him in this way through the Spiritual Exercises. Augustine, and then Origen—to say nothing of the other Greek and Latin Fathers—increased his familiarity with this practice. The friendship of Fr. de Lubac encouraged him in this at the time of his theological formation at Lyon (Fourvière). For him, as for them, the unity between theology and sanctity is inviolable. "Their division is the worst disaster that has happened in the history of the Church", he affirmed in 1984 before Pope John Paul II at the time of the reception of the Paul VI Award. He had affirmed this as early as 1948, in an article in *Dieu Vivant,* and in *Wort und Wahrheit.* This unity of theology and sanctity he had received from the great Catholic tradition and from his penitent. It is not an abstract unity; it is the "heart of the world", which he will celebrate in the theological poem bearing this title. It is therefore Christ, incarnate Son of God, seated at the Father's right hand, acting in the world thanks to the Spirit, who animates the Church. This unity is also the mission in Christ of whoever devotes himself to the glory of God and to his service.

Finally, by way of ending this second comment, such a unity of exegesis and contemplation does not allow of any return to the past, any nostalgia for the former state of the disciplines. Fr. von Balthasar deals with modern exegesis with the same seriousness he does the theology of St. Thomas. He knows the principal interpretations, he discerns the methodological difficulties which we have brought up, and without haste, with artisan-like and artistic skill, he places each fragment in the mosaic he forms. As a valuable example of all this, let us mention the unforgettable meditation on the Old Testament done for the glory of God in volume four of *Herrlichkeit.* In this case, to which many others could be added, we also can recognize the liberty *in* which he reads Scripture: this ancient history is that which Israel has lived for all mankind; to the degree that the figures of Christ are outlined, just so far the place that Christ alone will be able to fill is determined. In such a history as this, one which never comes to completion, von Balthasar recognizes "the humility of the Spirit" (Henri de Lubac), of which scientific exegesis only notices the objective shell. Just as his exegesis takes possession of the advance posts of research, it also is able justly and heartily to value the charisms and actual movements which, for a scientific exegesis, are enigmas or even aberrant realities in relation to the word of God—a word which evidently is not filled with the Spirit, but constricted within the word of the exegete.

"To Know as I Am Known"

Exegesis and contemplation: neither of these terms is weakened in the thought of our author. Exegesis should not serve a preconceived spirituality, nor contemplation consist in pious variations on scriptural themes. It is a question of understanding with all available exegetical methods what the letter of Scripture makes known of the history of God with his people in order to contemplate there the trinitarian love toward all humanity as it springs forth from the intimate life of God himself—in brief, to contemplate "the heart of the world" with all those who have also contemplated it, and first of all with the Mother of God.

These two terms, exegesis and contemplation: How does von Balthasar connect them? Or rather, how does he find them connected in the very revelation of God in which the Church knows them and precisely contemplates them? Between the two questions we note the change of perspective, or rather that conversion which St. Paul expresses in these terms: I know as I am known. There is no contemplation of God in Scripture if the one who searches it does not allow himself to be determined and measured by the knowledge that God has of him (the exegete) in revealing himself. It is consequently necessary—it is inevitable and indispensable—to consider in Scripture the figure of revelation in its center, which is Christ and his "objective evidence".

> The expression the "centre of the form of revelation" does not refer to a particular section of this form however central which, in order to be read as form, would then essentially need to be filled out by other more peripheral aspects. What the phrase is intended to denote is, rather, the reality which lends the form its total coherence and comprehensibility, the "wherefore" to which all particular aspects have to be referred if they are to be understood. The fact that Christ is this centre—and not, for instance, merely the beginning, the initiator of an historical form which then develops autonomously—is rooted in the particular character of the Christian religion and in its difference from all other religions.[2]

In the terms of a theological aesthetic, von Balthasar formulates thus the very principle of Christian exegesis: in its center, the historic Fact of Christ (the Great Fact, as Henri de Lubac says) is not a fragment, even though central, of revelation; it needs no prolongation any more than antecedent causes. It is in itself the plenitude of revelation and it completely illuminates it in such a fashion that each of its prior and subsequent moments only find their

---

[2] *The Glory of the Lord: A Theological Aesthetics,* I: *Seeing the Form,* trans. Erasmo Leiva-Merikakis, ed. Joseph Fessio and John Riches (London: T & T Clark; San Francisco: Ignatius Press, 1982), 463.

position in it, and only find their intelligibility in its light. In the Christ, history is the Spirit, the literal meaning is the spiritual meaning—that by which the Christian religion is distinguished from all others, and first of all from the religion of Israel, at the very moment when it brings that to completion. In fact, to proceed with von Balthasar, "Judaism has no such centre: neither Abraham, nor Moses, nor one of the Prophets, is the figure around which everything else is ordered. Christ, by contrast, is the form because he is the content."[3] By the virtue of what he is in his singular Person and in his unique Fact, he gives form and therefore intelligibility to Abraham, Moses, the Prophets, and likewise to his Church. "This holds absolutely", von Balthasar continues, "for he is the only Son of the Father, and whatever he establishes and institutes has its meaning only through him, is dependent only on him and is kept vital only by him."[4] His Person is divine, and the Great Fact is a trinitarian event—by which his person is distinguished from Abraham, Moses, and the Prophets, and in which the Fact of Christ distinguishes itself from the history which led up to it.

Only objective evidence offers a foundation of indestructible solidity capable of supporting such an edifice. The central figure of revelation ought to be self-evident. Such indeed is the nature of objective evidence: it issues, it radiates, from the phenomenon itself; it does not have as its basis the satisfaction of the needs of the subject. "The form that we encounter historically is convincing in itself because the light by which it illumines us radiates from the form itself and proves itself with compelling force to be just such a light that springs from the object itself."[5]

How does one perceive such evidence?

First case: one does not perceive it, because it "says nothing to me". Still, "the fact that Christ 'says nothing to me' in no way prejudices the fact that, in and of himself, Christ says everything to everyone."[6] Here it would be a matter of a subjectivity closed upon itself and thus not open to that which is objective. In this case not only is contemplation impossible, but even knowledge. This is simple narcissism.

Second case: take the Fact of Christ as one among many objects of knowledge and apply to it a scientific method. One will not know it as it is, for its status is predetermined by the method that one applies to it. There would be a certain scientific knowledge, but not contemplation, that is to say, knowledge of the Fact of Christ as he gives himself to be known. Such a knowledge (the third case) requires that he who desires to know should correspond to him

[3] Ibid.
[4] Ibid.
[5] Ibid., 464.
[6] Ibid.

who makes himself known,[7] that he not hide himself from him who lays himself open, that he not squint but open himself up and stand fast.[8]

Such correspondence does not allow the perceiver to intervene in the makeup of the objective evidence, or to modify it or substitute something for it. "In theology, even the most existential form of Kantianism must distort and thus fail to see the phenomenon."[9] This makes the martyr impossible, for no one dies for Christ if in one fashion or another he has created him in his mind. This is the theme dealt with acutely in *Cordula*.

But could we not invoke the scholastic axiom, *"Quidquid recipitur, secundum modum recipientis recipitur?"* No, for "if Christ is what he claims to be, then he cannot be so dependent on subjective conditions as to be hindered by these from making himself wholly understandable to man nor, contrariwise, can man, without his grace, supply the sufficient conditions of receiving him with full understanding."[10] Even he who claims that Christ says nothing to him receives the wherewithal to understand him, and he who claims to know him scientifically does not offer him conditions sufficient for understanding and accepting him. Thus every privilege of the knowing subject is excluded, as is the idea that the knowledge of Christ is patterned upon discursive knowledge, constructed on the opposition of the object and subject. In spite of all of this, the knowledge of Christ is not *a priori,* like that of first principles; nor is it intuitive, like aesthetic perception where subject and object are united. There is indeed an antecedent comprehension, but von Balthasar proceeds:

> The prior understanding is fundamentally not something which the subject applies as a contribution to Christian knowledge: it is something which arises necessarily from the simple and objective fact that God becomes man and, to this extent, corresponds to the universal human forms of existence and of thought. But, within these universal forms, God can make known that which he specifically is only on his own initiative.[11]

Such an antecedent comprehension and its relation to the comprehension that the Christ gives of himself remains obscure if one does not recall two theses and their epistemological consequences. Created in the image of God, man, a spiritual creature, is through the ceaseless movement of his spirit open to God. He desires to know him such as he is, and yet he can do so only by virtue of the self-revelation of God, which is also his auto-communication. And this revelation fills the opening up of the spirit even beyond its capacity, which it expands.

[7] Ibid.
[8] *Neue Klarstellungen* (Einsiedeln: Johannes Verlag, 1979).
[9] *The Glory of the Lord* I: 465.
[10] Ibid.
[11] Ibid.

This alliance of God and man possesses consequently a dialectic characteristic of the contemplation of God. By virtue of its structural opening on God, man is able, in fact, with St. Anselm, to recognize himself as he who *"rationabiliter comprehendit incomprehensibile esse"* (*Monologion*, 64), and can recognize God as *"id quo maius cogitari nequit"* (*Proslogion* 3), and then, in delight, *"quiddam maius quam quod cogitari possit"* (*Proslogion*, 15). Then von Balthasar points out that if these formulas are valid for the knowledge of God "they are fully valid there where God reveals himself to humanity in a definitive manner". That which was affirmed *a priori* in the movement of the spirit reflecting upon itself as turned towards God, is now verified *a posteriori* through the experience of the revelation of God. Von Balthasar explains:

> Man who in faith seizes for what is the revelatory work of God in Christ ought also to be capable of noticing that there appears here something *"Quo maius cogitari nequit"*, the manifestation of absolute love, leaving obviously behind anything that man could find more sublime than revelation. What miserable figures, for example, are all the initiations into divine mysteries in the gnostic apocalypse, compared to the love of the Son of God, who would die for all sinners, and for me, in that hell of the dark night of abandonment! The obviousness thus perceived of being faced with the ultimate limits of love is not vitiated by the objection that God, in his liberty and power, could have found and set to work something greater. [This is the objection drawn from the opposition between what God can do *de potentia absoluta* and *de potentia ordinata*.] The figure that God proposes, this play between his own liberty and that of his creature, whom he permits to commit sin because he is and ought to be free—and whom he can yet search out in love, without doing violence to him or destroying him by his omnipotence—this figure has in itself the evidence of a highest good. No, it is not possible to conceive of a thing so great. It is nevertheless comprehensible. *Comprehendit.* Not only affectively, in enthusiasm, but in the clear light of a spiritual intelligence. *Rationabiliter comprehendit.* But what is thus represented is recognized as unsurpassable, "incomprehensible", and turns out to be, according to the second formula of the *Proslogion*, *"quiddam maius quam quod cogitari possit"*....
>
> Here the distinctively Christian twist appears, which is distinguished from all abstract speculation about God.... This turning consists in the fact that the philosophical incomprehensibility of the being of God, expressed in the formulas of "negative theology", is transformed into a "theological" incomprehensibility of the love of God—for the Christian knows what the philosopher does not, that God is love. It is radically incomprehensible that absolute love, heaped up in the fullness of the trinitarian view, could, because of the sinner that I am, strip itself of its diverse traits in order to go to death in the deepest darkness. Confronted with this ridiculous absurdity, all negative theology is an innocent naïveté.... [That which is recognized by faith] is the obvious presence of the Unknowable which no concept can

contain and of which nevertheless we know that it manifests itself even here in its own originality, through a manifestation that any other figure, any other event, cannot replace, or even rival. *Rationabiliter comprehendit incomprehensibile esse* is the paradox that St. Paul expresses by the same dialectic, *scire supereminentem scientiae caritatem Christi* (Eph 3:19). That Christ, by his completely obedient attitude, should not present himself as the supreme source of love; that he should not make of his human existence the revelation of his own eternal love but the transparent medium of the love of the Father—that makes the paradox at one and the same time definitively impossible to conceive and nevertheless susceptible of being existentially understood. On the one hand the Person who obeys finds himself borne away in God and becomes the Son in the Trinity, and the Word of the Father; but on the other hand this form of existence-in-obedience gives to the believing disciple a point of entry that allows him to seize that which comes next, it opens a gate of access to him.[12]

And it is for the same reason that Christ fulfills the history of the Old Covenant by saving it from its infidelities. It is by virtue of the fact that his final obedience surpasses that of the particular figures of prophet, king, priest, sacrificial lamb, servant of Yahweh, and Son of Man that he fills them out and gives them their intelligibility. This integration of particular images in the total image is not the nucleus of the objective evidence itself (that is Christ), but it allows this evidence to be understood rationally according to the relation between promise and fulfillment, or, further, between the Old and the New Testament, between history and spirit, between the literal sense and the spiritual meaning.

At this point it becomes strictly impossible to distinguish between subjective and objective, between apologetic "proofs" which are based on exterior data and what we call the interior light of faith, which reveals to us the hidden justice of facts and words, and the coherence of their meanings. The simple eyes of faith see the truth that shines forth, not initially in them interiorly but in the objective presence of the Gospel. They can come across it there in various ways, but this light of truth shines for them, enters them, and finally shines inside them. And there is not any discordance between that which is recognized externally and that which gives itself internally to recognition. The two coincide [in a fully objective contemplation].[13]

To believe, therefore, von Balthasar repeats, is not to divest oneself of that which is offered, but to offer oneself and stand fast. "That's all there. Most people only consider things from a bias. They have already judged before having heard the reasons adduced. The prejudged word here falls short of the mark." In brief, "Jesus has no need of apologetics; everything is clear in his

[12] *La foi du Christ* (Paris: Aubier-Montaigne, 1968), 107, 110–11.
[13] *Neue Klarstellungen: Nouveau Pouef de refères* (Paris: Fayard, 1979), 153.

subject. He enlightens every man who comes into the world (Jn 1:9), and who does not intentionally determine otherwise."[14]

Thus the first condition necessary for understanding is at one and the same time that of faith and of science. "The first prerequisite for understanding is to accept what is given just as it offers itself. If certain excisions are practised on the Gospel from the outset, the integrity of the phenomenon is lost and it has already become incomprehensible."[15] But the Gospel presents the figure of Christ in such a way that all elements cohere: hidden life, public life, Passion, Resurrection, ascension, gift of the Spirit are tied together among themselves in such a way that the Christ of faith makes no sense unless internally identical with the Jesus of history.

> The first, earthly form is legible only if we see that it is to be wholly "used up" in death and resurrection. But death and resurrection (which constitute a strict ideal unity) are comprehensible only if they are understood as the transformation of this earthly form by God's power, and not as the form's spiritualisation and apotheosis. Neither the one nor the other half is the "Word of God", but both halves together, and both together only to the extent that the Word is understood from the outset as the bearer of the Spirit, and the Spirit as the spiritualiser and transfigurer of the Word and, thus, as the Spirit both of the Word and of the one who has spoken (sent) the Word. Or if the trinitarian dimension is excluded from the objective form of revelation, then again everything becomes incomprehensible.[16]

We would separate in fact at one and the same time that which contemplates, that which is contemplated, and the love in which the contemplation develops. For, in communicating himself to his Son, the Father contemplates him, and reciprocally the Son contemplates the Father in accepting himself from him and in giving him thanks; and their reciprocal gift, the Spirit, is the satisfaction of the Father with the Son and the action of thanks by the Son for the Father, united as their personal fruition.

Also, "there is a strict unity between all the theological traits. There is no Christology without the Trinity and vice versa, or history of salvation from the faith of Abraham to the Church, there is no Incarnation of the Word without the Cross and Resurrection. We must then react against the parcelling-out that believes itself to be scientific, and against all Neoplatonizing spiritualism, even to that of the most sublime mysticism."[17]

---

[14] Ibid.
[15] *The Glory of the Lord* I: 467.
[16] Ibid.
[17] Instituto Paolo VI, *Hans Urs von Balthasar: Premio Internazionale,* Paul VI, 1984.

The Tradition Renewed and Enriched

We know enough of the theology of Fr. von Balthasar to understand the reason why his contemplation is scriptural and his exegesis contemplative. We must yet show further that this reason overcomes the reasons for the separation between exegesis and contemplation which have been at work since the sixteenth century at the latest.

Exegesis, we repeat, forms a unit with contemplation because it accepts what is given just as it offers itself.[18] The "datum" is not the pure datum which science—in particular, exegesis—makes its object, determined by a subject which itself is potentially transcendental precisely inasmuch as it determines the object. The datum manifests what is given, and instead of submitting it to its determination, the subject receives it in its "givenness", with an openness which, on the one hand, corresponds to the opening of the human spirit to God and, on the other hand, is strictly Marian: the acceptance is interior like the "Thy will be done" of the Mother of God. Scientific exegesis, then, is in no way excluded. There is a datum, and fidelity to the object is the first condition of scientific explanation. Only, this fidelity to the object is subsumed under the Marian acceptance appropriate to the spirit of the gift which offers itself, that is to say, in the attitude of contemplation.

This attitude is manifest in the act of giving oneself to God: in Christ, the central figure of revelation. All that might possibly reintroduce the subject as determining the evidence is rigorously set aside. We must allow the Creator to communicate without interference with his creature.[19] Such is the decisive situation of divine and human liberty.[20] Fr. von Balthasar, quite supple in every other area, is inflexible here. And man prepares himself for this communication from God only by opening himself up, or as Ignatius of Loyola says, by indifference. This is what makes the Christian, even though it might take a long time, as with *Cordula*. This is what makes the *Theologos*, of whom John is the perfect model.

> The most profound interpreter of the mystery of Christ, John, was designated by the ancient Church as the theologian par excellence. At the climax of his redemptive work on the Cross, Jesus, with a truly testamentary deposition, confided his Mother to John, in order that he might form of these two the primitive living cell of his Church. John, following a long and profound contemplation, recognizes in his Gospel that Jesus is the Word of God; he effaces himself totally from his epistles in order to refer only to Christ; and finally, in the visions of the Apocalypse uniting the Old and the

[18] *The Glory of the Lord* I: 467.
[19] Annotation 15 of the Spiritual Exercises of St. Ignatius.
[20] Election of the first mode in the Spiritual Exercises.

New Covenant, in setting out from the immolated divine Lamb, unrolls the whole drama of salvation.[21]

The *theologos,* then, contemplates God such as he gives himself in himself and in the world, not God such as man discovers him through a purely *a priori* opening-up of his spirit and of the lived reality of salvation (Rahner), nor God such as the Christological curvature of the world manifests him (Teilhard). It is not that von Balthasar rejects these two ways of approaching the matter. On the contrary, he integrates them in his contemplation: he "shows the unique character of Christ in relation to all religions, and demonstrates thus that all philosophical anthropology can only culminate in the light of the perfect man, the Son of God, who allows us to go beyond our mortal birth with a new birth to immortal trinitarian life".[22] But he sees that these two ways— anthropological and cosmological—are not strictly appropriate to the *theologos,* and he remains fearlessly where God has placed him. This is precisely the place in which the Christian contemplates God in the Scriptures.

In this place, united with Henri de Lubac who effaces himself before the profundity of the mystery, he is close to Thomas Aquinas, Luther, Hegel, and Barth. With John he knows that the Spirit is received entirely through the faith of the Mother, open to God, and that united by the Lord to the Mother, John the apostle is the witness to it. Contrary to what Luther said, the objective Spirit thus is united with the ecclesial subject in constituting it according to the liberty that God gives to the human spirit.

Concerning this liberty von Balthasar holds the thesis of St. Thomas, recovered by Henri de Lubac. And, on this basis, he says, it is important to "reconquer a philosophy beginning with theology".[23]

Between God, who gives himself, and man, who in the Son offers himself in return, is knitted a dialectic not of appropriation and construction (as with Luther and Hegel) but of superabundance and contemplation, inside of which man lives even at the moment when he is transcended, because this dialectic follows the rhythm of the life and the logic of the Trinity (on this point von Balthasar sides with Hegel against Aristotle). This dialectic is that of analogy: *in similitudine maior dissimilitudo* (Lateran IV), *analogia libertatis,* such as Karl Barth could hardly conceive.

And so, the area of contemplation never ceases to expand, the texts of the Church broaden, the soul is dilated. Contemplation is not only presupposed in the mission (*Contemplata tradere*), it is coextensive with it. The more it is interior to the act of God which is revealed and given, the more it reveals and

---

[21] *L'Institut Saint-Jean,* 98–99.

[22] *Hans Urs von Balthasar: Premio Internazionale,* 28.

[23] "Regagner une philosophie à partir de la théologie", *Pour une philosophie chrétienne* (Paris: Lethielleux, 1983), 175–87.

hands over God, the more also it is turned toward time and already in it. Fr. von Balthasar loved to repeat the translation that Buber made of Isaiah 7:8: ("if you do not believe, you will not hold fast"): "he who believes will hasten nothing". This is consonant with a counsel of Adrienne von Speyr, which he repeats as readily: "Let things happen." Mission is the true name of contemplation. It is as much temporal as eternal.

We conclude with a citation from *Das betrachtende Gebet:*

> He who has once entered within the radiation of the divine Word remains enclosed in it; he knows, having proved it himself, that this Word not only transmits a knowledge about God, but itself possesses—hidden within the vestment of the letter—divine qualities. It manifests in itself, in an irresistible manner, the infinity and the truth of God, the majesty and the love of God. Its appearance forces the hearer to his knees. He thought he would be acting on a word which, like the other great and deep words of humanity, he could judge and take the measure of. But, entering into the circle of influence of this Word, he himself has become the judged and measured. He wanted to go to Jesus nevertheless in order to see him ("Come and see!"), and, under Jesus' gaze, he was compelled to feel that he had already for a long time been seen, transfixed, judged, and received in grace by him, to the extent that there remained nothing for him to do but fall on his knees and adore the Word: "Master, you are the Son of God; you are the King of Israel." But this experience in which we feel ourselves irresistibly mastered becomes the point of departure of something that only begins there: "You will see greater things than this. . . . Henceforth you shall see the heavens open, and the angels of God descending and ascending on the Son of Man" (Jn 1:46–51). It is through the word of Scripture that the Jacob's ladder of contemplation begins, and no step leaves behind the hearing of the Word.[24]

---

[24] *Das betrachtende Gebet* (Einsiedeln: Johannes Verlag, 1955), 6.

PETER HENRICI, S.J.

The Philosophy of
Hans Urs von Balthasar

People are always surprised when they are informed that Hans Urs von
Balthasar was never a professor at a university and that he did not earn a
theological doctorate. Yet the "doctor of philosophy" given to the student of
German literature contained more than a small portion of philosophy and, out
of love of theology, von Balthasar remained faithful to philosophy until the
end of his life. To plumb and present this philosophy remains a task too vast
for doctoral dissertations, let alone a brief essay. Let it suffice to set up a few
markers that will stake out its dimensions in rough outline.

The Works

From the first to the last, von Balthasar's books are permeated by philosophy.
His doctoral dissertation begins with "Historical Presuppositions"[1] that trace
the philosophical development from the Middle Ages to the modern age. It
continues with a preparatory chapter about "The Alternative: Kierkegaard
and Nietzsche".[2] The final reworking of the same materials in the three
volumes of *Apokalypse der deutschen Seele* (Apocalypse of the German soul)[3]
achieves above all a widening and deepening of the philosophical background
of the dissertation. The largely philosophical volume one contains monographs
about Herder, Kant, Fichte, Schelling, Hegel, and concludes with the chapter
on "Kierkegaard and Nietzsche" which is taken over "almost unchanged" from
the dissertation.[4] Volume two, entitled "In the Sign of Nietzsche", presents
Bergson, Klages, and again Nietzsche (face to face with Dostoevsky). The
final volume, "In the Sign of Death", deals with Scheler, Heidegger, and Karl
Barth. Volume four was to be a theological volume, but it was never written.

Translated by Michael Waldstein.

[1] See "Geschichte des eschatologischen Problems in der modernen deutschen Literatur"
(Dissertation, Zurich, 1930), 4–10.

[2] See ibid, 10–33.

[3] *Apokalypse der deutschen Seele. Studien zu einer Lehre von letzten Haltungen* (Salzburg: A.
Pustet, 1937–1939).

[4] *Apokalypse* I, 17.

Between the first version of the dissertation and the full version of *Apokalypse* von Balthasar studied scholastic philosophy for two years in Pullach near Munich "chaperoned from afar by Erich Przywara".[5] One cannot sense much of that in *Apokalypse,* except for occasional references to Thomas Aquinas and the weight given to Scheler, Heidegger, and Barth. By contrast, von Balthasar's theological studies, which were completed in the same intermediary period, resulted in a second group of works, the trilogy (never published as such) about Origen, Gregory of Nyssa, and Maximus the Confessor. Von Balthasar reads them as pertinent to the present and therefore emphasizes the philosophical aspects of their work, "so that problems of existential philosophy come face to face with Gregory of Nyssa, problems of German idealism point back to Maximus the Confessor, while the fundamental questions of contemporary Catholicism are given an almost threatening clarity in the light of Origen".[6] The volume on Gregory of Nyssa accordingly bears the subtitle, *Essai sur la philosophie religieuse de Grégoire de Nysse* (Essay on the religious philosophy of Gregory of Nyssa), and deals extensively with the distinction between existence and essence in the framework of a philosophy of becoming, of love, and of image—all of them in increasing transition to pure theology. The volume on Maximus, with the subtitle *Höhe und Krise des griechischen Weltbilds* (Apex and crisis of the Greek world view) represents the extension of the Chalcedonian formula to a cosmic formula and sees this formula (in the new edition of 1961) as a prototype of the encounter between East and West, in fact between Asian and European thought.

The three following writings, all of them from von Balthasar's first period at Basel, constitute the heart of his philosophical writings. The first is the long essay published in 1946, "Von den Aufgaben der katholischen Philosophie in der Zeit" (On the tasks of Catholic philosophy in our time),[7] von Balthasar's true *Discours de la méthode*. Published shortly after the critical review of his Gregory of Nyssa book by Fr. Labourdette,[8] the essay can be taken as an implicit response to the charge of anti-scholasticism. Von Balthasar understands Christian philosophy as philosophizing within faith and with a view toward theology. He sees its specific achievement in the history of philosophy in two things, "the art of *opening* all finite philosophical truth toward Christ, and the art of clarifying transposition"[9] achieved in exemplary fashion for modern philosophy by Maréchal, Sertillanges, and Przywara. After pointing

[5] *Unser Auftrag. Bericht und Entwurf* (Einsiedeln: Johannes Verlag, 1984), 32.

[6] *Kosmische Liturgie: Höhe und Krise des griechischen Weltbilds bei Maximus Confessor* (Freiburg: Herder, 1941) vi.

[7] "Von den Aufgaben der katholischen Philosophie in der Zeit", *Annalen der Philosophischen Gesellschaft der Innerschweiz* 3 (1946–47) 2/3; 1–38.

[8] See M. Labourdette, "La Théologie et ses sources", *Revue Thomiste* 46 (1946): 353–71.

[9] "Von den Aufgaben der katholischen Philosophie", 9.

out the special difficulties of an encounter between Catholic and modern as well as contemporary thought, von Balthasar concludes by sketching the tasks and possibilities of an encounter with *Lebensphilosophie*, existentialism, and "the modern spirit of history".[10] He sees the presuppositions of a mutually fruitful encounter in the scholastic doctrine of the transcendentals and in the real distinction between existence and essence. The highly dense article is hardly dated and deserves to be republished.

One year later von Balthasar published his systematic-philosophical main work, *Wahrheit, Bd. 1: Wahrheit der Welt*[11]—in the same year in which Karl Jaspers, at that time also in Basel, published his monumental work *Von der Wahrheit*. It is von Balthasar's only purely systematic-philosophical work, his only work without references to other authors, but thoroughly reflected and secretly always in dialogue, especially with Thomas Aquinas and Heidegger. The book is concerned with a phenomenology of truth. According to the mutual indwelling (*circumincessio*) of the transcendentals, the nature of truth is seen in the encounter between the lover and the beloved; truth manifests itself thus as revelation, as unveiling and veiling, but also as sheltering participation. Forty years later this work could be reprinted unchanged, only a new introduction being added, as the first volume of *Theologik*—while the second volume announced already in 1947, *Wahrheit Gottes* could apparently be written only as the conclusion to the whole trilogy.[12]

As the third and final work of the first Basel period there follows *Karl Barth: Darstellung und Deutung seiner Theologie*[13]—prepared by the Barth chapter in *Apokalypse*. Since it was the goal of this book to resume and continue the interrupted dialogue between Barth and Przywara, the philosophical problem stands in the foreground even here. The dialogue had failed due to the sharp opposition between *analogia entis* and *analogia fidei*. This opposition had to be questioned, the form of Barth's thought had to be understood as it derived from German idealism, and it had to be confronted with the Catholic form of thought that links philosophy and theology, nature and grace (in each case with a "relative autonomy" of the first) as attested above all in Thomas Aquinas. Von Balthasar's book on Barth, the work that comes closest to academic theology, also shows most clearly how he concretely conceives the interpenetration of philosophy and theology.

Ten years of a transitional period follow in von Balthasar's work until the first volume of the trilogy. These were his first years after leaving the order. In these years he published, first, his lectures on *Die Gottesfrage des heutigen*

[10] Ibid., 37.

[11] *Wahrheit, Bd. 1: Wahrheit der Welt* (Einsiedeln: Benziger, 1947).

[12] *Theologik II: Wahrheit Gottes* (Einsiedeln: Johannes Verlag, 1985).

[13] *Karl Barth: Darstellung und Deutung seiner Theologie*, 4th ed. (Einsiedeln: Johannes Verlag, 1976).

Menschen,[14] a book he himself was not content with, in which he attempts to explain "to this modern man his specific religious situation . . . in contrast to earlier situations".[15] Of course, many philosophical issues had to be discussed in this book; at a later point they were integrated in more systematic and reflected form in the short apologetics written for *Mysterium Salutis.*[16] Secondly, von Balthasar collected a few of his scattered essays in the first volumes of *Skizzen zur Theologie (Explorations in Theology)* where again much philosophy flowed into the methodological reflections on the basis of theology.[17] Special mention should be made of the essay "Philosophie, Christentum, Mönchtum"[18] which is the philosophical counterpart of the frequently quoted article "Theologie und Heiligkeit",[19] inasmuch as it explains the patristic and monastic understanding of *philosophia* as Christian life. The final work that we wish to count as part of this transitional period is the sketch of a theology of history, *Das Ganze im Fragment: Aspekte der Geschichtstheologie*[20] which develops the earlier study *Theologie der Geschichte*[21] by giving it a philosophical foundation. In the discussion of the (primarily Augustinian) understanding of time and of the perfectibility of the human person, the relation to Heidegger is unmistakable.

From von Balthasar's late or mature period we only need to mention his theological trilogy consisting of the Aesthetic, Dramatic, and Logic, the composition of which occupied him for more than a quarter century until his death. Philosophical elements found in smaller writings of this period are really only rays proceeding from the main work. Apart from the continual references to the history of philosophy and thought that are characteristic of von Balthasar's work, there are six places in the trilogy where philosophy occupies center stage. The most obvious is *Herrlichkeit Bd.* III/1: *Im Raum der Metaphysik,*[22] the purpose of which is to embed theological aesthetics in European intellectual history. Although "metaphysics" refers to myth, philosophy, and natural religion, the history of philosophy provides the guiding thread of

[14] *Die Gottesfrage des heutigen Menschen* (Vienna: Herold, 1956).

[15] *Rechenschaft 1965* (Einsiedeln: Johannes Verlag, 1965), 26.

[16] "Zugang zur Wirklichkeit Gottes", in *Mysterium Salutis, II. Grundriss heilsgeschichtlicher Dogmatik,* ed. J. Feiner and M. Löhrer, 3rd ed. (Einsiedeln-Cologne: Benziger, 1978) 15–43; republished as "Bewegung zu Gott", in *Spiritus Creator (Skizzen zur Theologie III)* (Einsiedeln: Johannes Verlag, 1967), 13–50.

[17] *Verbum Caro (Skizzen zur Theologie I),* 2nd ed. (Einsiedeln: Johannes Verlag, 1965); *Sponsa Verbi (Skizzen zur Theologie II),* 2nd ed. (Einsiedeln: Johannes Verlag, 1971).

[18] "Philosophie, Christentum, Mönchtum", in *Sponsa Verbi,* 349–87.

[19] "Theologie und Heiligkeit", in *Verbum Caro,* 195–225.

[20] *Das Ganze im Fragment: Aspekte der Geschichtstheologie* (Einsiedeln: Benziger, 1963).

[21] *Theologie der Geschichte* (Einsiedeln: Johannes Verlag, 1959).

[22] *Herrlichkeit. Eine theologische Ästhetik. Bd. III/1: Im Raum der Metaphysik,* 2 vols., 2nd ed. (Einsiedeln: Johannes Verlag, 1975).

THE PHILOSOPHY OF HANS URS VON BALTHASAR

the whole account, and the final chapter, "Vermächtnis und christlicher Auftrag"[23] is entirely focused on philosophy because myth and natural religion cannot be brought back in the Christian era. After this great prelude (in which one may see an ample reworking of *Apokalypse*) the other philosophical passages appear more modest, even though they have important and new things to contribute. *Theodramatik* II/1[24] offers elements of a philosophical anthropology in its chapters "Unendliche und endliche Freiheit"[25] and "Der Mensch".[26] *Theodramatik* III,[27] in its chapter "Pathetische Weltbühne",[28] offers a sketch of a philosophy of history which is substantially enriched in comparison with the earlier sketch. We already pointed out that *Theologik* reproduces the earlier book *Wahrheit*. In the theological volume two[29] one finds again two philosophical pieces about "Göttliche und menschliche Logik"[30] and "Trinitarische Differenz und Seinsdifferenz".[31] The *Epilog*,[32] finally, is again centrally philosophical by offering an entry into theology from philosophy.

The little volume *Glaubhaft ist nur Liebe*,[33] probably the densest summary of von Balthasar's thought, had done the same thing, with a less central role of philosophy. After a historical survey, two chapters unfold a philosophy of love and its human failure,[34] in order to be able to understand love as revelation. Among the lectures and essays of this period, the lecture "Regagner une philosophie à partir de la théologie"[35] deserves special mention, because it brings to light especially clearly von Balthasar's position on the theory of knowledge and science. Finally, the little posthumous volume, *Wenn ihr nicht werdet wie dieses Kind*[36] contains a dense chapter about the human child.[37]

---

[23] See *Herrlichkeit* III/1: 2. Teil: *Neuzeit*, 941–83.

[24] *Theodramatik* II: *Die Personen des Spiels*, 1. Teil: *Der Mensch in Gott* (Einsiedeln: Johannes Verlag, 1976).

[25] See ibid., 170–288.

[26] See ibid., 306–93.

[27] *Theodramatik* III: *Die Handlung* (Einsiedeln: Johannes Verlag, 1980).

[28] See ibid., 67–186.

[29] See *Theologik* II.

[30] See ibid., 27–57.

[31] See ibid., 159–70.

[32] *Epilog* (Einsiedeln-Trier: Johannes Verlag, 1987); chap. 2: "Die Schwelle", 35–66.

[33] *Glaubhaft ist nur Liebe*, 5th ed. (Einsiedeln: Johannes Verlag, 1985).

[34] See ibid., "Der dritte Weg der Liebe", p. 33–39 and "Das Versagen der Liebe", 40–48.

[35] "Regagner une philosophie à partir de la théologie", in *Pour une philosophie chrétienne. Philosophie et théologie* (Paris: Lethielleux, 1983) 175–87.

[36] *Wenn ihr nicht werdet wie dieses Kind* (Ostfildern: Schwabenverlag, 1988).

[37] See ibid., 12–20.

The Form (Gestalt)

Method

Our list illustrates two points. First, that von Balthasar evidently made an important contribution to Christian philosophy, secondly that he makes this contribution less as a systematic thinker than as an interpreter of the history of thought. In an interview he says about his relation to Karl Rahner,

> First of all, I consider Rahner the greatest theological power of our time. And it is evident that he is far superior to me in speculative strength. . . . But our starting points have really always been different. There is a book by Simmel called *Goethe und Kant*. Rahner has chosen Kant, or if you will, Fichte, the transcendental approach. And I have chosen Goethe, my field being German literature. The form (*Gestalt*), the indissoluble unique, organic, developing form—I am thinking of Goethe's poem "The Metamorphosis of Plants"—this form, which Kant does not know what to do with, even in his aesthetics. . . . One can walk around a form and see it from all sides. One always sees something different, and yet one sees the same thing.[38]

Thus we must attempt to glimpse the form (*Gestalt*) of von Balthasar's philosophy itself by observing how he himself sees the great figures (*Gestalt*) of the history of thought but also the form (*Gestalt*) of the central philosophical contents.

In seeing figures (*Gestalt*), von Balthasar's philosophical method cannot be called systematic—let alone conceptual-analytic or conceptual-constructive—nor really historical. It is closest, as he himself pointed out, to phenomenology—with a good measure of literary criticism. At the beginning of *Apokalypse,* von Balthasar describes the method as follows:

> The characteristic feature of the following studies is . . . that they use the historical structures of world views like stones to build a building which has a trans-historical meaning. They thus stand between history and system in a middle which is different from Hegel only because this middle appears as highly unstable, that is, as creaturely—as the middle of the mythical, not of absolute spirit . . . fundamentally, therefore, their method is the now inalienable phenomenological method, applied to the leaders of German intellectual and spiritual life . . . it is an act of listening which is, as mentioned above, passive-objective precisely when it sees creatively.[39]

The difficulties of presenting von Balthasar's philosophy hereby become evident. This philosophy can be approached neither in a historical-analytical nor in a conceptual-reconstructing manner. The only thing to do would be to

---

[38] "Geist und Feuer. Michael Albus: Ein Gespräch mit Hans Urs von Balthasar", in *Herder-Korrespondenz* 30 (1976), 75–76.

[39] *Apokalypse* I, 10, n. 2.

redraw the figures (*Gestalt*) seen by him. Yet, even this approach is unsatisfactory. A figure lives from its concrete richness; every simplifying sketch is an impoverishment and even a falsification. The difficulty increases due to the concrete historical form (*Ausprägung*) of his historical-phenomenological thought. The individual figures (*Gestalt*) are not significant in themselves; what he sees and draws is, rather, a historical movement which is a meaningful form (*Sinngestalt*) above all in its goal, its peripeties, and errors, and above all in the decisions it includes. What we would have to do, therefore, is to condense once again a movement which is drawn in condensed fashion. Above all, von Balthasar himself keeps himself outside of this movement: he embraces it from a contemplative vantage-point; he allows one to see certain value-judgments about this or that peripety and decision—not, however, on the basis of absolute (perhaps theological) "knowing better", but on the basis of historical knowledge about the eventual outcome and being struck by this outcome. He does not read history so much—as one might be inclined to think—from his own preconceived opinion, but he lets his own views be formed step by step by the course of history (as well as by his own countermovement to it). One can assume that this was the origin of his philosophy as well as of his literary theory, namely, to allow himself to be taught by the great writers and by their spiritual adventures, but at the same time, in the distant light of a theological, or rather, believing point of orientation, to preserve the freedom to think differently or even to think the opposite. In this way many of the figures he draws are anti-figures (*Gegen-Gestalten*) and von Balthasar's thought defines itself in opposition to them—in a thoroughly irenic attitude without entering into polemics or refutations with those who think differently.

In order to do some justice to this method, which must bring every academic mind (and all dissertations) to despair, but which is perhaps precisely thereby a true philosophical method, we want to focus in what follows on a few figures whose presence shapes the whole of von Balthasar's work. It is in their realm, eye to eye with the decisions that erupt in this realm—often as an anti-image of these figures—that von Balthasar's thought must be situated. We encounter it thus first as something "other" than these figures that is difficult to grasp, something "other" that is nevertheless akin in profoundly sharing what strikes them.

Figures

Plato—Plotinus—Hegel

Von Balthasar found his first deep access to philosophy in Hans Eibl's lectures on Plotinus in Vienna. His own philosophical eros ignited itself, characteristically,

by contact with a thinker who is as much a theologian as a philosopher; von
Balthasar treats him under the rubric "religion" in *The Glory of the Lord:*
" . . . philosophy, and yet more than that, for he gathers into it all the values of
myth, of religion . . . and he does so in a passionate return to the origins where
everything lies together without distinction."[40] Plotinus becomes a permanent point of reference for von Balthasar's thought, not only in *Glory*. Already
in *Apokalypse* he read Fichte, Schelling, and Bergson as continuations of
Plotinus, and in *Glory* he adds Erigena and Nicholas of Cusa. Yet he sees
Augustine and Gregory of Nyssa as answers to Plotinus and never misses an
opportunity for mentioning Plotinus as the source of some idea.

The vista which was opened up by Plato but remained ambiguous—namely,
his philosophy of eros, in which "the horizontal relation of the sexes was
raised up vertically" because it "dares to apply the model of mutual love to the
relation with the absolute",[41] and the issuing of all philosophy into myth,[42]
which points ahead to Christian revelation, but which nevertheless ends in
Plato's work in pure albeit dialectical knowledge and in an intra-cosmic
harmony between the divine and the human[43]—all of this is integrated and
preserved/cancelled/lifted above itself (*aufgehoben*) in the insurmountable difference between the source and what streams forth from it.

> It is only with Plotinus that the light rises again anew and great, in that the
> spirit (the world of ideas) is moved in hitherto unheard-of fashion by the
> eros of a needy/needless longing, a longing for the unthinkable, the unique,
> the good, the source of all beauty, even though the One itself does not even
> "deign to be beautiful". Thinking and love are one, and both are the light of
> the world; however, this light breaks forth from something inaccessible
> which is a groundless ground and source and which is therefore non-light or
> darkness or over-light. Certainly, being is identified with thought, but both
> exist by grace of the One, and both exist only in the manner of eros,
> penetrated by nothingness . . . and only in this manner are both a releasing
> ground for particular beings as "soul" and "nature".[44]

Yet even about Plotinus questions arise and then also criticism—more restrained
in *Glory*, more explicit in *Theo-Drama* and *Theo-Logic*. On the one side, the

---

[40] *Herrlichkeit* III/1. Teil: *Altertum, 252.*

[41] Ibid., 175f.

[42] Cf. ibid., 179: " . . . the only way from here (from the Platonic myths) leads forward
into Christian revelation which is the only thing that can achieve the synthesis between
poetry (myth) and philosophy. Until that point philosophy remains in this position, namely,
that it must at the same time project myths as its own conclusion and critically take them
back; that it must, at one and the same time, posit certain things in its erotic and inspired
excess which it cannot sustain in the return of reflection."

[43] See ibid., 195.

[44] *Herrlichkeit* III/1: 2, 967f.

theological side, the issue is God's freedom, "the Absolute One of Plotinus, whose freedom is absolute, but vibrates only in itself. . . . Such a God who has a fixation with being free from everything cannot *give* freedom, even if there is something like freedom outside himself, due to his radiance."[45] On the other hand, and even before this, the philosophical question arises whether the encounter with God in Plotinus is anything but the encounter with the spirit's self. "When the spirit in its infinite movement through all *noemata* (objects of thought) seeks the One, but returns in all departures into the identity of self-encounter, has it found what it seeks? If thinking (and thus reason, *nous*) is and remains secondary, then it must certainly transcend itself; but if one calls this transcending the eros that sets thinking into motion, is this eros anything more than the thinking or only its inner dynamism?"[46]

This question, which remains open in Plotinus, confronts us with the "European decision:"[47] whether the successors, as would be evident, tend toward a philosophy of identity (whose highpoint is Hegel, but whose influence already pervades—and falsifies?—Christian mysticism) or whether they interpret Plotinus in terms of the "suspended-adventist" features of his thought, namely, in terms of "the difference between the level of the spirit and the level of the One" with which Plotinus crowns his entire philosophy. "It is, in fact, theological in a sense that is difficult to pin down."[48] The task of making visible even today this Plotinian "divine revelation . . . which breaks forth from the center and depth of being itself . . . rests on the shoulders of those who have been permitted to see God's glory in the flesh, namely, the Christians; for it is their task to find God in all things".[49]

It has already become clear, therefore, why Hegel is a third great point of reference for von Balthasar. The post-Platonic line of false decision leads by way of Fichte and Schelling directly to him and finds its unsurpassable conclusion in "absolute knowledge". Just as Plotinus concludes the thought of antiquity, Hegel concludes that of modernity; his philosophy always stands before von Balthasar's eyes as the possibility which is infinitely proximate to the Christian thinker, but cannot be accepted. From his first book to his last, von Balthasar thinks eye to eye with Hegel. The verdict is clearer than in the case of Plotinus, because in Hegel, after Christ, there is no longer any suspended openness, but Christianity is clearly preserved/cancelled/lifted above itself (*aufgehoben*) into philosophy. However, von Balthasar's portrayal of Hegel is more multi-faceted. It reaches from the analysis of the "existentiality" of Hegel's thought in *Apokalypse* (in the end Hegel evaporates the "seriousness"

[45] *Theodramatik* II/1, 180f.
[46] *Herrlichkeit* III/1: 1, 265.
[47] See ibid., 262ff.
[48] Ibid., 270.
[49] Ibid.

of the dialectical sacrifice into the "cunning" of the mere spectator, "here love, there the spectator"[50]) by way of the sketch of the origin of his thought in *Glory* (where von Balthasar shows how Hegel "[1] proceeds from Christian revelation, [2] expels biblical glory from it in three steps, and [3] identifies the remaining doctrine of the Holy Spirit with the absolute [divine-cosmic] spirit"[51]) to the confrontation between dialogic and theologic[52] and the detailed consideration of Hegel's Spirit-Christology which can only be combated theologically.

> Hegel's thoroughly serious attempt of setting up the doctrine of the Trinity as the central proposition of his theological philosophy . . . threatens to turn into modalism, due to his universally applied dialectical method. For to the degree that creation is drawn into the immanent Trinity, the other *person* (*der* Andere) in God must be replaced by the other *thing* (*das* Andere) as whose peak the other *person* (*der* Andere) emerges only in the Incarnation; that person would, therefore, not exist as the divine Son without the evolution of the world.[53]

Against Hegel's attempt "to construct something like a system of truth" which "whether knowingly or not, contains a feature of blasphemy, at any rate a feature of anti-Christianity", von Balthasar raises up Christ,

> who called himself the Way and the Truth . . . and who confirms Hegel's statement that everything that is real is reasonable . . . in a sense that goes beyond everything that can be constructed on the basis of a system and in a completely different way, namely . . . by . . . being able to unite in a single act the absolutely divine and the absolutely anti-divine, not in the insanity of a titanic-superhuman gesture, but in the simplicity of his obedience.[54]

Kierkegaard and Nietzsche

The Kierkegaardian cadence of this final passage in the second volume of *Theologik* is unmistakable. Granted, in the trilogy Kierkegaard and Nietzsche do not occupy the dominating and orienting place they had in *Apokalypse*. In *Apokalypse,* the chapter "Kierkegaard and Nietzsche" had provided the *leitmotif* of volumes two and three; post-Hegelian philosophy as a whole was treated in

[50] *Apokalypse* I, 615. One could be tempted to consider J. Flügge, *Die sittlichen Grundlagen des Denkens. Hegels existentielle Denkgesinnung* (Hamburg, 1953) dependent on von Balthasar.
[51] *Herrlichkeit* III/1: 2, 907.
[52] See *Theologik* II, 42: "Both forms of theologic can be called such, because they establish and at the same time explode the model of an *imago trinitatis* in the world and thus integrate God in some form (or pre-form) into the model: in Hegel, all syntheses point vicariously to the final synthesis of absolute (divine) knowledge . . . "
[53] *Theologik* III: *Der Geist der Wahrheit* (Einsiedeln-Trier: Johannes Verlag, 1987), 40.
[54] *Theologik* II, 330f.

the light of this either-or. In the trilogy it could step into the background in favor of the "European decision" which begins already with Plotinus; everything is thereby anticipated, with less pathos, but no less radically, and Kierkegaard and Nietzsche are at best emblematic for a decision that has already been made.

Nevertheless, the either-or could perhaps become evident only in the example of Kierkegaard and Nietzsche—where it presented itself in inescapable existentiality without being mistaken for a purely speculative question which one could survey and therefore easily overlook.

Von Balthasar came to know Kierkegaard in Berlin in a course taught by Romano Guardini; his radical Christianity again and again moved him profoundly. "Unfortunately, since my youth coincided with the Kierkegaard wave—Guardini explained him to us in Berlin—I have read in Kierkegaard that the apostle of Christ (and who does not claim this name today?) is one who lets himself be beaten to death for Christ."[55] *Cordula*[56] and already *Wer ist ein Christ?*[57] were written with this Kierkegaardian radicality. In quite a different direction, also the Aesthetic stands eye to eye with Kierkegaard. It answers the challenge implied for von Balthasar, the musician, in Kierkegaard's condemnation of the aesthetic (and thus of Mozart and of eros). Nietzsche, on the other hand, was so important to von Balthasar that he dedicated three volumes to him in the European "Final Reserve" of the Klosterberg collection (no other author was given this honor!). It is clear that he is again and again fascinated by him, although it was clear from the outset (even clearer than in the case of Hegel) that no Christian can follow his thought. It is thus not surprising that in the Kierkegaard-Nietzsche chapter of *Apokalypse*[58] one finds all the themes that most deeply touch von Balthasar's own thought: theatrical drama,[59] music and eros,[60] the themes of love,[61] of dialogue,[62] of childhood,[63] of the call,[64] and finally even hell and a glance at a possible trans-valuation of the fire of hell, "Death and hell are new birth, rebirth. And the fire of condemnation rises as the fire of praise . . . "[65]

Perhaps we may read the account of these two thinkers in some way as autobiographical, as the genesis of von Balthasar's own form of thought

[55] *Rechenschaft* 1965, 12.
[56] *Cordula oder der Ernstfall*, 4th ed. (Einsiedeln-Trier: Johannes Verlag, 1987).
[57] *Wer ist ein Christ?* 4th ed. (Einsiedeln: Johannes Verlag, 1983).
[58] "Der Zweikampf", *Apokalypse* I, 693–734.
[59] See ibid., 698.
[60] See ibid., 705.
[61] See ibid., 715, 724, etc.
[62] See ibid., 723, 726.
[63] See ibid., 726.
[64] See ibid., 730.
[65] Ibid., 733.

(*Denkgestalt*). The three "jousts" in which von Balthasar lets Kierkegaard and
Nietzsche face each other (after having drawn out their inner kinship which
reaches into most profound depths) would then be stages on the way of von
Balthasar's discovery of his own philosophy. In fact, already in the first round
the issue is the true form (*Gestalt*) of love: Nietzsche's titanic "power-love"
encounters in Kierkegaard "the descending power and love" of the Crucified
"that offers itself even to death".[66] "Even for Nietzsche man is killed, sacrificed
—to the over-man. For Kierkegaard, however, the individual can perish 'in
self-annihilation before God' and rise as a new creature by God's power. And
nevertheless as the same man. For nature and supernature are only one man.
Man and over-man, by contrast, are two. And yet, even the over-man is man,
while supernature is no longer nature."[67]

This is still expressed a little formally and with a play on words. Nevertheless,
the ordering of nature (and thus of man and thus of philosophy) to supernature
remains a fundamental theme of von Balthasar, and already here he says that
he sees the "supernatural" essentially in God's loving descent. This is why in
the second round the issue is, more existentially, the understanding of existence itself. "From the Socratic question of truth the way leads into the ethical
problem of the good."[68] Truth and good exist only in dialogue, and thus the
fight is fought out as a dialogue.

> Our relation to God is only untruth, Nietzsche cries. Yes, Kierkegaard
> responds, and it even becomes more so, the more we deal with him. But
> God's relation to us is truth—*our* truth! Truth is *in* us; it does not approach
> us from the outside, Nietzsche responds. God is *in* us and comes into us from
> the inside, Kierkegaard replies. Then God is *my* ground of soul, Nietzsche
> says. Then the ground of my soul is a streaming openness to God, Kierkegaard
> answers. What ambiguity! Nietzsche exclaims . . .[69]

In order to proceed further, von Balthasar must probe with his questions
behind the imaginary conversation. And then one sees, "What happened here
was *dialogic,* in a decisive sense and in a decisive depth. But then one must be
able to show the precise place in Nietzsche where he is no longer able to
sustain this category. Then a primacy of dialogic must reach down through
the antithetic of good/evil all the way to that of truth/untruth."[70]

Although the conversation was imaginary, it still reveals that Nietzsche's
thought stands unwillingly, as it were, in a conversation—and thus expressly
closes itself against love: " . . . you *resist* some ultimate peace", von Balthasar

---

[66] Ibid., 717.
[67] Ibid.
[68] Ibid., 723.
[69] Ibid., 725.
[70] Ibid., 726.

quotes Nietzsche as saying [71] — while Kierkegaard is from the outset open, and remains open, to dialogue (with God). "For, man, this creation of the Logos, has been planned from the ground up in dialogic fashion, and any monological self-interpretation must destroy him. In *Sickness unto Death* (1849) Kierkegaard gave an unsurpassed description of this entire structure . . . " [72] The dialogical principle as an all-encompassing and all-decisive category thus becomes the forming principle (*Formprinzip*) of the trilogy. "The world of myth was fundamentally dialogical: from the personal-divine sphere, glory radiates upon man who dares to interpret his temporal existence in this light. All original artistic creation has its origin in this space", yet, "where philosophy begins in a historically perceptible form, the dialogical act of prayer breaks off in a single stroke." [73] This is the background of the "European decision", and we understand why *Theologik* can epitomize this decision once again in the opposition between dialectic and dialogic. [74]

But the decision reaches still deeper. A third and final round which follows the other two leads beyond philosophy into personal life. It is more an act of wrestling with oneself than with the partner. For the issue is to bring one's existence into harmony with the interpretation of existence. In this act, the existence of the two thinkers "becomes the *sign* of the whole intra-dialogical truth". This leads into "the abyss of the tragedy of man whose existence is supposed to be a sign"; [75] it leads into the necessity of having to "write" one's own existence. "There is only one consolation: that this *whole,* poet and poem, is the whole truth in the decisive dialogue, or better, that it can be found and counted such, that this torture is made meaningful through a *call,* that the fiery sign truly *signifies.*" [76] However, this implies a consumption of the self—in melancholy and madness—for the call. From here the lines point ahead to the heart of von Balthasar's life and work, "Theology and Holiness", "Philosophy, Christianity, and Monasticism", the writings about mission and the call, and especially to von Balthasar's own mission, [77] for which he consumed himself in obedience and which was recognized only so slowly and with hesitation by the Church.

[71] Ibid., 727.
[72] *Theodramatik* III, 133.
[73] *Herrlichkeit* III/1:1, 143f.
[74] See *Theologik* II, 40–53.
[75] *Apokalypse* I, 728.
[76] Ibid., 730.
[77] See *Unser Auftrag.*

Thomas Aquinas

Ecclesiality provides a final key word. The alternative between Nietzsche and Kierkegaard could mislead one into dissolving philosophy into pure existence, into an attitude without contents. However, this contradicts not only the entire Western tradition of thought, but also the structure of revelation itself. Normative in this respect is a final figure who points back from the existential to being, from theology to philosophy, Thomas Aquinas. He does not really appear as a "figure" (*Gestalt*) in von Balthasar's work; his figure is never drawn as such.[78] Although the thinker Thomas does not appear, his thinking is omnipresent, evidenced by explicit citations. In *Apokalypse,* Thomas' role is still subterranean, but evident characteristically at the two concluding highpoints, as a counter-image to Hegel and Karl Barth. The only thinker cited expressly (and repeatedly) in *Wahrheit* is Thomas. The article "Von den Aufgaben der katholischen Philosophie in der Zeit" turns around Thomas. Von Balthasar's commentary on Thomas (again his only work of the kind on which he spent a seemingly infinite amount of learning and care) does not deal with any philosophical issues, but with "special charisms and the two paths of man's life".[79] Nevertheless, the commentary intends to be exemplary for *how* one should read Thomas: on the background of his sources and in the framework of the debates of his time.

Von Balthasar's relation to Thomas is neither that of an enthusiastic admirer and follower, nor a mere exercise in ecclesiastical duty. He does not understand himself as a "Thomist" nor does he want to back up his own thought at all cost by means of quotations from Thomas. A certain intellectual kinship with Thomas cannot be denied: both attempt to "order" a vast treasure of Tradition which they reverently receive; that is, they attempt to interpret it in terms of what they see as the truth. Yet in this work von Balthasar integrates Thomas' thinking, rather than being himself integrated by it: he situates it historically without sterilizing it historically. He sees in it a key turning point of the history of Christian thought.

> Thomas is . . . a *kairos* as a historically passing moment between an old world that thought in monistic terms, inasmuch as it saw philosophy and theology (both in their Greek and their Christian forms) as a whole, and an approaching dualistic world that attempted to posit a separation (both in Christian and post-Christian ways) between philosophy and the theology of revelation and turn each of them into a totality. However, the historically

---

[78] Apart from the brief account, concentrated exclusively on the issues themselves, in *Herrlichkeit* III/1:1, 354–70.

[79] *Thomas von Aquin. Besondere Gnadengaben und die zwei Wege menschlichen Lebens. Kommentar zur Summa Theologica II–II,* 171–182 (German Thomas-Edition, vol. 23; Heidelberg und Graz: F.H. Kerle/A. Pustet, 1954).

transitional form can still hold them together, provided it is conceived and shaped with sufficient comprehensiveness.[80]

Von Balthasar's intellectual kinship with Thomas is connected with three of his themes, one of them classically Thomistic, the second controversial, and the third often forgotten.

> Thomas' main creative achievement was the distinguishing of *esse* (to be) in relation to essences. . . . However, inasmuch as Thomas understands "esse" as the non-subsisting fullness and perfection of all that is real and as the highest "similitude of the divine goodness", so that God can in no way be seen any longer as the being of things, except as their efficient, exemplary, and final cause, God is removed in a new and much more radical way beyond all being of the world, beyond all that can be calculated and aimed at from the real and ideal structures of the world, as the truly Wholly Other.[81]

Precisely in this absolute distance, the second thing comes to bear, namely, the natural desire for the vision of God, inasmuch as "Thomas sees man, who is given the capacity to think about being, in a characteristic suspension between nature and supernature—for he is by nature ordained to God's gracious self-revelation and cannot be definitively fulfilled without it, even though he has no claim upon it: this is precisely what his nobility consists in."[82] Thirdly—or, more precisely, in the first place—it becomes evident that Thomas is in the first place and above all a theologian and "thus wants to understand all metaphysics as ordered to 'theology' ".[83]

These observations provide an entry to the understanding of the form proper (*Eigengestalt*) to von Balthasar's philosophy. He too is in the first place a theologian, and he sees reflection about being as ordered to revelation.

The Proper Form (Eigen-Gestalt)

Philosophy in View of Revelation

That von Balthasar considers the passage through the history of thought as more important than his own systematic construction indicates (apart from a characteristic closeness to Hegel) a first unmistakable feature of his thought. He always sees philosophy in the light of revelation—not as an understanding of revelation after the fact (that would be theology), but as a conscious and unconscious approach to revelation. He sees all other thinkers in the contrasting light of this goal (from which they turn away on occasion in the post-

[80] *Herrlichkeit*, III/1:1, 356.
[81] Ibid., 354.
[82] Ibid., 356.
[83] Ibid., 357.

Christian era), and this is why they are important and even indispensable to him. His own thinking stands in the same contrasting light. He does not philosophize on the basis of an attitude of "I know better as a believer" (which would make the philosophical act impossible or would secularize faith), but he attempts to see in the beauty of being the reflection of the divine glory.

For this reason his philosophical doctrine of knowledge (*Wahrheit der Welt*) explains the truth of revelation and the process of knowledge as disclosure/concealment. He sees the fundamental philosophical act as wonder, amazement about what cannot be constructed by thought (*"id quo maius cogitari nequit"*, — that beyond which nothing greater can be thought). In this way his entire philosophizing can be called an *intellectus fidei,* as in the case of Anselm (to whom he is perhaps closest, from a methodological point of view). Yet it is an openness, not to individual mysteries, but to revelation as such, and not as an imaginary dialogue of the believer with the *insipiens,* but as a sharing in seeing that which even the nonbeliever (or the one who no longer believes) sees of the glory of God in the reflection of being and in the drama of human freedom.

This means on the one hand that von Balthasar's philosophizing is thoroughly "apologetic", in the same sense as Blondel's: that for him there cannot be any philosophy which is not oriented by its very essence toward Christianity. "If . . . biblical revelation rests on the ground of the original difference between God and the world, and thus on the ground of metaphysics, and comes to light from this ground, then conversely metaphysics is fulfilled in the event of revelation if it does not want to finalize itself and thus disastrously harden itself on preliminary levels."[84]

Another point is implied: the inner relation to revelation (which is often unconscious) confronts the thinker again and again with a decision. For von Balthasar, philosophy is *always* existential, as he shows in the example of Kierkegaard/Nietzsche, but also in the example of early Christian *philosophia* and monasticism. And yet truth is not "subjective" for him as for Kierkegaard; what is decisive is not the attitude itself, but the attitude faced with the decisive contents: whether being is perceived in such a way that the glory of God can shine in it. Forgetfulness of being means for von Balthasar profound "forgetfulness of God".[85]

Philosophy of Being

The above already makes clear why von Balthasar's philosophy, expressly and with insistent emphasis, is a philosophy of being. A philosophy which is

[84] *Herrlichkeit* III/1:2, 958.
[85] See "Die Gottvergessenheit und die Christen" in *Hochland* 57 (1964), 1–11.

oriented toward the objective content of revelation (and which precisely in this respect differs from Karl Rahner's transcendental philosophy, which reflects on the subjective orientation) must reflect on that in which God first reveals himself to thought. Even the supernatural form of revelation (*Offenbarungsgestalt*) can and must be inserted into this naturally revealed and revealing light. This revealed and revealing light, however, is being—the wonder "that there is anything at all rather than nothing". Three consequences flow from this perception of being.

First of all, being must be seen as filled with value. The issue is being itself and not beings, not ontology, but metaphysics. Being unfolds itself as endowed with value in the transcendentals, and again among them first and foremost in their epitome, namely, beauty, which includes the values of truth and goodness in itself. In this light one can see the reason for the structure of the theological trilogy—quite far from the systematic order characteristic of the schools, not only because the traditional order of the transcendentals is rearranged (the first is that at which all partial revelation of being aims), but especially because the transcendentals are not exemplified in academic examples, but seen in the living history of the human race.

Since what manifests itself in the transcendentals is not merely being itself, since von Balthasar sees them, on the contrary, as the vessel and frame for the revelation of the glory of God, the doctrine of the ontological difference [between *Sein* and *Wesen, esse* and *essentia*] must be the heart of his philosophy. Not only does he dedicate the final chapter of the metaphysics volumes of the Aesthetic to it,[86] but he also sees the entire history of metaphysics under this aspect. Already in the early essay "Von den Aufgaben der katholischen Philosophie in der Zeit", the real distinction is portrayed as the center of Catholic philosophizing. In this context, von Balthasar does not see the difference merely as a difference between "factual" and "self-evident", between beings and being, between essence and being, but at root as the difference between universal being and God. *This* difference raises the decisive question in Western history of thought; it affects and penetrates also the transcendentals, and thus it makes revelation possible in the first place through the simultaneous distance and relation between the beauty of being and the glory of God.

This point opens up the view toward the third aspect of von Balthasar's philosophy of being, the one most frequently discussed, namely *analogia entis*. Without a doubt, he learned about analogy from Erich Przywara. Yet we saw how he overcomes Przywara's position in his book on Barth and is able to take analogy more deeply into the event of revelation, so that it turns for him more

[86] See "Vermächtnis und christlicher Auftrag", *Herrlichkeit* III/1:2, 943–83.

and more into a "cata-logy"[87] inasmuch as the ontological difference(s)
become increasingly evident in the light of, and are increasingly grounded
in, the trinitarian and Christological difference. Analogy has thereby become definitively more than a mere structure of creaturely metaphysics;
it is anchored in being itself, because it is rooted in God himself. We
understand von Balthasar's later hesitation about the "pure rhythmician"
Przywara.[88] It is only in theological terms that one can speak adequately
about *analogia entis.*

> God's gift of being is fullness and poverty at the same time: fullness as being
> without limits, poverty in archetypal fashion in God himself, because he
> knows no clinging to himself, poverty in the act of being, which is given as
> a gift, because this act exposes itself without defense to finite beings (because,
> here too, it does not cling to itself). The beings invented by God are
> likewise fullness and poverty at the same time: fullness in the power of
> sheltering and guarding the gift of the fullness of being (as "shepherd of
> being"), albeit poorly, because in limited fashion; poverty again in twofold
> fashion, inasmuch as what captures being experiences its inability to empty
> out the ocean in its small vessel and inasmuch as, taught by this experience,
> it understands "letting go" of being—i.e., letting be, letting stream, passing
> on the gift—as the inner fulfillment of the finite being. It is here that,
> through the greater dissimilarity between finite and infinite being, the
> positive face of *analogia entis* shows itself which makes of the finite a shadow,
> trace, simile and image of the infinite . . . [89]

But the Greatest Is Love

The text above, which is a condensed expression of von Balthasar's philosophy of being, points beyond itself to something he has said again and again in
unmistakable ways and which has, nevertheless, been heeded so little: being is
intelligible only as love; the philosophy of being points beyond itself to a
philosophy of love. This can be shown—in preliminary fashion—in three
ways: in the Western history of thought with its hinge in Plotinus and his
philosophy of love;[90] in the individual genesis of the understanding of being
and of the world—when the child awakes in the experience of the "you" and
"sees the absolute, 'God', first in his mother, in his parents;"[91] and finally,

---

[87] See *Theologik* II, 159ff. (The Greek preposition "ana" found in "ana-logy" often
signifies upward movement; the preposition "kata", by contrast, often signifies downward
movement—TRANS.)

[88] See *Herrlichkeit* III/1:1, 37.

[89] *Herrlichkeit* III/1:2, 956.

[90] See above, 156–57.

[91] *Herrlichkeit* III/1:2, 946.

catalogically, in God's gift of being which must be understood, not as a natural capacity, but as a freely given, personal gift.[92]

All of this is more than "personal ontology" (or even more superficially, "personalism"); it is more than mere dialogic.[93] It is a metaphysics of love, the outlines of which become clear in the counter-light of a theology of love. Love alone is "credible" because it is the only thing that is truly intelligible, in fact the only thing that is truly "rational", *"id quo maius cogitari nequit"*. For its wonder lies beyond all that can be constructed by thought, and yet it is no less real, in fact it is the ground of all that is real. Here lies, in both open and hidden fashion, the key to von Balthasar's whole work and thus also to his philosophy. Only when we succeed in seeing being as love—both as the poverty of eros and as selfless gift of self—only then do the perspectives of this immense thought come together into a simple and impressive form (*Gestalt*). Since being is love, the center of the trilogy is not the Aesthetic, but the Dramatic.

---

[92] See ibid., 954.

[93] If we raise the question of the sources of von Balthasar's dialogical philosophy of love, his "beloved friend Rudolf Allers" must be mentioned first; he saw the happiness and healing of the person in opening to the "you". "Whatever there may be of value in the following discussions has matured in this friendship", von Balthasar writes in the preface to his dissertation.

WOLFGANG TREITLER

True Foundations of Authentic Theology

Hans Urs von Balthasar's rich literary activity in his productive life culminated in a theological synthesis, the trilogy, on which he spent the final decades of his life. What we find formed (*gestaltet*) in this work is the enthusiastic will of a theological mission which was entirely captured by the divine glory (*kabod*), led into contemplation by that glory, and thus made to dwell in the solitude of the inescapable encounter with God's truth as it forms itself (*gestaltet*) in its drama.[1] This may be the reason why von Balthasar's work was always full of the youthfulness found in the saints, who never grow old in spirit and attitude. This youthfulness shines through his whole creativity, which he saw as a gift of God.[2] Here lies the inexhaustible power of the sustained breath that allowed von Balthasar to complete his main work with a consistent and stringent conception.

The trilogy, which realizes itself in the analogy of the series of transcendentals of truth, goodness, and beauty, conceived by von Balthasar in reverse order, unfolds God's one saving mystery *pro nobis* from the perspective of form (*Gestalt*)—corresponding to the analogate of beauty; of its self-realization—in the analogy of the good; and of its logic—analogous to truth. *The Glory of the Lord,*[3] *Theo-Drama,*[4] and *Theo-Logic,*[5] as well as the *Epilogue,*[6] which is an appendix rather than a conclusion, constitute a methodically specified circling around God's absolute self-revelation in its distinct aspects. These aspects can be formulated on the basis of the analogical character of the given in this world. Already a survey of the structure of this theological composition quickly shows that von Balthasar did not work in arbitrary fashion. It is, therefore, not out of place to ask this completely enthusiastic theologian what theological method he considers most appropriate to its divine content. Such a question is legitimate, further, because only a dialectical relation between

---

Translated by Michael Waldstein.

[1] See *Gelebte Kirche: Bernanos,* 3rd ed. (Einsiedeln-Trier: Johannes Verlag, 1988), 36.
[2] See "Jung bis in den Tod", in *Homo creatus est* (*Skizzen zur Theologie V*) (Einsiedeln: Johannes Verlag, 1986), 179.
[3] *Herrlichkeit. Eine theologische Ästhetik* (Einsiedeln: Johannes Verlag, 1961–1969).
[4] *Theodramatik* (Einsiedeln: Johannes Verlag, 1973–1983).
[5] *Theologik* (Einsiedeln: Johannes Verlag, 1985–1987).
[6] *Epilog* (Einsiedeln-Trier: Johannes Verlag, 1987).

content and form (*Form*) can ensure the true validity of the content as well as an authentic method developed on its basis. Of course, this thesis already includes the logical primacy of the content inasmuch as it becomes the mold of the form by entering the form and making it thus its own form. In this perspective one must say, "Christ is the form because he is the content."[7] We have already approached the center, and we shall first express this center in a thesis and then unfold it. Theology realizes itself with authenticity of method to the degree that it receives its form entirely from the content that molds it; in other words, theology must relate as theology in the Holy Spirit to the comprehensive space of creation and salvation history; theology must be a catalogically/analogically[8] mediated integration.

Catalogical Analogy

In his theological dissertation about Bonaventure, A. Gerken introduced the concept of catalogy.[9] It seemed to him necessary, because he saw that Bonaventure grasped something as the presupposition of theology that bears the *analogia entis* as well as the *analogia fidei* in itself, but can no longer be appropriately expressed by this category, threadbare as it has become in controversy. This presupposition lies in man's entry into God *per Christum* as the absolute mediator. The following implication is contained in this thesis. If this entry *per Christum* is inescapably tied to this God-man, then it must necessarily take on his form (*Form*); expressed in biblical language: he is the way, and no one comes to God, the Father, except through him (Jn 14:6). If he is the one who descended from the Father, the Son sent as man into the world, then the entry into God *per Christum* must be understood as a process of being drawn into this descent of the Son: as a *condescensio*[10] of human beings with the incarnate Son. *This* process is understood by Bonaventure as the positive presupposition of all valid theologizing. More specifically, even the theological form derives its measure from this *condescensio;* it must, therefore, have the form of descent within itself. The concept of "catalogy" is used, not that of *"kenosis"* (emptying) (i.e., "kenotic theology" versus "catalogy"), because, despite the close unity between content and form, one must maintain a distinction between defining the method's form and expressing the content.

As we have already stated: for von Balthasar everything in the realm of

---

[7] *Herrlichkeit* Bd. I: *Schau der Gestalt* (Einsiedeln: Johannes Verlag, 1961), 445.

[8] The Greek preposition *"ana"* contained in the traditional concept "analogy" usually signifies upward movement; by contrast, the preposition *"kata"* in the neologism "catalogy" usually signifies downward movement—TRANS.

[9] See A. Gerken, *Theologie des Wortes. Das Verhältnis von Schöpfung und Inkarnation bei Bonaventura* (Düsseldorf, 1963), 320–27.

[10] Ibid., 328.

method stands and falls with the fundamental presupposition that the content determines the form in a union with the form, which bears in itself the difference between the two. There is no abstract identity between them, but they mediate themselves to each other through each other in the primacy of the content. At the same time we must note that the primacy of the content cannot be seen in its determinacy except inasmuch as it appears as *self*-formed (*selbst*geformt), and thus as containing within itself that absolute mediatedness which cannot be comprehensively captured by any subsequent reflection on it. This point must be firmly maintained already at this stage, in order to resist even the appearance of any hubris of excessive claims made by method and its methodology. What remains true of method is this: its measure is not absolute knowledge, but faith which must always follow, even to the very end. It is in faith that theologians have their content; it is in faith that they have the form which is molded by *kenosis*. And inasmuch as theology relates itself to this kenotically-formed mediation, it does so in a primacy of catalogy. Catalogy as a theological concept of method formulates thus the awareness of a theological methodology that God's self-expression in the incarnate Son can only be read truly from above downward as a formed process of following the divine *kenosis* in theological re-flection (*Nach-Denken*).

It thereby becomes evident how much the concept of *kenosis* has become the fulcrum of both the content and the form of theology for von Balthasar. In ways that must be further described below, the concept of *kenosis* is in this respect a total determination of God by means of which God can be approached in his infinite mystery as absolute love. An important implication must be pointed out: since God's kenotic self-being happens out of infinite love in which God has room for his other person (*seinen Anderen*), the Son equal in essence in the unity of the Holy Spirit, as well as for his other (*sein Anderes*), creation, his *kenosis* has nothing to do with any necessity of divine self-mediation in virtue of which God would come to himself. Any alleged overview gained through the power of emptying *gnosis* is made impossible, because God's truth presents itself from itself as a mystery and resists rational resolution. There is, rather, a permanent mediation between truth, knowledge, and faith, and thus between knowledge and mystery; and this mediation resists even the impression of an insight that would abolish the mystery.[11]

The determination of *kenosis* is highly differentiated in von Balthasar. He speaks of three forms (*Formen*) of *kenosis,* the first of which is intratrinitarian and as such is the foundation of all the others. He says of this form, "This primal *kenosis* provides the fundamental possibility of God's other *kenoses* into the world, and they are mere consequences of it."[12] Von Balthasar defines it

---

[11] See *Theologik* I: *Wahrheit der Welt* (Einsiedeln: Johannes Verlag, 1985), 193–99.
[12] *Theodramatik* III: *Die Handlung* (Einsiedeln: Johannes Verlag, 1980), 308.

as the generation of the Son in the equality of essence; the eternal Father gives himself to this Son and thus foregoes the solitary possession of the divine nature on his behalf.[13]

The act in which God, who is two-and-one in the Holy Spirit,[14] exists kenotically is the intradivine presupposition for seeing the economic forms of divine descent as *kenoses* of God and not as mere displays and abstract appearances. For, only inasmuch as God is himself kenotic is he not surpassed by any economically determined descent and not "forced" to anything by any event which happens in his creation.

The second *kenosis,* namely creation, has thus found its place. According to von Balthasar, God descends in creation inasmuch as he gives another out of love the freedom of self-actualization, which reaches a negative peak in human beings where they do not want to owe themselves to God's primal *kenosis* within this kenosis, but want to actualize an abstract autonomy.[15] In other words, the unheard-of opposition against God in sin is a realized possibility of something that lies in the positing of free creatures. From God's perspective this positing, which is man, has kenotic character, and it has its hardness in this: that it not only can and did become other than God, but it even became opposed to God. Here lies the economic beginning of the theo-dramatic process of God's contact with sin, first in the covenant with Israel, the hard election of a people, in order to allow the power of sin as well as the superabundant power of God to actualize themselves in it: Israel's pro-existence.[16] "But my people did not listen to my voice; Israel did not want me. So I abandoned them to their hardened hearts, and they acted according to their own plans" (Ps 81:12f). The extended history of violating the covenant brought Israel into the "empty time",[17] at the end of which God descended in the unique one and thus entered his final engagement.

This is the third *kenosis,* according to von Balthasar, and at the same time the *kenosis* which is posited economically by the intradivine presupposition. The incarnate Son, who gives himself completely away on the Cross, stands in the world as God's own descent in which the final battle occurs in "the confrontation between the groundlessness of God's love and the groundlessness of human sin".[18] The peak of this *kenosis* is reached in the death of Christ

---

[13] See ibid, 306f.

[14] See "Offenbarung und Schönheit", in *Verbum Caro* (*Skizzen zur Theologie* I) 2nd ed. (Einsiedeln: Johannes Verlag, 1965), 124.

[15] See *Theodramatik* III, 306.

[16] See *Theodramatik* II: *Die Personen des Spiels,* 2. Teil: *Die Personen in Christus* (Einsiedeln: Johannes Verlag, 1978), 372.

[17] See *Herrlichkeit* Bd. III/2, 1. Teil: *Alter Bund* (Einsiedeln: Johannes Verlag, 1966), 337–45.

[18] *Theodramatik* III, 309.

where all hope in God is extinguished in God's emissary.[19] Here he suffers unsurpassable forsakenness by God in the descent of his mission *ad inferos*, and he thereby traverses *pro nobis* the infinite spaciousness which the trinitarian God is, in and for himself.

In this light it becomes clear how much the concept of *kenosis* becomes a key determination of God in von Balthasar, a key determination of God's theo-dramatics both within himself and in the history of salvation. If one reflects authentically on this key determination, it leads in free, divine necessity to a catalogically constituted form of theology. Analogy stands within catalogy and its dialectical presupposition. The presupposition is dialectical because it remains clear at the same time "that we have no access whatsoever to the immanent Trinity except from its economic self-revelation".[20]

In catalogic fashion we have thus found the framework and at the same time the explicit criterion for assigning the proper theological place to the formula of analogy which was formulated by the Fourth Lateran Council against Joachim of Fiore. The Council considered the analogical understanding of theological terms necessary, "for between Creator and creature no similitude can be noted, however great it may be, without noting a greater dissimilitude" (*quia inter creatorem et creaturam non potest tanta*[21] *similitudo notari quin inter eos maior sit dissimilitudo notanda* [Denzinger-Schönmetzer, no. 806]). Von Balthasar thus sustains this formula, but at the same time he attempts to give a catalogical foundation to it and thus to remove it from the false alternative between the analogy of being (*analogia entis*) and the analogy of faith (*analogia fidei*). This alternative is fruitless because on the one hand the proponents of *analogia entis* (e.g., Thomas Aquinas and Erich Przywara) are accused of attempting to secure for themselves an indissoluble relation of the world to God by means of a (neutral) concept of being,[22] while on the other hand the proponents of a radical *analogia fidei* or *verbi* are subject to the charge of negating creation as a ground of meaning,[23] a negation which Vatican I rejected in the well-known canon: "If anyone says the one true God, our Creator and Lord, cannot be known with certainty by the natural light of human reason through the things that are created: *anathema sit.*" (*Si quis dixerit, Deum unum et verum, creatorem et Dominum nostrum, per ea quae facta sunt*

---

[19] See *Herrlichkeit* Bd. III/2, 2. Teil: *Neuer Bund*, 2nd ed. (Einsiedeln: Johannes Verlag, 1988), 207–17.

[20] *Theologik* III: *Der Geist der Wahrheit* (Einsiedeln: Johannes Verlag, 1987), 192; cf. 127; cf. also *Theodramatik* III, 301f.

[21] In recent editions of DS, *"tanta"* has been struck from the text as inauthentic — TRANS.

[22] See, for example, Karl Barth, *Kirchliche Dogmatik* III: *Die Lehre von der Schöpfung*, 2 (Zurich, 1948), 330.

[23] See, for example, *Karl Barth. Darstellung und Deutung seiner Theologie*, 4th ed. (Einsiedeln: Johannes Verlag, 1976), 175–81.

naturalis rationis humanae lumine certo cognosci non posse: anathema sit [DS, 3026]).

This fruitless alternative could thus be overcome by "catalogical analogy", which at the same time integrates in itself the legitimate aspects proposed by *analogia entis* as well as by *analogia fidei*. Catalogical analogy thus affirms two things: first, it negates the formation of any analogy that sustains itself, as it were, by means of an abstract substrate of a concept of creation that has been degraded to pure nature, and that fails to reflect for its specificity on creation as the *kenosis* of God or within God and on its necessary determination by the event of the covenant in salvation history and the peak of that event in the salvific event, Jesus Christ. Rather, the positive formation of analogy, as the opening up of the world's truth and thus of its character as analogy to God, can only be gained in the vision of this world's being which is reached in the *condescensio* of God himself. This implies at the same time that, precisely because being proves to be analogous by way of cataloly, more is attributed to it than it is from itself and for itself, namely, analogous speech as speech capable of reality.[24] Secondly—and this point takes the analogy within creation into account—in this catalogical analogy there occurs at the same time the disclosure of what lies in being as a creation from God (and thus again catalogically), namely, that it must *have been* able to be prepared for the new reality which could no longer be deduced from it and which can therefore be determined in its truth only by way of cataloly. The use of the perfect tense in this statement derives its logic immediately from the cataloly of analogy: it is and was impossible to know ahead of time that to which creation, if it was to be adequately at its Creator's disposition, had to be further opened up in view of the history of salvation which occurs in creation and at the same time draws it into itself.

When von Balthasar thus gives a catalogical foundation to analogy, it is part of the stringency of his thought that he ties the methodical determination of cataloly to the content of *kenosis,* so much so that the criterion and measure of cataloly is found in the place in which content and form were one or, in other words, where God has become a man. Jesus Christ is, therefore, according to von Balthasar, the absolute analogy or the concrete analogy of being,[25] and thus all analogy is given a Christocentric determination by Christ. And yet, here too we must observe a triple step made by von Balthasar which lies in the stringency of the two aspects of catalogical analogy.

I. According to von Balthasar, Jesus Christ, as the eternal Son who descended from God, is the dwelling of the divine ideas for creation[26] as well as of their

---

[24] See J. Reikerstorfer, "Zur Logik analoger Glaubensrede", in H. Nagl-Docekal, ed., *Überlieferung und Aufgabe. Festschrift für E. Heintel,* 2 (Vienna, 1982), 426.

[25] See *Theologie der Geschichte,* 6th ed. (Einsiedeln: Johannes Verlag, 1979), 53f.

[26] See *Theologik* II: *Wahrheit Gottes* (Einsiedeln: Johannes Verlag, 1985), 146; also *Theodramatik* III, 308.

analogical character. This analogical character lies, more specifically, in the fact that, due to the so-called *distinctio realis* (i.e., the non-identity of essence and existence), creation cannot close itself in its finiteness; on the contrary, because it is, but need not necessarily be, it awaits in the wonder of its being another who founds it. Since, however, it is creation from God, precisely inasmuch as it stands, as finite, in the real distinction, its difference still says something analogously about God himself. The triune God bears within himself a difference of persons who thus cannot be reduced to each other such that one absorbs the other, just as created reality cannot gain power over its essence through its existence.[27] The individual being is not something closed in itself, and thus it is no *ens univocum,* yet neither is it something that has its concept completely outside of itself, and thus it is no *ens aequivocum.* It is a being which is open to the totality that transcends them, because it is posited by this totality in its determinateness. It is an *ens analogicum.* In other words, it has its unity in distinction from this totality which grants to it its own analogous totality; this proper totality consists in this: that it is identical with itself in such a way that in its own identity and self-possession the difference from the totality of Being becomes apparent, inasmuch as this totality needs the individual realization of beings, and conversely each being needs the totality of Being as that from which it receives its specificity.[28] The analogical character of this real distinction of being in relation to God is thus present, because it is posited from God and in God; it can, therefore, be correctly understood in its manifest specificity only in catalogical terms. Since the being, to the degree that it is not identical with itself, points to its final foundation, its character as *ens analogicum* allows one to see the breaking in of affirmative analogicity which can be approached in catalogical terms. In this way, the return in analogy to the foundation proves to be a step toward that primal reality from which one must then proceed to think. This is the trinitarian God whose divine persons are distinct from each other and stand in relation to each other in the unity of the divine essence: in the unity of the Spirit of both, the eternal Father "kenotically" generates the Son who is equal in essence. He thereby posits an eternal primal *kenosis* in which all economic *kenosis* is included, founded, and made possible. Also creation, as a kenotic act of God, is therefore included and founded in this primal *kenosis.* In this way the Son proves to be the dwelling of all ideas for creation and therefore, of course, the dwelling of their analogical character, as he himself is "analogical" toward the Father, "God from God, Light from Light, true God from true God, begotten, not created, one in essence with the Father" (similitude), but also "for us and for our salvation he came down from heaven, took flesh from

27 See *Theologik* II, 166–70.
28 See *Epilog,* 38–41.

the Virgin Mary and became man" (dissimilitude), as the Creed says. And what becomes visible in the economy is founded in God himself: the sameness of essence stands within the greater difference of persons which makes an abstract monotheistic coincidence unthinkable. At the same time, difference appears within the more embracing unity, because it is only in this way that it can exist in its relatedness as difference. It is in this sense that, according to von Balthasar, the Son must be conceived as the dwelling of the divine ideas for creation.

2. How does the affirmative character of analogy show itself in the descending Son in catalogic fashion? On the basis of the formula of analogy as well as the Christological definition of the Council of Chalcedon (DS 301f.), one can say:

In terms of analogy: in this determinate man, Jesus of Nazareth, in whom God is present in unsurpassable and unique manner as himself (*similitudo; indivise, inseparabiliter*—similarity; undividedly, inseparably[29]) God is revealed as the *Deus semper maior,* God who is ever greater (*maior dissimilitudo; inconfuse, immutabiliter*—greater dissimilitude; unconfusedly, unalterably).

In terms of catalogy: in the Son of God sent from God (true God from true God) the truth of free and sinful humanity before God becomes completely manifest (*similitudo; indivise, inseparabiliter*), but in such a way that God has nothing in common with sin but, as the one who infinitely towers above sin, he brings sin into an annihilating and saving judgment (*maior dissimilitudo; inconfuse, immutabiliter*).

Since, however, the definiteness of this catalogical analogy lies in the Son who descended, it remains clear that analogy is really founded in catalogy even here. Analogy, understood in these terms, goes completely through Jesus, the Christ, according to von Balthasar, and thus Christ himself is analogy in a catalogically discernible specificity: absolute analogy, thus *analogia entis,* but also *analogia libertatis* and *analogia salutis,* the absolute catalogical analogy.

3. An important implication follows: if Christ is absolute analogy, posited in a descent from God, then he must be understood as the totality that sums up everything in itself, and as the center that brings everything to its goal in itself and relates everything to itself. The totality of this absolute analogy refers to the inexpressible beginning (the divine ideas of creation posited in the eternal Son) as well as the execution (the mission of the God-man in the history of salvation), and to perfect reconciliation as the absolute result (being brought home into salvation into the Father's kingdom *per Christum*). We see here a

---

[29] According to the Council of Chalcedon, "one and the same Christ, Son, Lord, Only Begotten [is] acknowledged to be unconfusedly, unalterably, undividedly, inseparably (Latin: *inconfuse, immutabiliter, indivise, inseparabiliter*) in two natures . . ." (DS 302)—TRANS.

complete Christocentrism which results, according to von Balthasar, from the understanding of catalogical analogy. As the absolute figure (*Gestalt*) set up by the Father in the world and interpreted and expressed in the Holy Spirit and by it for all of history,[30] Christ becomes the fulcrum for everything which can be called theological analogy, because everything is gathered in him. It remains true that a philosophical analogy *remoto Christo* (on the supposition that Christ is removed) possesses its legitimacy as a guardian of the mystery that remains unspeakable to such philosophical analogy. However, the theologian knows about the necessary Christocentrism and must reflect about it. Von Balthasar expresses the point from the perspective of the history of salvation and revelation as follows: "That Christ is this center—and not merely the beginning, the initiator of a form (*Gestalt*) that goes on to unfold itself independently—lies in the specific character of the Christian religion and its contrast with all others: Judaism does not have such a center; neither Abraham nor Moses nor one of the prophets is the figure (*Figur*) around which everything else is ordered. Christ, however, is the form (*Form*), because he is the content. This is absolutely true, because the only Son of the Father is he . . . "[31]

Since Christ, according to von Balthasar, is such a totality, namely a protological, temporal, and eschatological summation, this requires a theological form as integration which is realized catalogical analogy that attempts to do justice to the claim of absolute revelation in its specificity. Von Balthasar expresses this in a simple saying when he writes, "The one who sees more truth is more deeply right."[32] This statement is free of misunderstanding only if and when the criterion of integration, which has been found here in catalogical analogy, has been clarified. Its measure is the divine Spirit, and the freedom of that Spirit prevents integration from freezing into a spiritual integralism: integration is not concerned with a system of theoretical propositions.[33] Such a system, according to von Balthasar, is based on the fallacious assumption that revelation is presented as a compendium of propositions to be believed. This is the assumption on which the spirit of systems depends, the spirit that forces everything into itself and in which the form of the system is "placed above the content, power above the Cross".[34]

This is not the aim of integration as realized catalogical analogy. Rather, such integration becomes the negation of all integralist temptations due to its catalogy as and in analogy that has its measure in the absolute analogy, in Jesus

---

[30] See *Theodramatik* III, 142–50.

[31] *Herrlichkeit* I, 445; see also *Licht des Wortes. Skizzen zu allen Sonntagslesungen* (Trier: Paulinus-Verlag, 1987), 142.

[32] *Epilog*, 11.

[33] See "Integralismus", in *Wort und Wahrheit* 18 (1963), 738.

[34] Ibid., 739.

Christ as absolute totality. He is totality, because creation has been posited in him, as we have seen. However, von Balthasar does not rest content with this theological assertion, but carries it out in detail for the Son in his mission. According to von Balthasar, he is the real recapitulation of the inorganic (he calls himself the cornerstone), of the vegetative ("I am the vine, "... the bread of life", etc.), of the animal (the scapegoat driven out of the city), of the human (the Incarnation of the Son realized itself through all the stages of human life from conception to death), of the religious (he stood in the religion of the fathers, and he is, at the same time, the final divine word-form [*Wort-Gestalt*]), of the historical (fulfilled promise), and of the cosmic (everything consists in him and is through him and for him),[35] and thus he is the eschatological fullness of all as the risen one who sent his Spirit. This unity can be characterized as Spirit-Christ,[36] and Christ thereby expresses the permanent presence of his eschatological fulfillment in time, which is a presence of the nature of Spirit and only in this way a fitting presence. In this way Christ in his concreteness is the Spirit of theology so that, for this reason, one must necessarily speak of a theology in the Holy Spirit.

Theology in the Holy Spirit

Theology in the Holy Spirit is required for two reasons, according to von Balthasar. First, Christ liquified his own totality completely into the interpretive Spirit that testifies to him, because he completed the utterance of the Word, which he is himself.[37] According to von Balthasar, "the Spirit knows the voice of God in the Word of the Son (in fact, he lets it resound over the whole world) and he gives to the responding human voice its correct meaning and sound." This implies "that a theology, however learned or simple it may be, can be authentically developed only in the Holy Spirit".[38]

Secondly this implies the following: if theology does not have its object without faith, if faith is brought about by the divine Spirit,[39] and if theology is the appropriate reflection of that Spirit,[40] then it can only be true if it realizes itself in the same Spirit of faith.

This means that if the absolute form of revelation (*Offenbarungsgestalt*) is, as

---

[35] See, e.g., *Das Weizenkorn,* 3rd ed. (Einsiedeln: Johannes Verlag, 1957), 56; *Herrlichkeit* III/2:2, 70f.; *Herrlichkeit.* Bd. II: *Fächer der Stile.* I. Teil: *Klerikale Stile,* 3rd ed. (Einsiedeln: Johannes Verlag, 1984), 51–55.

[36] See *Theologik* III, 64.

[37] Ibid.

[38] Ibid., 26.

[39] See "Wahrheit und Leben", *Concilium* 3 (1967): 41.

[40] Cf. also K. Hemmerle, *Theologie als Nachfolge. Bonaventura—ein Weg für heute* (Freiburg, 1975).

we have just seen, an antecedent given for theology within faith, and if it is true of faith that it does not happen in fatalistic manner, but awaits free acceptance inasmuch as it is brought about by the Spirit[41] and is thus in need of conscious decision, then theology stands under the same claim inasmuch as its foundation lies in a faith that mediates the absolute form of the word (*Wortgestalt*). Its only appropriate assimilation stands thus on the foundation of the same decision of faith. Von Balthasar expresses this point as follows: "It belongs to the nature of this, and *only* this, science that its scientific objectivity rests on the decision of faith, that (from the point of view of theology) there can be no neutral objectivity in order to treat the object of faith also without faith or in a way that abstracts from faith or lack of faith."[42]

In order to be able to recognize the absolute form of revelation, which communicates itself to faith, the corresponding organ of knowledge is required, namely faith, in which alone the truth of the form is communicated in the impact of its glory. This very correspondence between the object of knowledge and the organ of knowledge which is formed (*gebildet*) through the object turns out to be theological scientific objectivity. This objectivity consists in this: that its truth occurs in the communication of truth to the believing theologian—there is no other theologian[43]—by the Holy Spirit, which is the one Spirit. By way of conclusion, we thus face the problem which organically arises for theology from catalogical-analogical integration, namely, how theology, faced with the one Spirit, can legitimate and sustain itself as plural in its exercise.

Does what von Balthasar intends with his characterization of catalogical analogy not lead to contradictions in the face of all the necessary implications that lie in it? The one Spirit and the multiplicity of theology: if one takes both of these together, does this not lead either to the dissolution of the one Spirit of God, to his transformation into an empty postulate, or to a uniformity of theological thought which loses its power and perspectival nature to the empty repetition of one and the same thing?

First of all, the thesis must be sustained that the one Holy Spirit gives the one interpretation which is the only one appropriate to God's absolute form-word, for "the Spirit was, as it were, the most attentive listener of the Word"[44] who is therefore also able to universalize it in the correct manner.[45] Now, no finite concept is able to master the infinity of this form-word which

---

[41] See "Fides Christi", in *Sponsa Verbi* (*Skizzen zur Theologie II*) 2nd ed. (Einsiedeln: Johannes Verlag, 1971), 53–64.

[42] *Einfaltungen. Auf Wegen christlicher Einigung*, 4th ed. (Einsiedeln-Trier: Johannes Verlag, 1988), 46f.

[43] See *Theologie der drei Tage* (Einsiedeln: Benziger, 1969), 58.

[44] "Wort, Schrift, Tradition" in *Verbum Caro*, 12.

[45] See ibid., 17.

has been revealed to us and becomes manifest to us as a permanently valid mystery. Already the theologians of the New Testament attest this fact inasmuch as they place everything and everybody "into the never bounded space of an ever greater truth",[46] which not only makes different approaches possible, but also demands them. Choosing these approaches is not subject to the willful arbitrariness of the individual, but to the communication of God by the Holy Spirit. In the Spirit, God is powerful enough to "present his own hermeneutics."[47] Theology comes in view here as a question of mission, precisely in the face of the problem of God's one Spirit and the multiplicity of approaches to the one mystery of the absolute form-word. It is the mission of individuals, according to von Balthasar, that they labor, each from their own necessary perspective, for the glory of theology rooted in the glory of God.[48] They are fulfilling from their perspective the one service of theological meditation. The multiplicity of perspectives is thus rooted in the fact that the one Holy Spirit providentially assigns the expression of the absolute revelation in each case to a determinate time, i.e., that he gives it to certain persons who must think, speak, and pray according to their situation.

Nevertheless, von Balthasar excludes the possibility that the synthesis of all finite and momentary expressions would produce the "absolute concept" which would still end up dissolving the mystery. This dissolution is excluded because God's truth is itself infinitely unfolded; it is "symphonic". "That the Christian truth is symphonic is perhaps the most necessary truth which must be proclaimed and taken to heart today. Symphony does not at all mean saccharine harmony without tension. Great music is always dramatic; it is always a compression and higher resolution of tensions."[49] This form of the dramatic manifests itself theologically precisely at the point where the perspectival nature of theology becomes more intense: for to the degree in which the perspectives become more comprehensive and more numerous, and in which the ways of access become wider, to that degree the revealed absolute mystery shines up more clearly: *Deus semper maior*,[50] not only, von Balthasar insists, for us and for our power of knowledge, but also for God himself.[51] For otherwise one would always have to assume a not yet

[46] "Einheit und Vielheit neutestamentlicher Theologie", *Internationale katholische Zeitschrift Communio* 12 (1983): 108.
[47] "Heilsgeschichtliche Überlegungen zur Befreiung", in K. Lehmann, ed., *Theologie der Befreiung* (Einsiedeln: Johannes Verlag, 1977), 108.
[48] See "Der Ort der Theologie", in *Verbum Caro*, 171.
[49] *Die Wahrheit ist symphonisch. Aspekte des christlichen Pluralismus* (Einsiedeln: Johannes Verlag, 1972), 13.
[50] See *Theodramatik* II/1, 235.
[51] See *Theologik* III, 146.

revealed remnant of God that would make him a riddle, not an absolute revealed mystery.

Accordingly, theology will never possess its mystery in a final way in a concept, neither in theological-aesthetic concepts, nor in those of transcendental theology or liberation theology or dialectical theology, nor in those of historical criticism. For this mystery remains the one, it is communicated to the Church in the Holy Spirit; she approaches it with her thought in the Holy Spirit in ways that differ in each case.

This is what the catalogical analogy means: in von Balthasar it is understood as the linguistic expression of the *condescensio* into which the individual is taken as an elect. The determinateness of election is no longer his own concern; it is enough if he knows about it and practices again "a praying and kneeling theology".[52] However, he will know about it only if he also formulates election in the catalogical primacy and thereby follows the deed God performed upon him as it has come to be for him in God's Spirit. All theological content thus offers itself to thought in catalogical/analogical form; it is a content which God brings about in the individual through Christ in the one Spirit.

We see thus that von Balthasar introduces an eminently theological method whose claim stands high without limit and that nevertheless thereby reminds us insistently of what makes theology Christian theology. It does not forego mediations because the proven certainty is inscribed in it that the negation of mediations leads to bad and indefensible forms of positivism. If the beginning and the forming principle (*Formprinzip*) of the method is God's primal *kenosis*, it is, at the same time, certain that, "in order to approach the trinitarian event in God, there is no other way than to feel one's way back to the mystery of the absolute from what is revealed in God's *kenosis* in the theology of the covenant—and thus of the Cross."[53] In view of this "way" the theologian is compelled, according to von Balthasar, to think of theology in the form of *condescensio* (catalogically) and of co-rising (analogically). And according to the totality of the absolute analogy, which is the divine Son, this means that theology is a form of catalogical/analogical integration. The truth and determinacy of the form of this integration realized by individual theologians lies in the appropriation of the mystery through the one Holy Spirit. Each individual expression will find its criterion in its openness to other theological approaches and in its capacity to remain open to the ever determinate, mysterious God and to liberate all meditation toward him rather than closing it in itself.

This presents the specific service of theology as von Balthasar saw it and defined it methodologically. For this reason it is no accident that his theology

[52] "Theologie und Heiligkeit", in *Verbum Caro*, 224.
[53] *Theodramatik* III, 301.

contains the immediate enthusiasm of the divine Word not only in its content, but also in its form and style. We can thus follow P. Eicher's insight, with certain restrictions, when he pointedly writes with reference to von Balthasar's understanding of theology, "... the Logos which reflects *out of* the received Word of God (believing reason) about God (general rational reason) becomes here a Logos that speaks quite consciously only *out of* the Word and that gives itself up willingly in order to give voice and hearing to the Logos of Jesus Christ himself."[54] The fact, however, that von Balthasar was able to reflect this specific immediacy to the absolute word-form of God in methodological terms shows the great relevance of this approach for the doing of all theology. The claim of catalogical/analogical integration does not favor a mere intuition or incantation, but it stands for true justification of a theology that must legitimate itself in scientific terms.

---

[54] P. Eicher, *Offenbarung. Prinzip neuzeitlicher Theologie* (Münich, 1977), 341f.

LOUIS DUPRÉ

The Glory of the Lord

HANS URS VON BALTHASAR'S THEOLOGICAL AESTHETIC

Divine Form

Hans Urs von Balthasar's seven-volume *Herrlichkeit,* completed in 1969, ranks among the foremost theological achievements of our century. The whole work has now been competently translated into English under the general title *The Glory of the Lord.*[1] The important first part, *Seeing the Form,* defines the scope, method, and intention of the entire work, and includes a general theological discussion of what the author calls "the form of the Lord Christ". Volumes two and three contain historical elaborations of this aesthetic ideal— "reflected rays of glory" (II, 13)—by representative theologians of the early and medieval tradition (II: *Studies in Theological Style: Clerical Styles*) and by modern poets and "lay" thinkers (III: *Lay Styles*). Volumes four and five deal with the broader metaphysical context in which the Christian form could appear or which, by its absence in the modern age, prevented it from appearing, while six and seven treat the theology of the Old and of the New Testament. Theology in this majestic work fully regains the central position which it held in the unfolding of Western culture. It extends far beyond the borders of the intellectual ghetto into which an increasingly secular climate has sequestered it. To grasp its full scope as von Balthasar does we must return to Plato and Aristotle, for whom it referred to what we now call metaphysics, as well as to ancient Israel where society itself formed the source and content of all religious speculation. From this wider perspective von Balthasar approaches the New Testament in a masterful spiritual exegesis but not before having first studied the successive, expanding circles of its impact through the centuries in

Communio 16 (Fall 1989). © 1989 by *Communio: International Catholic Review.*
     The Glory of the Lord: A Theological Aesthetics (San Francisco: Ignatius Press, 1982–1991). References to the volumes translated into English will be by Roman numeral for the volume and by Arabic number for the page. The English titles are: I: *Seeing the Form* (1982); II: *Studies in Theological Style: Clerical Styles* (1984); III: *Studies in Theological Style: Lay Styles* (1986); IV: *The Realm of Metaphysics in Antiquity* (1989); V: *The Realm of Metaphysics in the Modern Age* (1991), VI: *Theology: The Old Covenant* (1991); and VII: *Theology: The New Covenant.* The translation, a joint American-British enterprise, stands under the (1990), direction of Joseph Fessio, S.J. and John Riches. All volumes were published in the United States by Ignatius Press. All volumes were published in German by Johannes Verlag in Einsiedeln (1961–1969).

the Greek and Latin Fathers, scholastic philosophy, and modern metaphysics, and, most outstandingly, in his sensitive analyses of great literary works from Dante to the present. At the basis of this comprehensive reflection on our entire Christian culture lies a judgment on the present as well as a hope for the future. Whichever verdict history may reserve for von Balthasar's critique and expectation, the unique conjuncture of a staggering erudition, a refined taste, and a powerful vision, secures for his accomplishment both timeliness and survival.

At the center of von Balthasar's enterprise stands a simple idea. By assuming human nature God transformed the very meaning of culture. Henceforth all forms have to be measured by the supreme form of the Incarnation. Theology itself, indissolubly united to this visible form, thereby acquired an aesthetic quality. It would have to show in its very structure and diction "the diversity of the Invisible radiating in the visibleness of Being of the world" (I, 431). In fact, however, it has moved in the opposite direction. It has become satisfied with a rational interpretation of Scripture (exegesis), of nature and history (fundamental theology), and of the ecclesiastical tradition (dogmatic theology). By thus neglecting the *form* of the Incarnation it has failed to do justice to revelation itself as Christians have concretely received it. The form thereby becomes reduced to a mere sign pointing toward a mystery that lies entirely beyond it. For von Balthasar, on the contrary, the revelation in Christ manifests a divine "super-form" (I, 432). His theological project is intended to reintegrate grace and nature, thought and feeling, body and mind, culture and theology within a synthetic, comprehensive, theological reflection on form.

This, then, is what *Glory* (*Herrlichkeit*), the title word that carries the theme throughout these seven volumes, denotes: "The divinity of the Invisible radiating in the visibleness of Being of the world" (I, 431). The important introduction to the first volume on metaphysics explains: "The openness of every beautiful form, which always expresses more in the most perfect and determined expression than what goes into the thing formed itself (namely, the infinity of glory), makes the beautiful as such available as a form of revelation" (IV, 34). As it functions in the revelation, aesthetic form does not arbitrarily restrict what in itself is formless. Rather than pointing to an Absolute beyond itself, it *manifests* the divine "super-form" (I, 432). In Christ, God himself appears as expressive in his very nature. The aesthetic form, then, lies at the very heart of the Christian mystery: it reveals substantially and definitively (IV, 33). "The kingdom of *beauty* ... is as a whole, as being, transparent to a divine *esse subsistens* [subsistent Being] only comprehensible as *mysterium,* which is, as a hidden primordial ground, radiant glory" (IV, 375).

But can theology ever become genuinely "aesthetic"? Does it not belong to the essence of the Christian message not to take the form of this perishing world as definitive, much less as divine? Is a "theological aesthetic" not a contradiction? In the subjective sense which the new theory of beautiful form, characteristically called *aesthetics* (i.e., science of perception), acquired in the eighteenth century, undoubtedly! For when that term began to be used for referring to a theory of beautiful form, it shifted the meaning from the form itself to a particular mode of *perceiving:* the human subject achieves a temporary harmony with the perceived object by endowing it with its own interiority. In that short-lived union, form becomes spiritually transparent while the human subject becomes intimately united with the world or some part of it. But such a subjective perspective allows no theological aesthetic, since form becomes reduced to self-created "inner-worldly" beauty (IV, 35). At best it may yield an "aesthetic theology", not basically different from Matthew Arnold's vision of Christianity.

But von Balthasar unambiguously repudiates the "impressionist" subjectivism of an aesthetics based more on the harmonious relation which the human subject establishes toward the form than on the form's intrinsic quality of radiance. For him, as for the Greek Fathers (and, indeed, for Plotinus), the light of beauty breaks forth from the form itself, not from the subject's perception of it (IV, 31). Beauty, as a transcendental quality belongs to Being itself and is, indeed, its primary manifestation. This ontological nature, the opposite of any aestheticism, disposes it to reveal the depth of God's presence in all forms. Modern *aesthetics* has lost its ontological significance. Its subjectivist attitude has turned away from that "sure light of Being" (St. Thomas), and has reduced poetry and art to formalist exercises or private expressions, marginal to the deeper concerns of human existence. Since religion is concerned with ultimacy, poetic and artistic form have ceased to serve as its primary expressions.

Clearly aware of this modern predicament, von Balthasar defends an earlier theory capable of revitalizing aesthetics as well as of restoring a more holistic concept of theology. Not in the subject, but in Being itself, does the aesthetic illumination of form originate. But, unlike today's philosophical critics of modern subjectivism, von Balthasar sees the ontological culminating in the theological. Beautiful form, beyond manifesting Being, reveals the non-manifest depth of a divine presence (I, 443). "Being itself here unveils its final countenance, which for us receives the name of trinitarian love; only with this final mystery does light fall at last on that other mystery: why there is Being at all and why it enters our horizon as light and truth and goodness and beauty" (I, 158). Yet if not even Being itself provides a grammar for determining the structure of that ultimate mystery, how can it be said to manifest at all? Not until the end of volume two does the author explain what a manifestation of God's hiddenness must mean. With St. Bonaventure he agrees that the essence of form lies not in its being a potential object of sense perception, but rather in its intrinsic power *to express* — whatever mode of appearance the expression may take. In the Incarnation God essentially expresses himself in a manner that allows us to

speak of a *divine form,* even though the expressing God remains hidden within
the expressive form. What the form reveals in Christ and through him in all
finite forms, is not a direct "resemblance" between the visible and the invisible,
but that the divine source of this expression in visible form is itself *formally*
structured.

> It is in their being light and in their act of self-expression that the substances'
> resemblance to God lies; in this they express God, though it is rather he who
> expresses himself in them. This mystery of light as the creative power of
> revelation is broken up into the colors in their various illuminations, and
> into the forms, which ultimately are only various stamps of expression (II,
> 346).

What any given form reflects, then, is not one attribute of God or another, but
his inexhaustible, ever mysterious expressiveness itself.

Bonaventure declares the world a *vestigium,* a "trace", and Cusanus a
"cipher", not an image, because God resembles none of the things that
manifest him. The various, often conflicting forms reveal him as the one
whose very nature is expressive. In the *Itinerarium Mentis,* Bonaventure measures the beauty of visible things by their power to manifest an archetypal
reality that transcends all form. Nor does this transcendent reference destroy
the finite's own expressiveness, for the form constitutes no attempt to copy its
divine source, but to manifest a God who remains hidden, and precisely in its
ability to do so lies its *formal* (i.e., aesthetic) perfection. Beings appear
theologically "beautiful" not through a particular proportion of their being,
but simply through their being itself. As a theological category, beauty is a
transcendental attribute of Being itself (I, 30). No more than truth or goodness
or unity, can it be lifted out of the totality of Being to mark only the
privileged exception.

Still, the reader wonders, why should we call any form expressive of the
unmanifest Mystery "beautiful", particularly when that divine life in the
ultimate expression of Christ's Cross conflicts with accepted aesthetic standards?
"The Christ *epiphaneia* of God has nothing about it of the simple radiance of
the Platonic sun of the good. It is an act in which God utterly freely makes
himself present, as he commits to the fray the last divine and human depths of
love" (II, 12). At this point one either abandons the project of a theological
aesthetic as being too far removed from the common understanding of aesthetics,
or one rebuilds it on a wholly different footing. Von Balthasar has followed
the latter course. Rather than rendering his theological aesthetic a *subspecies* of
that tradition which has developed from Plato to Heidegger, he has set up an
analogous order that, while sharing the general norms of expressive form,
establishes its own laws from above, so to speak. As in Eckhart's theory and in
that of most Christian mystics, this analogy between the divine and the

human order does not move in an ascending line (from the creatures to God), but in a descending one that views creation in a divine, revealed light. Von Balthasar's theology of form plunges its roots more deeply in the New Testament than in a philosophical aesthetic. The suffering and death of Christ, far from being the exception they would be in a worldly aesthetic, here become the *model*. They have, in fact, opened new form perspectives on "the nocturnal side of existence" for which earlier theories had no place. The entire volume on the New Testament (VII) presents the divine glory as essentially consisting in the *kenosis* of God's Word. That Word was from all eternity destined to silence—first in Christ's hidden life, then in his Passion and death, finally in the descent into hell. Cross and damnation thereby come to belong to the very essence of divine form. A theological aesthetic describes how God's perfection becomes *actually* manifest, and Scripture reveals it to consist in the "correspondence between obedience and love, between self-emptying into hiddenness and being raised up into manifestness" (VII, 261).

Yet, if the *analogia crucis* is to penetrate our entire vision of the real, it must, at some point, link up with an idea of God based upon the *analogia entis*. Von Balthasar agrees with Barth that a Christian aesthetic must start from the Cross. He differs from him, however, in not admitting any definitive *caesura* between this theology of form and a philosophical aesthetic. Revelation sets up a new analogy which, rather than separating it from transcendental aesthetics, establishes new norms and criteria for it. Do the consciousness and the language available within our culture still allow an aesthetic of grace? Has "the perspicuity of the *analogia entis*" not been destroyed by the modern world picture? To be sure, to the pious mind there continues to exist an analogy "from above", descending from God to the creature—and in this respect the believer may perceive God in the creature today as much as before. John of the Cross, at the end of *The Living Flame,* exclaims: "Here lies the remarkable delight of this awakening: the soul knows creatures through God, and not God through creatures. This amounts to knowing the effects through their cause, and not the cause through its effects" (IV, 4). But a theological *aesthetic* requires more than an inward vision: it must be able to *present the world as manifesting God's presence.* This requires the analogy from above to be complemented by some analogy from below. Only the latter can provide the symbols and images to concretize that theological vision and extend it to the entire world. In modern culture this has become exceedingly difficult. More and more, faith tends to depend exclusively on revelation and/or on the inner experience. God has to be known through his revelation and through his inner voice, so to speak, in isolation from the world. The battle cry of the Reformation—*sola fide*—first expressed this mentality of the modern age. Even the Catholic representative figures presented in volume three perceived the natural link between God and cosmos as broken. John of the Cross and

Pascal resist the *sola fide* doctrine by stressing the inner *experience* of faith, not by reconnecting faith with cosmic experience.

Form and the Mystery of Being

Theological *form* has increasingly come to be reduced to the "formal" aspect of the expression rather than revealing itself in the very experience of the cosmic structure. Where the link between God and cosmos has ceased to be visible, the theological expressiveness of worldly form becomes impaired. When von Balthasar criticizes Pascal's "harsh dualism of the future . . . between science and supernatural piety" (III, 189), he describes in fact a common situation which threatens the success of his own enterprise. Our world is no longer illuminated by the light of grace—whatever divine light reaches the modern believer's mind illuminates mostly the inner realm of the soul. The separation between the realms of nature and grace, as well as the "desincarnation" of all theology in the modern age, are not coincidental phenomena. They express a separation which exists *de facto* in the modern mind. How does von Balthasar evaluate these restrictions imposed by our age?

The first obstacle blocking the kind of aesthetic vision of reality as a whole required for a theological aesthetic is the loss of the *mystery of Being.* At the end of the Middle Ages philosophy ceased to be metaphysical and became scientific—either a positive science or an *a priori,* deductive one. In the important introduction to volume four, von Balthasar outlines the conditions for a genuine metaphysical awareness of Being within which alone the universality of God's glory may become manifest. By metaphysics, the study of the Being of beings, von Balthasar understands, in the Greek tradition, not merely the purely rational mode with which we have come to identify philosophy, but any reflection on ultimate foundations, including the mythical and the poetic. All fundamental thought on Being as such and on its transcendental attributes of truth, goodness, and beauty holds metaphysical significance. Hence Homer and Virgil, Cervantes and Tasso, even Goethe, Hölderlin, and Rilke feature in von Balthasar's discussion of metaphysics next to Plato, Aristotle, Descartes, and Kant. Somewhat surprisingly, von Balthasar even includes the mystics of the late Middle Ages, Eckhart, Tauler, Ruysbroeck, Julian, Catherine of Siena, and Catherine of Genoa. In his view, all of them probe Being in its totality rather than remaining satisfied with articulating the content of Christian revelation, as theologians do, or with discussing the subjective constitution of objectivity or value, as modern philosophy tends to do. One may consider such a comprehensive list arbitrary. But under it lies the solid idea that genuine metaphysics requires a thematic awareness of the total mystery of Being. Only to a reflection that approaches reality from a sense of wonder about the mysteriousness of Being, can the beautiful remain an essential attribute of Being. The sense of mystery and the transcendental nature of beauty go hand in hand. Without it the aesthetic becomes reduced to the effect of a subjective disposition.

> ... From Homer and Pindar, through Plato and Aristotle, Plotinus, the Christian early medieval period and high Middle Ages, up to the Renaissance and the Baroque period; we term this intuition here 'transcendental aesthetics', in the sense that the *kalon* (as what is whole, sound, shining, beautiful) is one of the transcendental determinations of being *qua* being. The biblical revelation can and must enter into dialogue with such transcendental aesthetics; by the same token it can have no interest in a partial aesthetics that is confined within the boundaries of this world (IV, 19–20).

Such a dialogue alone secures the continuity of the aesthetic of revelation, as it creates the space needed for receiving the divine form. In its transcendental beauty, Being radiates its fundamental graciousness (*"Im Dichterischen wird die Welt als Charis offenbar"*[2]) within which alone the divine form is able to reveal its own radiance. Form and Being remain indissolubly united, because any form—even that of revelation—must be viewed in the totality of Being if it is to possess any ontological power (*Seinshaft*) at all (IV, 31).

In its formal aspect Christian revelation constitutes a contracted representation of the Absolute that sheds a new light on Being as such. With other forms it shares an aesthetic radiance. Yet it differs from them in that the revealed form not merely *points* to the Absolute, but expresses it centrally and definitively. (III/1, 34). By the same token it transforms our contemplation of the mystery of Being itself, as well as displacing all other forms we perceive in its light. Comparing its effect to the inherited Greek view of the cosmos, we see it breaking down the relative identity between that cosmos and its absolute foundation. Henceforth only one revealing *Subject* directs the manifestation of the cosmos. How the cosmos manifests the ultimate mysteriousness of Being must, in the final analysis, be learned from that divine Subject itself. Its intradivine being is not revealed in the sheer radiance of the cosmos alone. With the Christian revelation the transcendental aesthetic assumes a wholly new perspective, one not given in the mind's natural aesthetic perceptiveness. Henceforth that natural perceptiveness fulfills a necessary yet mediating role. This transformation of our perspective on Being revolutionized Western metaphysics. It took the Fathers and scholastic philosophers centuries to implement it within the traditional frame of thought. By the time of the High Middle Ages they had succeeded in doing so.

Their philosophical successors were less successful in coping with the

---

[2] *Herrlichkeit*. Bd. III/1: *Im Raum der Metaphysik* (1965), 24. This volume corresponds to the English volumes four and five.

process of disintegration which, at the end of the Middle Ages, eroded the metaphysical frame itself. Von Balthasar presents Nicholas of Cusa (fifteenth century) as the last metaphysician to attempt a synthesis between Christian revelation and cosmic manifestation. In his magisterial work we already perceive that return to an older, pre-Christian cosmic theology which began during his lifetime. At the dawn of the modern era, Plato and Plotinus who had, of course, played an important part all through the Christian ages, were assigned the new, even more substantial task of reestablishing the divine immanence in that cosmos of which late medieval theology had deprived it. A line of religious thought begun in Eckhart had tended to skip the cosmic reality in its attempt to establish an unmediated union of the soul with God. What accounts for this was less an ill-directed theology than a spiritual response to a philosophy (and philosophically oriented theology) that had lost touch with the original *mystery* of Being and reduced the world to a mere effect of an arbitrary divine causality. The return to antiquity that marked the humanist movement constituted on a different level a response to the same predicament: a cry for help uttered by a Christian culture that had felt its traditional foundation slipping away. Where Being lost its mystery the cosmos allowed no more genuine divine immanence. Hence the split between, on the one hand, an unworldly theology—spiritual-empirical or dogmatic-positive— and, on the other, a new philosophy which, mostly based on pre-Christian sources, defended a cosmic immanence of God that bypassed the revolutionary transformation in that immanence wrought by the biblical revelation. The former led to an acosmic kind of theology, the latter to a pantheistic or at least, by Christian norms, insufficiently transcendent, view of the relation between God and the world. Both excluded the very possibility of a properly Christian aesthetic. As soon as philosophy acquired a method that enabled it not to rely on any sources of reality outside the philosophizing mind itself, speculation about God soon lost the cosmic character which had briefly marked it during the Renaissance. It then came to consist in a purely *a priori* form of ratiocination only to reveal in the end (late eighteenth century) what it had been all along: a titanic human construction (V, 248).

Theology proper has suffered no less from the disappearance of its metaphysical background. While once revelation constituted "the inwardness of absolute Being, the mystery of its life and love" (I, 148), breaking forth as "the self-revelation of the mystery of Being itself" (I, 145), by the end of the Middle Ages theology had become detached from the natural mystery of Being. Natural "piety of Being" (I, 447) ceased to mediate "supernatural" piety. Yet only if grace fully *penetrates* the natural order, can finite form become able to express the divine. That divine life itself, as revelation teaches in the mystery of the Trinity is, more than an absence of form, an "infinitely determined super-form" (I, 482) which introduces a new mode of divine *presence* in the form of nature.

Following de Lubac's critique of the supernatural as an independent order of the real, von Balthasar founds his theological aesthetics on a more intimate harmony of nature and grace than the one that has dominated the theology of the past four centuries. Though the divine mystery remains *intrinsically* concealed—the more God becomes manifest in his revelation, the more he remains hidden—a revelation of the divine manifests human nature, and indeed all of nature, to itself. Conversely, nature, if seen in the revealed perspective of the Cross, reveals something of God's very being. Thus Irenaeus, with whom Christian theology originated, insists, against Valentine's gnostic spiritualism, on seeking the figure of grace in nature itself. The flesh is "not without the artistic wisdom and power of God", but "God's hands are accustomed, as they have been from the time of Adam, to give their work a rhythm and hold it strongly, to support and place it where they choose" (*Adv. Haereses* 2, 330–31, cited in II, 73).

The Witness of Theology

Von Balthasar devotes his second volume (on "Theology: Clerical Styles") to exploring the often surprising way in which ancient theologians have developed the theme of the transformation of nature by divine grace. He has deliberately selected theologians who have been traditionally interpreted as challenging such a transformation, either by their negative theory (Denys the Areopagite), or by the opposition of grace to a corrupt nature (Augustine), or by the one-sidedly rational quality of their thought (Anselm). His inspired discussion of Denys shakes long-established positions by a straightforward defense of this controversial writer. Instead of regarding him as a rather too faithful follower of Proclus, who under a fraudulent authority succeeded in releasing straight Neoplatonism upon an unsuspecting Church, von Balthasar presents him as an original, authentically Catholic thinker. He exculpates Denys' work from the charge of a dangerously radical negative theology by showing how it gravitates toward a theology of form rather than foundering on a formless absolute. The essays on Irenaeus and Denys show how solidly von Balthasar's own theological aesthetic remains anchored in an earlier, Greek tradition which it effectively recaptures.

His efforts to rescue the early Western tradition from its later dualist interpretations encounter greater difficulties. Here also the author displays a masterly control over his material, often forcing us to correct our reading as well as our reading perspective. Nevertheless they do not always succeed in dispelling all doubts about the solidity of the Latin synthesis, especially in the cases of Augustine and Anselm. Bonaventure, with whom the second volume concludes, alone perhaps in the West, approaches the core of what constitutes von Balthasar's essential insight. From the vision of the crucified Seraph at its center, this theology of form radiates its aesthetic light over all of nature and history. One may regard his synthesis as the foundation in the Western tradition of von Balthasar's own work.

In the modern age when theology became abstractly rationalist, the author turns to poets and "lay" thinkers for support of his theological aesthetic. At the threshold of that new tradition stands Dante, his feet still firmly planted on medieval soil, yet his eyes already gazing at a remote future. He first declared literary *form,* the harmony of linguistic expressiveness, imaginative power, and symbolic content, to be the essence of poetic creation, at a time when Cimabue and Giotto were accomplishing a form revolution in painting and Andrea Pisano in sculpture. Yet it was the mystical quality that gave Dante's aesthetic its unique character, decisively elevating it above the courtly tradition in which it had originated. "In Dante the ethos of the *cor gentile,* originally an obscure, esoteric, and unreal form of thought, burst its limits, became concrete and universal."[3] This aesthetic vision gave birth to the most perfect synthesis of nature and grace in the Middle Ages. At the same time Dante already anticipated and in a way resolved some of the tensions of the emerging modern culture.

His poetic development moved from a Platonic spiritualism that merely allegorized corporeal beauty to a fully symbolic mystical vision. The changing role of Beatrice clearly marks the stages of this development. Already in his *Vita Nuova,* Dante attempted to christianize an *eros* that with the ideal of courtly love and its verbalization by the Provençal poets had suddenly entered European culture. His loving remembrance of Beatrice established the basis for a new religious humanism that incorporated *eros* into *agape* rather than renouncing it. But not until the *Comedia* did he succeed in fully uniting the spiritual meaning with Beatrice's physical presence. Mediating between heaven and earth, she finally allowed him to embrace the earth without turning away from heaven. In *Paradiso,* Beatrice no longer escapes earthly love: she fulfills it in a perfect union of nature and grace. In Beatrice, Dante conveys physical form and existential meaning to his Christian faith. Sensibility and eros become part of the *Sponsa Christi* (III, 52). Human beauty now rises to express divine goodness. This synthesis of nature and grace likewise appears in Dante's disconcerting use of ancient cosmology in the structuring of Paradise. The planets and spheres of heaven transform the cosmos itself into a symbol of God's love. Dante clothes everything in Paradise with *form,* even if it requires deviating from established theology. His souls are clearly more than bodiless spirits waiting for the general resurrection.

---

[3] Erich Auerbach, *Dante, Poet of the Secular World* (Chicago: University of Chicago Press, 1961), 64.

Their clarified bodies remain subject to feeling and emotion. Beatrice weeps in Paradise, Peter fumes against his successors, Benedict complains about the present state of his order.

Sobered by the wave of naturalism which submerged the early Christian humanism during the Renaissance and which continues to inundate modern culture, modern poets, while still glorifying the harmony of the Christ event with the entire history of mankind, nevertheless avoid intrinsically mixing ancient mythology with the Christian world view. By and large, their "syntheses" display a greater complexity, as becomes almost painfully evident in Gerard Manley Hopkins' intimate but tortured embrace of nature and grace. Through the Incarnation permanently embedded in nature, grace reshapes cosmos and history into a Christological form. Henceforth all events in this world become inspired, stimulated, and forwarded by a power that rules their order yet surpasses them. But the transforming mystery of the Incarnation culminates in the Cross, "the fundamental, ontological presupposition of all natural processes that all, knowingly or not, intrinsically signify or intend by pointing beyond themselves" (III, 394). The challenging task of the Christian poet consists in rendering sensible what in itself must remain completely transcendent. When the Word became flesh the mystery of God ceased to hide *behind* the forms of this world: it became one of them and affected all others (III, 393). The divine reality remains mysterious and Christ's Incarnation made it even more so. His death on the Cross, so contrary to the drives immanent in nature, results in constant struggle and never-ceasing pain. This very tension, expressed in the violence Hopkins does to language, defines a poetic ontology in which the "ciphers" of reading must receive their definitive sense from Christ's transformation.

Compared to Hopkins, Péguy appears more serene, poetically almost sedate. Yet the comprehensive scope of his theological vision renders his work into a Christian *Summa*. More perhaps than any other writer of our time, he perceived the earthly ramifications as well as the historical consequences of God's entering this world and transforming its entire configuration. For Péguy, the Christ event, both his person and his message, reaches beyond the historical Jesus to the biblical and classical horizon. Christ inherited not only Israel, but all ancient philosophy as well as the Greek *polis* and the Roman Empire. They permanently enshrine his form. The ancient world proleptically points at the coming Incarnation from which it was destined to receive its definitive meaning. The formal perfection of Greek art prepared matter for receiving the ultimate imprint of Spirit, while the roads of Rome radiating outwards "like the cracks in a glass mirror into which someone had thrust the shaft of a spear", were to become the highways of God's expanding grace. In unforgettable verses the long poem *Eve* sings of the Roman legions marching over the entire civilized world to prepare the coming of the Savior: *"C'est pour toi qu'ils ont marché."* Péguy's poetic message aimed at the restoration of nature as much as at the acceptance of grace. If the modern world has closed itself to redemption, it is not because of its greater respect for nature, but because of its systematic destruction of the natural order, the very soil of grace. Reducing the natural "rightness" of things to mathematical equation, modern culture has equalized, quantified, depersonalized, and formalized human life. The full embodiment of the Christ event requires not only that it be solidly attached to the cultures that preceded and followed it, but, even more, that it plunge its roots deep in the historical soil in which it has been planted. Péguy urges the Church in France to return to its roots, to hold on to its national models, and to venerate its local saints—Jeanne d'Arc, St. Louis, St. Geneviève. Everywhere Péguy shows a profound respect for the given order of nature and history—"the climate of grace".[4] His poetry most consistently places the order of grace firmly *within* the natural world (III, 404).

Hamann, the contemporary of Kant and Herder, understood, alone with the poets, how a God who dies on a Cross transforms history and language. The Bible's poetic disorder reflects the Spirit's adjustment to "the regular disorder of nature" (III, 275). Nature serves as an antehamber to the direct revelation of Scripture. History in its great figures symbolically anticipates and follows the supreme, historical event of the Incarnation. Thus, Hamann finds Socrates' ultimate significance in his relation to Christ. Socratic ignorance presymbolizes the death of natural reason in faith. In revelation God empties himself. Hamann refers to Scripture, the *kenosis* of the Holy Spirit, as "the still small voice that we ... hear in our hearts" shrunk to fit the "small understanding of men".[5] "All history is like nature, a sealed book, a concealed witness, a riddle that cannot be solved unless we plow with some heifer other than our reason."[6] Language, particularly poetic language, responds to the word God addresses to us in creation. It must be understood in analogy with the definitive interpretation of his work in Scripture. Hamann's theological aesthetic unites nature and grace in a relationship at once hidden and open. "The categories he imposes on nature have so radical and sweeping an effect, because, ultimately, they derive from the sphere of supernatural revelation. Poetic inspiration is (hidden) prophecy. Language is (hidden divine) revelation" (III, 276).

Despite his profound affinity with Hamann, von Balthasar claims a greater autonomy for nature. The Protestant thinker, he feels, tends to "overpower" nature all too hastily and to "replace" it by Scripture (III, 277). In defending the relative autonomy of the finite against an inadequate *information* of the

[4] Charles-Pierre Péguy, *Eve* in *Oevres poétiques complètes* (Paris, 1941), 813.
[5] Johann G. Hamann, *Biblische Betrachtungen* (Nadler) I, 121.
[6] Hamann, *Sokratische Denkwürdigkeiten* (Nadler) I, 65.

divine in nature, von Balthasar revives the medieval controversy whether theology ought to study nature in its own right, or merely as a branch of Scriptural theology. While respecting the autonomy of the natural form, however, theology ought not to remain satisfied with aesthetic principles derived only, or even mainly, from nature. To measure the Christian mysteries by criteria of the natural form is to aestheticize them. Precisely for that reason a great work like Chateaubriand's *Génie du christianisme* remains permanently inadequate, while Pascal and John of the Cross, for all their distrust of the finite form as expression of an infinite mystery, may nevertheless be considered authentic "form" artists of the divine. The case of John of the Cross, in particular, vividly illustrates how precarious the balance between a formless supernaturalism and a naturalist formalism had become in the modern age.

As von Balthasar presents him, John of the Cross came at a time when the new view of nature had already destroyed the symbolic analogy of the cosmos that had shaped Dante's *Comedia*. The Spanish mystic proposes a theology as austere as that of the Reformation's salvation by faith alone. As the soul progresses in her spiritual ascent she gradually must discard all images and forms — not only the terrestrial ones, but even more the supernatural visions, illuminations, and consolations. God can be known only through God himself in the night of senses and imagination (III, 105, 109). Despite these form-destructive principles, von Balthasar grants John of the Cross a significant position in the theological aesthetic of the modern age. What the content of the mystic's work rejects, its poetic form reinstates (III, 120). In his poetry, which contains the essence of his message, the natural images, so severely banned from spiritual life, become the very medium for expressing the imageless state for which he aims. With him the theology of form moves toward a new center. The Spirit, though no longer appearing as the *anima mundi*, achieves a new harmony of nature and grace as the source of poetic inspiration. "Who can divide the spheres of supernatural and natural inspiration? Why shouldn't the direct inspiration of the Holy Spirit at the same time awaken all of the powers of artistic enthusiasm and creative inventiveness where such powers exist?" (III, 124). And yet, such a mystical aesthetic hides a deep tension, for the poetry merely induces one to abandon the poetic vision and to surpass all sensuous images. The final chapters of *The Ascent of Mount Carmel* on religious art disclose how far John of the Cross' theology is from granting any kind of sacramental presence of God *in* the icon. He is intoxicated by beauty, yet the only permanent abode of beauty he accepts is one that rises above all earthly forms. In the end, von Balthasar feels, his "paradox" yields no universal Christian truth. John's way to God, however admirable, cannot serve as a model, even in the modern age.

Pascal's witness appears equally complex. Because of a distorted reading of St. Augustine, he admits no natural "illumination" in the order of grace —

whether from science or philosophy. Such a "harsh dualism" (III, 189) between science and piety would seem to disqualify him for significantly contributing to a theological aesthetic. But von Balthasar convincingly shows how his austere Jansenist theology rests on an anthropological basis which bridges the irreconcilable opposition between grace and nature. The assumption of their deeper union supports Pascal's entire moral and intellectual structure. The ideal of the *honnête homme,* the person who observes the proper form, the just proportion, the right relation in his dealings with the world, presupposes that the Christian is able to translate the vision of grace into the order of nature (III, 201). Pascal's vision of the human condition reveals what his theology tries to suppress. The science of the heart balances the two infinites between which human existence moves. The person "hovers as a spirit in a void that he cannot understand" (III, 208): his condition can be clarified only from within an infinite which he himself is unable to grasp. This insight, however dimly perceived, urges the person to accept a transcendent reality without which his existence fails to make sense. Where man can understand himself only through God, existence itself justifies faith.

Even the God of faith, however, remains "a hidden God" and faith merely *manifests* the hiddenness both of an incomprehensible God and of an incomprehensible sinfulness. Scripture itself reveals in "ciphers", rather than in clear statements.

> The Old Testament is a cipher, certainly in the first place insofar as it relates to the New as nature does to grace, . . . but more deeply it is not simply pure nature, but the incomprehensibly encoded medium (*le milieu*) between nature and grace, between paganism and Christianity, which can produce no picture of itself except when it passes over into the truth to which it refers (III, 226).

Even the New Testament and the Church, while providing the "code" to the biblical ciphers, prefigure only the eschatological revelation of glory. They themselves remain full of mystery and darkness. Love alone renders the mystery transparent, because the God of love can reveal his truth only to love (III, 228). On this oscillating dialectic, then, of hidden manifestness and manifest hiddenness rests Pascal's theological aesthetic. One of those lapidary descriptions in which von Balthasar's essays culminate expresses it beautifully: "His greatness is that of Romanesque architecture, throwing bridges across abysses and indeed incorporating the void within its structures" (III, 234). The *Pensées* constitute a living exercise in what he himself defined as "rhetoric": right measure of presentation, of utterance, of deporting oneself, in short, existential proportionateness on all levels. Pascal supports von Balthasar's thesis that a Christian aesthetic transforms all appearances in the light of the Christ form. Christ himself, the form of God in this world, should become the measure not only of revelation but even of the "natural" forms of cosmos and history. Indeed, the light derived from the very divine-human form which appears in it transforms our vision of cosmos and history.

Revelation and Experience

Thus far we have simply *assumed* that the Christ form must provide the final principle for an aesthetic of revelation while the natural forms offer no adequate basis for such a theological aesthetic. Yet how could revelation lay an independent foundation for a theological aesthetic without reducing its vision to a "natural" one and its theology to an aestheticism? Is the very concept of the *aesthetic* not grounded in a natural ability to perceive "natural" forms? Von Balthasar, fully conscious of the decisive significance of this question, has devoted the most profound pages of his *opus* to an attempt to answer it. To repeat, he does not deny the relative autonomy of the natural form, but he assumes this natural aesthetic into an aesthetic of grace which, while fully respecting the autonomy of nature, nevertheless in the light of the Christian mysteries aesthetically transforms the natural. Revelation itself radiates the light in which we see its form. *In lumine tuo videbimus lumen.* "The light of faith stems from the object which revealing itself to the subject, draws it out beyond itself—into the sphere of the object" (I, 181). God's revelation establishes both its content and the believer's ability to comprehend it. Christ reveals as the God who expresses, and stands revealed as that which he expresses. Unlike the Socratic teacher he does not merely teach the truth: he *is* what he teaches. His form conceals as much as it reveals, but that concealment belongs essentially to the nature of what he reveals. The light, then, within which the believer apprehends God's manifestation entirely originates in the manifestation itself. So does the believing response to it: faith does not exist *alongside* Christ's word, but is God's own response to it given by one "enacted" by God (Eph 2:10). The believer assents "within the object of his faith" (I, 192), thereby partaking in the eternal Yes the Son speaks to the Father. The union of the believer with Christ links the two constituent parts of the act of faith—the object and the response to it. The eye with which the believer sees God, as Eckhart forcefully expressed it, is the eye with which God sees himself. In modern language, the conditions for the possibility of "theological" knowledge are the very conditions that constitute the "theological" object, with this important restriction that the object itself provides the conditions for its knowledge. "The light of faith cannot . . . be thought or even experienced as a merely immanent reality in our soul, but solely as the radiance resulting from the presence in us of a *lumen increatum,* a *gratia increata,* without our ever being able to abstract from God's Incarnation" (I, 215).

As von Balthasar presents it, that faith, far from standing opposed to experience (as past theology frequently implied), creates its own experience. The Eastern Church, with its theology of God's uncreated light that became manifest in Jesus' transfiguration, has never ceased to proclaim this supernatural experience of faith. Even in the West, particularly in Augustine, faith originally included experience as an essential part of itself. Not until Suárez was the "supernatural" quality of that experience disputed and lowered to a psychological level. The unity of the two is crucial to von Balthasar's thesis. If experience does not belong to the essence of faith itself, the form construed on the basis of that experience possesses no theological standing whatever. A study of theological form then, turns into a branch of natural aesthetics (as it did in the aesthetic theologies of the romantic era) wherein the form functions only as the *appearance* of a totally different, supernatural reality. For von Balthasar, the *gnosis* of theology grows entirely out of the experience of faith and belongs to the same order. "Theology deepens *pistis* into *gnosis* so far as this is possible on earth, and it does this through a contemplative penetration of the depths of individual facts" (I, 601). Precisely because it originates in the *experience* of faith all Christian theology possesses both an aesthetic and a mystical quality. All too often modern theology has restricted faith to a set of divinely communicated principles which theology, then, by purely rational methods, develops into an autonomous system. Following the older tradition, von Balthasar regards faith as a comprehensive, supernatural experience in its own right—intellectual, volitional, emotional—through which God's Spirit takes possession of the human mind. "The 'gifts of the Holy Spirit' bestowed seminally by grace, lead the believer to an ever deeper awareness and experience both of the presence within him of God's being and of the depth of the divine truth, goodness, and beauty in the mystery of God. This experience is usually referred to as Christian *mysticism* in the most general sense of the term" (I, 166). God's revelation, for von Balthasar as for Augustine, establishes its own *sensorium* in the soul (I, 249, 163).

Nor should this experience of faith be separated from the *natural* experience which it fulfills and transforms. The impact of the object of faith affects the mind's natural orientation toward Being. "Along with the ontic order that orients man and the form of revelation to one another, the grace of the Holy Spirit creates the faculty that can apprehend this form, the faculty that can relish it and find its joy in it, that can understand it and sense its interior truth and rightness" (I, 247). The encounter in faith transforms the soul's ontic dynamism into a direct receptivity for the Christ form. Though fulfilling the mind's natural aspirations, the experience of faith emerges from *within* faith, is conducted by the standards of faith, and results in seeing the form of faith (I, 225–27). Even as a great work of art imposes its own spiritual *a priori* upon the viewer or the hearer, faith conveys its own intrinsic necessity to the entire natural order (I, 164).

Yet grace "imposes" its form without doing violence to nature. The revelation in Christ occurs within a divinely created nature which already in its own being manifests God's eternal presence. Hence revelation must not only adopt the form of this world; it completes that form by extending it to its ultimate archetype, God's triune nature. Hence the highest form quality of the Christ, his divine relation to the Father and the Spirit, stands not opposed to the structure of this world: it appears as a form *within* this world, yet one from which that world itself must receive its definitive form. I write "definitive", because Christ is not a sign pointing beyond itself to an invisible God: he himself, the indivisible God-man, *is* the reality he signifies, "man insofar as God radiates from him; God insofar as he appears in the man Jesus" (I, 437). Being ultimate, the Christ form should not be measured by other forms: it becomes itself the measure of all. For von Balthasar, as for Bonaventure, the Son is archetype of all things because he is absolute expression. "The likeness which is the truth itself in its expressive power ... better expresses a thing than the thing expresses itself, for the thing itself receives the power of expression from it."[7]

The Incarnation would not constitute the *definitive* form if Christ's humanity had merely been a randomly adopted form, extrinsic to God's inner life. To be definitive the God-man must express God's own form (I, 480). An Infinite wholly inexpressible would leave the Incarnation no more than a docetist significance. What Christ reveals in his own reality, however, is that intradivine relationship whereby God himself is form. "In the Son of Man then appears not God alone; necessarily there also appears the inter-trinitarian event of his procession; there appears the triune God ... " (I, 479). God is able to express *himself* in Jesus *because he is expressive in his divine nature,* and Christ's humanity, far from being a concession made to human frailty in God's self-revelation, *is* the divine reality itself as it becomes manifest. What remains concealed in him (his divinity) has not been withdrawn from manifestation, but rather *manifests* the inscrutable, divine mystery itself. As in the work of art, no ulterior reality hides *behind* the form: the form, totally manifest, adduces its own evidential power. Incomprehensibility constitutes as much a positive property in the form of God's revelation as the continuing mystery does in a beloved person (I, 186). Both the concealed and the revealed become object of the *perception* of faith. "Visible form not only 'points to' an invisible, unfathomable mystery; form is the apparition of this mystery, and reveals it while, naturally, at the same time protecting and veiling it. ... The content does not lie behind the form but within it" (I, 151). The entire mystery of Christ becomes *visible,* including its trinitarian origin. Only the aesthetic perception of form fully transcends the

[7] Bonaventure, *In I Sent.,* Distinction 35, qu. 1 ad 3. In II, 293.

otherwise persistent dualism between the external sign of faith and the internal light: the light breaks forth from the form itself.

The Foundation of Scripture

Not before the final volumes on the Old and the New Testament (VI and VII) does von Balthasar give the definitive justification of these principles. Only scriptural exegesis can convey what the "divine form" has concretely meant, first in the revelation of Israel's destiny as God's chosen people, then in the inspired power and amazing diversity of its written formalization, finally in that one individual who in his person expresses the fullness of God's inner life. I know no more powerful description of God's form-giving activity in history than the volume devoted to the Old Testament. In it we become aware of the awesome complexity of a divine election operative in the concrete cultural context of primitive, half-nomadic tribes slowly unified by a series of theophanies in an isolated trek through the desert. In unforgettable pages von Balthasar evokes the *tremendum* of these founding events whereby Yahweh becomes Israel's God and Israel becomes his people. Next we learn of Israel's doubtful response to this high vocation in the violence and barbaric crudeness (suggested in Judges) of the tribes' attempt to settle down in the newly conquered land. Once some civilized order was established under a reluctantly accepted kingship the successful exchange with neighboring tribes poses the even greater threat of cultural assimilation.

The Bible reflects these successive stages in a literature which, while expressing Israel's God-given identity—and as such partaking in the sacred form— nevertheless more and more opens itself to a universal near-Eastern humanism that occasionally stands in flagrant opposition to its own founding principles. Thus, next to the powerful language of transcendence in the Prophets and the Pentateuch we find the sceptical deism of Qoheleth, the unrestricted eroticism of the Song of Songs, the courtly wisdom of Proverbs, perhaps even the despair in the face of suffering in Job and some of the Psalms. Yet all these strands, however secular if taken by themselves, have entered the one sacred expression that formalizes the experience of the God-shaped nation. Most remarkably von Balthasar has compelled the far-reaching conclusions of radical biblical criticism into a fundamental, all-comprehensive religious vision. This enables him to read the entire Bible as an anticipatory symbol of God's full revelation in the form of Christ. The final part of the volume on the Old Testament is entirely devoted to the longing for a divine glory "that was not present": the "empty time" of Israel's waiting for the messianic era. During that concluding biblical epoch the principles of the Covenant began to expand beyond the cultural borders of the nation into the universal space of the Hellenistic commonwealth. So the last section of this work on God's glory in the Old Testament bears the provocative title *"Das Heute ohne Herrlichkeit"* ("The Present Day without Glory") which takes the idea of a divine form to its furthest limits where it is no more than the empty space that waits to be filled.

The discussion of the New Testament follows a wholly different course. Here the form appears perfect and fulfilled from the start. While the form-giving process in the Old Testament consisted primarily in a reception of words, in the New Testament it immediately attains full expression in the one, incarnate Word. The Church continues to find models and images for this physical presence in the Bible and will continue to meditate on its mystery until the end of time. But the presence is there from the beginning (VII, 89–103). This initial completeness of the revelation, however, does not result in a single theology. Already the New Testament itself displays a variety of approaches to the mystery of the Incarnation depending on the different cultural settings in which it was to be embedded. Matthew's theology of Christ as the fulfilled promise of the Old Testament is clearly distinct from John's doctrine that opposes the true *gnosis* of the Gospel to the gnostic systems of late paganism. Later, theological reflection introduces further distinctions to a point where one cannot speak of *the* theology of the New Testament.

Yet, through it all runs the unifying thread of Jesus' own life, a life of poverty, humility, and total obedience. In it the biblical idea of glory receives a new, paradoxical meaning. In Christ a loving God assuming the sinfulness of the human race in his own body becomes himself the victim in a sacrifice of propitiation. Precisely this *kenosis* manifests a heretofore hidden splendor of God's inner life. "Glorified in him God will also glorify him in himself" (Jn 13:32), Christ says at the Last Supper. And: "Glorify your Son that the Son may glorify you" (Jn 17:1). That same kenotic glory descends over the entire sacred community of the new Israel.

In discussing the New Testament von Balthasar changes his approach to Scripture. His treatment of the Old Testament fully allowed for a condition characteristic of all *verbal* expression, namely that it requires *interpretation.* The words of Scripture, though unique in their revealing capacity, are not separated from other discourse. They originate in a concrete, historical setting and are addressed to humans who speak a language of their own, not necessarily that of the ancient narrative, prophecy, or legislation. Hence they call for hermeneutic clarification and historical criticism. In practice Christians have never questioned the need for interpretation beyond the words of the Bible. From the beginning they have provided a new reading of the Old Testament text. Yet with respect to the New Testament their attitude has been more hesitant. Since it constitutes the definitive and closed revelation of the one Word, it stands in a class by itself. For von Balthasar this uniqueness implies that, rather than relying upon external interpretation, the words must be allowed to provide their own light. No hermeneutic or philological methods *independent of the living faith of the Church* (the only authoritative reader of the Word) can truly enlighten the believer. Being itself the normative standard, the New Testament recognizes no external authority. For von Balthasar, the sacred text is itself a "super-form" of which the various parts illuminate each other while refusing any other source of light to penetrate the inner *sanctum*. This does not lead him to a *sola Scriptura* doctrine, for the authoritative Tradition which helped to shape that form retains its definitive jurisdiction over its interpretation. Since Scripture must be read in the Church, it cannot claim "a form which can be understood and apprehended in itself" (I, 546). Yet it does imply that external sources of reading must not be allowed to interfere with past tradition or the ecclesial Magisterium. Hence von Balthasar, despite a command of exegetical and philological method equaled by few, rejects much recent historical scholarship in his reading of the New Testament. He knows it, occasionally refers to it, but rarely applies it. Thus the authorship of the Epistle to the Hebrews and of the pastoral letters is unflinchingly attributed to St. Paul, as is that of the two Petrine letters to St. Peter himself. Most Protestants and many Catholics refuse to follow him in this regard. For them *words,* even the words of revelation, always require *more* words than the text's own content provides. Any "universe of discourse", they maintain, is by its very nature, permanently open-ended, and hence in need of further interpretation. In adopting a more restrictive attitude von Balthasar reasserts the traditional view of Scripture as a *form* in its own right, a view which many Catholics feel has been somewhat sacrificed in the Reformation's emphasis on the openness of the word. But Protestants are likely to respond that the *word* forever resists being fully identified with any *closed form,* because of the peculiar complexity of its own form—expressiveness. One of the initial objectives of the Reformation had been precisely to defend the unrestricted open-endedness of the word against any definitive closure—even by the authentic interpreters of the tradition.

Von Balthasar's different mode of interpreting the words of the New Testament differs not only from the one he applies to the first Testament, but also removes it from the total openness of the Christian world view (nevertheless based upon the New Testament) with respect to philosophical systems—so magnificently illustrated by von Balthasar himself in the volumes dealing with the "space of metaphysics". In volumes four and five he displays not only the full scope of his awesome erudition (which merited him to be called—by Henri de Lubac—the most learned man in Europe), but also his exceptional openness toward any trend of thought (including modern atheism) that, from near or far, ever entered into dialogue with Christianity. The few lines devoted to that encyclopedic work in the second section of this essay may suggest the scope of the enterprise, but convey no idea of von Balthasar's all-embracing Christian humanism. Surprisingly, when it comes to other faiths his attitude becomes less conciliatory. Here I occasionally feel a revival of the old tension between nature and grace which he himself so effectively strove to remove. The principle of harmony forces the author to recognize the religious significance and even the indispensability of other religions in the economy of grace (e.g., I, 213). Christ becomes "the measure, both in judgment and redemption, of all other religious forms in mankind" (I, 171). Yet von Balthasar's own treatment reflects more judgment than redemption. Of course, the nature of a theological *aesthetic* requires a clear delineation of the specific *form* of the Christian message. But his concern for formal clarity has led him to paint the contrasts in rather harsh tones. His opposition increases when faiths threaten to dissolve precise form and thereby to jeopardize the very possibility of a theological aesthetic—as, in his view, Hinduism and Buddhism do.

Still, if the *particular significance* of the Christian form lies precisely in its ability to *harmonize* nature and grace, then it also would seem to demand religious openness toward other faiths. Instead von Balthasar unqualifiedly rejects "non-Christian mysticism" as lacking in objectivity (I, 216), Hinduism as "dancing [all forms] away" (I, 217), Buddhism as being a religion that "climbs up toward the divine" (I, 496) rather than waiting for a divine message from above. Indeed, he questions "anything which passes for an analysis of religious existence outside Christianity" (I, 231). Outside Christianity, he feels, the supremacy of the whole almost inevitably results in a shattering of finite form (I, 193). Evaluations of this kind now seem unnecessary for preserving the form of Christian faith. Von Balthasar rarely engages in a real dialogue with other faiths.

Even a general typology which places the Christian form within the context of other religious forms—Judaism, the religious movements of Mesopotamia and Egypt, Hellenistic culture—von Balthasar distrusts as potentially dangerous to its uniqueness.

> This form . . . does not appear as something relatively unique, as might be said of the creations of other great founders. Qualitatively set apart from them, the Christ form appears absolutely unique; but on the basis of its own particular form, the Christ form relates to itself as the ultimate center the relative uniqueness of all other forms and images of the world, whatever realm they derive from (I, 507).

Though he claims that Christ mediates all other forms (I, 527ff.), they appear to lose their religious justification once the Christ form appears. Not to accept that form amounts to "objectively misapprehending it either in whole or in part" (I, 509)—a misapprehension which "cannot be exempt from a certain kind of guilt" (I, 510). This severe argument rests upon the dubious assumption that the Christ form "*appears* absolutely unique" (I, 507). But how can any *form* appear as *absolutely* unique? Does form not by its very nature relate to a formal context from which it can never become completely detached? It is undoubtedly true that in the form the divine mystery appears. The Incarnation would not "truly" reveal if in Christ we did not actually apprehend the irradiation of God's inner form. Yet must we not distinguish the form actually *perceived* "with the eyes of faith" from the invisible form *believed* to be present on the basis of that perception? The German term *Gestalt* hides a fundamental ambiguity. In Christ *appears* the form (*Gestalt* here approaches *Bild*); but we *believe* the mystery of God's internal life to possess a trinitarian *Gestalt* (not *Bild* and hardly *Form*). While fully accepting the presence of a *gnosis* in faith we still may distinguish the *gnosis* of perception from that of "dark knowledge". Here perhaps lies an element of truth in negative theology not sufficiently appreciated by von Balthasar.[8] In volume four he defines *Gestalt,* with Cusanus, as a "contracted representation of the 'absolute' " (29). But for the Renaissance mystic the contracted expression never surpasses the *docta ignorantia* in which what we know does not formally appear.

Conclusion

With a feeling of awe the reader closes the final volume of this last great *Summa,* so original and so traditional, in which Tridentine theology attains its final, perhaps most beautiful expression. Von Balthasar's work concludes a theological epoch of the Catholic Church—a period of solid scholarship, enormous erudition, and deep piety. Displaying the majestic grandeur of a Byzantine liturgy, its religious culture sufficed to those inside the tradition while it remained relatively inaccessible to outsiders. By the time von Balthasar began writing the pressure upon the self-contained structure had become severe and cracks began to appear. There had been crises before—the one caused by Vatican I, the modernist crisis—yet each time the structure had shown its remarkable resilience. What occurred around the middle of this century was different. The pressure came from within the main body, not from a few recalcitrant elements. Among them were those in the vanguard of Catholic theology and philosophy, those who "taught" von Balthasar (especially Henri de Lubac). He himself experienced the tension and felt the need to

---

[8] I have dealt with this more extensively in my *The Common Life* (New York, 1984) and in "Negative Theology and Affirmation of the Finite" in *Experience, Reason, God,* ed. Eugene Thomas Long, Studies in Philosophy and the History of Philosophy, no. 8 (Washington, DC: Books on Demand UMI, 1980), 149–57.

remedy the situation that caused it. Yet his strategy differed from that of others. Rather than attempting to expand the limits of orthodoxy, he strengthened the internal unity of the structure by mobilizing those elements that had remained unused and that may well have constituted the Tridentine Church's greatest asset. Primary among them was the aesthetic creativity dispersed over various areas of the Christian experience. The period immediately preceding World War II, when von Balthasar received his formal training, witnessed a veritable outburst of Catholic art and literature, an emergence of patristic, liturgical, and mystical studies, and the creation of a dynamically original yet also respectfully traditional Catholic philosophy. Most of those elements the stubbornly monolithic school theology of the previous decades had failed to integrate. Von Balthasar rallied those *disiecta membra* to the support of a Christian identity which he perceived as being in extreme danger. This design gives his work a polemical edge. Yet the very purpose of strengthening the internal coherence of the structure and widening its base, removes it from the controversies with a secular society and mostly from a direct dialogue with it.

A project of this nature runs the risk of yielding to integrist rigidity and/or to aesthetic constructivism. Von Balthasar has avoided these pitfalls throughout the seven volumes of *Herrlichkeit*. One may call his attitude "conservative" in the sense that he attempts to "conserve" a tradition which he, unlike many who claim the title, thoroughly *knows*. His name has occasionally been used as a rallying cry for reactionary forces in Roman Catholicism. Unjustifiably, it seems to me. A theology of glory can never be "fundamentalist", we learn in the volume on the New Testament (VII, 113–14), because the immediate encounter between God and the Christian precedes doctrinal articulation. The Magisterium interprets revelation: it does not lay its foundations. Its pronouncements "do not aim at constructing a system which eventually would come to replace Scripture either in whole or in part" (I, 555). In fact, they possess no autonomous form of their own. Even Scripture constitutes only a part of the revelation. It can claim no form "which can be understood and apprehended in itself" (I, 546). Nor is von Balthasar's traditionalism uncritical. His views on Augustine's theology of damnation, on Dante's hell ("the *reductio ad absurdum* of scholastic theology" [III, 90]), of Christ's descent into hell to suffer the pain of the damned and to liberate the captive souls (VII), move far from the center of Tradition.

Von Balthasar writes with the flair of an artist, a very learned one, but an artist nevertheless. In his essays he practices what his theory preaches. They are brilliant exercises in theological aesthetics. Rather than abiding by the rational structures of dissertational writing, they obey the more adventurous order of the creative imagination, shaping each intellectual profile into an aesthetic construction in its own right, fiercely independent of established norms or opinions and free to follow the meandering course of its subjective inspiration. This approach yields marvelous results. Often an idea displays itself more advantageously in the half-light of poetic metaphor than in the full glare of rational conceptualization. To be sure, the method also creates a logical elusiveness potentially discomforting to the philosophically exacting reader. Von Balthasar has repeatedly proven (for instance, in his study on truth[9]) his ability of sustaining a rigorous argument. The *Glory of the Lord,* while bearing an even more impressive witness to his formidable powers, occasionally displays an equal intellectual *desinvolture* if an argument fails to warrant the author's patient attention. Von Balthasar's masterpiece contains some passages (his use of Heidegger's thought in volume one and his reconstruction of Soloviev's in volume three) that will do little to lift the philosopher's traditional skepticism with respect to a theological use of his categories. Yet small criticism is out of place where great thanks are due. *The Glory of the Lord* is a glorious work: a continuous challenge to read and a continuing joy to remember.[10]

[9] *Wahrheit.* Bd. I: *Wahrheit der Welt* (Einsiedeln: Johannes Verlag, 1947) reprinted as *Theologik* I: *Wahrheit der Welt* (Einsiedeln: Johannes Verlag, 1985).

[10] This article includes material published by the author in *Religion and Literature* 19, no. 3 (Autumn 1987): 67–81, and in *Theological Studies* 49 (1988): 299–318 — Ed.

JOHN O'DONNELL, S.J.

Hans Urs von Balthasar: The Form of His Theology

The Enigma of Man

It is sometimes said that von Balthasar's theology, centered as it is on Christology and firmly rooted in the *Catholica,* is incapable of dialogue. Moreover, one could think that his rejection of Rahner's transcendental method, with its Kantian heritage of the turn to the subject, implies that von Balthasar's theology is not anthropological in its scope and interest. Yet a closer reflection reveals that both judgments are too facile and are lacking in nuance.

If, for Rahner, the starting point for philosophical and theological reflection is the subject's self-consciousness and the questioning of his world, for von Balthasar the primordial human experience is that of the Thou, the moment when the child for the first time becomes aware of the smile of its mother and so becomes *Geist.* In that moment the child becomes an I. And with the experience of the I is given also the experience of the world and the experience of the Thou. Thus the primary word is love. And in this initial experience of love the child is given a glimpse that an infinite love is possible. In spite of subsequent disappointments and even the realization that the mother's love is finite, the original intuition abides. And in that intuition lies the origin of the person's religious pilgrimage.

For von Balthasar, the spirit of man which is awakened in the original encounter with the Thou is inevitably religious and oriented to God, for spirit is as such an openness to the Infinite. But if man is thus openness to God, how is he to realize union with the Infinite who always recedes with every human attempt to grasp him?

Here von Balthasar utilizes the resources of his Christian Faith to enter into dialogue with the great ways of salvation which the human spirit has produced in the course of its history. First, there is the way of the primitive religions. In these religions we note a number of elements. First, they are polytheistic. The gods of these religions always represent some aspect of human need, the need for protection from the perils of nature, the need for defense in battle, the need for love. The gods are always gods in service of

Communio 16 (Fall 1989). © 1989 by *Communio: International Catholic Review.*

man. In fact, von Balthasar observes that the gods are basically projections of some aspect of finite experience onto the realm of the divine. Another aspect of these primitive religions is mythology. The myths are important for two reasons. First of all, for their view of time. The myths narrate events, but events which do not take place in history but in a primeval time. On the other hand, the language of myth is always the language of this-worldly time based on imagery derived from our spatiotemporal world.

The way of these primitive religions is doomed to failure, for at some point man will inevitably realize that the gods he has fashioned are finite and hence are not worthy of worship. The way of the gods is the way of idolatry. Moreover, since the gods are always projected to satisfy human needs, the way of the primitive religions has a built-in tendency to magic. As regards myth, the true problem here is that of temporality and the value of the world. Since mythological events take place in an *Urzeit*, real temporality is not taken seriously. At the same time, myth's enfleshment in worldly language is a reminder that man who is an incarnate being can never leave this world behind in his pilgrimage to God. If myth does not offer an adequate response to man's religious question, nonetheless Christ has come not merely to destroy but to fulfill. Christ shatters the mythological view of time by becoming incarnate in our history, but Christ integrates myth into himself by redeeming the world so that the world becomes a genuine means of salvation.

In the history of Western culture, the moment when man realized the self-defeat of the way of the religions became a glorious moment in that man attempted a new way to God, namely the way of philosophy. With the emergence of Greek philosophy, man broke with the myths and placed his hope in reason. The nobility of this tradition consisted in its radical attempt to purify man's religious desire and to seek the true God, the God who is beyond everything finite. For Plotinus this could be nothing less than the radically simple One beyond all duality. The transcendent God of the philosopher is the God who can be sought only by the way of radical negation, in which the self in an ultimate act of abandonment cuts itself loose from everything finite and loses itself in the infinite abyss of the nameless one.[1] Such an abandonment has a sublime nobility, but according to von Balthasar its founders for two reasons, both of which are linked to love. First, the self has to abandon its original intuition, for in the primordial experience of the mother's smile, the I was born. Now philosophy seems to be calling for the annihilation of the I. Secondly, von Balthasar argues that although it is possible to abandon oneself to the nameless one, it is not possible to love a faceless Infinite. Here once

---

[1] Von Balthasar makes a similar critique of the Eastern religions. Whereas in Eastern religions everything depends on transcending the world and annihilating the self, the Christian Faith is centered on the fact that God addresses humanity in his Word.

again the original intuition of love is denied. And so it would seem that man's religious search ends in an *aporia*. Neither the way of the gods nor the mystical way of the philosopher can recuperate the original intuition of love. For the Christian Faith this enigma can only be resolved in Christ, for it is only in Christ that the reality of God is revealed as the mystery of love. But to understand this point, we must plumb the depths of Jesus' identity and his trinitarian origins. Let us, then, approach this mystery by looking more closely at how von Balthasar proposes to comprehend the person of Christ.

Christology: "He Was in the Form of God" (Phil 2:16)

One of von Balthasar's major contributions to Christology is his attempt to employ aesthetic categories to illuminate the mystery of Christ. For von Balthasar the aesthetic experience consists of two essential dimensions, the form with its harmony, proportion, and measure, and the ecstasy which results when the perceiver is drawn into the form. Important here is the fact that the unity of the form transcends its parts. The perception of the form consists in seeing the totality of the form which is greater than the elements of which it is made up.

It is faith's judgment that Jesus is the form of God revealed in the flesh. In developing this point, von Balthasar reveals his preference for the fourth Gospel. According to St. John, "No one has ever seen God; the only Son, who is in the bosom of the Father, he has made him known" (1:18). The key here then is that Jesus is the visibility of the invisible God. In this context, von Balthasar is fond of citing the Christmas preface: "In him we see our God made visible and so are caught up in the love of the God we cannot see." Looking at the history of Jesus, one sees many elements. One sees, for example, an itinerant Jewish preacher, a wonder-worker, a condemned criminal. But faith asserts that one has not really seen what is there to be seen until one sees Jesus as the God-man, as the visible manifestation of the invisible God.

If there is any key which unlocks the mystery of Jesus' identity, for von Balthasar it would be Jesus' obedience vis-à-vis his heavenly Father. Time and again, von Balthasar returns to such Johannine texts as 4:34: "My food is to do the will of him who sent me, and to accomplish his work"; and 6:38: "I have come down from heaven, not to do my own will, but the will of him who sent me"; and 8:29: "I do always the things that please him." Here we see that the center of Jesus' existence is his obedience. So much is this the case that von Balthasar says that Jesus' "where" is in the Father. He writes, "The Son's 'where', which fixes his state, is always clear, regardless of whether he is in the bosom of the Father or on the paths of the world: it is the mission, the task, the will of the Father. He can always be found here, because he himself is the epitome of the Father's mission."[2]

Two points call for comment here. The first is that von Balthasar's understanding of the person is rooted in the concept of mission. On the human level, von Balthasar distinguishes between a *Geistessubjekt* and a person.[3] A *Geistessubjekt* has intellect and will. But the *Geistessubjekt* becomes a person in his uniqueness in the mission which he receives from God. This understanding of the human person has its origins in the divine person of Jesus. He is person *par excellence* because his whole being is his obedience to the Father. Jesus' sonship and his obedience go hand in hand. It is his being as Son to be totally available for the will of the Father. Because Jesus is Son, he is radically open to the Father's mission.

The other comment which is required here is that such an understanding of Jesus' sonship and mission makes sense only within a trinitarian context. In the same passage cited above, von Balthasar notes, "The mystery of the Son's mission in the world is a purely trinitarian mystery."[4] In other words, for von Balthasar, what happens here on earth in the terrestrial ministry of Jesus is the unfolding of Jesus' eternal relation to the Father. Jesus in his eternal being is always a coming forth from the Father and a returning to the Father in an eternal response of love. Thus during his earthly life, his coming forth from the Father is not the memory of a distant past event which recedes as he grows in his human history but rather this coming forth is continually present to him as the eternal source from which he lives and derives his energy. Here one could also mention, in order that the full trinitarian dimension be glimpsed, that the Spirit is in no way absent from this experience, for it is precisely the Spirit who manifests to the earthly Jesus the promptings of the Father's will. It corresponds to the nature of the Son's obedience to let himself be guided by the Spirit. Only in the power of the Spirit can Jesus fulfill his human mission, and so great is Jesus' surrender to the Father's will that he is ready to face even the human failure of his mission on the Cross and to entrust the rescue of that mission to the Spirit after the Resurrection.

From Incarnation to the Paschal Mystery

We saw above that, relying on St. Paul's affirmation, von Balthasar develops his theological aesthetic vision according to which Jesus is the form of God

[2] "Das Wo des Sohnes, das seinen Stand festlegt, ist also, mag er sich im Schosse des Vaters oder auf den Wegen der Welt befinden, stets eindeutig: es ist die Sendung, der Auftrag, der Wille des Vaters. Hier ist er jederzeit anzutreffen, weil er der Inbegriff der väterlichen Sendung selbst ist." *Christlicher Stand* (Einsiedeln: Johannes Verlag, 1977), 149.

[3] See *Homo creatus est* (Einsiedeln: Johannes Verlag, 1986), 100–101.

[4] "Das Geheimnis des weltlichen Auftrags des Sohnes ist ein rein trinitarisches Geheimnis" *Christlicher Stand,* 149.

revealed in the flesh. Building upon the same hymn in Philippians, von Balthasar stresses as well the *kenosis* of Jesus, or the self-emptying of the Logos, even to the point of the Cross. As St. Paul says, he did not consider his equality with God a thing to be grasped, but emptied himself becoming obedient unto death, even death on the Cross (see Phil 2:6–8). Like St. Paul, von Balthasar joins together the self-emptying of the Incarnation and that of the Cross. Indeed, he would go so far as to say that Jesus became incarnate in order to die for us.[5] The idea lying behind this affirmation is that in Jesus' identifying himself with us and our human condition he not only took on flesh (*verbum factum caro*), but indeed took on the condition of a sinner (*verbum factum caro peccati*). Here another Pauline text strongly influences von Balthasar's thought: "For our sake he made him to be sin who knew no sin, so that in him we might become the righteousness of God" (2 Cor 5:21). Thus the death of Jesus was no accident but was the inevitable outcome of the clash between God's love and sinful humanity's refusal to accept that love.

Among contemporary theologians, von Balthasar is one of the few who has dedicated his energies to plumbing the depths of what God's identification with sinful humanity entailed for Jesus. Von Balthasar pursues this reflection in his well-known treatment of the theology of Holy Saturday. To appreciate this theology, we could first begin by noting the contrast with the theology of Good Friday. We know that from an anthropological viewpoint, human death is not just a fate which the human person undergoes but is rather the supreme act of his liberty, that moment in which he sums up and expresses the whole meaning of his life. This fact becomes all the more clear when we realize that death is not just a biological end but the horizon in which the person lives at every moment and in which he realizes his freedom. According to the well-known phrase of Heidegger, *Dasein* is a being-toward-death. In the Gospels as well, Jesus' death is seen as the supreme act of his liberty. As Jesus says, no one takes his life from him. He lays it down of himself (Jn 10:18). Moreover, Jesus expresses this death as an act of love: "Greater love has no man than this, that he lay down his life for his friends" (Jn 15:13).

But this active self-surrender of Good Friday must be balanced by the radical passivity of Holy Saturday. For von Balthasar, Holy Saturday represents Jesus' complete identification with man in his sinfulness. As identified with the condition of a sinner, Jesus is dead, helpless, cut off from God, incapable of redeeming himself. Jesus so identifies with the God-forsaken that, as Paul says, he is made sin. Thus he experiences the radical powerlessness and helplessness of the sinner. As von Balthasar puts it, Jesus becomes a cadaver obedience.

---

[5] See "Mysterium Paschale", in *Mysterium Salutis,* ed. by J. Feiner and M. Löhrer, vol. III/2 (Einsiedeln: Benziger, 1969), 133–326.

To express these ideas more concretely, von Balthasar appeals to the scriptural image of Jesus' descent into hell which is mentioned in I Peter 3:19 and 4:6. But instead of interpreting these passages as a triumphal journey of Jesus into the underworld, as was common in the Middle Ages, von Balthasar prefers to see in this journey a symbol of Christ's total identification with the sinner, even to the point of experiencing God-forsakenness. And he illuminates this image by appealing to the Old Testament category of Sheol. By evoking a whole host of Old Testament texts, von Balthasar shows how Sheol is the realm of darkness, dust, silence. It is the pit and the land of forgetfulness. The dead are cut off from the living. They have no life-force or vitality and no longer praise the Lord. All of these images express Jesus' solidarity with the sinner in the dark night of the Cross.

So great is this solidarity with the God-forsaken that von Balthasar can say that Jesus experienced hell in the Cross. In fact, he notes that hell is a Christological concept. What it means to be separated from God has to be understood by looking at the crucified Jesus. His experience cannot be interpreted in quantitative terms. It was a qualitative experience which as such was timeless. Looking both backwards and forwards from the Cross, we can say on the one hand that hell as such was not known in the Old Testament, for the first Covenant never knew a situation of complete abandonment and despair. In the darkest moments of the history of the Old Covenant, there was always the light of the promise of the coming Redeemer. Looking forward from the Cross, our vision is one of hope. Christ has died for the sinner and taken his place in hell. He has suffered the judgment in our place. Thus the Christian lives with a radical hope both for himself and for all others. Solidarity with the whole human race, indeed solidarity in hope, is possible. We can and must hope that everyone will be saved. Von Balthasar does not deny that it is still possible to reject God's love but he nonetheless affirms that we may hope that no one has done so. He asks: May we not hope that even the most hardened sinner, in the moment of his death, will be brought face to face with the crucified Christ and so be converted from selfishness to love?

Apropos of the theology of Holy Saturday and Jesus' journey into the underworld, von Balthasar finds in this experience of the Lord the divine response to the conundrum of human freedom. The history of God with the world is a dramatic confrontation of two freedoms, the divine and the human. Does man have the capacity to utter a final No to God? If not, he seems not to be free. If he does, then human freedom seems to have the final word over God by undermining his project of love. Does God's freedom have the final victory over man's hardheartedness? If so, then human freedom does not seem to be taken seriously. Von Balthasar finds the answer to this dilemma in the Cross. God does indeed take human freedom seriously. He allows man to utter his No to the kenotic offer of love. He lets man choose radical isolation and aloneness. But in the Cross, God comes in love to disturb the solitude of the hardened sinner turned in upon himself. God does not violate the sinner's freedom but God's presence with the sinner in his abandonment disturbs his narcissistic solitude. The sinner finds himself in hell to be sure, but he is no longer absolutely alone. His solitude has become a co-solitude (*Miteinsamkeit*).

Trinitarian Love

We began this overview of von Balthasar's theology with a reflection upon the enigma of man and have explored how Christ is the resolution of this enigma. We must now pursue the trinitarian dimension of the Christ event, for it is only in the Trinity that the mystery of man is fully illumined.

We have already seen that the primordial intuition given in childhood is that of love awakened by the smile of the mother. Even on the human level, therefore, the person will seek the meaning of his existence in human community. In our own day the dialogical philosophers have pointed us in the direction of the human community as the context for understanding the meaning of the person, but von Balthasar asks whether a dialogue between I and Thou offers the final solution to the mystery of man. Is there not a danger here of ending up in a double monologue? In von Balthasar's view, the philosopher who has come closest to the real solution is Ferdinand Ebner with his emphasis upon the Word. For Ebner, the Word which is spoken by the I to the Thou is made possible by the *zwischen* which enables communication to take place. Here we find a foreshadowing of the ultimate trinitarian resolution.

On the basis of Christology we can see that Jesus' identity is rooted in an eternal trinitarian community. The Father is *grundlose Liebe,* the source of love, whose hypostasis as Father consists precisely in giving himself away totally to the Son. The Son in turn is a radical response to the Father's love. The Son holds nothing back from the Father. Their mutual love in turn overflows in the love of the Holy Spirit. The Holy Spirit can thus be defined as the fruitfulness of the divine love. This fruitfulness is as infinite as the divine life itself.

Since in Jesus we are enabled to say that God is love and since in him we come to know who God is, Christian faith enables us to proclaim that ultimate reality is love. Thus the classical problem of philosophy, the problem of being, turns out to be the mystery of love. The Trinity teaches us that being is love. To be sure, God is, as the mystical negative tradition has taught, the one beyond the world. But here we see that the one is not an undifferentiated one. Plurality is as primordial as unity. The ultimate mystery of being is the mystery of community.

One of von Balthasar's principal desires (*Anliegen*) is to think God's being, and hence the trinitarian processions, in terms of love. In this regard he criticizes the Augustinian-Thomistic tradition on two counts. First, this tradition, while not totally excluding the communitarian model for God, prefers as the prime analogate of the divine life the human mind with its acts of intellect and will. In this sense this tradition is guilty of a certain *Ich-Geschlossenheit.* On the other hand, the Thomistic tradition conceives the procession of the Word as an intellectual procession whereas the procession of the Spirit is regarded as a procession of love. But if the immanent Trinity must correspond to the economic Trinity and if God's giving of his Son to the world is an act of love, must not then the eternal generation of the Son by the Father be an act of love? However, if the first procession is a procession of love and if the Father has already given everything in generating the Son, how are we to distinguish the first procession from the second? Here von Balthasar appeals to the theology of Bonaventure. According to Bonaventure, the generation of the Word takes place *per modum exemplaritatis.* The Father so gives himself away that he impresses his form on the Son, enabling the Son to be his perfect reflection in the world. But if the Father has given everything to the Son, there is nonetheless a new possibility for the Father to give himself, namely with the Son. This new mode of love is the Holy Spirit, the mode of ecstatic, overflowing love, which Bonaventure describes as *per modum liberalitatis.*

Since the Holy Spirit is the ecstatic openness of the Father and the Son beyond themselves, the Holy Spirit can also be described as the place of the world. The world has its place in the open space between the Father and the Son.[6] As Adrienne von Speyr has expressed it, "The relations of the three divine persons to each other are so spacious that the whole world has room in them."[7] Looking at the world in trinitarian perspective enables von Balthasar to resolve a number of classical conundrums. First, God is not in need of the world, for God already has his "other" within the Trinity itself. Thus the creation of the world is in no way necessary to his being. Secondly, this trinitarian vision grounds the abiding value of the world. If the philosophical mystic is tempted to leave the world behind in his flight to the One, and if the atheist in the end must confess that all finite reality is doomed to extinction, the Christian is able in Christ to see the world as God's theophany, as the sphere of divine glory. Since Jesus has assumed the world in becoming flesh, the world has an abiding value. The redeemed creation will last forever in the trinitarian life.

Before concluding this reflection on the Trinity as the foundation of von

[6] See *Theodramatik* IV: *Das Endspiel* (Einsiedeln: Johannes Verlag, 1983), 53ff.
[7] "Das Verhältnis der göttlichen Personen zueinander ist so weit, dass die ganze Welt darin Raum hat." Cited by J. Moltmann in *Kirche in der Kraft des Geistes* (Munich, 1975), 77.

Balthasar's theological hermeneutic, we should show how the Trinity also provides the ultimate context for understanding the event of the Cross. At least two points call for comment here. First, as we have seen, von Balthasar's vision of the God/world relation is dramatic. The rapport between God and his creation is that of a drama in which the encounter of two freedoms is played out. We have already seen that this drama culminates in the crash where Jesus is crucified in God-forsakenness. The second point follows directly from the first. Since Jesus dies with the cry of abandonment upon his lips, we must ask whether we end up in fact with the vision of God which Luther called *Deus sub contrario*. Does the Cross imply a split in God? Is God torn apart in the event of the Cross? Does he become his contradictory so that love becomes hate and holiness sin?

The answer of von Balthasar is clear. The drama between God and the world which culminates in the Cross can be understood consistently without falling into the Lutheran *Deus sub contrario* only if we base the historical drama of salvation upon the inner trinitarian drama. For von Balthasar the inner trinitarian life is anything but static. It is a dramatic encounter of love which already includes within itself the possibility of love's encounter with a world of darkness. In one of von Balthasar's most moving passages, he writes:

> That God (as Father) can give away his divinity to such an extent that God (as Son) does not merely receive it as something borrowed, but possesses it in the equality of essence, implies such an unspeakable and unsurpassable "separation" of God from himself that every other separation (made possible by it!), even the most dark and bitter, can only occur within this first separation.[8]

Thus the drama of the Cross can only be understood within the eternal drama of love which admits of no contradiction. The drama which unfolds on Calvary is thoroughly consistent with this eternal drama of love. God does not become his own contradictory. Indeed he remains love, but now love poured out to the end upon sinful humanity which rejects love. God's love remains consistent with itself. And remaining consistent with itself, in the face of such massive rejection, love can only suffer. But because love remains itself, the Cross is the supreme instance of God's glory, even if this glory is a hidden glory, concealed under the suffering and disfigurement of the divine Beauty. The glory of the Lord is hidden, but for the eyes of faith, the glory shines out, as the glory of the eternal trinitarian love.

---

[8] "Dass Gott (als Vater) seine Gottheit so weggeben kann, dass Gott (als Sohn) sie nicht bloss geliehen erhält, sondern 'gleichwesentlich' besitzt, besagt eine so unfassbare und unüberbietbare 'Trennung' Gottes von sich selbst, dass jede (durch sie!) ermöglichte Trennung, und wäre es die dunkelste und bitterste, nur innerhalb ihrer sich ereignen kann" *Theodramatik* III: *Die Handlung* (Einsiedeln: Johannes Verlag, 1980), 302.

The Mystery of the Church: Body and Bride

If the Cross is the revelation of God's trinitarian love, love even to the end, it is also the basis for an understanding of the mystery of the Church. According to the fourth Gospel, at the moment of his death, blood and water flowed from the side of Christ. Moreover, at that moment, Jesus entrusted his Mother to the beloved disciple. Following the patristic tradition, von Balthasar finds in these images rich resources for understanding the mystery of the Church.

The Church is born from the side of Christ dying upon the Cross. The blood and water are symbols of the sacraments of baptism and the Eucharist. Mary is seen as the Mother of the Church and an archetype of the Church's fecundity. Mary combines in her person the role of the Bride and of the Mother. She is at once the bridal response of love to Christ and the womb from whom Christ is born in the hearts of believers. The imagery of John must be combined with the Pauline image of Ephesians where Paul sees in matrimony an image of the spousal relationship between Christ and his Church (Eph 5:32).

If we ask who is the Church, a question which supposes that the Church is a subject and not a thing, the bridal image can help us to find an adequate response.[9] On the one hand, a bridal relationship presupposes two persons. Hence Christ and his Church do not form a hypostatic union where the distinction between Christ and his Church becomes confused. On the other hand, the goal of the matrimonial relationship is that the two become one flesh and this relationship should express the complementarity of the sexuality of the spouses. In the case of the Church this means that Christ takes the initiative. He bears the seed of eternal life which is to be planted in the womb of the Church. The Church as Bride is wholly feminine in her being. Her call is to say Yes, to receive the seed, to gestate it in her womb. Her role is receptivity, but not a passive receptivity. Rather this receptivity calls for the active *disponibilité* to let God's Word fructify in her life. The sexual imagery is so important for von Balthasar that he even says that the Church must avoid everything which is masculine (grasping, active, determining) in its relationship to God and to Christ, otherwise it falls into a type of religious homosexuality which perverts the fundamental nature of the God-man relationship. This is the subtle error of non-Christian forms of mysticism which seek to reach union with God by means of techniques and of primitive religions which strive to manipulate the divine through magic. For von Balthasar as well there is a masculine principle in the Church, but it has validity only insofar as it is at the service of the feminine character of the Church. The

[9] See von Balthasar's essay "Wer ist die Kirche?" in *Sponsa Verbi* (Einsiedeln: Johannes Verlag, 1960), 148–202.

masculine principle is embodied in Peter and expresses itself in authority, in the *ex opere operato* of the sacraments, in the teaching office, and in the canon of Scripture. From the point of view of the finality of the Church what is important to note is that the masculine principle is always subordinate to the feminine principle and exists that the Church might fulfill her feminine identity, namely her bridal response of love to her Lord.

The background and condition of possibility for the spousal relationship with the Church is God's trinitarian love for the world. As we have seen, the ultimate reality is love and this love is nothing less than the trinitarian love of the divine persons. The Trinity wishes to enter into unity with humanity itself. And this union is realized in the Church. But as von Balthasar notes, the Church in this sense represents humanity itself. The Church whom God predestined is nothing less than the entirety of humanity. If the Trinity is the ground of the Church, the triune community also helps us to explain the nature of the bridal union between Christ and the Church. This unity consists in the Holy Spirit who is the bond of union between the Father and the Son in the inner trinitarian life. The Holy Spirit is their unity in person. As third person of the Trinity, he both allows the other two persons to remain distinct and joins them together in an unbreakable bond of love. In this sense, von Balthasar can speak of the Holy Spirit as *coincidentia oppositorum*.[10] The Holy Spirit also fulfills the same role in the Church. As the ultimate subject of the Church (the who of the Church), the Spirit respects the distinctness of the believers while uniting them in Christ.

This unity is so intense that the bridal image is not sufficient to illuminate the mystery of the Church. Among other images which shed light on the mystery is the Johannine one of the vine and the branches. The branches are grafted on the vine, they exist in the vine, and only in this way do they share the life of the vine and bear fruit. And then there is the crucial image of the Body of Christ. So united is the Church with her Lord, that with him as Head of the Church she forms one Body. If the image of the bride stresses the distinction of the persons, the image of the body stresses the unity which is superior to the greatest unity imaginable for finite creatures, namely the sexual union of spouses. Here the believers actually become the limbs of the Body of Christ. It is Augustine who exploits this image to the full. The union between Christ and his faithful is so great that Head and members are one Body, the *totus Christus*.

Here von Balthasar meditates upon the patristic idea of the *corpus triforme* of Christ, namely the physical Body of the Lord, the mystical Body of the Church, and the sacramental Body of the Eucharist. If the goal of God's dealings with the world is *connubium*, then this union is realized when by

---

[10] Ibid., 202.

baptism the believer is inserted into Christ's Body. In that moment Christ impresses his form upon the Christian. From that moment the life of the Christian consists in the daily letting himself be molded by the archetypal figure of Christ. The culmination of this conformation to Christ is the celebration of the Eucharist in which the Marian spousal image and the Pauline bodily image coalesce. In offering the Eucharist, the Church can do nothing of herself.[11] She has nothing of her own to give God. All she can do is to say: Let it be. She can only say Yes to what Christ does, to his death on her behalf. Her action is the active receptivity of Mary. And yet because the feminine Church is also the Body of Christ, in him she can offer Christ to the Father, for it is the living Christ, the *totus Christus,* Head and members, who offers the sacrifice. The Eucharist is the perfect embodiment of the *admirabile commercium* between God and man. The Church presents her emptiness to the Father, and she in turn is filled with Christ, the Bread of Life. And the bread which she eats is the Body which she becomes, Christ's Body visible in the world. As St. Augustine says, *"Hoc est sacrificium christianorum: multi unum corpus in Christo."*[12]

Christian Life: Being Molded into Christ

To appreciate the goal of von Balthasar's theology, we must always bear in mind that he was formed in the school of the Spiritual Exercises of St. Ignatius. These Exercises culminate in the meditation for obtaining the love of God in which the exercitant is invited to contemplate God's presence indwelling his creation and is summoned to offer his entire being to the Lord so that from henceforth he can find God in all things.

We have already seen how von Balthasar's theology is focused upon the idea of the *connubium* of God with the world. At the end of the first volume of *Herrlichkeit,* von Balthasar notes that myth understands the God/world relationship as a theophany. Christianity too sees this relation as a theophany, but a theophany rooted in Christ and in his Incarnation. In Christ the world radiates the glory of God. Eschatologically the world is being assimilated to Christ, so that it too is becoming the theatre of God's glory. This process takes place as the human person lets himself be molded by the form of Christ. Such receptivity to Christ's informing action is what von Balthasar means by faith. He writes, "Participation in Christ's mission and form of existence, a participa-

---

[11] For von Balthasar's understanding of the Eucharist as sacrifice, see "Die Messe, ein Opfer der Kirche?" in *Spiritus Creator* (*Skizzen zur Theologie* III) (Einsiedeln: Johannes Verlag, 1967), 166–217.

[12] *De Civ. Dei* X. 6 as cited by von Balthasar, *Theologik* III: *Der Geist der Wahrheit* (Einsiedeln: Johannes Verlag, 1987), 270.

tion that bridges the permanent difference between him and us, is possible when a believer is ready through the assent of faith to receive and live his existence as mission."[13] Let us then examine this participation in Christ's form of existence in three stages: the meaning of faith, the significance of obedience, and the nature of mission.

First of all, we note that for von Balthasar faith is not an intellectual act but rather an existential surrender of the whole person. By this surrender the person hands over his whole being to Christ. Although faith in this sense is the most personal act imaginable and therefore an intensely personal experience in which one knows the Lord, it is in no sense a self-centered or introspective act. Faith is in no way preoccupied with itself. Therefore von Balthasar rejects the whole Lutheran idea of faith as security. Rather faith is an act of expropriation, wholly centered on another, namely on Christ. The paradigm for this understanding of faith is Paul. Paul, speaking of his faith in Christ in the Letter to the Philippians, says that he seeks to know Christ and the power of his Resurrection and affirms his willingness to share now in Christ's sufferings and death. Acknowledging that this goal is still something to be attained, he writes, "One thing I do: forgetting what lies behind and straining forward to what lies ahead, I press on toward the goal for the prize of the upward call of God in Christ Jesus" (Phil 3:13–14). Von Balthasar comments, "Everything is founded upon the suspension of having let go of oneself and of existing only in the flight toward the goal."[14] Such is the nature of faith's expropriation that it is existence poised in flight.

But if faith is thus other-centered, it can also be described as obedience. Just as Christ's form was his abiding openness to the will of the Father, so the Christian's being, informed by Christ, consists in his radical availability to do the will of the Father. Here we see again that the form of faith will always be Marian, the receptivity to let God do in me what he will.

But this reflection brings us finally to the notion of sending. If faith in general can be described as obedience, this obedience becomes concrete in the mission which each one receives from God. We recall that, for von Balthasar, a *Geistessubjekt* becomes a person in the concrete, unpredictable mission which he receives from God.[15] Man is created with the faculties of intellect and will but he becomes a person only through the dialogical relation. The supreme

---

[13] "Teilnahme an der Sendung und Existenzform Christi wird, über die bleibende Differenz zwischen ihm und uns hinweg, dort möglich, wo ein Glaubender im Jawort des Glaubens seine Existenz als Sendung zu empfangen und zu leben bereit ist" (*Spiritus Creator*, 309).

[14] "In die Schwebe dieses Sich-los-gelassen-habens und erst im Flug auf das Ziel hin Existierens ist alles gestellt" *Herrlichkeit* Bd. I: *Schau der Gestalt* (Einsiedeln: Johannes Verlag, 1961), 219.

[15] See above, p. 210, note 3.

dialogical partner is God through whom the person receives the mission by which his freedom becomes concrete. By stressing the unique project of love which God has for each individual, von Balthasar once again deepens the Ignatian tradition of the Exercises whose central focus is the election. From all eternity God knows each man or woman with a particular love which is realized in a unique mission which no one else can fulfill. In this way the person's own holiness is fulfilled by responding to the mission, and at the same time holiness is never a grace for oneself but is always a gift given for the upbuilding of the Church.

Thus we see that if the religious question arises for man in that primordial moment in which his I is awakened by the mother's smile, thereby giving him the intuition to love, the resolution of this question is found in God's address to man in Christ. In Christ and in his Cross we see the form of God's love for the world. Responding to that love, in faith and in obedience, to a mission planned for no one else who ever was or will be, the person discovers the meaning of his freedom, a freedom which in the response becomes concrete and informed, thus enabling him to verify in his own experience the truth that Being is love.

ELLERO BABINI

Jesus Christ: Form and Norm of Man according to Hans Urs von Balthasar

Besides being one of the most characteristic traits of the theological position of the great, recently deceased thinker, Hans Urs von Balthasar, the particular type of relation he has constructed between Christology and anthropology, the bond he has found and brought to light between the reality of Christ and the reality of man, is one of the most precious supports for the renewal of theology along the lines of sound and authentic Catholic Tradition. Nevertheless, that relation, which constitutes one of the cruxes for the theology of every historical epoch and especially for contemporary theology, has remained among the least examined aspects of his theology within the panorama of critical studies (growing constantly in recent years). Too often, we confine ourselves to an almost exclusive consideration of the theological "aesthetics" elaborated in the seven volumes of *Herrlichkeit*,[1] forgetting that they represent only the first part of a trilogy which continues with *Theodramatik* and finally with *Theologik*,[2] which the author managed to complete shortly before his sudden and regrettable death.

It is precisely with *Theodramatik* that von Balthasar succeeds in elaborating a complete and systematic doctrine of man and his connection with Christ, the Redeemer of man, as he affirms in the second volume. Therefore, in this essay I would like to confront the problem of the relation between anthropology and Christology in the wake of *Theodramatik*, with passing glances at other— earlier or later—works which shed light on that connection.

What sort of bond unites man to Christ? How are Christology and theological anthropology interrelated? Together, they take three steps, as if deepening the discourse in three successive stages. These steps on one path may be summed up in three words which I believe to be key words in von Balthasar's

Translated by Thérèse M. Bonin.

Communio 16 (Fall 1989). © 1989 by *Communio: International Catholic Review.*

[1] English translation under the title *The Glory of the Lord: A Theological Aesthetics* (San Francisco: Ignatius Press 1983–91).—TRANS.

[2] These volumes are being translated into English under the names *Theo-Drama* and *Theo-Logic* by Ignatius Press.

thought. Thus we will come to see how Jesus Christ is the "form" and "norm" of man.

Mission

Jesus Christ presents himself as the man who lives and dies to fulfill the mission received from his Father in the Holy Spirit, as the man who identifies himself with his mission ("My food is to do the will of him who sent me and to accomplish his work" [Jn 4:34]). In the Christology of *Theodramatik,* even more than in the works preceding it, the key concept, the basic idea, is provided by the divine *mission,* which animates anthropology by reflex action. Consequently, the Christian, like Christ, becomes one sent: "As the Father has sent me, so I send you" (Jn 20:21). Christ is the principal actor or protagonist of the "drama", and he enables man to recite his part in turn and become a *Mitspieler,* a co-actor. As in Christology, so in anthropology the keystone is provided by the category "mission", of which the category "role" is a theatrical prefiguration. That is to say, man is a being in the process of becoming (to use biblical language, he is an *image* of God destined for an ever fuller *likeness* to him; he is an *Abbild* called to conform more and more to his *Urbild*): on a philosophical level, we can say that he is originally a *Geistessubjekt,* i.e., a spiritual subject, called to become truly a "person". And he becomes a person—a mature subject responsible for dramatic, existential action—by virtue of the mission, the existential task received from and in Christ, the real protagonist of the theo-drama, of which God the Father is the author, and the Holy Spirit the director.

By means of the mission received, man discovers why he has been made and who he really is, since it is in mission, received as gift from an "other", that he hears himself called as an "I" by a "Thou", and (made responsible by this latter) called to a response. The responsibility (which engages the freedom of the person, and in which the human subject reaches maturation and arrives at his adult stature) is responsibility for a charge, for a mission received, for a work which involves and is inseparable from the person's whole existence. In this work there is clearly expressed and found a concrete verification, a practical realization of that "response" which man as such is in his creatureliness. If man as creature is *Antwort* (a response) to God who has created him, this starting point is realized existentially, dramatically, in a *Verantwortung,* a responsibility.

That responsibility is carried out by "corresponding"—or not—to the role received, i.e., to one's own vocation. And this philosophical category of *Entsprechung* (correspondence) finds its more properly theological counterpart in the category of "obedience".[3] By his obedience, Christ realizes his redemptive mission. If the keystone of Christology, its formal, determining characteristic, is mission (*Sendung*), then its content, or, better, the historical coloration it assumes, is obedience. More precisely yet, it is *Liebesgehorsam,* an obedience of love.

This obedience (in the first place a Christological key, and then, consequently, an anthropological one) is, at bottom, nothing but the practical translation of that fundamental, vital attitude of filial dependence which the creature has before his Creator: von Balthasar calls it *Angewiesenheit,* i.e., return to God, vital dependence on him, inescapable reference to him.

All this is very far from making the drama monotonous, from suppressing or thwarting that original freedom which distinguishes man. Indeed, the very reception of his own, personalizing mission by following Christ and participating in his central role empowers man for a conscious and significant exercise of his freedom[4] and makes him enter into a living, existential co-involvement in the universal, dramatic event of which the protagonist is Christ, and the backdrop is heaven and earth, history and eternity.

If the human person is primarily defined, not so much by his constitution in body and soul, but rather, from the personalizing mission, then there results a living anthropological picture, dynamic, moving, everything but static! And so it is a matter of truly becoming a person, of being ever more a person. Certainly, being always remains at the foundation: man is ontologically, by his constitution, a spiritual subject. But this being is animated and moved by a tension, a becoming.

Thence arises a dynamic conception of man as an open being, moving toward his fulfillment, growing toward his personal maturity and toward the full appropriation of the truth about himself. Since man is, by origin, *angelegt auf Gott,*[5] oriented toward God and dependent on him as a finite freedom posited in act and contained by an infinite freedom, he arrives at self-realization through correspondence to his original vocation, a growing, existential adequation to his being *imago Dei,* a practical verification of the *analogia entis* which grounds it, by conforming himself to Christ who is the *Analogia entis* become concrete.[6]

---

[3] Cf. *Theodramatik* II: *Die Personen des Spiels,* 2. Teil: *Die Personen in Christus* (Einsiedeln: Johannes Verlag, 1978), 175, 485; III. *Die Handlung* (Einsiedeln: Johannes Verlag, 1980), 58, 210, 460; IV. *Das Endspiel* (Einsiedeln: Johannes Verlag, 1983), 77 (where the fundamental presupposition—that, in the intratrinitarian life, freedom is equivalent to "correspondence"—is clarified).

[4] Cf. *Theodramatik* II/2, 47, 393, 487; III, 57, 444.

[5] Cf. *Theodramatik* III, 126, 130. See also *Pneuma und Institution* (*Skizzen zur Theologie* IV) (Einsiedeln: Johannes Verlag, 1974), 23.

[6] Cf. *Theodramatik* II. 1. Teil: *Der Mensch in Gott,* 243; III, 444; *Theologie der Geschichte*

The axis about which everything revolves is, then, this conception of the *analogia entis*, which has its center in the Christological dogma of Chalcedon— with its decisive adverbs *"inconfuse"* and *"inseparabiliter"*—and its clarifying development in Lateran IV: *"Inter creatorem et creaturam non potest similitudo notari, quin inter eos maior sit dissimilitudo notanda"*[7] (DS 806). In other words, the just and correct relation of loving dependence of man before his Creator is safeguarded and defended thanks to this underlining of the *maior dissimilitudo,* i.e., of the distance which alone makes possible a true union of love, the *admirabile commercium,* the meeting and the exchange between God and man, by avoiding the risks of the mysticizing and nullifying fusion of contours and personal identity typical of every ancient or modern form of *"gnosis".*[8]

This *analogia entis* crosses the incandescent nucleus of the hypostatic union and is verified, reformulated, and elevated by it.[9] In Christ, union and distance, proximity and remoteness between man and God, are carried to their extreme point, until they reach the unthinkable cry of Jesus on the Cross: "My God, why have you abandoned me?" (Mk 15:34). They go deeper yet, descending into hell, the place of extreme remoteness from God or, rather, of his absolute absence. Precisely by this journey toward the most extreme remoteness, a new and unimaginable nearness, intimacy, and communion between God and man is reestablished and recreated.

At this Christological level, the original axis, the *analogia entis* into which the Son, becoming incarnate, had entered, is surpassed and inserted within another relation, which is revealed as more original, indeed as grounding the creaturely relation of the *analogia entis:* the trinitarian relation of the Son with the Father in the Holy Spirit. The distance between man and God, between the world and God, is contained within the intratrinitarian distance between the Son and the Father, which is a communion in the Holy Spirit who proceeds from both and who maintains union even in remoteness.[10]

(Einsiedeln: Johannes Verlag, 1959), 53; *Verbum Caro* (*Skizzen zur Theologie* I) (Einsiedeln: Johannes Verlag, 1960), 191.

[7] Latin: Between the Creator and the creature, no likeness can be noted without there being a greater unlikeness to be noted—trans.

[8] Cf. *Theodramatik* II/1, 368; II/2, 202–11; III, 354f. This underlining of the "distance" is clarified quite well in the work *Christlicher Stand* (Einsiedeln: Johannes Verlag, 1977). English translation by Sr. M. Frances McCarthy under the title *The Christian State of Life* (San Francisco: Ignatius Press, 1983), 51f., 104.

[9] See especially *Theodramatik* II/1, 373; II/2, 186, 209. R. Vignolo, too, has given evidence of such Christological centering of the *analogia entis* in *Estetica e singolarità* (Milan, 1982), 146–66 and 443f. For von Balthasar, see also *Christen sind einfältig* (Einsiedeln: Johannes Verlag, 1983), 32.

[10] Cf. *Theodramatik* II/2, 20: "The creature's obedient distance before his Creator and

Thus, the *analogia entis* finds its *ubi consistam,* its crystallization and verification in the Christological dogma of Chalcedon. And this constitutes a proof of the validity of the assertion that the category "mission" is an exhaustive interpretative and explanatory factor as much in Christological as in anthropological truth. Before the Father, the Son presents himself as sent, and, in his turn, he sends to the whole world the men who have followed him. As much for Christ as for man, the road to self-realization, to perfection, lies in fulfillment of the mission.[11]

Substitution

The second key word of the relation between Christology and anthropology, the second step on the way to deepening the bond which links Christ and man, is provided by the theological term *Stellvertretung,* i.e., "representation" or, better, vicarious "substitution", a classical term in the history of Christian doctrine concerning soteriology.

It clarifies and deepens on a soteriological level what has been made plain about the first point, mission.

The decisive importance of von Balthasar's adoption and maximization of Chalcedon's Christological dogma, which informs the philosophical axis (the *analogia entis,* understood in *Theodramatik* especially as an *analogia libertatis*), is increased by his use of the soteriological model of vicarious substitution. Taken from St. Anselm's *Cur Deus homo?* and completed with the Thomistic theory of the *gratia Capitis* and the patristic theory of the *admirabile commercium,* it allows one properly to locate the terms of the soteriological relation between man and Christ, and between these latter and the Father.[12] Indeed, it is precisely on the supposition of the Chalcedonian formula, *"vere Deus et vere homo",* that a real assumption of human nature by the person of the Son becomes possible—an assumption unto a perfect and real substitution, a putting oneself in the other's place and representing him before the divine "justice" in perfect terms.

Thus in meeting the demands of a soteriology which does not rest content with the bland image of a God "already always" reconciled with man (a superficiality which von Balthasar believes to be a risk present in Rahnerian transcendental theology), and which takes with the utmost seriousness the

---

master becomes transparent with the intradivine distance of the Son to the Father in the Spirit." See also *Theodramatik* II/1, 238–46.

[11] Cf. *Christlicher Stand,* 64.

[12] Cf. *Theodramatik* III, 212–395. The importance of von Balthasar's use of the soteriological model of *Stellvertretung* has been stressed by K. Lehmann as well, in his article "Er wurde für uns gekreuzigt", *Theol. Quartalschrift* 162 (1982), especially 303–17.

whole human drama in its radical need for salvation, the category of substitution simultaneously furnishes a model for explanation and a criterion for verification of man's radical *belonging* to Christ, of the intimate insertion of anthropology into Christology.

This utilization of the Anselmian model of vicarious substitution—amplified and complemented by a trinitarian background in which the "economy", and therefore the mission of the Son and of the Spirit, is rooted in the immanent Trinity, characterized by an eternal attitude of devotion and self-offering (*Selbsthingabe*) of one divine person to the other—represents an essential contribution of von Balthasar to contemporary theology. Thereby anthropology receives a more precise Christological centering in a soteriological mode.

By virtue of the fact that Christ, "true God and true man", according to the dogma proclaimed at Chalcedon, suffers and dies not only on man's behalf, but, indeed, *in his place* (this is the most radical sense of *crucifixus etiam pro nobis*[13]), as representative of all humanity and of every man, he is truly the new man, the new Adam; and man is thus truly and fully reconciled with God the Father, beyond every extrinsicism and every justification by mere "imputation".

Therefore, anthropology and Christology do not remain simply parallel, one beside the other; instead, they are merged one with the other, intimately connected and indissolubly linked—and that by virtue of the substitution based on the Christological dogma of Chalcedon.

The fruit which stems from the sacrifice of the Cross in the supreme act of self-dedication, of trinitarian self-giving, is finally manifest as the fundamental, universal element, as what is most original: the new man who offers himself to the Father in the Holy Spirit on the Cross is simultaneously the one in whom and for whom all things were made. He is the Omega, and, at the same time, the Alpha.

Thus a certain dichotomy is overcome and eliminated, that dualism between a primarily creationistic (or philosophical) anthropology and a primarily Christological anthropology, founded principally on the redemption effected by Christ. G. Colombo finds this dualism somehow present even within the conciliar constitution *Gaudium et spes*.[14] In *Theodramatik*, these two aspects or accentuations of anthropology are certainly both present, but they are not simply juxtaposed; rather, they are harmoniously integrated, founded on a unitary design. One can see this not only from the central volume, *Die Handlung* (III), where soteriology is the matter at hand, but already in the introductory volume of the anthropology, *Die Personen des Spiels: Der Mensch*

---

[13] Latin: He was crucified for us. (From the Latin text of the Constantinopolitan creed; see DS 150.)—TRANS.

[14] Cf. G. Colombo, "La teologia della 'Gaudium et Spes' e l'esercizio del Magistero", *Scuola cattolica* 98 (1970): 477–511.

in Gott (II/2). Moreover, this profound insertion of anthropology into Christology, achieved on the basis of the soteriological model of *Stellvertretung*, is very far from cutting off the discourse of anthropology in advance or absorbing it prematurely and unduly, taking away man's space for autonomous action in the manifestation of his original freedom. On the contrary, the *Stellvertretung* acted out by Christ makes possible for man a full display of his freedom, opening for him a space for action and offering him the possibility of exercising his co-responsibility, of being an authentic *Mitspieler,* a co-actor in the drama.[15]

Here is the *n*th verification of how anthropology is "normed" by Christology, informed, and vivified by it: thanks to Christ's sacrificial self-offering, and in virtue of man's union with him and consequent partaking of his destiny, in the Eucharist and in the Church's *communio,* man acquires a new and unexpected possibility of self-realization, of authentic exercise of his original freedom.

We may note, too, how the categories "correspondence" and "participation" assume a new worth and a particular importance—categories which had already animated both the great current of Neoplatonic-Areopagitic tradition (the heavenly and earthly *hierarchy*) and the Thomistic tradition (the ideas of *adaequatio* and *participatio*).[16] Here, in *Theodramatik,* they are appropriated and utilized from a new viewpoint: that of the human/divine drama, in which man is called to recite his part, corresponding with responsible freedom to the role received, and thus participating in the drama of which Christ is the protagonist and principal subject, who creates space and offers a role to other and always new co-actors as well.

Singularity

We find the third step, the third deepening or explication of the connection between Christology and anthropology, in von Balthasar's particular emphasis on and use of the category "singularity" (*Einmaligkeit*). This singularity refers, first and foremost, to Christ, being his typical and inalienable quality in his original, unrepeatable, *unique* position as mediator between God and the world,[17] between the Father who has sent him and humanity to which he has been sent and which he represents in himself before the Father. But, as a consequence, there suddenly emerges man's singularity, by virtue of the unconfusable originality of the call and the personal (and personalizing)

---

[15] So, too, K. Lehmann, "Er wurde für uns gekreuzigt", 315.

[16] Cf. L. B. Geiger, *La participation dans la philosophie de St. Thomas d'Aquin* (Paris, 1942).

[17] K. Lehmann, too, speaks of "einzigartiges und letzlich analogieloses Ereignis der Erlösung Jesu Christi" in *Er wurde für uns gekreuzig,* 303.

mission he receives from God through Jesus Christ. Every man has a task and a unique vocation, planned expressly for him, to which he alone can respond. It is a matter of a "unicity", an analogical participation in the unicity of the mission of Christ and of the ecclesial figures who, by virtue of their mission, are closest to him: Mary in the first place, and then the saints, beginning with the twelve apostles.

Not only in *Theodramatik,* but also in *Herrlichkeit* and in minor works, von Balthasar insists on underlining this unicity, singularity, incomparability, which is typical of the Christian "figure" (*Gestalt*), a distinctive element of the Christian event. Thus, its intrinsic novelty stands out: the salvation accomplished in and through Christ, man's redemption, is something absolutely new, a gratuitous gift, surprising and irreducible to what was already known, even if it finds an inchoate correspondence and a meeting point in man's waiting and in his needs, in his *desiderium.*

An obstacle to this dimension of novelty, and therefore a polemical objective von Balthasar never ceased to address, is the *immer schon gewusst* present in the foundations of Karl Rahner's transcendental Christology. It is the risk of considering Christian salvation, God's reconciliation with the world, as something which was, at bottom, already known, presaged and intuited by man in various forms, even if unconsciously and "anonymously". The tendency to *Verallgemeinung,* i.e., to the generalization of what is and remains the distinctive, specific, and inalienable element of the Christian event, is an obstacle to the perception of its singularity. The Christian element cannot be reduced simply to what is universally human, to the human in general.

Here one must make an important qualification. Sometimes a distinction is drawn between "general" (which is in danger of being diluted to "generic") and "universal", between *allgemein menschlich* (universally human) and *universal.* I believe that one of the conquests and fundamental acquisitions of *Theodramatik* (already foreseen in *Herrlichkeit*) was having made plain the original and irreducible *subjectivity* characteristic of the Christian *Gestalt* and of the Christian event, which has its center in Christ. This subjectivity, as such, brings with it its inalienable *singularity.* Christ is in fact the singular, *einmalig,* unique subject of the theo-drama; man is a singular subject by derivation and analogy with respect to Christ. Now, this dimension of irreducible subjectivity, in its original singularity, makes Christ (and man, who, in the ecclesial sequel, participates in him) capable of "integration" and therefore of universal meaning and worth. The universality of the redemption worked by Christ cannot be severed from its particular unicity; indeed, its universality derives from its singular position. The universal integrative capacity characteristic of the Christian subject depends on his original singularity and his unconfusable identity. Thus, the universality deriving from the capacity of the original Christian subject for harmonious integration is guarded and protected from the risk of dilution in a formless generality, in a "genericity", in something universally "common".[18]

The soteriological category of vicarious substitution, as appropriated by von Balthasar, allows for manifestation of the aspect of universality typical of Christian redemption, while simultaneously preserving and highlighting the singularity of Jesus Christ. His original position is irreducible to some generally human position and therefore immune to any attempt at *Verallgemeinung,* at generalization. His very singularity and unicity, his *Einmaligkeit* and *Einzigartigkeit* as God's Son made man, grants him universality, allowing him really to represent in himself, by substitution, all humanity and each man in particular.[19]

From this singularity, from this original Christian subjectivity, a people, a community takes its origin, as was the case with the types of the Old Testament (from Abraham and Moses to the symbolic figure of the Servant of Yahweh, who "will see his descendants . . . will receive the multitudes as his reward[20] . . . because he has consigned himself to death" [Is 53:10–12]). The Christian subject generates communion by virtue of his Christian identity.

But this is possible because, in fact, there is already a communion at the beginning: the intratrinitarian communion between the Father and the Son in the Holy Spirit, a communion which is at the origin of everything, from the plan for salvation history to the world itself. Von Balthasar always asserts and sheds new light on the trinitarian implications and presuppositions of every phase in salvation history and every aspect of Christian life, giving them a relief and an importance not often seen in contemporary theology. Adrienne von Speyr excelled at teaching the trinitarian implications and the role of the trinitarian mystery in every part of theology and of Christian life.[21]

The Christian subject, the theological personality, has a communal origin.

---

[18] German has the adjective *allgemein* (= general), whence derives the pejorative *gemein* (= common, current, vulgar)—TRANS.

[19] We can find confirmation of this in the Church's recent teaching; e.g., *Gaudium et spes,* 22: "By his Incarnation, he, the Son of God, in a certain way united himself with each man", and *Redemptor hominis,* 13: "Jesus Christ becomes present with the power of the truth and the love that are expressed in him with *unique, unrepeatable* fullness." (It is interesting to note that, in the German text of this papal encyclical, the two adjectives are the very ones on which von Balthasar insists: *in einzigartiger und einmaliger Fülle . . . .*)

[20] The author seems to be following an Italian translation of the Septuagint: *dia touto autos klēronomēsei pollous* — TRANS.

[21] For a global view of Adrienne von Speyr's theological thought, see Hans Urs von Balthasar, *Erster Blick auf Adrienne von Speyr* (Einsiedeln: Johannes Verlag, 1969), English translation by Antje Lawry and Sr. Sergia Englund under the title *First Glance at Adrienne von Speyr* (San Francisco: Ignatius Press, 1981). See also the acts of the symposium on her ecclesial mission, held at Rome in September of 1985: *Adrienne von Speyr und ihre kirchliche Sendung* (Einsiedeln: Johannes Verlag, 1986). For a study of her influence on von Balthasar's theological production, see *Unser Auftrag* (Einsiedeln: Johannes Verlag, 1984), especially 81–97.

From beginning to end there is a communion,[22] that communion which is a participation in the trinitarian life, itself a communion of persons.

Thus, the theological elaboration of *Theodramatik*, still more clearly than *Herrlichkeit*, seems a timely answer to the need for a *theocentric* anthropology expressed by the encyclical *Dives in misericordia*: "The more the Church's mission is centered upon man—the more it is, so to speak, anthropocentric—the more it must be confirmed and actualized theocentrically, that is to say, be directed in Jesus Christ to the Father."[23]

With *Theodramatik*, von Balthasar has fulfilled the theological program (begun in 1952 with the small but precious *Theologie der Geschichte*) of showing how Christ is the "form" and the "norm" of man and of history, the model and rule for man, for each man, on an ontological as well as an ethical level. His particular manifestation of the unbreakable bond between Christology and anthropology is certainly one of the most important contributions he has made to Catholic theology.

---

[22] Cf. *Theodramatik* II/1, 374, 382; III, 378; IV, 53ff., 341ff.

[23] *Dives in misericordia*, 1. An analogous judgment on von Balthasar's theology is expressed by R. Vignoli, who, in the study cited above, speaks of "Christocentrism oriented in a trinitarian perspective, which anthropological feature is, in turn, to be interpreted theocentrically, always beginning from Jesus' filial obedience to the Father" (*Estetica e singolarità*, 442).

MARC OUELLET, S.S.

The Foundations of Christian Ethics according to Hans Urs von Balthasar

Introduction

Since the Second Vatican Council the Church lives under the sign of dialogue with the modern world. Her *aggiornamento* seeks to communicate better the Gospel to the man of today. But the encounter is not proceeding without difficulty, because modern culture is anthropocentric. Karl Rahner is undoubtedly the theologian who has made the greatest effort to express revelation in this category. His anthropological approach has modified the posing of ethical problems, and many moralists, especially in the United States, are grateful to him for this.[1] We find in his thought a concept of man as fundamental liberty which allows us to transcend a strict ethics of action toward a deeper ethics of the person. But the integration of this perspective brings difficulties which are apparent from documents from the Magisterium, in the domain, for example, of sexual morality.[2]

Hans Urs von Balthasar is a theologian who has attempted an expression of Christian revelation that transcends the anthropocentric framework of contemporary culture. This is undoubtedly the reason why his thought has been assimilated so slowly into the discussion of current problems, especially those which touch ethics. His "Nine Propositions for a Christian Ethics"[3] has been acclaimed as "a gem",[4] "remarkable in its Christological and biblical aspect" but, according to Jean-Marie Aubert, "very vague on the subject of concrete

Translated by Mary F. Rousseau.
Communio 17 (Fall 1990). © 1990 by *Communio: International Catholic Review.*

[1] Richard McCormick "Moral Theology 1940–1989: An Overview", *Theological Studies* 50 (1989): 3–24.

[2] Joseph Cardinal Ratzinger, "The Difficulties of Faith in Europe Today", *Osservatore Romano* [English ed.], July 24, 1989. A. Regan, C.Ss.R., "Grappling with the Fundamental Option", *Studia Moralia,* 27, 1 (1989): 103–39.

[3] "Nine Propositions on Christian Ethics", in Ratzinger, Schürmann, von Balthasar, *Principles of Christian Morality* (San Francisco: Ignatius Press, 1986), 77–104; hereinafter referred to as *PCM* and cited simply by the paragraph numbers.

[4] P. Delhaye and J. Ratzinger, *Principes d'Éthique chrétienne* (Paris: Sycomore/Lethielleux, 1979), introduction, 11–12.

norms".[5] The same author expresses surprise at the secondary and relative place given to reason and the natural law, and attributes this fact to a "pessimistic idea of human nature".[6]

My proposal here is not to supply what is wanting to the "Nine Propositions", nor to show concretely how they apply in particular ethical situations. I am seeking, rather, to clarify what is given so succinctly in the "Propositions" in terms of the entire work of von Balthasar, but especially the *Theodramatik,* where he presents the core of his theological anthropology.

I would like, by this more formal approach, to disengage the general sense of Christian ethics as it is manifested in this drama, which studies the confrontation of divine liberty and human liberty in the theater of salvation history. The central question addressed in this work is the unity of the person in his constitutive relationship to Jesus Christ, to the Church, and to the world. We shall begin by briefly presenting Christ as the supreme ethical norm and center of the integration of persons into the divine freedom. As a conclusion we shall see how Christian ethics is located and modified theologically.

Von Balthasar claims to offer in his *Theodramatik* the point of convergence of currents of contemporary theology which are discordant and yet convergent.[7] "The confrontation of God's freedom with man's reaches a critical point, their encounter reaches the center—a center that is finally dramatic—of the problem of existence."[8] How, then, does Christian ethics find itself modified and fecundated?

Christ, the Supreme Ethical Norm

"Christian ethics must be modeled on Jesus Christ. . . . " (*PCM,* 1.1).

This abrupt affirmation which begins and gives the tone to the "Nine Propositions" assumes a special meaning for von Balthasar that distinguishes his approach from that of a Barth, a Häring, and most of the contemporary moralists who refer to the law of Christ. The structure of the nine propositions clearly reflects his Christocentric perspective. He begins by showing "the accomplishment of morality in Christ" (four propositions), and then shows "the Old Testament elements of the future synthesis" (two propositions), in order to end with "fragments of an extra-Biblical ethics" (three propositions).

This original structure follows an eschatological perspective which goes beyond the historical-chronological viewpoint in order to situate the Chris-

---

[5] J. M. Aubert, "Débats autour de la morale fondamentale", *Studia Moralia* 20, 2 (1982): 207–8.

[6] Ibid, 208.

[7] *Theodramatik* I: *Prolegomena* (Einsiedeln: Johannes Verlag, 1973), 23–47.

[8] Ibid., 46.

tian "in the 'last age' " in which he must "strive beyond those elements within him that are preliminary and seek to embrace things of ultimate validity" (*PCM,* preliminary note). Von Balthasar thus begins from the fullness of Christ and proceeds to consider, by a sort of subtraction, we might say, what remains of elements and fragments of an ethics when we abstract from the fulfillment of man in Jesus Christ.

His point of view is neither purely ascending, as that of those authors who begin with a philosophical anthropology in order to discern what the Christian dimension adds to an ethics already largely constituted; nor is it purely descending, as that of authors who overlook the mediation of reason and tie themselves to a pure ethics of faith. It is a perspective of integration beginning with the Covenant concluded in Jesus Christ at the center of the history of the world. It is an integration of nature and grace, an integration of human freedom into divine freedom which leaves the necessary room (the analogy of being) for an autonomous and authentic "play" of human freedom that is interior to the "dramatic action" of the divine freedom. "God does not recite the drama of the world as a soliloquy; he makes room in it for his human co-protagonist." [9]

Jesus Christ is the supreme norm of this double dramatic action in which God and man truly encounter each other. Von Balthasar calls him "the concrete categorical imperative" (*PCM,* I.I), the one who is to be followed and obeyed absolutely because he is the unique measure and the archetype of divine love and of the human response to it. Thus he is not only a "universal and formal" norm of moral action, but a "concrete and personal" norm. The concrete existence of Jesus, from his birth to his death, constitutes the "personal Word" of God to mankind, the "Call" both transcendent and immanent who reveals the entire love of the Father and accomplishes in his own existence all that the Father expects from men. "Christ himself was a manual laborer for thirty years, and a spiritual worker for three years, before the three days of his Passion, his death, and his Resurrection." [10] He himself fulfilled the law of the creation by working in perfect solidarity with the most common conditions of real humanity. But at the end of his earthly stay he carried creation to its eschatological fulfillment.

But we can still ask by what precise title Christ as norm acquires a "concrete and personal" character that is valid for and applicable to all ethical situations. The answer to this question requires us to be precise about the soteriological link between Christ and sinners. According to the author of *Theodramatik,* it is not enough that the Word of God be a partaker of our

---

[9] *Theodramatik* II. *Die Personen des Spiels,* I. Teil: *Der Mensch in Gott* (Einsiedeln: Johannes Verlag, 1973), 81; hereinafter referred to as *TD* II/1.

[10] *Theologie der drei Tage* (Einsiedeln: Johannes Verlag, 1969), 188.

human condition through the Incarnation, nor that he be the meritorious cause of our salvation; nor is it enough to see in Jesus crucified the real symbol of the divine mercy offered to each man, nor to discover in him the unsurpassable model of a trusting abandonment to God in death. It is necessary that in him the authentic Covenant between divine love and fallen freedom be realized. Now, this Covenant is realized through the obedience of Jesus, which is the historical-eschatological place where the truth of God is revealed and where the Yes of sinners is pronounced for all, in all truth.[11] In brief, by his divine-human obedience, Jesus has become "the Covenant in person",[12] who attests his truth and his fecundity in the outpouring of the Spirit.

However, this obedience comprises a very specific content which must be stated precisely in order to clarify further the concrete, personal link between Christ and sinners. Von Balthasar holds very strongly to the radical significance of the *pro nobis* of the Cross. According to him, the New Testament statements about the Son delivered into the hands of sinners, about the Christ who was made sin for us, must not be softened into meaning only that God acted in our favor, in solidarity with us. He insists that the realism of the *pro nobis* means "in our stead", in the sense of a substitution.[13] It is literal truth that Christ took upon himself the sin of the world and that he emptied it of its injustice and its offensiveness by the superior force of his obedience of love. Von Balthasar sees here the necessary condition for the establishment of a true Covenant between God and man (*TD* III, 296ff.).

This superhuman mission clearly requires that the Christ be the unique Son of the Father (*homoousios*) and not just an eschatological prophet announcing the divine mercy. Von Balthasar notes that some Christologies that do not take seriously the *pro nobis* tend also to understand the hypostatic union in a reductive way.[14] Christology and Trinity stand or fall together. And the salvation of men depends entirely on the articulation of these two mysteries.

We must say that the assumption of the sins of all men into his own humanity and their dissolution by expiatory suffering, death, and descent into hell creates a very concrete bond of knowledge and love between Christ and sinners, one which contains an ethical imperative for every man.[15] St. Paul

[11] Cf. Michel Beaudin, *Obéissance et Solidarité, Essai sur la christologie de Hans Urs von Balthasar* (Montreal: Fides, 1989).

[12] *Pâcques, le Mystere* (Paris: Cerf, 1981), 205.

[13] *Theodramatik* III: *Die Handlung* (Einsiedeln: Johannes Verlag, 1980), 309–15; hereinafter cited as *TD* III.

[14] See for example the critique of the soteriology of Karl Rahner in *TD* III, 253–63, where he observes that the Cross is interpreted as a *pro nobis* of God rather than a *pro nobis* of Christ (255, 260), and where he expresses reservations about the conception of the hypostatic union as the insurpassable "case" of an anthropology conceived as the self-communication of God to man (259).

[15] *Kennt uns Jesus—Kennen wir ihn?* (Freiberg: Herder, 1980).

expressed it eloquently: "My present life in the flesh I live by faith in the Son of God who has loved me and has been delivered up for me" (Gal 2:20).

By the force of substitution Christ has penetrated in advance, through love, into the "private sphere" of the sinner, into his prison, in order to deliver him from within. That is why "the sword-point of anti-Christian sin is directly aimed at the center of the personal norm. It pierces the heart of the Crucified which represents the concreteness, in the world, of trinitarian love in its self-surrender" (*PCM*, 4.3). That is also why the return of the sinner, his conversion, rests entirely on the power of this suffering love, which calls him even to the end, with the greatest respect for his freedom (*TD* III, 326ff.).

Christ is, then, the concrete and personal norm in virtue of this obedience which reveals the whole depth of the trinitarian love that expiates sin. But this love bears another dimension, that of freeing the sinner for the sake of a liberating mission. As principal actor in the theo-drama, Christ is also the supreme norm in that his archetypical mission is "the principle of distribution of roles for the other actors".[16] In taking sin upon himself, Christ gives in exchange the grace of reconciliation with God, the grace of filiation which means always a participation in his mission. These two dimensions of the substitution establish, consequently, a very personal and concrete link between Christ and sinners, justifying his truly being "the concrete categorical imperative".

How is the connection made between the norm and the ethical situations of each person? There must be a historical appropriation produced, thanks to mediations, between a man in a situation and the Christ event. "On the basis of the Cross we have been given the Holy Spirit of Christ and of God" (*PCM*, 2.3). Here is the indispensable mediation for the universal and personal application of the Christological norm. The Holy Spirit universalizes the "form" of the Christ, which would otherwise remain an inaccessible model of morality. His role as mediator in the very existence of Jesus allows him to extend into us the obedience of the Savior, which he made possible from the first moment of the Incarnation until his death and descent into hell. In the event of the Resurrection, the Spirit glorifies this obedience, universalizes it, and brings it into the capacity of each man.

The Eucharist is the privileged place where this marvelous exchange is actualized and where the community of sinners is joined to Christ as a Body to its Head. Von Balthasar sees in this mystery the necessary complement of substitution: "In it, the realism of belonging as a mystical member of Christ appears clearly . . . but we also see that he who gives his body and his blood does so in an 'exchange', returning to us what he has taken from us and transformed into himself" (*TD* II/2, 223).

---

[16] *Theodramatik* II, 2. Teil: *Die Personen Christus* (Einsiedeln: Johannes Verlag, 1978), 238; hereinafter cited as *TD* II/2.

The "how" of this mediation remains a mysterious reality outside of the visible boundaries of the Church. She is the arena instituted to sacramentally realize this appropriation. Von Balthasar reacts against the modern tendency to separate the Spirit and the institution by showing the profound inter-penetrations of these two realities. His work *Pneuma und Institution,* along with the last volume of *Theologik,* The Spirit of Truth, develops this idea by showing the objective and subjective dimensions of the Spirit. The objective dimension is found in the institution of sacramental forms and the liturgy, in the norms of Tradition-Magisterium-Scripture, in canon law and theology. The subjective dimension appears in prayer, forgiveness, the experience of the gifts and charisms of the Spirit, and the witness of life. Thus all these mediations serve to constitute the Church as Body of Christ united to her Head in the Spirit.[17]

In summary, Christ is the supreme ethical norm inasmuch as he has accomplished the Covenant of mankind with God in introducing human situations, concretely, by his obedience, into the interior of "the interpersonal exchange of divine life" (*PCM,* 3). That is why the believer finds in the Crucified the source and the personal norm of his own obedience, "who, in virtue of his suffering for us and his eucharistic surrender of his life for us (which imparts it to us—*per ipsum et in ipso*), empowers us inwardly to do the Father's will together with him (*cum ipso*)" (*PCM* 1.1). In addition, the Golden Rule (Mt 7:12; Lk 6:31) of brotherly love which commands the entire moral life of a Christian becomes practicable for him in virtue of the gift of God which is, "as a result of the outpouring of the Holy Spirit of the Father and Son—the Spirit of the divine 'We'—into the hearts of believers, . . . an even more profound a priori assumption (Rom 5:5)" (*PCM,* 2.3).

Persons in Christ

The Christocentric and trinitarian soteriology of von Balthasar reflects directly on his anthropology. It entails a modification of the problematic that is expressed in the very question of man: not the philosophical question, "What is man?" but the theological question: "Who is man?" and even "Who am I? Why am I precisely this I?"[18] It is the question of the unity of the person that occupies the center of the *Theodramatik.* Von Balthasar treats it in an eminently theological fashion which extends the patristic doctrine of the *imago Dei* and the Thomistic anthropology of the natural desire for the Vision, restored to honor by Henri de Lubac. His approach seems similar to that of Cardinal

[17] *Theologik* III. *Der Geist der Wahrheit* (Einsiedeln: Johannes Verlag, 1987), 294–380.
[18] *Pneuma und Institution* (*Skizzen zur Theologie IV*) (Einsiedeln: Johannes Verlag, 1974), 18.

Wojtyla in his fundamental book, *The Acting Person*,[19] which reverses the connection between person and action by beginning with action in order to penetrate the interior of the person. Von Balthasar begins with mission, which is the fundamental concept of the *Dramatik,* allowing a synthesis of dogma and ethics.

The main point of his approach is an integration within the formal constitution of the person of the fundamental determination of the Word of God addressed to each man in Jesus Christ. Declaring the long controversy about the philosophical distinction between person and nature to be unresolved, von Balthasar introduces a new distinction between subject (*Geistessubjekt*) and person, transferring the properly personal determination to the side of grace. In the light of the Christological Archetype, he holds that the uniqueness of the person does not rest, in the final analysis, on an *a priori* structure of the spiritual creature but on an *a posteriori* determination that is given in Christ. "When God says to a spiritual subject who he is for him, the true and eternal God; when he tells him in the same act the end for which he exists—thus conferring on him a divinely sanctioned mission—then one can say that that spiritual subject is a person" (*TD* II/2, 190). A man discovers who he is when he accepts the Word which gives him at once his name and his mission (*TD* II/2, 190ff.). The vague subject constituted by self-awareness and self-determination acquires his qualitative uniqueness in accepting, in faith, his place and his mission in the Body of Christ.

Hence the Balthasarian identification of person and mission. On the basis of the Christological archetype, whose "universal mission is a temporal modality of his eternal procession" (*TD* II/2, 184, 487), von Balthasar conceives the mission of each person, in Christ, as the temporal modality of his integration into the filiation-mission of the Word made flesh. In his opinion, to be "born of God" (*Geburt aus Gott*) and to be incarnated into history are the two inseparable dimensions of divinization.

Between Christ and the Christian, as between God and a creature, there is no univocity but an analogy, i.e., a certain similarity but only within the greatest dissimilarity.[20] There is an analogy of being, but also an analogy of acting and of attitudes. In Christ, the person-mission identity is given *a priori* by the grace of the hypostatic union which is expressed humanly in his absolute and immemorial consciousness of *being sent* into the world by the

---

[19] Karol Wojtyla, *The Acting Person. Analecta Husserliana,* X (1979), 18ff.

[20] See Georges de Schrijver, *Le merveilleux accord de Dieu et de l'homme. Etude de l'analogie de l'être chez Hans Urs von Balthasar* (Leuven: BETL, 1983). The author shows that the thread of Ariadne that runs through the various stages of the thought of von Balthasar is the analogy of being, taken especially in the mystical sense of a situation "where finite liberty allows itself to be seized in its interior by the victorious hold of the love of infinite liberty" (47).

Father in the Spirit (*TD* II, 151ff.). In us, this identification is worked out temporally, in an *a posteriori* synthesis between our natural subjectivity and the "I of the mission"[21] that is a participation in the identity of Christ. "I live now not I, but Christ lives in me" (Gal 2:20). Briefly, we *become* persons in Christ, by a gift of our freedom to the mission which likens us to, and associates us with, the gift of God. The ethical decision in response to the call of grace constitutes a theological person.

Realization of this personalizing gift does not depend only on the result of the mission of Christ, namely, the creation of a space/time of grace for an infinity of objective missions analogous to his own. It comes about also through the action of the Holy Spirit who adapts indecisive, impotent, or rebellious subjects, through conversion and sanctification, to their objective and most intimately personal identities.[22] In giving their consent in faith, hope, and love, they allow themselves to be conformed to Christ as members of his body, and put to its service their entire unique charisms as these correspond to their personal vocations.

The advantage of this theological conception of the person is that it establishes at once both uniqueness and ecclesiasticality. "A human subject, inasmuch as he becomes a theological person by a unique call and mission, is simultaneously deprivatized, socialized, and made the location and the bearer of community" (*TD* II/2, 249). The identification with Christ through the mediation of the Spirit communicates a constitutive specific solidarity to persons, the "communion of saints" that resembles the trinitarian communion. In this participated trinitarian communion it becomes manifest, von Balthasar adds, that not only the goods and the values belonging to persons become common property, but "the very persons themselves" (*TD* II/2, 321).

The immanence of the reciprocal belonging of persons in community is one of the main themes of Balthasarian anthropology. But in order to appreciate its value and importance we must recall its anchor point in the structure of human freedom. Here is where von Balthasar makes use of Henri de Lubac to deepen the paradox of man as a finite liberty oriented toward the openness of the infinite liberty but incapable of postulating it by himself: the natural desire for the vision of God (*Desiderium naturale visionis*), according to the formulation of Thomas Aquinas, restored to its original meaning by Fr. de Lubac.[23] The originality of von Balthasar lies in uncovering the moment of inter-

---

[21] *Sponsa Verbi* (*Skizzen zur Theologie II*) (Einsiedeln: Johannes Verlag, 1971), 177.

[22] *Das Ganze im Fragment: Aspekte der Geschichtstheologie* (Einsiedeln: Benziger, 1963), 91. [For an English translation, see *A Theological Anthropology* (New York: Sheed & Ward, 1967).]

[23] Henri de Lubac, *Surnaturel* (Paris: Aubier, 1946), and *Le mystère du surnaturel* (Paris: Aubier, 1965).

subjectivity which occurs in the consciousness of one who is called into existence by infinite freedom. In his view,

> Man, that is to say, extra-Biblical man, is awakened to a theoretical/practical self-awareness thanks to a voluntary and loving challenge on the part of his fellow man. In responding, he experiences (in the *cogito/sum*) both the radiance of reality as such (which is true and good), manifesting itself and beckoning man toward it, as well as the fact that his freedom is part of his relationship to his fellow men (*PCM*, 7.1).

At the very source of consciousness of self there is a call from God mediated by the call of another. The most eloquent illustration of this fact appears in the mother-child relationship which von Balthasar uses as his phenomenological starting point.[24] The "other" human person thus plays a role in the access to self of each freedom. The "I" is always indebted to a "we". It never exists as a monad but only as a transcendental relation to a divine You that includes the constitutive relation to a human you. "Human communality and the immediate relation of each individual to God are inseparable from each other" (*TD* II/1, 359). The fact that one discovers *a posteriori* that the other human person is a being who has also been awakened to himself leaves unbreakable the primordial transcendental unity of these two inclinations (*PCM*, 7, ad 1c).

On this point von Balthasar refuses the closed circle of modern consciousness confined to "the charmed precincts of the *Cogito*" (Ricoeur) and restores the rapport with the other and with the world which gives back to man an awareness of his dependence, of his cosmic and communitarian roots. The modern drift toward liberty as an emancipation of a finite subject in a liberal individualistic or Marxist collectivist sense is here corrected in its root. The analogy of being applied to the drama of limited freedom and its inclusion into infinite freedom remains the key to this advance. It blocks the Promethean identification of man with the Absolute and keeps him aware of his finitude and poverty.[25]

This transcendental dialogical character of human freedom constitutes, according to von Balthasar, the natural foundation of a "positive" revelation of God in the Old and New Testaments that is meant, in principle, for all mankind. Indeed, this character is inscribed in the image of God that is human freedom, an image created from the beginning for the sake of its likeness to

[24] "Bewegung zu Gott" in *Spiritus Creator (Skizzen zur Theologie III)* (Einsiedeln: Johannes Verlag, 1967), 13–50. This access to God by intersubjectivity is proposed by the author explicitly as a way to surpass the transcendental viewpoint of Kant and Maréchal. See also *TD* II/1, 357 ff.

[25] See the synthesis of his analysis of German idealism in de Schrijver, *Le merveilleux accord*, 73–138. Von Balthasar rejects this philosophy of the subject to the extent that it "issues into a quasi-mystical enthusiasm, as an energy apt to elevate itself to the level of the Absolute", 77.

Christ (*TD* II/1, 211; *TD* III, 354). But the image bears within itself the trace
of the Archetype, a certain knowledge of its infinite liberty but in terms of a
natural desire for the vision of God, "an impulse toward him who alone—in
infinite freedom—can give himself as a positive infinite freedom" (*TD* II/1,
219). Without the positive revelation of God in Christ, the intersubjective
nature of the image retains an incomplete character, an enigmatic quality
which puts it into an insoluble dilemma because of sin and the death which
destroys the outlines of the meaning of human love.

Here is the reason why von Balthasar emphasizes the unachieved, and
inachievable, character of human freedom on the natural level of its concrete
relations. Such is the result, for example, of the analysis of the tensions that
characterize human existence pulled between the flesh and the spirit (*GF,* 63;
TD II/1, 332–33); also in the male-female relationship, in the treatment of the
enigma of the strict tie between sexuality and death (*TD* II/1, 341–43); and,
finally, in the rapport, impossible to establish in a definitive fashion, between
individual and community.

According to von Balthasar, the anthropological impasse finds its culmination in the death of the individual, which renders impossible a complete
synthesis between his personal accomplishment and his social integration
(*PCM,* 9.3). Only the Resurrection of Christ brings the light that definitively
illumines the fragmentary character of these relations and their transcendent
achievement.

Some characterize this anthropological consideration as pessimistic—for
example, Jean-Marie Aubert in regard to "the essentially relative character of
natural law" in von Balthasar.[26] But in fact the view is entirely consistent
with his Christocentrism. Man is one who awaits a Word that he cannot
invent for himself, despite the thirst for the Absolute which haunts him. The
norm of the Good inscribed in the nature of the first Adam orients him
towards a gift and a renunciation of himself whose definitive measure is found
in the second Adam. Von Balthasar does not fall into the "Christologic
narrowness" (*Christologische Engführung*) of Karl Barth because his doctrine of
the analogy of being defends precisely the proper consistency of human
nature even if it remains relative.[27]

In the same order of ideas he affirms the natural capacity of man to know

[26] Aubert, "Débats autour", 209. In regard to the influence of Barth on this aspect of von
Balthasar's thought, the author mentions in a note that Barth himself evolved toward a more
positive concept. It is well to note here that this evolution is in good part the fruit of his
dialogue with von Balthasar on the analogy of being. See von Balthasar, *Karl Barth:
Darstellung und Deutung seiner Theologie,* 4th ed. (Einsiedeln: Johannes Verlag, 1976), 93–181
[for an abridged English translation, see *The Theology of Karl Barth* (New York: Holt,
Rinehart & Winston, 1971)].

[27] *Karl Barth,* 278ff.

God, beginning with his own freedom, but he underlines more than others the necessity of grace for perceiving the call of the God of grace. For von Balthasar, man does not have a point of departure in a common nature with his fellows for a dialogue with God. If God speaks to him, he is not "capable" of understanding by reason of his simple natural intelligence. He needs grace to elevate his intelligence to the height of the Word which is addressed to him. He has within himself a certain passive aptitude which, however, contains a primordial knowledge of being and its transcendental properties, on the basis of which an immediate access to infinite liberty is opened for him.[28]

These anthropological considerations explain the theological perspective of von Balthasar, who conceives man, on the basis of revelation, as an essentially dialogical being who is thus unachievable by himself, because destined to achieve himself, in an unforeseeable fashion, by the Word of God in Jesus Christ. When he receives this Word in faith and allows himself to be defined as a member of the Body of Christ with a personal charism for the service of others, he becomes a person in Christ and takes his place in the bosom of a communion that is at once divine and human. This communion heals and fulfills the inchoative intersubjectivity of the image by his insertion into the trinitarian likeness.

Here we see how, in the Balthasarian conception, the person is found at the confluence of nature and grace at the precise point where the fundamental ethical decision of each subject called by grace determines the meaning of the theological person. We cannot explain here the themes which have led to this synthesis, mainly the development of functional analogy and the existential unity between grace and charism and the accent on the unity between justification and mission.[29] Let us simply note that he advances beyond the Protestant individualism of justification by faith and the Catholic individualism of merit by recovering the essential implication of community in the occurrence of grace.

Let it suffice to evoke here, at the conclusion of this rapid glance, the figure of Mary as archetype of the theological person (*TD* II/2, 276ff.). Von Balthasar takes up the patristic vision of the *perichoresis* Mary-Church, based on her universal mission as the new Eve. In a discreet way, subordinate but immensely fruitful, Mary collaborates as Mother and as Spouse with the archetypical mission of the New Adam. Her unconditioned *fiat* in the fullness of the Spirit is the secret of her archetypal fecundity. She espouses without reserve the gift and renunciation of self which constitute, in God, the unity of person and relation. That is why, in her life, personal grace and social charism are one and

---

[28] "Bewegung zu Gott", 33ff.
[29] Marc Ouellet, "L'existence comme mission, L'anthropologie théologique de Hans Urs von Balthasar", Pontifical Gregorian University (Rome, 1983), 33–56.

the same. Her entire existence is lived as a mission: Behold the handmaid of
the Lord. This archetypal mission associates her so intimately with Christ that
her theological personality acquires a universality that embraces the whole of
the ecclesial communion. That is why von Balthasar boldly designates her
"the inchoative subjectivity of the Church" (*TD* II/2, 324).[30]

This Mariological illustration of the person-community integration is the
high point of the theo-dramatic perspective of von Balthasar and the archetype of all the personalizing missions in the Church. It teaches us that a
Christological ethics will always be, at the same time, Marial—that is to say, a
realization of the person that begins with grace accepted without reserve and
put at the service of others by a pledge that is total and without calculation.

What Kind of Ethics for Christians?

After these soteriological and anthropological presuppositions, we must ask
what sort of ethics results for Christians. Let us note well at the beginning of
this inquiry that it is a question of an ethics for Christians. Von Balthasar's
perspective is Christological. He does not take his departure from a natural
ethics "within the bounds of universal reason", and then ask what can be
added that is specifically Christian. He begins with the eschatological event of
Christ who transforms and remodels the ethical dimension of human existence.
We shall explain here the meaning of this transformation by using from the
start the trinitarian horizon of ethics, and then employ its theological and
historical dimensions in order to conclude with several particular applications.

According to the vision of von Balthasar, the Alpha and Omega of the
salvific plan is the trinitarian love that manifests its glory and gives itself in
participation. This plan is a drama in which God engages personally in order
to liberate captive freedoms; a "trinitarian drama" in which the divine persons
include the creature, assume its decadence, and secretly transform its history
by the force of their exchange of love that is opened to us in Jesus Christ (*TD*
III, 328, 337). "The reciprocal trinitarian gifts are the place of the creature."[31]
The ultimate meaning of the salvific plan consists in the mutual glorification
of the Divine Persons which is accomplished in the very involvement of each
Person in their work *ad extra*.[32] The result of this mutual glorification in
Christ leads to the participation of man in this intratrinitarian mystery of
glorification. By Christ and in Christ, human existence is found transplanted,
so to speak, between God and God, between the Father and the incarnate Son,

[30] See also *Sponsa Verbi*, 188–89.
[31] *Herrlichkeit. Eine Theologische Aesthetik.* Bd. III/2, 2. Teil: *Neuer Bund* (Einsiedeln:
Johannes Verlag, 1969), 484.
[32] *Spiritus Creator*, 100–101.

where it participates in the divine life in a way that goes beyond what the heart can conceive.[33]

This participation in intratrinitarian love is realized in this life by the loving faith which acts in the hope of pleasing God and serving him. The theological virtues are the modes of this participation: "They form, in the last analysis, the act which renders to God what he expects from man: above all God himself, but with man's participation."[34] With this expansion of perspective, we go entirely beyond the anthropocentric viewpoint of desire towards a theo-dramatic ethics, an ethics of serving God in all things.[35] What counts in this perspective is not primarily the satisfaction of human desire, even the desire for God; it is, rather, the satisfaction of God's desire, which commands a permanent spiritual attitude of conversion.

Now, God's desire is for the integration of all of creation into the beatitude of his trinitarian exchange. From this ultimate horizon there springs the meaning of human existence as "praise and service" to the glory of God, an Ignatian definition which von Balthasar accepts by explaining its trinitarian meaning.[36] In the interhuman love where God is hidden under "the sacra-ment of the brother", it is possible to "serve God" by participating mysteriously in God's own gift to the world. "With his own engagement, the Christian lives within the engagement of God for the sake of liberating the world."[37]

The original meaning of Balthasarian ethics is, then, the insertion of human liberty, fallen but not destroyed, into God's engagement, that is, into the Christ sent into the world. This perspective lends validity to the view in revelation that it is true that not only does God have significance for man, but man also has significance for God.[38]

The trinitarian horizon of human existence which we have just evoked is the foundation of ethical decisions. Von Balthasar has dedicated a great part of his theological effort to illuminating this ultimate trinitarian foundation of the

---

[33] *Pneuma und Institution,* 431.

[34] Von Balthasar takes from John of the Cross a bold expression which says a great deal about the meaning of this service: "As God gives himself to her [the soul] freely and gratuitously, she senses, for her part, that her will is more free, more generous, the more she is united to God. Thus . . . she gives, so to speak, God to God" (*Living Flame of Love,* strophe III, vv. 5–6). Cited in von Balthasar, "Bewegung zu Gott", 41.

[35] *Homo creatus est* (*Skizzen zur Theologie V*) (Einsiedeln: Johannes Verlag, 1986), 22ff.

[36] Ibid., 11–26.

[37] *In Gottes Einsatz leben* (Einsiedeln: Johannes Verlag, 1971), 89. [For an English translation, see *Engagement with God* (London: Society for Promoting Christian Knowledge, 1975).]

[38] This last aspect is treated in von Balthasar's *Theodramatik* IV: *Das Endspiel* (Einsiedeln: Johannes Verlag, 1983), in regard to the problem of eternal damnation: "So wurde etwa das Problem der ewigen verdamnis nicht sosehr vom anthropologischen Gesichtspunkt gestellt 'was verliert der Mensch, wenn er Gott verliert?,' als vom Standpunkt Gottes: " 'Was verliert Gott, wenn er den Menschen verliert?' ", 463. The masterly conclusion appears under the title: "Was hat Gott von der Welt?", 463–76.

Christian life. "Dogma brings to light, by the light of revelation, the conditions for the possibility of Christian action."[39] In order to grasp the theodramatic meaning of Christian ethics, that is to say, the positive insertion of human liberty into Christ, it was necessary to show this trinitarian horizon which leads to the articulation of mission and person that we mentioned above.

Its power consists in indissolubly uniting the two dimensions, historical and eschatological, of ethics. It does not propose a theological ethics detached from history, nor a natural ethics extrinsic to grace. It proposes a Christiform integration which acquires and elevates the natural virtues, but not without elevating in man the norm of their harmony and perfection. That norm is "the love which 'organizes' man, and not the reverse; love makes of man—who always resists—its instrument".[40] This integration shows that nature passes over into the service of grace, following "the order that is rooted in the person of Christ: nature as the expression of, and at the service of, the supernatural. In that service she does not perish."[41]

This viewpoint makes explicit the fundamental structure of Christian ethics: its character as a response from within the Covenant. Von Balthasar's partner of God is not the residue of a Barthian Christocentrism, overwhelmed by the triumphal glory of God. He is a true partaker in a covenant, in an "analogy of liberty" which the author takes from Anselm, Thomas, and Ignatius of Loyola. That analogy makes human freedom, even though sinful, capable of giving itself and choosing what God chooses for it, in an "analogy of choice" which incarnates the covenant relationship. The response of Christ on the Cross, on behalf of all, does not remove the necessity of the faith which freely ratifies what he has done for us.[42] And this ratification does not eliminate anxieties, perplexities, existential decisions because Christ the second Adam assumed the first man with the whole moral problematic that is proper to him (PCM, preliminary note).

An adequate response to being called is known as faith. Von Balthasar conceives the original act of subjecting oneself to grace as a unique attitude of disponibility that is part of the faith-hope-charity triad.[43] A Christian theodramatic ethics primarily cultivates this disponibility, which is called faith: "In essence, it is a disposition which allows love to operate: not just allowing it to

---

[39] *Glaubhaft ist nur Liebe* (Einsiedeln: Johannes Verlag, 1963), 75. [For an English translation, see *Love Alone* (New York: Herder and Herder, 1969).]

[40] *Glaubhaft ist nur Liebe*, 89.

[41] *Verbum Caro* (*Skizzen zur Theologie I*) (Einsiedeln: Johannes Verlag, 1960), 180. [For an English translation, see *Explorations in Theology*, vol. 1: *The Word Made Flesh* (San Francisco: Ignatius Press, 1989).

[42] *Epilog* (Einsiedeln-Trier: Johannes Verlag, 1987), 93f.

[43] *Das Ganze im Fragment*, 115–16.

have its way, but willing what it wills, i.e., wishing to be seized by it".[44]
When the believer allows himself to be drawn by the Spirit into the "archetypal
faith" of the Savior, he enters into the mystery of the birth of the Word and
the fecundity of the Spirit.

Von Balthasar's insistence on a living faith as the right attitude before
God constitutes one of his major contributions to the foundations of Christian ethics. Orthopraxis is rooted in orthodoxy. But he deepens orthodoxy
when he opens up his third "aesthetic" way to a doctrine of faith as a
perception (*Wahrnehmung*) of revelation that leads to a rapture (*Entruckung*),
that is to say, to an adoring and fecund contemplation. "The third way
is indivisible. For either the character of Christian revelation is seen and
grasped in its entirety as the glorification of absolute love by itself, or it is not
perceived at all."[45]

No one has provided a doctrine of contemplation so profound and so
liberating for human reason, imprisoned in a critical and rationalist age, when
man no longer knows how to pray.[46] Christian ethics can be rooted only in
an attitude of acceptance, or respect, and of adoration of a mystery of such
manifest holiness.

One's mission proceeds from authentic faith, that is, from the reception of a
personal charism for the service of unity in the Body of Christ. Here is
another feature of a theo-dramatic ethics: a disponibility for letting love have
its way. This disponibility is particularized in as many missions as there are
persons chosen by Christ to take part in his universal mission (*TD* II/2, 248).
There is no general rule over and above the personal call of Christ, who
invites one to follow him. The unity of the whole is guaranteed, however,
because love is the living substance of all particular missions—the Golden
Rule which commands the realization of a "catholic" community whose unity
rests in the Trinity.

The moral activity of Christians seeks to realize the ecclesial "we" which
incarnates the trinitarian "We" in history. According to von Balthasar, the
mutual love of Christians is not just a simple, extrinsic celebration of
God, but "possesses an intrinsic relation to his essential glory".[47] That
reminds us that there is an indissoluble unity between the love of God and the
love of neighbor. "One's faith requires him to see, in the less significant

---

[44] *Herrlichkeit* III/2: 2, 375.

[45] *Glaubhaft ist nur Liebe*, 39.

[46] "The rationalist can no longer pray, only rationalize, and in the end only criticize. But
he who can no longer pray is incapable even of beginning a dialogue with one of the world's
religions, let alone of showing in this discussion that more truth, because more absolute love,
is present in the Christian religion" (Von Balthasar, *Convergences to the Source of Christian
Mystery* [San Francisco: Ignatius Press, 1984], 14).

[47] *Herrlichkeit* III/2: 2, 373.

I-thou relation, the actualization and the 'sacrament' of the eternal I–Thou relation." [48]

In the light of this mysterious covenant between interhuman love and trinitarian love, we can deepen the sacrament of marriage as a privileged sign of the eternal I-thou-we relation. Von Balthasar offers a short meditation on Ephesians 5 that clarifies theologically the doctrine of *Humanae vitae* on contraception. He emphasizes the fact that according to St. Paul, "the decisive norm for the husband-wife relation is a theological one" which follows from the model relation of Christ and the Church which marriage ought to symbolize even in the conjugal act itself. [49] To limit in advance the total gift of persons by contraceptive means is equivalent to refusing to respect the nature of love, its indissolubly corporeal and spiritual fecundity, and the presence of trinitarian agape that is expressed and communicated in the bodily intercourse of spouses. In his view, the realm of sexuality is not exempt from the demand to follow Christ. "The sexual dimension as Eros must express Agape, and Agape always includes an element of renunciation, precisely for the sake of transcending the limits placed by subjects in their gift of themselves." [50] The theo-dramatic mission of spouses consists in responding to the call of the Creator in Christ, in putting their love at the service of the trinitarian Agape, which it achieves by including it in the sacramental expression of its proper fecundity.

Finally, a theo-dramatic ethics bears a social dimension of combat for the sake of the deprived and the marginal. "The fight for social justice for the poor and the oppressed is a strict Christian duty, a 'work of mercy' both corporal and spiritual according to which the Christian and every other man will be judged" (*TD* III, 453). In order to carry it on according to his Faith, the Christian does not prescribe ready-made recipes; "he must, along with others, struggle to decipher the enigmas of nature and of history". [51] He has at his disposal a certain image of man which orients his own choices, but these have to take account of the resistance of the structures of this world and of their proper laws: "He must not forget their contingency, and, for example, demand total disarmament and non-resistance or pacifism, in virtue of Christian charity and Christian communion, while overlooking all political prudence." [52]

---

[48] *Herrlichkeit*, Bd. III/1: *Im Raum der Metaphysik*, 2. Teil: *Neuzeit* (Einsiedeln: Johannes Verlag, 1965), 977.

[49] *Neue Klarstellungen* (Einsiedeln: Johannes Verlag, 1979), 122, 119 [for an English translation, see *New Elucidations* (San Francisco: Ignatius Press, 1986)]. See also Michel Séguin, "Nouveau point de vue sur la contraception", *Nouvelle Revue théologique*, (March–April 1990) 202–23, and (May–June) 394–415.

[50] *Neue Klarstellungen*, 128.

[51] *In Gottes Einsatz leben*, 97.

[52] Ibid., 93.

Here as in other areas an ethics of faith and of love applied to social life does not produce the economy of a rational reflection, of a calculus of relations of power, of a scientific and technological knowledge, because Christians live always in the structures of the old world which are not abolished but taken up and brought to their fulfillment in Christ.[53] They are not spared the painful experience of ethical choices, with their perplexities and anxieties, because it is precisely the experience of the "passing over" and "the fulfillment" of the old in the new. The Christian can surely count on the Holy Spirit in order to see clearly in ambiguous situations, but he must exercise prudence and discernment "without slicing through the complexities of profane domains from the outside, with the blade of a theological argument, for example. . . . One of the attributes of the Spirit is that he advances and clarifies earthly matters from within (Rom 8:28)."[54]

Von Balthasar thinks, along with Moltmann, that the social and historical dimension of Christian hope "has always been neglected in the history of Christianity, because we have ceased to think eschatologically and have left the task of proposing eschatological anticipations for the world to fanatics and to enthusiasts."[55] The New Testament vision of "patience" signifies "certainly more than a passive waiting; it contains a considerable element of impatience as well in the struggle of resistance and in the effort to act and to transform the world."[56]

But important though the economic and political dimension of this struggle might be, which Latin American theology has made primary, in von Balthasar the drama of liberation reaches its deepest level in the participation by the Church in the "battle of the Logos" (*TD* III, 399ff.), in this spiritual struggle against the forces of evil which manifest their power in history. Participation in the Passion of Christ through heroic charity, the contemplative and consecrated life, the prayer and vicarious suffering of the communion of saints are still efficacious weapons for the salvation of the world (*TD* III, 434ff.; *TD* II/2, 400–408).

It is the radiance of this Christian ethics of absolute love which reflects most purely the essence of the Church as the self-communication of God to the world. Von Balthasar has never ceased to recall that the credibility of Christianity does not rest primarily on a teaching, a wisdom, or an organization guaranteed by a revelation from above. It rests above all on Someone who acts and who allows action at the heart of history by holiness, Someone who manifests his own transcendence by the transcendence of Christian love.[57]

---

[53] Ibid., 92ff. See also *TD* III, 444f.

[54] *In Gottes Einsatz leben,* 100.

[55] Jürgen Moltmann, *Theologie de l'espérance* (Paris, 1970), 354. Cited in von Balthasar, *Theologie der drei Tage.*

[56] *Theologie der drei Tage,* 188.

[57] *Glaubhaft ist nur Liebe,* 46.

No *Weltanschauung,* no "pretence of catholicity" can rival the transcendence of this love. Facing the escape on high of Asiatic mystics and the flight to the future of Marxism, Christianity exalts a liberty of love that integrates the whole man into the service of the coming of the reign of God in history. Indeed, wherever Christian love, "eschatological love",[58] springing forth from the Eucharist, forms a solidarity with human suffering and the battle against the forces of evil, history reaches its fulfillment. History receives, in this theo-dramatic "analogy of love", its supreme dignity as covenant. It enters into "the hope of the God" (*Hoffnung Gottes*)[59] who wished to so give himself, with complete freedom, a created expression of his uncreated love.

Thanks to this eschatological light, von Balthasar makes human hope precise. The heart of man should not put its hope in an ambiguous and utopian, earthly "progress", nor in a flight from present history. It should locate its treasure in this vertical covenant which gives him the "whole into the fragment" (*das Ganze im Fragment*)[60] and which gives to each moment of time and of human labor a value that is eternal.

At the heart of this historical-eschatological covenant, those who agree to live their existence as a mission, i.e., as a service to absolute love, as saints, find their beatitude and their profound identity precisely in that service. They find, in wonderment and gratitude, that they "can" do something for God. They are not just turned toward God in an aspiration toward love; they are also turned toward the world, in God and with God, in a conspiracy with love. Even more, they find that they can not only collaborate with the pouring forth of trinitarian love into the world, but by an unfathomable grace, they can *also* and *thereby* serve the uncreated exchange between Father and Son in the Spirit.

The theological enterprise of Hans Urs von Balthasar seeks to surmount the spiritual and moral crisis of contemporary man. "We have run aground on the sandbanks of rationalism", he proclaims energetically, "let us back up in order to reach the rugged rock of mystery."[61] To achieve the *aggiornamento* sought by Vatican II, von Balthasar proposes a return to the center of revelation, a rediscovery of the mystery of trinitarian love incarnate and crucified. Human existence finds therein a completion of such incomparable meaning that nothing greater can be conceived.

It is only the proclamation of the true God that can de-center man from his unhealthy anthropocentrism and re-center him on Jesus, the one and only,[62]

---

[58] *Herrlichkeit* III/2:2, 406.

[59] *Theodramatik* IV: 160–67.

[60] *Das Ganze im Fragment,* 353.

[61] *Einfaltungen Auf Wegen christlicher Einigung* (Munich: Kösel Verlag, 1969), 9.

[62] J. Godenir, *Jesus, l'unique. Introduction à la théologie de Hans Urs von Balthasar* (Paris: Lethielleux, 1984).

who opens for him an infinite horizon of liberty, in love. The work of Hans Urs von Balthasar offers this center of integration to contemporary thought. Do we not have here a fecund seed for deepening a Christian ethics that takes account of the modern history of freedom and of the radical novelty of Christianity?

CHRISTOPH SCHÖNBORN, O.P.

Hans Urs von Balthasar's Contribution to Ecumenism

Who can measure the harvest of a life? As the sum of the Gospel, the Lord left us the image of that poor widow who, unaware that Jesus was watching her gesture, threw two copper coins, "everything she had to live", into the temple treasury (see Lk 21:1–4). Hans Urs von Balthasar liked to point to this widow.[1] She is an emblem of the Church, the embodiment of what counts in God's eyes. God's measures are evidently different from human measures, and yet, following the vision and words of Jesus and allowing ourselves to be led by his Spirit, we can approach these measures. The widow's two copper coins are worth more than many works, more than deeds that have an impact on world history, more than human fame. Christ brought about the salvation of the world in a deed which he saw prefigured in the widow's gift: he threw everything he had to live, his life itself, into his Father's temple treasury, and all times draw from this one gift, which was not noticed by the great ones of the world: Christ's inexhaustible "treasury of grace"!

If one dares to raise the question of the harvest of a life, one can do so only in view of this *one,* in whom all the treasures of wisdom and of knowledge are hidden (see Col 2:3), for what has not been gathered with him, is scattered by the wind of history. Enduring value lies only in that which has been done "in Christ". Only what can pass through the narrow gate remains of a life's work; everything else is ballast. Only what has been done in abandonment, in love, can enter through the door, through Christ. Love alone remains, according to the Apostle's words (1 Cor 13:8).

How can one measure what was lived in a human life in such a way that it was able to pass through this narrow door into eternal life? On the other hand, if one does not attempt to look back on a life from this perspective, one runs the danger of losing oneself in social "small-talk", the danger of seeing important things where there are none and of overlooking what is essential.

With these things in mind, the following is an attempt to look at the work and figure (*Gestalt*) of Hans Urs von Balthasar. I am raising the question of his

---

Translated by Michael Waldstein.

[1] See, for example, *Licht des Wortes. Skizzen zu allen Sonntagslesungen* (Trier: Paulinus-Verlag, 1987), 190.

contribution to ecumenism. If we wanted to point to results that can be measured in numerical terms, we would have missed the point. The question of what von Balthasar contributed to ecumenism cannot be answered by pointing in the first place to his publications on ecumenical themes and his activities in the field of ecumenism. The issue is much deeper: What has von Balthasar contributed so that Christians may be one in Christ, so that the wounds of division may be healed? The answer to this radical question can, of course, be given only in view of Christ and the coming of his kingdom. Who can give this answer?

Seen in this light, what is a contribution to ecumenism? When we approach our subject from this perspective, we may seem to be "overreaching" ourselves. And yet, I believe that we will do justice to von Balthasar's concerns only if we raise this question. A purely pragmatic view of ecumenism was always quite foreign to von Balthasar, which is why the theme "ecumenism" is rarely "associated" spontaneously with his name.

Our concern in what follows is to show that the high theological — in fact in a certain way mystical — claim with which von Balthasar approached the division of the Church constitutes an essential aspect of his contribution to ecumenism. I will therefore move our theme towards this center in three concentric circles:

(1) the external side of this work which appears at first glance "unecumenical"; (2) the ecumenical breadth of the whole work; (3) the "heart" or "hearth fire" of this work. Only from this innermost center will it be possible to appreciate the true significance of our theme.

Not in Favor of "Ecumenism"

At first glance von Balthasar does not appear "ecumenical" at all. Unfailingly faithful to his Catholic origins, always at home in Catholicism,[2] he remained to the end a thoroughly Catholic figure. The late honor of being nominated a cardinal was a compensation for the attacks which he had to sustain all his life in the Church. Painful as these attacks were, they never made him waver in his Catholic identity.

Von Balthasar was not an ecumenist in the sense of dialogue commissions and consensus documents. He remained a stranger to the "official" side of ecumenism. Theological compromise was an abomination to him. Against hasty attempts at unification he could be as polemical as Karl Barth, who will, of course, be further mentioned in this context.

The themes of von Balthasar's theology also make at first a thoroughly unecumenical impression. They are typically "Catholic" themes: *Mary*, on

---

[2] See *Unser Auftrag. Bericht und Entwurf* (Einsiedeln: Johannes Verlag, 1984).

whom he meditates again and again as the epitome of the Church and of faith; the papacy: von Balthasar's *Der antirömische Affekt*,[3] this firework of learned and suffering polemics, does not (out of ecumenical caution) evade clear insistence on the inescapable question of the papacy. Von Balthasar discusses all the controversial questions that present difficulties to ecumenism, often in several places of his work: intercommunion, women priests, the question of offices.

In ecumenical respects, the "outside" of his work makes a rather prickly and forbidding impression. There are other factors as well. Von Balthasar dealt in detail with many great figures of Christian history, but Luther and Calvin, the main figures of the Reformation, are not among them. Von Balthasar's knowledge of Luther relies largely on secondary literature, much of it controversial among experts (e.g., P. Hacker and T. Beer whose works were published by von Balthasar). With respect to Calvin the situation is similar. It is also curious that von Balthasar never carried out his plan to write a final volume of *The Glory of the Lord*. Its title was to be *Ökumenik* (Ecumenism). I do not know the reasons why he changed his plan. At the end of the '60s, when this volume was to be written, von Balthasar found himself in painful and sometimes angry opposition against what he saw as a tendency toward "selling out" Catholicism. It may be helpful to quote an example from the ominous year 1968. Karl Barth and von Balthasar had been invited to give the two opening addresses of the first session of the newly created Protestant/Roman-Catholic/Christian-Catholic commission in Switzerland on the subject of "deepening ecumenical work". On that occasion von Balthasar said,

> Today's ecumenical dialogue is understood often as a common search for the Christian truth in looking up to our common Lord, but occasionally also as a radical reduction to what is allegedly "essential", at the exclusion of all dispensable additions that hinder understanding. That the Catholic partner will necessarily get the shorter end of the stick on these presuppositions is quite clear, because the Reformation, even 450 years ago, began to relieve the ship of allegedly unnecessary "ballast", and today, given what is happening in the Catholic Church, it speaks, not without self-satisfaction, of a "need to catch up".

In contrast, von Balthasar demands another attitude:

> Ecclesial theology . . . needs obedient reflection on all aspects and the ability not to leave out complementing elements (complementing in view of the fullness of Christ!) when establishing a hierarchy of truths. Protestant and Anglican movements of our time are intensively engaged in regaining such integrating realities—e.g., Taizé, Grandchamps, the Anglican monastic

[3] *Der antirömische Affekt. Wie lässt sich das Papsttum in der Gesamtkirche integrieren?* (Freiburg: Herder, 1974).

movement, the new appropriation of Mariology, of the Mass also as sacrifice, of the Church's Magisterium, and the literal life of following Christ in the evangelical counsels—by contrast, it has become fashionable among Catholics to sell off all of that as if it were cheap trash.[4]

It is understandable that after such "deepening" von Balthasar was not heard so favorably in places where ecumenical euphoria carried the day. However, one should read what the old Karl Barth, in the year of his death, wrote into the ecumenist's guestbook on the same occasion. It testifies to a deep common vision shared with Hans Urs von Balthasar.

> I would have a little (not so little) question to raise here, this time addressed to the decree *Gaudium et spes* about the relation between Church and world, and also to the decree *De dignitate humanae personae,* which deals with the freedom of religion, and to a whole series of other Vatican texts and parts of texts. It is a question that we others, who are called Evangelical in the narrower sense, must address first of all to all that is called neo-Protestantism, even in its most modern variations, but now also to postconciliar Roman Catholicism—the following simple question: With respect to these windows opened to the world, is there not too much of a good thing being done by our "Protestants", but also during the last Council? For, if one makes too many windows and opens them up, the house is no longer a house. The salt must go into the dough. But the dough is not itself salt, and the salt must, in turn, not wish to turn into dough; otherwise the concept of Church could become so broad as to disappear in a dark cloud of unconscious Christianity. I am thinking here of a great neo-Protestant theologian, Richard Rothe in Heidelberg, but also of a great contemporary Roman Catholic theologian![5]

Von Balthasar and Barth speak a common language here. It is the expression of a spiritual kinship which leads us into the next circle of our reflections.

Ecumenical Breadth

For decades von Balthasar was engaged in an intensive theological dialogue with the other great German-Swiss theologian of this century, Karl Barth. Von Balthasar's monograph about Barth is a masterwork of theological conversation.[6] They have much in common: not only their love of music, for Mozart, not only the considerable number of pages contained in their

---

[4] Karl Barth and Hans Urs von Balthasar, *Einheit und Erneuerung der Kirche* (Ökumenische Beihefte 2; Fribourg, 1968), 36f.

[5] Ibid., 15. In 1966 von Balthasar had said similar things in *Cordula oder der Ernstfall* (Einsiedeln: Johannes Verlag, 1966).

[6] See *Karl Barth. Darstellung und Deutung seiner Theologie,* 4th ed. (Einsiedeln: Johannes Verlag, 1976).

works, the distance from all fashion in theology, from the busy bustle of the theological guild, which was often interpreted as elitism. Their kinship lies deeper. They also shared a passion for a theology that attempts to reflect first on the glory of God, of his Word, his revelation, a theology which can only be theocentric and Christocentric, because it is entirely absorbed in looking at the form (*Gestalt*) of revelation and because it seeks everything that theology has to say in Christ. This common theological orientation is reflected in a remarkably similar view of the criteria of ecumenical dialogue.

Von Balthasar was not an "ecumenist", but his theology has a rare ecumenical breadth, and it is able to further greater unity among the confessions as hardly any other theology in the twentieth century. I see three reasons for this.

1. I have already mentioned the first reason: an unconditional and unabashed *theocentrism*. Among the various mottos of the volume on the Old Covenant in *The Glory of the Lord* (vol. 6),[7] von Balthasar quotes Ignatius and Calvin, *"Ad majorem Dei gloriam"* and *"Soli Deo gloria"*. The "whole" von Balthasar is here; his entire work breathes this spirit. It is entirely concerned with God's glory, first contemplatively, in receiving the glory of God as it reveals itself [Aesthetic]; then adoring in the abandonment of obedience, of love [Dramatic]; finally in thought, in retracing God's revelation and the human response [Logic]. This theocentric orientation is the reason why von Balthasar's work has remained foreign to trends of fashion. To the very end there is nothing that seems more pressing to him than to speak of the mystery of the Trinity. Whether that pleases at the moment or not is unimportant. Von Balthasar is a contemplative and when he writes the reader always has the impression that he writes in the light of this vision. Such theology is ecumenical, because it is fascinated only by its "object" and because, for this reason, it wants to lead only to this object. The idea of seeking unity through a formula of compromise that covers the division of the Church was completely foreign to him. He could only agree with Karl Barth, "The step from separated confessions to one confession would have to be made absolutely without any compromise, and especially without assent to those forms and formulas of unity that merely conceal division instead of overcoming it."[8]

2. Von Balthasar's theocentrism finds its expression in an incomparable *reverence for the Word of God*. Sacred Scripture is without a doubt the center and medium of his theology or, as the Council wished for all theology, the soul of theology.[9] I say "incomparable" because among contemporary theo-

---

[7] *Herrlichkeit. Eine theologische Ästhetik.* Bd. III/2, 1. Teil: *Alter Bund* (Einsiedeln: Johannes Verlag, 1967).

[8] Karl Barth, *Die Kirche und die Kirchen* (Theologische Existenz heute 27; Munich, 1937), 18; quoted in von Balthasar, *Karl Barth*, 17.

[9] See *Dei verbum*, n. 24.

logians there are only few who are so naturally and completely at home in Scripture as von Balthasar. This becomes impressively clear in his many little books, e.g., *Kennt uns Jesus—Kennen wir ihn?*[10] or *Paulus ringt mit seiner Gemeinde,*[11] the latter book written as if from an interior vision, reexperiencing and reliving with the apostle. This familiarity with Scripture is vast and impressive in the two volumes *Alter Bund* and *Neuer Bund* in *Herrlichkeit,* which offers perspectives through Sacred Scripture as a whole written with greatest alertness to the inner diversity of the text. In the posthumous little volume, *Credo. Meditationen zum Apostolischen Glaubensbekenntnis,*[12] all nonscriptural references have been left aside. God's word simply speaks by itself, *sine glossa.* Such theology is ecumenical, because the only thing it wants to make heard is God's word. Anyone who wants to come to know von Balthasar's theology should read his simple, selfless meditations on Scripture.[13]

Von Balthasar's contemplative approach to Scripture passes beyond the problems of the historical-critical method. He knows much about contemporary exegesis and uses it, but he does not lose sight of the whole of revelation, of its "form" (*Gestalt*). How does he find a sure path between the reductionism of a one-sided use of the historical-critical method and the danger of fundamentalism? It is the inner unity of ecclesiality and spiritual experience that makes Scripture so "full of light" for him. On the one hand, he reads Scripture in the living Tradition of the Church as a whole—he knew this Tradition as hardly anyone else in our time; on the other hand, it is the living experience of the realities of which Scripture speaks that makes it possible for him to interpret Scripture "from within", as it were. Is such an interpretation of Scripture "scientific"? Von Balthasar reminds us untiringly that exegesis must subordinate itself to

> the simple rule of all sciences, namely, that the object determines the method appropriate to it and that only a method defined in this way can be considered "adequate" and "scientific". Here the object is Jesus Christ, certainly in human form (*Menschengestalt*), but with the claim of proclaiming God's definitive Word in the world. No purely worldly method can be the one demanded by this object, except to the degree that it subordinates itself

---

[10] *Kennt uns Jesus—Kennen wir ihn?* (Freiburg: Verlag Herder, 1980).

[11] *Paulus ringt mit seiner Gemeinde. Die Pastoral der Korintherbriefe* (Einsiedeln-Trier: Johannes Verlag, 1988).

[12] *Credo. Meditationen zum Apostolischen Glaubensbekenntnis* (Freiburg: Herder, 1989). The introduction by M. Kehl stresses this emphasis on the "original tone" of God's word; see ibid., 16.

[13] Especially in the two "testamentary" volumes, *Licht des Wortes* and *Du hast Worte des ewigen Lebens. Schriftbetrachtungen* (Einsiedeln-Trier: Johannes Verlag, 1989) in which von Balthasar "scatters the seed of God's word once again in rich fullness and in a final engagement . . . with trust in the vitality and healing power of this word" (*Du hast Worte des ewigen Lebens,* 5).

as a humble instrument to the only adequate response to this word, ecclesial faith.[14]

Von Balthasar's way of dealing with Scripture is exemplary. Here theology is truly "under God's word"; and it can be so completely "under", without falling into fundamentalism, because it listens to the word *in* the Church and because it reads Scripture in the Spirit in which it was written.[15]

3. A third aspect gives ecumenical breadth to von Balthasar's work. He was never a man for *commissions* of dialogue, but his whole work is *a unique dialogue*. I believe it is no exaggeration to say that something unique was given here, a gift that comes from God himself, who is triune dialogue of giving and receiving. "In dialogue," von Balthasar says with reference to Karl Barth, "being able to listen is even more important than speaking. This ability to listen is part of our faith, and thus of our obedience and our prayer, since these three form an inseparable unity."[16] Faith—obedience—prayer: the three sources of von Balthasar's apparently unlimited capacity for dialogue. In order to conduct a true dialogue with all the great figures of Christian spiritual history one must possess extraordinary selflessness, receptivity, and alertness. Intelligence and memory—von Balthasar was undoubtedly highly gifted with both of these—are not enough by themselves. Von Balthasar listens to the "heartbeat" in his dialogue partners, he enters into their innermost word, hears it, and allows himself to be addressed by it. What an extraordinary school of listening it is to read von Balthasar's monographs about the Fathers of the Church, the great authors of the Middle Ages, and the poets and philosophers of modernity! No violence is done. Authors are allowed to speak their word, von Balthasar lends them his ear, his heart, in order to let them speak. Criticisms are not made from the outside, but in the form of questions raised as he walks along with the other's thought. I am convinced that formation by von Balthasar's style of dialogue is a great school for listening and thus for true dialogue.

How important is such schooling! Here one learns that it is not enough to use labels and slogans to finish off the other's thought. To the very end von Balthasar did not grow tired of letting *others* speak—through his work as an editor and translator, through introductions and monographs, both small and

---

[14] *Kleine Fibel für verunsicherte Laien,* 2nd ed. (Einsiedeln: Johannes Verlag, 1980), 43.

[15] On this "hermeneutical key" set forth in the Constitution *Dei verbum* (n. 12), see the important essay by Ignace de la Potterie, "Die Lesung der Heiligen Schrift 'im Geist' ", *Communio* 15 (1986): 209–24; more in detail: de la Potterie, "L'interprétation de la Sainte Ecriture dans l'Esprit où elle a été écrite", in R. Latourelle, ed., *Vatican II. Bilan et Perspectives vingt-cinq ans après* (1962–1987) (Paris-Montreal, 1987), 235–76; cf. J. Cardinal Ratzinger, ed., *Schriftauslegung im Widerstreit* (Freiburg, 1989).

[16] *Karl Barth,* 27, with reference to Karl Barth, *Kirchliche Dogmatik,* III/3: *Die Lehre von der Schöpfung* (Zurich, 1950), 278–321.

large. His work stands before us as a great invitation to a truly ecumenical attitude of dialogue.

The Heart: The Catholica

Where did von Balthasar find the capacity and power for listening, for dialogue? In *Kleine Fibel für verunsicherte Laien* von Balthasar writes,

> The divided Church does not make a credible impression on the world; we must do everything to eliminate the scandal of schisms. However, a Catholic Church with inner divisions makes an impression on Christian dialogue partners which is no more credible. Only when we are certain that we can show forth the unity and fullness of catholicity within the Church, only then are we ready for dialogue. Those who labor for Catholic identity to find itself are laying a rich foundation for a meaningful ecumenical dialogue.[17]

Von Balthasar's concern is clearly characterized in these words. His work serves this idea: "for Catholic identity to find itself". At first glance this may seem like a "Catholic ghetto", like withdrawal behind safe bastions. This would be a complete misunderstanding. Von Balthasar's view of ecumenism can only be seen correctly in the light of his understanding of the catholicity of the Church. Given its origin and goal, the Church can only be *one*. She is the one, holy, catholic, and apostolic Church. In God's plan of salvation, carried out by Christ, enlivened by the Holy Spirit, there is only *one* Church, just as there is only one baptism, one faith, one Lord (see Eph 4:5).

Von Balthasar quotes Karl Barth, "One should not attempt to explain the multiplicity of churches as an unfolding of the riches of the grace given to the human race in Christ Jesus, as an unfolding which is willed by God and therefore normal. One should not attempt to explain the multiplicity of churches at all. One should treat it as one treats one's own sin and that of others. . . . One should understand it as guilt."[18] Concern about the division of churches must begin here: sin is always separation—from God, from one's neighbor, as a split in one's own life. *Ubi peccata, ibi multitudo,* is a saying by Origen that von Balthasar likes to quote.[19] Ecumenism can only mean conversion, asking for the forgiveness of sins. As long as sin is at work, there will be divisions. It is only in sanctity that the unity of the Church becomes visible, for sanctity is the victory of love, which alone can unite all. For this reason the saints are the great signs of

---

[17] *Kleine Fibel,* 91–92.

[18] *Karl Barth,* 16; see also *Theodramatik* II. *Die Personen des Spiels,* 2. Teil: *Die Personen in Christus* (Einsiedeln: Johannes Verlag, 1978), 407f.

[19] See, for example, ibid., 407; and "Absolutheit des Christentums und Katholizität der Kirche", in *Homo creatus est* (*Skizzen zur Theologie V*) (Einsiedeln: Johannes Verlag, 1986), 345.

unity, the ferment that heals division. Von Balthasar showed this untiringly in the great figures of the Church. It is in them that he finds the inspiration for paths toward unity. "Beyond all cross-pollination and mutual instruction among the 'churches', which is always possible, there is for the *Catholica* only *one* path of meaningful ecumenical activity, namely, the portrayal of its own principle in exemplarily lived sanctity."[20] If one were to condense von Balthasar's view of ecumenism into one principle, it could only be the following: *the saints are the path of ecumenism,* because it is in them, in the many-colored multiplicity of charisms, that the catholicity of Christian love is expressed.

Let us sketch at least briefly how von Balthasar sees this path. In his *Fibel,* von Balthasar mentions two aspects of ecumenical dialogue following the principle "for Catholic identity to find itself":

> On the one hand, non-Catholic Christian communities have been able to stress certain fundamental truths of the Gospel and have been able to preserve them in their exodus from the *Catholica,* truths that were obscured in the *Catholica* and not re-introduced with sufficient balance by the extreme counter-positions adopted in the controversies following the schism (catchword: "Counter-Reformation"). In this case, Catholics must listen to the voice of those who point out to us a missing or insufficiently realized piece of the whole of faith.[21]

In this way von Balthasar was a listener who was able to hear the voice of the *Catholica* even in apparently very distant voices—I am thinking here not only of confessional dialogue in the narrower sense, but also cultural dialogue (von Balthasar's attention to poets, e.g., Goethe, Rilke, Brecht; and to philosophers, e.g., Schelling, Nietzsche, and many others). Such realization of truth that has emigrated from the Catholic unity leads to a second element of the dialogue. "On the other hand, members of the *Catholica* must be aware that their 'separated brothers and sisters' can alert them only to things that have always rested in the fullness of their faith, things which were merely forgotten or lost through negligence or guilt. If this guilt is admitted, the claim to Catholic totality is possible without arrogance."[22]

That von Balthasar lived this claim, not as *his* private and personal claim, but as the claim of the Church's catholicity, was often interpreted as arrogance, elitism, and exclusivism. He attempted to live this claim "without arrogance", but with the claim's inexorable and uncomfortable force. Thus von Balthasar formulates sharply and unequivocally:

> All communities that left the *Catholica* rest, inasmuch as they are separated, on more or less drastic negations of elements that belong to the organic

[20] *Theodramatik* II/2, 409f.
[21] *Kleine Fibel,* 92.
[22] Ibid.

unity of the tradition of the faith. To show to others in Christian love that
elements subtracted by them really belong to the unity is something demanded
by theological sensitivity but also by the ethical attitude of the Catholic.
The Catholic must be able to show that the controversial points are a part,
indispensable even if relative, of the apostolic Creed.[23]

Von Balthasar has attempted to show this in many areas. He mentions two
areas that are considered specific ecumenical obstacles, namely, the Marian
dogmas and the question of offices, epitomized in the question of the office of
Peter. "It is not by abolishing the Marian dogmas or by the denial of the
apostolic succession that one brings about unity with Protestants, but by the
proper integration of these truths into the comprehensive Christological-
trinitarian whole. It is not by giving up the true primacy of the successor of
Peter that union with the Orthodox is achieved, but by living it in a credible
way in the spirit of the Gospel."[24]

Von Balthasar's numerous texts about the Mother of the Lord are exemplary here. They are theological meditations that are formed in a thoroughly
biblical manner and that show Mary as the believer, as the one who lives in
obedience toward God, who assents to the mission of her Son. Mary has
fundamental ecumenical importance, according to von Balthasar, because it is
in Mary that the Church appears as *ecclesia sancta et immaculata,* it is in her that
the Church's complete form (*Vollgestalt*), her catholicity, is not merely a
promise, an eschatological hope, but an already realized fullness. Von Balthasar's
Mariology is fundamental for ecumenical dialogue about the Church.

The second "critical point" is the question of the Petrine office.[25] Von
Balthasar's book *Der antirömische Affekt* has found a certain echo, if any
echo at all, only in its polemical aspects. The positive concern is expressed
in the subtitle: How can the papacy be integrated in the Church as a whole?
The key word is "integrate": not the bracketing of what one likes to portray
as a Catholic "surplus" and which therefore remains as "a troublesome
question" at the margins of ecumenical endeavors, but "integration" of this
seemingly troublesome aspect into the Catholic whole. The Church cannot be only Pauline; but also not only Petrine. She has been willed by
Christ in manifold (*vielgestaltig*) unity, as Marian and Johannine, Petrine
and Pauline Church. Such integration also prevents a certain narrowing
within Catholicism. It is possible, with the sure instinct of the Holy Spirit, *for
the saints.*

Karl Barth was worried and decisively rejected von Balthasar's attempt at

---

[23] Ibid., 92–93.

[24] Ibid., 93.

[25] See "Absolutheit des Christentums": "The distinctively Catholic element in comparison with other Christian communities lies, therefore, in these two points; they belong
together and point to each other" (347).

seeing the saints as the signposts for ecumenism. He had heartfelt praise for von Balthasar's Barth monograph, but he pointed a warning finger at the two monographs written by von Balthasar at the same time about Thérèse of Lisieux and Elizabeth of Dijon, in whose company he probably felt himself theologically misunderstood. In von Balthasar's reading of the saints, he sees the danger that the uniqueness of Christ might pale vis-à-vis the "representation" of Christ by the saints, [26] and so it was probably not possible for him to hear von Balthasar's concern in these books. In 1961 von Balthasar wrote: "*Elizabeth of Dijon* [1952] was juxtaposed as a Catholic counterpart to Barth's doctrine of predestination." [27] A passage from von Balthasar's book about Thérèse of Lisieux may clarify the manner in which von Balthasar shows that precisely the great figures of the saints succeeded in integrating the concerns of separated confessions.

> One would have to be blind not to see that Thérèse's doctrine of the little way directly faces the fundamental concerns of the Reformation and that it largely represents the daring and sure response of the Church to Protestant spirituality. The rejection of an Old Testament ethos of works; the deconstruction of one's own perfection as a whole in order to make room for God's perfection in us; transcendence in the structure of faith, the center of which remains in God and whose supernatural intentionality requires from the human person an increasing orientation toward God; the existential fullness of the act of faith, which implies more than the intellectual assent to the contents of faith, namely, an act of total personal faithfulness to God's personal truth; finally not taking one's own faults seriously, in fact joy about this in the sense of *"felix culpa"* — all of these are close ties between Thérèse and the Reformers. [28]

With his *view of ecumenism as integration into the whole of the* Catholica *realized in the saints,* von Balthasar has remained so far largely alone. "Academic theology" does not like being asked to submit to the schooling of Thérèse of Lisieux to learn *Catholic integration* from her. And yet *this* is the way on which Hans Urs von Balthasar walked untiringly to the end; this is the way he suggested for theology. I am thinking here of his edition of the works of Marie de la Trinité shortly before his death, [29] and especially

[26] See Karl Barth, *Kirchliche Dogmatik*, IV: *Die lehre von der Versöhnung*, 1 (Zurich, 1953), 858f.

[27] *Karl Barth*, 2nd. ed. (Cologne: Verlag Jakob Hegner, 1962), viii; see also the "Predestination" in *Schwestern im Geist. Therese von Lisieux und Elisabeth von Dijon*, 3rd ed. (Einsiedeln: Johannes Verlag, 1978), 365–99.

[28] *Schwestern im Geist*, 273f.

[29] See Marie de la Trinité, *Im Schoss des Vaters. Aufzeichnungen, ausgewählt und übertragen von H. U. von Balthasar* (In the Father's Bosom. Translated and introduced by H. U. von Balthasar) (Einsiedeln-Trier: Johannes Verlag, 1988).

of the gigantic work of Adrienne von Speyr.[30] In his activity as a translator and editor, von Balthasar edited many works by women of the past and present. More than other (male) theologians, he was engaged in a *theological* conversation with these women. He did not see their experiences and reflections as "spirituality", but as theological contributions. This manifold conversation should be looked at closely because it is also of great ecumenical significance.

Von Balthasar's concern to reintegrate theology and spirituality is an eminently ecumenical concern. An important work of the French Carmelite François Marie Léthel, which has just come out, would have pleased von Balthasar very much. (I am not sure whether one can rejoice in heaven about new theological publications, or whether one does not rather smile about them.) Its title can be translated "To know the love of Christ which surpasses all knowledge: The theology of the saints."[31] The book's protagonists are Irenaeus of Lyon, Anselm, Thomas, Jeanne d'Arc, Péguy, and Thérèse de l'Enfant Jésus—a program with which von Balthasar would certainly have agreed, since it is quite in line with what he did in the volumes on styles contained in *The Glory of the Lord.*[32] The programmatic first sentence of Léthel's book is, "All the saints are theologians; only the saints are theologians."[33] Here too I am certain of the great teacher's assent. Theology, speaking of God, is most exact when the speaker has become similar to what he speaks of. Only then does his word truly carry, only then does it really speak of God and strike human beings.

Hans Urs von Balthasar said much and wrote much. At the beginning we raised the question of what the yield of his life may be, and we know that we cannot know this. "The souls of the just are in the hands of the Lord." The reward is *always* incomparably greater than all merit. But to us, who are still pilgrims, the work and person of Hans Urs von Balthasar raise a question: What will *we* do with the gifts we received? Great witnesses of Christ are given to the Church so that the Church might renew herself. But will their testimony be accepted? Von Balthasar's contribution to ecumenism is an inexhaustible stream of "manifold wisdom" (Eph 3:10) which lives in the breadth of the *Catholica Ecclesia.* We were all allowed

[30] Last of all the great anthology, *Kostet und seht. Ein theologisches Lesebuch. Aus ihren Schriften ausgewählt und eingeleitet von H. U. von Balthasar* (Come and Taste. A Theological Reader. Selected from Her Writings and Introduced by H. U. von Balthasar) (Einsiedeln-Trier: Johannes Verlag, 1988).

[31] See F. M. Léthel, *Connaître l'amour du Christ qui surpasse toute connaissance. La théologie des saints* (Venasque, 1989).

[32] *The Glory of the Lord:* II: *Clerical Styles* (San Francisco: Ignatius Press, 1984) and III: *Lay Styles* (1986).

[33] Léthel, *Connaître l'amour du Christ.*

to receive from this fullness. Will our time see the ecumenical wealth[34] that lies ready here?

---

[34] We are aware that the reflections sketched here are a mere beginning. One essential aspect is missing. Without it, the theme of ecumenism would remain misunderstood in von Balthasar's work. Von Balthasar pointed again and again to the "original break" in the Church, in the one Israel of God, which consists in the nonrecognition of Jesus by a large part of Israel and which cleaves congenitally, as it were, to the Church. The overcoming of the many schisms will probably be achieved only with the closure of this break; see on this *Theodramatik,* II/2, 331–410, and "Absolutheit des Christentums".

APPENDIX

BISHOP KARL LEHMANN AND BISHOP WALTER KASPER

Preface to *Hans Urs von Balthasar: Gestalt und Werk*[1]

When Hans Urs von Balthasar suddenly left us on June 26, 1988 the world lost a man of a stature seldom found today. No less a person than Henri de Lubac considered him the most cultured man of our time. He was a man of the Gospel, of intellectual life, and of culture who uniquely encompassed the great Western and European heritage. Two days before he was to receive the insignia of Cardinal by which John Paul II wanted to honor this teacher of the Church, he took his farewell as if he still wanted to forego the honor which he had accepted in obedience: he was too shaped by the poverty and self-expropriation attested in the Gospel, especially with regard to himself.

This man fits no theological, academic, cultural, or political pigeonholes. He was at home everywhere, and yet he was on a restless spiritual journey without ever giving the impression of hectic haste. The usual classifications and political labels (left-right, progressive-conservative-reactionary) could never capture him. His life is a rich testimony of new departures that never brought him to waver in his faithfulness to what is original and essential. Here lies the source of the sovereign manner in which he could judge the spiritual currents and fashions of our time.

Although his work is inexhaustible in the abundant number of books he wrote, and although it developed with surprising freshness, it is always concerned with "the one thing" which he considered the one thing necessary, as his master did in the house of Mary and Martha. The deed of God's absolute love enraptured him unceasingly. Let us allow him to say in his own words where he saw the greatest gift given to the Church: "The deepest thing in Christianity is God's love for the earth. That God is rich in his heaven is something known also by other religions. That he wanted to be poor together with his creatures, that in his heaven, he wanted to and did indeed suffer for his world, and that through his Incarnation he enabled himself to prove the suffering of his love to his creatures: this is the hitherto unheard-of thing." His

Translated by Michael Waldstein.
[1] Edited by Karl Lehmann and Walter Kasper (Cologne: Communio, 1989).

every concern was to unfold this one center in its many dimensions and to refold the many figures and styles into the one mystery.

In one person, Hans Urs von Balthasar realized a number of callings each of which could have filled more than a whole life for others—supposing that they had comparable gifts of the spirit and of grace. These callings should at least be indicated: the *spiritual master* who accompanied many individuals and quite a number of communities with his discreet spiritual and pastoral care; the *theologian* who created an incomparable synthesis of manifold experiences of God in his main work in three parts and fifteen volumes, *The Glory of the Lord, Theo-Drama, Theo-Logic;* the *writer* who was given a rare "charism of writing" (Alois M. Haas) and had all stylistic forms and keys of human language at his disposal; the *translator* of many works from Greek, Latin, Spanish, and especially French—Paul Claudel and Henri de Lubac, to mention only two representative examples; the *editor and publisher* of the independent publishing house founded by him, Johannes Verlag, which published inalienable treasures of a spiritual Europe and who brought the German public into contact with great works of theology and spirituality, especially French works: a great builder of bridges between German and French culture; together with the Swiss physician and convert Adrienne von Speyr—whose life work in sixty volumes he edited—he became the *founder* and especially the *spiritual director* of the Community of St. John, an activity through which, together with his theological writings, he gave a great impetus to other secular institutes. What else should one mention? The scholar of German literature, the highly gifted musician, the friend of art. . . .

Communio was one of the things he founded. At the beginning of the '70s when Hans Urs von Balthasar launched this *International Catholic Review* together with friends associated with the International Theological Commission (the first number of the German edition appeared in 1972), he fulfilled a call that he had long sensed, often postponed, and almost abandoned. He gave to *Communio* not only its spiritual program and inner dimensions, but, from the beginning up to the last days before his death, he was also its guiding spirit. He not only convened and led the small annual editorial gatherings in Basel; even at the great international conferences he was spiritually the undoubted center in what had meanwhile grown into twelve editorial teams across the world. Only a future time will be able to assess how much Hans Urs von Balthasar contributed to the construction and cohesion of *Communio,* especially through his extensive correspondence and through his friendships throughout the world—for the longest time in close collaboration, at times filled with tension but always fruitful, with Franz Greiner, who was executive editor from the beginning until his death a year before von Balthasar and who was the organizational column of the whole.

This volume is intended as a sign of memory, of reverence and of gratitude for everything we owe to Hans Urs von Balthasar. At the same time it hopes to be a stimulus for the world of thought and of culture, and especially for Christians and theologians, to discover anew a figure who is unique in our century, in his wisdom superior to and independent from all fashions of the day. We hope for a new future in the figure and work of Hans Urs von Balthasar. He is a thinker of the Catholic Faith, of a sort that is urgently needed by the Church and the world.

HENRI DE LUBAC, S.J.

A Witness of Christ in the Church: Hans Urs von Balthasar

As Ludwig Kaufmann has justly remarked in a recent issue of *Orientierung*, it is disconcerting that from the first summons of the Council by John XXIII it did not seem to have occurred to anyone to invite Hans Urs von Balthasar to contribute to its preparatory work. Disconcerting and—not to put a tooth in it—humiliating, but a fact that must be humbly accepted. Perhaps, all in all, it was better that he should be allowed to devote himself completely to his task, to the continuation of a work so immense in size and depth that the contemporary Church has seen nothing comparable. For a long time to come the entire Church is going to profit from it.

Indispensable though such things undoubtedly are, Hans Urs von Balthasar is not a man for commissions, discussions, compromise formulas, or collective drafts. But the conciliar texts that resulted from them—of Vatican II and of all previous councils—constitute a treasure that will not be yielded up at a single stroke: the councils are the work of the Spirit, and so these texts contain more than their humble compilers were conscious of putting in them. When later the time comes to exploit this treasure it will be seen that for the accomplishing of this task no work will be as helpful and full of resource as that of von Balthasar.

One thing we see immediately: there is not one of the subjects tackled by Vatican II that does not find a treatment in depth—and in the same spirit and sense as the Council—in his work. Revelation, Church, ecumenism, priesthood, liturgy of the word, and eucharistic liturgy occupy a considerable portion. Valuable insights on dialogue, on the signs of the times and the instruments of social communications will also be found. . . . Before the Fathers of the Council had insisted that the dominant role of Christ be recognized in the schemas on the Church and revelation, von Balthasar had seen the need. His voice was an advance echo, as it were, of the voices that were raised in St. Peter's to ask for an adequate statement of the role of the Holy Spirit. The Virgin Mary in

From *The Church: Paradox and Mystery*, translated by James R. Dunne (Staten Island, N.Y.: Alba House, 1969). Reprinted by permission. All rights reserved.

the mystery of the Church, her prototype and anticipated consummation, is one of his favored contemplations. Gently, but with all the force of love, he has denounced those eternal temptations of churchmen, "power" and "triumph", and has at the same time recalled to all the necessity of witnessing through "service".

His spiritual diagnosis of our civilization is the most penetrating to be found. Though it would be going too far to claim that he had produced a complete outline of the famous Schema 13, he did, certainly, anticipate its spirit when he shows how "in the same way that the Spirit calls the world to enter into the Church, so he calls the Church to give herself to the world"; and he warns us that no good will come of a facile synthesis of the two. In many cases one would also find in his writings the means to avoid the pitfalls of false interpretation which inevitably follow upon a call to *aggiornamento*.[1] And if, finally, one is seeking (always in line with the Council) the doctrinal framework needed before beginning the dialogue with the non-Christian religions and the various forms of modern atheism, one can safely go to von Balthasar.

His work is, as we have said, immense. So varied is it, so complex, usually so undidactic, so wide-ranging through different genres, that its unity is difficult to grasp, at least at first blush. But, strangely enough, once you have got to grips with it, the unity stands out so forcefully that you despair of outlining it without betraying it. It is like a radiant impulse penetrating from a central point to all corners of his work. With the astonished perception of the immense culture he enjoys, displayed without pedantry, must go equal appreciation of the strong judgment that dominates this culture. The reader has to appreciate the breadth of thought that is never narrow or doctrinaire even when it had to be (or believed it had to be) hard and trenchant; and yet, at the same time the reader has to fell the rigorous balance of doctrine that is, in both senses of the word, profoundly catholic. And our problem does not end there: the reader must also be brought to see that he is never confronted with a purely theoretical construction; nor is von Balthasar a polisher of systems. Author of numerous books, some of them very long, neither is he a book factory! Every word he writes envisages an action, a decision. He has not the slightest time for "that certain economy of the mind which budgets and spares itself": everything is squandered that the "personal meeting" with God may be arrived at without delay.

This man is perhaps the most cultivated of his time. If there is a Christian culture, then here it is! Classical antiquity, the great European literatures, the

---

[1] We should state straightaway that he has courageously declared war on certain wild abandons that are a betrayal of the Council. Had more allies rushed to his flag, he would have had no need to write certain rather savage pages.

metaphysical tradition, the history of religions, the diverse exploratory adventures of contemporary man and, above all, the sacred sciences, St. Thomas, St. Bonaventure, patrology (all of it)—not to speak just now of the Bible—none of them that is not welcomed and made vital by this great mind. Writers and poets, mystics and philosophers, old and new, Christians of all persuasions—all are called on to make their particular contribution. All these are necessary for his final accomplishment, to a greater glory of God, the Catholic symphony.

Many of his books are historical studies or translations or anthologies: he likes to remain in the background of the pictures he commissions to serve as witnesses of the truth of man or of God. He was twenty-five when he published his first work, *Apokalypse der deutschen Seele,* which was a historical commentary of the whole of German thought. A new edition has since appeared. Another book was an anthology of Nietzsche. He has written commentaries on the Epistles of St. Paul to the Thessalonians and the pastoral Epistles. He has published his own translations of many of the Fathers: Irenaeus, the Apologists, Origen, Gregory of Nyssa, Augustine. To several he has devoted a special study that in each case gave new life to its subject: *Présence et Pensée,* for instance, on Gregory of Nyssa; *Kosmische Liturgie* on Maximus the Confessor. He has given us a commentary on part of Augustine's *De Genesi ad litteram,* and also on part of the *Summa Theologica* (Questions on Prophecy). His translations include the revelations of St. Mechtildis of Helfta, the *Spiritual Exercises* of St. Ignatius (whose devoted disciple he is), the *Carnets Intimes* of Maurice Blondel—as well as the greater part of Calderón's religious drama. His incomparable translation of the lyric poems and *Le Soulier de Satin* of Claudel are well known.

He had done critical studies on Martin Buber and R. Schneider, on Péguy and Bernanos (*Le Chrétien Bernanos* was one of the last books the Abbé Monchanin read in the summer of 1957 at Kodaikanal). The substance of a book (recently reprinted) which is a confrontation of the Protestant Reformation and Catholicism he owes to his close contacts with a neighbor in Basel, Karl Barth. He has discussed the message of the two French Carmelites, Elizabeth of Dijon and Thérèse of Lisieux. The second volume of the monumental work he was long engaged on, *Herrlichkeit,* consists of a series of twelve monographs in which Denys and Anselm meet Dante and John of the Cross, Pascal and Hamann meet Soloviev and Hopkins. . . .

Without ever abdicating his freedom to criticize, he is at ease with all, even those whose genius might appear most foreign to his own; but when the time comes to disagree with them he does not hesitate. He excels at highlighting the original contribution of each. He admires human wisdom wherever he finds it—but surpasses it. Sensitive to man's *Angst,* he emerges from it in faith. The light from so many ancient sources allows him to illuminate the present situation and the accumulated wisdom of the centuries allows him, if we may be permitted the metaphor, to bury his arrows ever deeper in our present reality.

The inner universe he introduces us to is thereby in its marvellous variety, perfectly unified. As in Tolstoy's epic, a broad and calm atmosphere prevails; as in Dostoevsky, this atmosphere is electric with sharp spiritual insight. All is patterned around a lofty and unchanging notion of truth, outlined in his beautiful work *Phénoménologie de la Vérité*. Truth is the cornerstone on which his theology of history is erected, more particularly in two essays. Finally, every word is designed to set in relief a basic anthropology relating to modern situations and the most pressing problems being faced by man today.

The contribution of the positive sciences is, perhaps, rather neglected, though scientific knowledge is assigned its proper place. The arts, it seems to von Balthasar, have more to offer by way of illuminating suggestion. He realizes, in fact, that the great works of art—and every great work is a work of art—go beyond so-called purely aesthetic categories and ought to be accepted, as they were conceived of by their artists, as efforts to complete a full image of man. Elsewhere he remarks that since the Renaissance, man is no longer thought of and understood in the cosmological context but in an openly anthropological one. And since "in an anthropological era the highest objectivity can only be attained by total engagement on man's part", we see the heightened dramatic character of all modern thought worthy of the name, a character that corresponds to the drama of existence itself.

Emerged from the cosmic development that nursed him, no longer in any way capable of regarding himself as one object among many, no longer having any home but his own fragility, man, von Balthasar thinks, is more predestined than ever "to become religious man" if he is to surmount this crisis of "dereliction" resulting from the new situation. His rapport with God acquires a sudden urgency; the biblical teaching of man made in God's image becomes better delineated in his eyes and without the stage of natural knowledge being destroyed in the process the revelation of Jesus Christ presents itself to him more than ever as the necessary response to the interrogation forever carried on by his being. In his existence in time and history that constitutes "the visible explication of the existence-form of the God-Trinity", Jesus comes to reveal this unknown that was in him to man; then "his features expand, are enlightened and deepened when he meets, not a mirror giving him back his own image, but his own supreme original".

It is quite impossible to summarize here the theological thought of von Balthasar; we shall confine ourselves to the essentials. What distinguishes it and gives it its most striking originality is its refusal to be labeled. It can neither be termed old nor modern; it derives from no school and repudiates all piecemeal "specialization". With no axe to grind, no single aspect of a given question is stressed to the detriment of the others, or rather, it refuses to delay over successive "aspects" while never forgetting to consider each. The indispensable technicalities are there, whether in criticism (certain work on Origen, Evagrius, or Maximus, for instance, is inspired guesswork followed up by the most rigorous verification), or in dialectic (as in the dialectic "of the unveiling and enveloping" to different degrees of revelation, or in the relation of negative natural theology to the knowledge of the "face of revelation" which is given to us in Christ). But, for all that, it retains a highly synthetic character which breaks down the barriers to the interior life of things where the classic theology of our times is usually bogged down. While it does not offer direct pedagogical models, his thought—and even the form of his thought—may be usefully meditated on in view of the new directions which Christian thought must take since the Council.

Not to labor the point, let us say that in a word his theology, like our ordinary credos, is essentially trinitarian. Not that the Trinity fragments the divine unity—it is revealed to us, after all, through its work of salvation which is itself perfectly one. The "seamless coat" and the "lance's thrust" are the symbols he uses to bring this home to us:

> A mystery that is broken up into aspects (*epinoiai*) will yield its secrets to the inquiring intelligence. But there is one mystery that absolutely refuses to do so, the irreducible mystery of the *persona ineffabilis*. From him the whole Church comes in his death, with the water and the blood—the Church which with all her truths, liturgies, and dogmas is only an emanation of the heart that broke unto death, as Origen better than anyone else understood.

For the "thrust of the lance on Golgotha is in some manner the sacrament of the spiritual thrust that wounds the Word and so spreads it everywhere. . . . The Word of God cast into our world is the fruit of this unique wound."

It is the Holy Spirit who ceaselessly introduces the Christian into the heart of this mystery. The Spirit's role is to "refresh daily the memory of the Church and to supplement it in a renewed manner" with all truth. It is he who realizes everything in the Church and in her individual members "as it was he who formerly realized the Incarnation of the Word in the womb of the Virgin". Also von Balthasar likes to point out the continuity between "the Marian experience" and "the maternal experience of the Church". He likes to speak of "the Marian dimension of the Church" or of "the Marian Church", and this simple expression we take as a condensation of his teaching which might also be said to be the teaching of the Church, or of the Virgin Mary, or of the Spirit, or of Christ, or of the Christian life.

His refusal of all biased "modernity" is by no means a refuge from present problems and the responsibilities they impose. The theologian must transmit a truth which is not his own and which he must guard against alteration, but transmitting this truth and watching over change to new situations demands from him a real involvement:

> One sees this very clearly in the manner in which St. Paul transmits what had been confided to him. Anyone who would wish to insert himself without danger in the chain of Tradition and transmit the treasures of theology, almost as children who switch their hot buns from hand to hand in the hope of not being burnt, would be the victim of a sorry illusion, quite simply because thoughts are not buns, or rather because from the morning of Easter combat was joined between the material and the spiritual.

This theology, so traditional, remains relevant today and indeed does not lack a certain audacity. Von Balthasar has recalled to the modern theologian the immense task that confronts him and that even demands that he give all his attention for the moment to the central core of the doctrinal question:

> The doctrines of the Trinity, of the Man-God, of redemption, of the Cross and the Resurrection, of predestination, and eschatology, are literally bristling with problems which no one raises, which everyone gingerly sidesteps. They deserve more respect. The thought of preceding generations even when incorporated in conciliar definitions is never a resting-place where the thought of the following generations can lie idle. Definitions are less the end than the beginning.... No doubt anything that was won after a severe battle will be lost again for the Church, which does not however dispense the theologian from setting to work immediately again. Whatever is transmitted without a new personal effort, an effort which must start *ab ovo*, from the revealed source itself, spoils like the manna. And the longer the interruption of living tradition caused by a simply mechanical transmission the more difficult the renewed tackling of the task.

The boldness of such a program, we can see clearly enough, does not lead us onto perilous or uncharted seas; it does lead us to the living center of the mystery. Its primary concern is for completeness. Von Balthasar's audacity is not an irresponsible appetite for novelty: it proceeds from a faith whose daring grows in proportion to the strength of its roots. He himself is one of those men of whom he has spoken, men who devoted the work of their lives "to the splendor of theology—theology, that devouring fire between two nights, two abysses: adoration and obedience". The denials and lack of comprehension of our age disconcert few people as little as him. Fashionable opinion does not intimidate him; he never entertains the temptation to water down the vigorous affirmation of doctrine or the rigorous demands of the Gospel.

There is no trace in him of that terrible inferiority complex rampant today in certain milieux among many Christian consciences. The Church, he has written, following St. Jerome and Newman, "like the rod of Aaron, devours the magicians' serpents"; and by her, at the same time, he says in an image borrowed from Claudel and which might also be described as Teilhardian, "the key of the Christian vault is come to open the pagan forest". And so von Balthasar has done. With calm assurance he displays to all, as far as he can, the entire Christian treasure. He does not hesitate to oppose, not criticism nor psychology nor technology nor mysticism, but all their unwarranted pretensions, and no one can accuse him of blaspheming what he does not know.

He knows the value of "human sciences", he admires their conquests but will not submit to their totalitarian claims. His many observations on scriptural exegesis, on the need for a spiritual intelligence, and, in particular, on the blindness of a certain historico-critical method of dealing with the meaning of the history of Israel and the person of Jesus, all deserve a wider audience. "The Holy Spirit", he writes, "is a reality which the philologists and philosophers of comparative religion are ignorant of or at least 'provisionally put into parentheses'." Von Balthasar removes the parentheses, or rather, he shows us how the Holy Spirit himself removes them.

Some of his criticisms—they are rare—might appear harsh. In every case they arose from his concern not to compromise in essentials. He is too far above pettiness, too heedless of passing modes and allurements—particularly those that arise from pseudo-science or a frivolus faith—not to find himself often isolated. In the end however his attitude is always positive. His "tough line" is the same as that he has pointed out in Christ, the revealer of love. He is being true to his own position when he warns us of the dangers of isolationism. He does not wish "through enthusiasm for the glorious past of the Church", or for any other reason, that the Christian "forsake the men of today and tomorrow. Quite the contrary. It is the duty of all who represent Jesus Christ—be they bishops or layfolk—to keep open their perspective on the human; never to allow any maneuver to push them back into isolationism or negative attitudes."

"We live in a time of spiritual aridity." The vital equilibrium between action and contemplation has been lost, to the apparent profit of the first but, for the very same reason, to its detriment. Von Balthasar has tried to reestablish this equilibrium. All his work has a contemplative dimension and it is this above all that gives it its profundity and flavor.

He introduced again into theology the category of the beautiful. But make no mistake, this is not to say that he surrendered the content of the Faith to current notions in secular aesthetics.[2] He began by restoring to the beautiful its position as a transcendental—this beauty "which demands courage and decision at least as much as truth and goodness, and which may not be

---

[2] He had already said in *Le Chrétien Bernanos:* "There exists a theological, an ecclesiological aesthetic that has nothing at all to do with aestheticism. In it pure human beauty meets with the beauty of the supernatural."

separated from its sisters without drawing upon it their mysterious vengeance".
He has not agreed with those theologians who based their work on the
separation of aesthetics from theology. His "theological aesthetics", however,
is not an "aesthetic theology"; it has nothing to do with any aestheticism
whatever. Moreover, in this mystery of the beautiful which men, not daring to
believe in it, converted into a mere appearance, he sees, as in the biblical
description of wisdom, the union of the "intangible brilliance" and the
"determined form", which requires and conditions in the believer the unity of
faith and vision.

The beautiful is at once "image" and "strength", and is so par excellence in
that perfect "figure of revelation" who is the Man-God. Faith contemplates
this figure and its contemplation is prayer. Von Balthasar has observed that
wherever the very greatest works were produced there was invariably "an
environment of prayer and contemplation". The law is verified in an analogous manner even in the pagan domain.

> The proud spirits who never prayed and who today pass for torchbearers of
> culture vanish, with regularity, after a few years and are replaced by others.
> Those who pray are torn by the populace that does not pray, like Orpheus
> torn by the Maenads, but even in their lacerations their song is still heard
> everywhere; and if, because of their ill-use by the multitude, they seem to
> lose their influence, they remain hidden in a protected place where, in the
> fullness of time, they will be found once again by men of prayer.

Jesus, "indivisible Man-God", is at once the object and model of Christian
contemplation. This is the burden of the great work, still uncompleted,
Herrlichkeit. The idea is put into action in a book like *The Heart of the World* in
which the heart of Jesus opens to us in a kind of lyrical explosion. It may be
seen even better perhaps in *Prayer,* an introduction to prayer that is at the same
time a complete—the most complete available—outline of the Christian mystery.
We shall restrict ourselves here to quoting just one passage, a passage of great
value in that it provokes reflection on the primordial importance of contemplation in the life of the apostle:

> All we have been able to attest to other men, our brothers, of the divine
> reality comes from contemplation; of Jesus Christ, of our Church. One
> cannot hope to announce in a lasting and effective manner the contemplation
> of Christ and the Church if one does not oneself participate in them. No
> more than a man who has never loved is capable of speaking usefully of
> love. Even the smallest problem in the world will not be solved by one who
> has not met this world; no Christian will be an effective apostle if he does
> not announce, firm as the "rock" Peter, what he has seen and heard: "We did
> not bring you the knowledge of the power and advent of our Lord Jesus
> Christ on the warrant of human fables, but because we have been privileged

to see his majesty. He received from God the Father honor and glory. . . . This voice (of the Father) we have heard when we were with him on the holy mountain . . . !"

And he continues, not without sadness:

But who today speaks of Tabor in the program of Catholic action? And who speaks of seeing, hearing, or touching that which all the zeal in the world cannot preach and propagate if the apostle himself has not recognized and experienced it? Who speaks of the ineffable peace of eternity beyond the conflicts of earth? But also, who speaks of the weakness and obvious powerlessness of crucified Love whose "annihilation" to the extent of becoming "sin" and "accursed" has given birth to all strength and salvation for the Church and mankind? Whoever has not experienced this mystery through contemplation will never be able to speak of it, or even act according to it, without a feeling of embarrassment and a twinge of conscience, unless, indeed, the very naïvete of such a basically worldly business has not already made this bad conscience apparent to him.[3]

On specifically Christian contemplation von Balthasar's judgment is equally lucid: "All the other unfathomable depths to which man's contemplation may penetrate, when they are not expressly or implicitly the depths of the trinitarian, human-divine, or ecclesial life, are either not real depths at all or are those of the devil." There is a kind of spiritual pride that is the most dangerous inversion of all; many so-called "mystical" states are no more than "artificial paradises" and as for those "sublime spirits" who search for the way apart from or above the humanity of the Savior, "what they experience in their ecstasies is the disguised ghost of their empty nostalgia". Even in the Christian spiritual life it may be opportune to recall that "the Gospel and the Church are not dionysiac: their overall impression is of sobriety; elation is left for the sects".

These reservations do not, however, tend in the slightest to "crush the Spirit". The Spirit must be received in the manner in which he gives himself, in a sort of tension between precision and enthusiasm:

The saints knew how to do it: it is precisely this precision of the image of Jesus as projected by the Spirit that they would wax enthusiastic about; and then their very enthusiasm, expressed with precision, would convey to all the fact that they had been gripped by this image. Even if they were full of indubitable truths that might express for all the world the truth of the Gospel, the saints were not arid textbooks: expressing the truth was the very life of the saints gripped by the Holy Spirit of Christ.

---

[3] He has also, most opportunely, pointed out the danger of a "liturgical movement" which would be "isolated and uncontemplative", just as he has also indicated his "contempt" for a war that has been declared against the contemplative tendency and that is sometimes waged in the name of eschatology.

Even for the humblest and weakest Christian it is in the simplicity of his *Yes* of acceptance and openness, in imitation of the *Yes* said by Mary to the Word, that the element of contemplation, inserted at the base of every act of faith by the Holy Spirit, is developed.

No matter what subject he is treating, and even if he never mentions any of their names, it is very clear that von Balthasar was formed in the school of the Fathers of the Church. With many of them he is on more than familiar terms; he has in many ways become almost like them. For all that, he is no slavish admirer: he recognizes the weaknesses of each and the inevitable limitations that result from the age in which each lived. With his customary frankness he criticizes even those he admires and loves most. But their vision has become his own. It is principally to them that he owes his profound appreciation of the Christian attitude before the Word of God. He owes them too that vibrant feeling of wonder and adoration before the "nuptial mystery" and the "marvellous reciprocation of contraries" realized by the Incarnation of the Word. He is indebted to them for that sense of greater universality (in the strictest orthodoxy) because "it would appear at first that the infinite richness of God contracts and centers in a single point, the humanity of Jesus Christ . . . but this unity reveals itself as capable of integrating everything".

This rhythm of reflection that combines confidence in received truth with a wide-ranging scope in investigation is also patristic. It is in spontaneous imitation of the Fathers that in him "the crystal of thought takes fire in the interior and becomes a mystical life". They have communicated to him their burning love for the Church: for them, as for him, "the Church is the exact limit of the horizon of Christ's redemption just as, for us, Christ is the horizon of God". This is why he considers it as futile to stress the many human faults "which are only too clear to anyone who looks", as it is vital "to bring to light the admirable secrets of the Church which the world does not know of and which scarcely anyone wishes to recognize".

The study of the "Church of the Fathers", in Newman's phrase, has confirmed him in an attitude as distant from "false tolerance" as it is far from "confessional narrowness", so that his work, to anyone who wishes to meditate on it, offers a profound ecumenical resonance. One of the great apostles of ecumenism, Patriarch Athenagoras, recognized as much when he sent a messenger to Fr. von Balthasar with a gift of the gold cross of Mount Athos. We may also be glad that as the Faculty of Protestant Theology at Edinburgh University had already done, the Faculty of Catholic Theology at the University of Münster asked him in 1965 to accept an honorary doctorate.

It seems that von Balthasar has felt a certain shared situation with that of the Fathers, not in any archaic sense, but in that he too seeks to harness all the features of the culture of his time to make them achieve their full flowering in Christ—though he does not forget, any more than the Fathers did, that all the "spoils of the Egyptians" are of no use and could, in fact, become a deadly burden if they are not received into a converted heart. For "it is not the greatest knowledge or the deepest wisdom that is right but the greatest obedience, the deepest humility"; not the sublimity of thought, but the effective simplicity of love.

Effective simplicity are the key words if we are not to give a false idea of where this theologian would wish to lead us: he is theologian only to be apostle. For him, the task of theology, as Albert Béguin has written, "is ceaselessly to refer back into humble practice the full significance of the revealed word".

We must confine ourselves here to his written work. As we have already insinuated this work is not narrow or inbred; its "Pauline passion" makes this very clear. Nothing pleases the author more than to wean his words away from dreams, from the illusion of some "spurious eternity", to immerse them in the "true temporality" which is the process of configuration to Christ by submission, *hic et nunc,* to his Gospel. This is shown in one of his latest works, a short treatise with the Kierkegaardian title: *Wer ist ein Christ?*

The other element of his makeup, besides the Fathers, is the influence of St. Ignatius of Loyola. The need for total commitment to the following of Christ and for fidelity to what one has received from him, these two great themes of the Spiritual Exercises were revealed to him by his teacher, Erich Przywara, in all their force. His own ever deeper study of the Exercises has strengthened this conviction, which he is forever communicating to others.

Read, for instance, his booklet, published some fifteen years ago, *Laïcat et plein apostolat;* follow it up with the splendid chapter he contributed to the symposium *Das Wagnis der Nachfolge* — "Zur Theologie des Rätestandes". One may, if one wishes, pass over the concrete plans for a secular institute proposed in it; such things are contingent, depending on circumstances of time and place and personal likes and dislikes. But at this moment, with so many clamoring voices whose Christianity seems marginal arising in the bosom of the Church, those who are troubled and anxious at the sight of all the spray in the wash of the great vessel, the Ecumenical Council, even if they have no stomach for the deeper reaches of his greater works, will find much comfort in this essay that recalls, so objectively and precisely, the laws of the Gospel. It will also show them what the true dignity of the layman is, in Christ.

They will also better understand why the Council decided to include in the Dogmatic Constitution on the Church, as though to contribute to the definition, the two chapters on the universal call to sanctity and on the externally organized spiritual life: just as the Old Testament was not confined to preparing men for the coming of Christ but also had the role of unfolding, even before the event, the dimensions of his person, so, and even more so, the Church does not restrict herself to the instruction of men with a view to the final return of Christ, but announces that his imprint must be placed on all creation, that a movement is under way which will end only under new skies and in a new land. "She is not only on her way to this event; as the 'mystical parousia' she is its beginning." And as for those who are determined to be true imitators of Christ in their apostolates, they will find themselves forewarned against the discouragement lying in wait for them when they hear the author say that for these true imitators, "Christian suffering will not be spared."

Effective simplicity, we were saying, *of love.* This last is not a word von Balthasar pronounces lightly: he feels its full weight. Even before he reckons up the conditions for a Christian to realize it, he sees the human impossibility of it. How could man love man? He would "perish at the stifling" contact:

> If in the other person nothing is offered but what one already knows fundamentally for oneself—the limitations inherent in his nature, his anguish before them, his constant buffeting by them: death, sickness, folly, chance; a being to whom this anguish can give wings to the most astonishing discoveries—why should the "I" lose itself for a "Thou" which the "I" cannot honestly believe is, at the deepest level, any different from itself? No reason at all, of course! If in my like it is not God I meet; if, in love, no breath of wind brings me the sweet scent of the infinite; if I cannot love my neighbor with any other love than that arising from my finite capacity; if therefore, in our meeting, that great reality that bears the name of love does not come from God and return to him—beginning the adventure is not worth the trouble.
>
> It rescues neither from his prison nor his solitude. Animals can love one another without knowing God because they have no consciousness of themselves. But as for those beings whose nature permits and forces this reflection, and who have learned to practice it so profoundly that not only an individual but all humanity can look itself in the face, for them love of another is impossible without God.

But Jesus came and, having promulgated his great commandment, diffused his Spirit.

> The Fathers of the Church and the medievalists were at considerable pains to explain why his coming was so late. We, on the contrary, ask why he did not delay his arrival till today when existence on this planet has become insupportable without him. Be that as it may, the seed he sowed pushes its way above the ground and becomes visible.

The hour of history has sounded when it has become evident that man cannot be loved except in God—and that God is only loved in "the sacrament of our brother". It is also the hour when it must be recognized—Jesus himself was explicit on this subject—that all Christian love implies a bursting out of enclosures and inner precincts, an outgoing to the world, to him who does not love, to the lost brother, to the enemy. The Church is the Spouse of Christ but will not be acknowledged as such except in the transcendence that is her love. *Glaubhaft ist nur Liebe.* In all that it is most intimate and pressing, Christian love surpasses "Christianity but this very action of surpassing is Christianity itself." [4]

And it is also God himself:

> ... If the supreme reality in God were truth, we should be able to look, with great open eyes, into its abysses, blinded perhaps by so much light, but hampered by nothing in our flight towards truth. But love being the decisive reality, the seraphim cover their faces with their wings, for the mystery of eternal love is such that even the excessive brilliance of its night cannot be glorified except in adoration.

We have barely touched on some of the many themes this immense achievement offers for our consideration, barely indicated some of its characteristics. We must now try to penetrate the secret of this highly personal thought, but whose personality consists solely in a loving search for an objective grasp of the mystery. Our reward (if we are successful) will be a heightened consciousness of the unique originality of our faith and, by that very fact, of every effort of the intelligence which wishes to be faithful to it. Since we cannot fully explore the whole, let us at least point out one of the avenues that leads to its center.

The precise nature of von Balthasar's invitation to us to look on the face of Jesus is conditioned by a rather rigorous interpretation of the Christological formula of Chalcedon. The "density of the human nature" of Christ is altered not a whit by its union to the divinity, no more after the Resurrection than during the earthly existence—and the personal unity is not so less perfect that the man Jesus is not the face expressive of God. "Not for a single instant is the glory of God absent from the Lamb, or the light of the Trinity from that of the incarnate Word". It follows that for the Christian, negative theology, even when pushed to its extremes, is not detached from its base, the positive theology that illumines that face.

No doubt, for him as for all, the divinity is incomprehensible: *Si comprehenderis, non est Deus.* The dissimilarity between the Creator and the creature will always be greater than the similarity. But the situation of the Christian is still not much different from that of the philosopher or any other religious man. He knows that God himself has a face. What appears in Jesus Christ "is

---

[4] A similar idea will be found in Karl Rahner, "Is Christianity an Ideology?" in *Concilium,* 1965: "Unlike an ideology, powerless of its nature to surpass itself, Christianity is, in a sense, more than itself: it is this very movement by which man abandons himself to the mystery at the ground of his being and which ceaselessly escapes him, but which he knows leads on to this mystery, that finds its effective realization in Jesus Christ: a love that draws near and envelops his existence."

the Trinitarian God making himself visible, an object of experience; the face
in revelation is not the limit of an infinite without face, it manifests an
infinitely determined face."

In Jesus the believer sees God. For him, therefore,

> what is incomprehensible in God no longer proceeds from a mere ignorance;
> it is a positive determination by God of the knowledge of faith: the daunting
> and stupefying incomprehensibility of the fact that God so loved the world
> that he gave us his only Son, that the God of all plentitude lowered himself
> not only in his creation but in the conditions of an existence determined by
> sin, destined for death, removed from God. Such is the obscurity that
> appears even as it hides itself, the intangible character of God that becomes
> tangible by the very act of touching him.

That cannot any longer happen in Christianity what *"cannot but happen"*
everywhere else: "that the finite is, in the last analysis, absorbed by the infinite;
the non-identical snuffed out by the identical"; religion devoured by mysticism.
Accomplished "once for all", the humiliation of God in the Incarnation
cannot be nullified. In the tension manifest in the face of Christ "between the
grandeur of a free God and the abasement of a loving one", "the heart of the
divinity" is opened before the Christian's eyes.

The entire trinitarian teaching and all theology of revelation are bound up
with this central vision; they explain one another through it and are themselves necessary for its understanding. As is normal, while the mind gives its
consent to all this by an intuitive impulse, it makes the intelligence alert,
satisfies it, and finally, like all fruitful thought, poses it more problems than it
answers. . . .

To finish what we set out to do we shall make another brief incursion, not
this time to the core of the doctrine, but to the heart of the spirituality that
corresponds to it. (Need we say that our efforts are no substitute for personal
reading of his works.) A single word defines this spirituality: it is a spirituality
of Holy Saturday.

" . . . There was a day when Nietzsche was right: God was dead, the Word
was not heard in the world, the body was interred and the tomb sealed up, the
soul descended into the bottomless abyss of Sheol." This descent of Jesus into
the kingdom of the dead "was part of his abasement even if (as St. John admits
of the Cross) this supreme abasement is already surrounded by the thunder-
bolts of Easter night. In fact, did not the very descent to hell bring redemption
to the souls there?" It prolonged in some manner the cry from the Cross: Why
have you abandoned me? "Nobody could ever shout that cry from a deeper
abyss than did he whose life was to be perpetually born of the Father."

But there remains the imitation of Christ. There is a participation, not only
sacramental, but contemplative in his mystery. There is an experience of the

abandonment on the Cross and the descent into hell, and experience of the *poena damni*.[5] There is the crushing feeling of the "ever greater dissimilarity" of God in the resemblance, however great, between him and the creature; there is the passage through death and darkness, the stepping through "the somber door". . . . In conformity to the mission he has received, the prayerful man then experiences the feeling that "God is dead for him". And this is a gift of Christian grace—but one receives it unawares. The lived and felt faith, charity, and hope rise above the soul to an inaccessible place, to God. From then on it is "in nakedness, poverty and humiliation" that the soul cries out to him.[6]

Those who have experienced such states[7] afterwards, more often than not, in their humility, see nothing in them but a personal purification. True to his doctrine which refuses to separate charisms and gifts of the Holy Spirit, the ecclesial mission, and individual mysticism, von Balthasar discerns in it essentially this "Holy Saturday of contemplation" by which the Betrothed, in some chosen few of her members, is made to participate more closely in the redemption wrought by the Spouse. We have arrived at a time in history when human consciousness, enlarged and deepened by Christianity, inclines more and more to this interpretation. The somber experience of Holy Saturday is the price to be paid for the dawn of the new spring of hope, this spring which has been "canonized in the rose garden of Lisieux": " . . . is it not the beginning of a new creation? The magic of Holy Saturday . . . Deep cave from which the water of life escapes."

Reading so many passages where this theme is taken up, we discern a distress, a solitude, a night—of the quality, in fact, as that experienced by "the Heart of the world"—and we understand that a work that communicates so full a joy must have been conceived in *that* sorrow.

Postscript:[8] It is hard to believe that ten years have passed since these pages were written. They were meant as a testimony and not as an exposition or critique of von Balthasar's writings. Had they been meant as such, how inadequate they would have proved to be! And how much less adequate they would be today!

In these ten years a monument has grown up before our eyes. As soon as the first volume of the projected triptych, *Herrlichkeit*, was achieved, work on

---

[5] Compare the analogous experience by Pierre Emmanuel in *La face humaine* (Ed. du Seuil, Paris, 1966), 277–78, and which he calls "the aesthetic of Holy Saturday".

[6] See also in *Question théologiques d'aujourd'hui*, vol. 2, 1965, 280–88: "Eschatologie".

[7] Cf. Jules Monchanin, "Spiritualité du désert" in *Dieu vivant*, I, 1945, 51: "A naked faith that includes, without knowing it, hope". Hadewijch, *Mengeldichte*, 16 (Poiron, 127–28), quoted by Jean Orcibal, *Jean de la Croix et les mystiques rhéno-flamands* (1966), 108.

[8] Translated by Andrée Emery, 1975.

the second volume was immediately begun. Apart from the prodigious quantity, the greatness of the work becomes more and more evident, even though the author's modesty makes him shun the marketplace of publicity. Despite the silent hostility that superiority invariably encounters, and despite the remarkable resistance of certain professionals to take note of this unclassifiable man and acknowledge him as one of their own, even in France, where translations are regrettably few, haphazard, and sporadic, appearing at a desperately slow pace, von Balthasar's thought has captured one by one the spirit of an elite youth.

Looking at von Balthasar's work as a whole, among the many traits which cannot be all described here, I discern two main characteristics that have stood out in the course of the past decade and that seem to become more momentous and more consequential to the present.

First: instead of engaging in a series of *a posteriori* skirmishes with diverse presentations of Christian origins by contemporary writers, or being content to dissect them one by one to reveal the frequently chaotic excesses, von Balthasar grasps their essence in one glance with astonishing acumen. He takes hold of them, so to say, in one fell swoop which in itself is an intellectual feat—and then, with keen discernment comes up with an altogether different and unexpected view. The person of Jesus, shining with radiant beauty, has an unmistakable affinity with the original interpretations of the evangelists' writings. There is a reversion of perspective, an application of Newman's method to an area that is even more fundamental than dogmatic development. The work is done with precision, with a spirit seeking understanding and rejoicing in what it finds. Never was the mysterious focal point, which is not the result but the source of unity, the unfathomable figure of Christ, the object of the Church Faith, made more clearly understandable to the historian.

Second: instead of, like many others, laboriously striving to rejuvenate scholasticism, for better or worse, by making gestures toward contemporary philosophy, or else abandoning, as so many others, all organized theological thought, von Balthasar shapes a fresh, original synthesis with radically biblical inspiration, without sacrificing any of the traditional dogmatic elements. His acute sensitivity to cultural developments and to the problems of our own times give him the necessary courage to do so. His intimate knowledge— witnessed to by his previous works—of the Fathers of the Church, of St. Thomas Aquinas, and of the other great spiritual writers, enables him to engage in this venture. He was nurtured by these great men and he follows in their footsteps, without servility and without falsification, because he has fully assimilated their substance. His enterprise is a far cry from the sporadic and futile experiments which bear the earmarks of subjective fantasies, or which, spawned by resentment against Tradition, secularize the tenets of the Faith or minimize them to the point of vanishing.

These two fundamental characteristics, described here somewhat awkwardly and certainly very sketchily, seem to me the more remarkable as they exactly answer the two basic insufficiencies of Christian thought today, and also because their beginning antedates the last Council's invitation to theology to start its own *aggiornamento*. It is a mark of great and necessary works to arise in this manner, unnoticed at first, without even the initiator himself perceiving their future import. They take shape and develop as if by natural growth and not by command.

The twofold aspect of von Balthasar's approach described above does not compromise the divine origin of Christian faith and the authenticity of Christian theology. Rather, the first is placed into a new light and the second is freed of naturalistic and "objectivistic" consequences which in modern times have often burdened and even disfigured it.

The irrepressible vitality of Tradition sweeps away scared conservatism. It is a fact that for nearly a century all attempts to complete the codification of scholasticism and seriously to renew it were stopped authoritatively. So much so, that today it seems to be withdrawn from circulation. Because of the magnitude of this phenomenon it would be futile to measure particular injustices. But it might be of historical interest to note that even if such an effort of discriminating discernment were made, it would not be capable of awakening new life. The debate held over this great body dissected it as a corpse, and many feel that they now face a great void. Still, few doubt that a new structure will arise in the service of an intact and renewed faith, which will salvage from our squandered heritage what was most valuable. And yet, even the admirers of von Balthasar's works more often than not see merely a series of stimulating and beautiful books, written on important subjects that are more or less timely. They miss seeing their true import.

Nevertheless, with the passing years Hans Urs von Balthasar emerges more and more clearly as what he always has been: a man of the Church, in the most beautiful sense of the word. And in the present trial of the Church torn asunder by her own children, in a crisis the seriousness of which cannot be underestimated anymore by anyone—no matter what interpretation they may give it or whatever current phraseology they may use—von Balthasar, with sensitive awareness, accepted from God the role that his quality as a theologian demands. As a result, marginally to his great theoretical works but not marginally to his essential plan, he wrote a series of small volumes, simple and accessible but not less important or less personal.

For the same purpose also his long and tenacious effort to create that International Theological Review, which under the title *Communio* endeavors to contribute to and strengthen the intellectual and spiritual vitality of Catholicism. For this also the many humbler works, sermons, intimate instructions, and communications.

All these reflect a virile strength of thought and, together with an unfailing serenity, a liberated, free spirit. Von Balthasar is sincerely seeking, is never discouraged, is always conciliating. He faces all situations with a generously understanding intelligence, and his heart is open to all who approach him.

"I feel as if I had always known him", said a recent visitor the day after their first meeting, surprised by the friendly reception that he received. And he added the picturesque words with which I shall conclude: "I felt as if I were walking with one of the Church Fathers who somehow wandered into Switzerland, and who counts among his ancestors the three Magi besides Wilhelm Tell . . . "

Telegram from Pope John Paul II

To my revered Brother, Cardinal Joseph Ratzinger, Prefect of the Congregation for the Doctrine of the Faith:

It is my particular desire, after manifesting my sincere sympathy at the sudden death of the esteemed Professor Hans Urs von Balthasar, to show the deceased, on the occasion of his burial services, a final honor through a personal word of commemoration.

All who knew the priest, von Balthasar, are shocked, and grieve over the loss of a great son of the Church, an outstanding man of theology and of the arts, who deserves a special place of honor in contemporary ecclesiastical and cultural life.

It was my wish to acknowledge and to honor in a solemn fashion the merits he earned through his long and tireless labors as a spiritual teacher and as an esteemed scholar by naming him to the dignity of the cardinalate in the last Consistory. We submit in humility to the judgment of God who now has called this faithful servant of the Church so unexpectedly into eternity.

Your participation at the solemn funeral services, very reverend Cardinal, will be an expression of the high esteem in which the person and the life work of this great priest and theologian are held by the Holy See. With all who commemorate him in sorrow and in gratitude, I beg for the dear departed eternal fulfillment in God's light and glory. Now that his earthly life is completed, may he, who was for many a spiritual leader on the way to faith, be granted the vision of God, face to face.

In spiritual union, I impart to all who participate by their prayers in this liturgy for the deceased, from my heart, my special apostolic blessing.

At the Vatican, June 30, 1988
John Paul II

Translated by Josephine Koeppel, O.C.D.

JOSEPH CARDINAL RATZINGER

Homily at the Funeral Liturgy of Hans Urs von Balthasar

We are gathered here in order to entrust our departed brother, Hans Urs von Balthasar, to the mercy of God. Mourning and consolation touch one another at the death of a believer. We mourn because he is no longer among us. Never again shall we be able to hold a conversation with him, never again obtain his advice. We shall need him so often, but shall seek for him in vain. But there is also consolation in this sorrow: his life has taught us how to believe. His witness is hope for him and for us: "I know that my Redeemer lives" (Job 19:25). We know that the souls of those who have died are alive in the resurrected Body of the Lord. The Lord's Body shelters and carries them toward the common resurrection. In this Body, which we are permitted to receive, we remain close to one another, and we touch each other.

On this occasion, we are not interested in paying honor to the life's work of our departed friend. What we want is to receive the consolation of the Word of God in the community of the Body of Christ, and to allow this consolation to come to us precisely from his life. Henri de Lubac has called von Balthasar possibly the most cultured person of our time.[1] Actually, the arc of his works spans from the predecessors of Socrates to Freud, Nietzsche, and Bertolt Brecht; it embraces the entire Western heritage of philosophy, literature, art, and theology. But in this vast adventure of the spirit, his interest was not the curiosity to know a great deal, nor the power that comes from having many skills. If he wished to gather the treasures of Egypt into the storehouse of our Faith (to speak in the language of the Church Fathers), he also knew that such treasures can bear fruit only in a converted heart,[2] while on the shoulders of the unconverted they become a destructive burden. He knew that fullness of knowledge turns to unhappiness in the face of the extent of the still unknown and to despair over our impotence to achieve the essential: being a person, life itself. What von Balthasar wanted may well be encapsulated in a single phrase of St. Augustine: "Our

---

Translated by Josephine Koeppel, O.C.D.

[1] Henri de Lubac, "A Witness to Christ in the Church: Hans Urs von Balthasar", 271–88, above. See p. 272.

[2] Ibid., 281.

entire task in this life, dear brothers, consists in healing the eyes of the heart so they may be able to see God."[3]

That is what mattered to him, healing the eyes of the heart so they would be able to see the essential, the reason, and goal of the world and of our lives: God, the living God. In this quotation from Augustine, the Johannine aspect of von Balthasar's soul is revealed in the sense of the words of the Gospel which we have just heard: "This then is eternal life: to know you, the one true God, and Jesus Christ, whom you have sent" (Jn 17:3).

Eternal life is not a life which comes hereafter—sometime later; for then it would not be eternal. It is the one true life. We live if we acknowledge him. Von Balthasar was concerned with that knowledge which is life, life itself. He was one who was alive, and so he was one who continually gave, for life is always creative and giving.

"This is eternal life, to know you." All the reaching out of his soul is a search for truth, a search for life. He sought the traces of the Holy Spirit everywhere, the radiation from his truth, the windows that will open up to allow access to him. Everywhere, von Balthasar sought to discover ways which would lead out of the prison of finitude into the whole, into truth itself. But just because he did that, he knew the limits of our ability, knew that the living God will rise only out of the helpless collapse of our concepts, for we cannot invent him.[4] Finally, it is always God himself who manifests himself to us and gives us what exceeds all of our thinking. That is why von Balthasar coined the expression: theology on its knees. He knew that theology is suspended between the abysses of adoring obedience and of humble love. He knew that theology can come into action only at the touch of the living God, which happens in prayer. Precisely because he knew that God is greater than all our thoughts and our hearts, he submitted himself to the concreteness of God, who, in the human face of Jesus Christ, looks at us in greater and more infinite measure than in all the negations of an unformed mysticism which remains, finally, within the person alone.

This obedience of thought, which allows itself to be led away even from the highest peaks of mysticism by the true God, was very concretely part of von Balthasar's life. He himself had not wished to become a priest, far less had he thought of a career in theology or as a man of the Church. He studied

---

[3] Sermo 88.6 PL 38.542; this text is found in the fine selection which von Balthasar first published, with Benziger in 1942, under the title *Augustine. Das Antlitz der Kirche,* Text 290, 351 (new ed. 1955).

[4] Gregory of Nyssa, "The Sealed Fountain. Commentary on the Song of Songs". A shortened version was translated and introduced by Hans Urs von Balthasar, in *Christliche Meister* 23 (Einsiedeln: Johannes Verlag, 1983), 17 in the introduction. See also Werner Löser, *Im Geiste des Origenes. Hans Urs von Balthasar als Interpret der Theologie der Kirchenväter* (Frankfurt, 1976), 109.

Germanistik, and his choice alternated between music and literature, until he found his "fig tree". It was under a tree in a remote woods on the outskirts of Basel that certitude struck him like lightning: You must become a priest, you must be an Ignatian one.[5] The tie to obedience was what was Ignatian in his whole life. He did not follow the path of his own will; he went the way along which he was led against his own wishes, until, in this manner, his will and his being came to be increasingly free and pure. Because he lived out of obedience, it was at once obvious to him that theology does not live from what one thinks but from what one receives. Therefore, in the deepest sense of the word, he was a man of the Church.

He knew the Church's weaknesses and her misery, not only theoretically. He had hard and painful experience of it throughout his lifetime. He knew Augustine's phrase: "Our winter is the hiddenness of Christ." What he wrote about Holy Saturday certainly depended somewhat on his contact with the mystical experiences of Adrienne von Speyr, but at the same time it was nourished as well by his own painful experience of the apparent absence of God within his Church. But von Balthasar knew, with Augustine, that even "in wintertime, the root lives on",[6] and that we live if we live from that root.

He therefore had little regard for a theology which tries to make itself interesting through the options it can devise, and which thereby, for all that, grasps at what is incongruent, unproven, and empty. He thought little of a pluralism which in reality resembles the disintegration of decomposed matter. He knew that only a pluralism which is living and manifold in the unity of the one who is alive will bear any weight. He knew how indigent was that progress which Gregory of Nyssa compared to an ascent of the sand dunes of the desert in which one makes no headway at all.[7] Here, too, the concreteness of dogma was for him the guarantee of the eternal and inexhaustible Truth which is never lessened by a new expression, but rather imposes greater tasks and opens perspectives which enable us, slowly, to surmise the immensity of the whole in what lies fragmentarily before us.

Von Balthasar had a great reverence for the Petrine, for the hierarchical structure of the Church. But he knew, too, that this is not her entire nor her deepest aspect. Von Balthasar spoke of the Church as Bride, as person. The

[5] Löser, *Im Geiste des Origenes*, 7, n. 6.

[6] Augustine, Sermo 36.4, *PL* 38.216; in the collection of texts mentioned above, Text 278, 342ff.

[7] "What is terrestrially-unending is similar to 'child's play in the sand. The pleasure in what has been built is extinguished at the same time as the joy in building, . . . the sand collapses and leaves no trace of what was erected with so much care.' The soul resembles, then, 'those who climb up a dune: even when their feet seem to cut through long stretches, they struggle in vain; repeatedly the sand runs down, so that, although there is strenuous movement, there is no progress of any kind' " (Gregory of Nyssa, in Hans Urs von Balthasar, *Christliche Meister* 23, 14).

Church is herself totally in persons, and exists most purely and entirely in her, out of whose Yes she was formed; in Mary, the Mother of the Lord. Von Balthasar, the Johannine and Ignatian Christian, was above all a Marian person. He knew about the charismatic element of the Church, about the ever new movement and working of the Spirit, which creates new life precisely where we would not seek it, and where, frequently, it does not please us at all. He knew of the significance of the feminine in the Church, of the great symbolism of the virginal and the maternal. From Mary, he learned the humility of obedience, but also the responsibility of putting into action an embodied, effective love. He allowed her to tell him, and he told us in turn, that Christianity is spiritual only insofar as it is an ever new incarnation of the Spirit. In his commentary on the Marian encyclical of the Pope, he coined the phrase that Mary—who was assumed bodily into heaven—may not be elevated by us into someone "too heavenly". Rather, we must learn precisely from her how our faith is to be enfleshed and how it is to be responsible in temporal matters.

From Mary, finally and foremost, he learned that the origin of all fruitfulness in the Church is contemplation, without which action becomes empty activity. He learned that God's word dwells in silence and in waiting, and only in these can it grow to its greatest fertility.

Von Balthasar was a contemplative, but he was not, as many probably imagined him to be, a Jerome in his hut, in the way depicted in Dürer's portrait which von Balthasar has so lovingly described. Out of his contemplation grew action in a wholly Marian and Ignatian spirit: in obedience and without any outward show, hidden and without seeking to make a name for himself. After the Council, he began to collect friends in order to build up with them a powerful source for correct renewal as opposed to its counterfeit forms. That is how he came to be the actual father of the large *Communio* family, which is at work, today, on all the continents, and which, despite its still being a tiny seed, represents a force for community, for life, for change and renewal. His activity as a publisher was also animated by the same will: producing books was not the important issue, much less did he labor for a commercial interest—for that he had no aptitude at all. It was because he wanted to set the energy of the best sources in opposition to the flood of empty talk, to offer living water and good bread which nourishes in the time of drought. And increasingly he traveled back and forth, giving retreats in order to open persons for the living bread, to heal the eyes of their hearts so that they might see God. It was this same care that led him to collect, as his living legacy, the Community of St. John, the women and men, lay persons and priests, who, living out of this same spirit which was at once Johannine, Ignatian, and Marian, should be cells for renewal in the Church and the world.

Von Balthasar was hesitant in opening himself for the honor intended for him by his being named to the cardinalate. This was not motivated by a coquettish desire to act the great one, but by the Ignatian spirit which characterized his life. In some way, his being called into the next life on the very eve of being so honored seems to show he was right about it. He was allowed to remain himself, fully. But what the Pope intended to express by this mark of distinction, and of honor, remains valid: no longer only private individuals but the Church itself, in its official responsibility, tells us that he is right in what he teaches of the Faith, that he points the way to the sources of living water—a witness to the word which teaches us Christ and which teaches us how to live.

"Christ is my life." This word taken from today's reading from the Letter to the Philippians (1:21) sums up the whole course of his life. And since it is the truth of his interior biography, we may be certain that the sentence that follows, "For me to die is gain", also counts for him; and that his death is not a leave-taking from the community of the living, for whom he was ever available, but is rather a new way of his being close in the strength of the presence of God's love, in unity with all the members of Christ's Body. Let us ask the Lord to enable us to keep the great witness of this, his servant, ever alive and to carry it on. We beg the Lord to reward him for all he did and suffered out of the humility of his hope-filled love. Amen.

In the Hofkirche, Lucerne,
July 1, 1988

BIBLIOGRAPHY

English Translations of German Titles by Hans Urs von Balthasar[1]

Der antirömische Affekt. Wie lässt sich das Papsttum in der Gesamtkirche integrieren (Freiburg: Herder, 1974)
The Office of Peter and the Structure of the Church (San Francisco: Ignatius Press, 1989)

Apokalypse der deutschen Seele. Studien zu einer Lehre von letzten Haltungen (Salzburg: A. Pustet)
Bd. I: *Der deutsche Idealismus* (1937)
Bd. II: *Im Zeichen Nietzsches* (1939)
Bd. III: *Die Vergöttlichung des Todes* (1939)
Apocalypse of the German soul: Studies for a doctrine of final attitudes. Volume I: German idealism; volume II: In the sign of Nietzsche; volume III: The divinization of death.

Das betrachtende Gebet (Adoratio 1) (Einsiedeln: Johannes Verlag, 1955)
Prayer (San Francisco: Ignatius Press, 1986)

Christen sind einfältig (Kriterien 66) (Einsiedeln: Johannes Verlag, 1983)
Christian simplicity.

Christlicher Stand (Einsiedeln: Johannes Verlag, 1977)
The Christian State of Life (San Francisco: Ignatius Press, 1983)

Cordula oder der Ernstfall (Kriterien 2) (Einsiedeln: Johannes Verlag, 1966)
The Moment of Christian Witness (New York: Newman Press, 1968)

Credo. Meditationen zum Apostolischen Glaubensbekenntnis (Freiburg: Herder, 1989).
Credo: Meditations on the Apostle's Creed. (New York: Crossroad/Continuum, in process)

---

[1] This list does not include all of von Balthasar's works, just those books mentioned herein. For a complete bibliography see *Bibliographie, 1925–1990* (Einsiedeln: Freiburg, 1990). In the following list, if English titles are given in italics they have been or soon will be published.

Du hast Worte ewigen Lebens. Schriftbetrachtungen (Einsiedeln-Trier: Johannes
   Verlag, 1989).
   You Have Words of Eternal Life (San Francisco: Ignatius Press, 1991)

Einfaltungen. Auf Wegen christlicher Einigung (Kriterien 73) (Munich: Kösel-
   Verlag, 1969) (neuauflage, Einsiedeln: Johannes Verlag, 1985)
   Convergences: To the Source of Christian Mystery (San Francisco: Ignatius
   Press, 1984)

Elisabeth von Dijon und ihre geistliche Sendung (Cologne-Olten: Jakob Hegner
   Verlag, 1952).
   Elisabeth of Dijon (London: Harvill Press, 1956)

Epilog (Einsiedeln-Trier: Johannes Verlag, 1987).
   Epilogue (San Francisco: Ignatius Press, 1992)

Erster Blick auf Adrienne von Speyr (Einsiedeln: Johannes Verlag, 1968)
   First Glance at Adrienne von Speyr (San Francisco: Ignatius Press, 1981)

La foi du Christ: Cinq approches christologiques (Paris: Aubier-Montaigne,
   1968).
   The faith of Christ: Five Christological approaches.

Das Ganze im Fragment. Aspekte der Geschichtstheologie (Einsiedeln: Benziger,
   1963)
   A Theological Anthropology (New York: Sheed and Ward, 1967)
   Man in History (London: Sheed & Ward, 1967)

Gelebte Kirche. Bernanos (Einsiedeln: Johannes Verlag, 1971).
   Lived Church: Bernanos.

Geschichte des eschatologischen Problems in der modernen deutschen Literatur (Zurich:
   1930 dissertation).
   History of the eschatological problem in modern German literature.

Glaubhaft ist nur Liebe (Einsiedeln: Johannes Verlag, 1963).
   Love Alone: The Way of Revelation (London: Burns & Oates, 1968)

Die Gnostischen Centurien des Maximus Confessor (Freiburg: Herder, 1941).
   The gnostic centuries of Maximus the Confessor.

Die Gottesfrage des heutigen Menschen (Vienna: Herold, 1956).

The God Question and Modern Man (New York: Seabury Press, 1967)

Herrlichkeit. Eine theologische Ästhetik (Einsiedeln: Johannes Verlag)
 Bd. I: *Schau der Gestalt.* (1961)
 Bd. II: *Fächer der Stile* (1962)
  1. Teil: *Klerikale Stile* (1984)
  2. Teil: *Laikale Stile* (1984)
 Bd. III/1: *Im Raum der Metaphysik* (1965)
  1. Teil: *Altertum* (1975)
  2. Teil: *Neuzeit* (1975)
 Bd. III/2: 1. Teil: *Alter Bund* (1966)
 Bd. III/2: 2. Teil: *Neuer Bund* (1969)
 The Glory of the Lord: A Theological Aesthetics (Edinburgh: T & T Clark;
San Francisco: Ignatius Press)
  I: *Seeing the Form* (1985)
  II: *Studies in Theological Styles Clerical Styles* (1984)
  III: *Studies in Theological Styles Lay Styles* (1986)
  IV: *The Realm of Metaphysics in Antiquity* (1989)
  V: *The Realm of Metaphysics in the Modern Age* (1991)
  VI: *Theology: The Old Covenant* (1991)
  VII: *Theology: The New Covenant* (1989)

Das Herz der Welt (Zurich: Arche, 1945).
 The Heart of the World (San Francisco: Ignatius Press, 1980)

Homo creatus est (Skizzen zur Theologie V) (Einsiedeln: Johannes Verlag, 1986).
 Homo creatus est (*Explorations in Theology,* vol. 5) (San Francisco: Ignatius
 Press, in process)

In Gottes Einsatz leben (Einsiedeln: Johannes Verlag, 1971)
 Engagement with God (London: Society for Promoting Christian Knowledge,
 1975).

Karl Barth. Darstellung und Deutung seiner Theologie (Einsiedeln: Johannes
 Verlag, 1951).
 The Theology of Karl Barth (New York: Holt, Rinehart & Winston, 1971)
 New edition in process (San Francisco: Ignatius Press)

Katholisch. Aspekte des Mysteriums (Kriterien 36) (Einsiedeln: Johannes Verlag,
 1975).
 In the Fullness of Faith: On the Centrality of the Distinctively Catholic (San
 Francisco: Ignatius Press, 1988)

Kennt uns Jesus — Kennen wir ihn? (Freiburg: Herder, 1980).
  Does Jesus Know Us? Do We Know Him? (San Francisco: Ignatius Press, 1983)

Klarstellungen. Zur Prüfung der Geister (Freiburg: Herder, 1971).
  Elucidations (London: Society for Promoting Christian Knowledge, 1975)

Kleine Fibel für verunsicherte Laien (Einsiedeln: Johannes Verlag, 1980)
  A Short Primer for Unsettled Laymen (San Francisco: Ignatius Press, 1985)

Kleiner Diskurs über die Hölle (Ostfildern: Schwabenverlag, 1987)
  A Short Discourse on Hell, appendix to *Dare We Hope "That All Men Be Saved?"* (San Francisco: Ignatius Press, 1988)

Kleiner Lageplan zu meinen Büchern (Einsiedeln: Johannes Verlag, 1955).
  A brief overview of my books, included in translation of *Mein Werk* (San Francisco: Ignatius Press, in process)

Kosmische Liturgie: Höhe und Krise des griechischen Weltbilds bei Maximus Confessor (Freiburg: Herder, 1941)
  Cosmic liturgy: Apex and crisis of the Greek world view in Maximus the Confessor (San Francisco: Ignatius Press, in process)

Der Laie und der Ordensstand (Einsiedeln: Johannes Verlag, 1948)
  The layman and the religious state.

Licht des Wortes. Skizzen zu allen Sonntagslesungen. (Trier: Paulinus-Verlag, 1987)
  Light of the word: Outlines for all the Sunday readings.

Neue Klarstellungen (Einsiedeln: Johannes Verlag, 1979)
  New Elucidations (San Francisco: Ignatius Press, 1986)

Parole et Mystère chez Origène, ed. du Cerf (Paris, 1957)
  Word and mystery in Origen.

Paulus ringt mit seiner Gemeinde. Die Pastoral der Korintherbriefe (Kriterien 83) (Einsiedeln-Trier: Johannes Verlag, 1988).
  Paul Wrestles with His Community (San Francisco: Ignatius Press, 1992)

Pneuma und Institution (Skizzen zur Theologie IV) (Einsiedeln: Johannes Verlag, 1974)

Spirit and institution (*Explorations in Theology*, vol. 4) (San Francisco: Ignatius Press, in process)

Présence et pensée. Essai sur la philosophie religieuse de Grégoire de Nysse (Paris: Beauchesne, 1942).
Presence and thought: Essay on the religious philosophy of Gregory of Nyssa.

Prüfet alles—das Gute behaltet (Ostfildern: Schwabenverlag, 1986)
Test Everything: Hold Fast to What is Good (San Francisco: Ignatius Press, 1989)

Rechenschaft 1965 (Einsiedeln: Johannes Verlag, 1965)
"In Retrospect" in *Communio: International Catholic Review* (Fall 1975) 197–220
Included in *Mein Werk* which is being translated by Ignatius Press, San Francisco

Reinhold Schneider. Sein Weg und sein Werk (Cologne-Olten: Jakob Hegner Verlag, 1953)
Reinhold Schneider: His way and his work.

Schleifung der Bastionen. Von der Kirche in dieser Zeit (1952)
Razing the barriers.

Schwestern im Geist (Einsiedeln: Johannes Verlag, 1970)
Two Sisters in the Spirit: Thérèse of Lisieux and Elizabeth of Dijon (San Francisco: Ignatius Press, in process)

Spiritus Creator (Skizzen zur Theologie III) (Einsiedeln: Johannes Verlag, 1967).
Spiritus Creator (*Explorations in Theology*, vol. 3) (San Francisco: Ignatius Press, in process)

Sponsa Verbi (Skizzen zur Theologie II) (Einsiedeln: Johannes Verlag, 1960)
Church and World (New York: Herder and Herder, 1967)
Essays in Theology II: *Word and Redemption* (New York: Herder and Herder, 1965.
Spouse of the Word (*Explorations in Theology*, vol. 2) (San Francisco: Ignatius Press, 1991)

Die Stille des Wortes. Dürers Weg mit Hieronymus (Einsiedeln: Johannes Verlag, 1979)
The silence of the word. Dürer's path with Jerome.

Theodramatik (Einsiedeln: Johannes Verlag)
    I. *Prolegomena* (1973)
    II. *Die Personen des Spiels,* 1. Teil: *Der Mensch in Gott (*1976)
    II. *Die Personen des Spiels,* 2. Teil: *Die Personen Christus (*1978)
    III. *Die Handlung* (1980)
    IV. *Das Endspiel* (1983)
    Theo-Drama: Theological Dramatic Theory (San Francisco: Ignatius Press)
    I: *Prolegomena* (1988)
    II: *Dramatis Personae: Man in God* (1990)
    III: *Dramatis Personae: Persons in Christ* (in process)
    IV: *The Action*   (in process)
    V: *The Last Act*   (in process)

Theologie der drei Tage (Einsiedeln: Benziger, 1969) (Also: *Mysterium Paschale* in *Mysterium Salutis*)
    Mysterium Paschale (Edinburgh: T & T Clark, 1990)

Theologie der Geschichte (Einsiedeln: Johannes Verlag, 1950; Neue Fassung, 1959)
    Modern Catholic Thinkers (extract) (New York: Harper & Brothers, 1960)
    A Theology of History (New York: Sheed and Ward, 1963)

Theologik (Einsiedeln: Johannes Verlag)
    I: *Wahrheit der Welt* (1985)
    II: *Wahrheit Gottes* (1985)
    III: *Der Geist der Wahrheit* (1987)
    Theo-Logic (San Francisco: Ignatius Press)
    I: *The Truth of the World* (in process)
    II: *The Truth of God* (in process)
    III: *The Spirit of Truth* (in process)

Therese von Lisieux. Geschichte einer Sendung (1950)
    Thérèse of Lisieux: A Story of a Mission (New York: Sheed & Ward, 1954)

Thomas von Aquin. Besondere Gnadengaben und die zwei Wege menschlichen Lebens (1954)
    Thomas Aquinas: Special charisms and the two paths of man's life.

Unser Auftrag. Bericht und Entwurf (Einsiedeln: Johannes Verlag, 1984)
    Our Task (San Francisco: Ignatius Press, in process)

Verbum Caro (Skizzen zur Theologie I) (Einsiedeln: Johannes Verlag, 1960)

Essays in Theology I: Word and Revelation (New York: Herder and Herder, 1964)
II: Word and Redemption (1965)
The Word Made Flesh (*Explorations in Theology,* vol. 1) (San Francisco: Ignatius Press, 1989)

Wahrheit. Bd. 1: *Wahrheit der Welt* (Einsiedeln: Benziger, 1947)
Truth: The truth of the world (See *Theo-Logic III*)

Die Wahrheit ist symphonisch. Aspekte des christlichen Pluralismus (Kriterien 29) (Einsiedeln: Johannes Verlag, 1972)
The Truth Is Symphonic: Aspects of Christian Pluralism (San Francisco: Ignatius Press, 1987)

Was dürfen wir hoffen? (Kriterien 75) (Einsiedeln: Johannes Verlag, 1986)
Dare We Hope "That All Men Be Saved"? With a Short Discourse on Hell (San Francisco: Ignatius Press, 1988)

Das Weizenkorn. Aphorismen (Lucerne: Josef Stocker, 1944)
The grain of wheat: aphorisms. (San Francisco: Ignatius Press, in process)

Wenn ihr nicht werdet wie dieses Kind (Ostfildern: Schwabenverlag, 1988)
Unless You Become Like This Child (San Francisco: Ignatius Press, 1991).

Wer ist ein Christ? (Einsiedeln: Benziger, 1965)
Who Is a Christian? (New York: Newman Press, 1968)